MANNING MARABLE is perhaps the best-known Black
Marxist in the US today. He is currently Professor of
Political Sociology and Director of the Africana and
Hispanic Studies Programme at Colgate University,
Hamilton, New York. A political activist and journalist,
his column 'Along the Colour Line' appears regularly in
150 newspapers. In the past decade Manning Marable
has written over a hundred scholarly articles for
sociology, economics, political science and history
journals. His major publications also include *From the
Grassroots* (1980), *Blackwater* (1981), *How Capitalism
Underdeveloped Black America* (1983) and *Race,
Reform and Rebellion: The Second Reconstruction in
Black America, 1945–1982* (1984).

Manning Marable

Verso

Black American Politics
From the Washington Marches to Jesse Jackson

Verso is the imprint of **New Left Books**

British Library
Cataloguing in Publication Data

Marable, Manning
Black American Politics: from the Washington Marches
to Jesse Jackson.
Vol. 1: Afro-American social protest and
electoral movements.
1. Afro-Americans——Politics suffrage   2. United
States——Politics and government——1933–1945
3. United States——Politics and government——1945–
I. Title
306′.2   E185.61

First published 1985
© Manning Marable

Verso
15 Greek Street, London W1V 5LF

Typeset in Times by
PRG Graphics, Redhill, Surrey

Manufactured in the United States of America

10 9 8 7 6 5 4 3 2   86 87 88

ISBN 0-86091-108-X
      0-86091-816-5 pbk

Contents

Preface

'The problem of the twentieth century is the problem of the colour line — the relation of the darker to the lighter races of men in Asia and Africa, in America and the islands of the sea,' wrote W.E.B. Du Bois in *The Souls of Black Folk*, first published in 1903. But half a century later, in a brief introductory preface to the work, Du Bois added: 'I still think today as yesterday that the colour line is a great problem . . . But today I see more clearly than yesterday that back of the problem of race and colour lies a greater problem which both obscures and implements it: and that is the fact that so many civilized persons are willing to live in comfort even if the price of this is poverty, ignorance and disease of the majority of their fellowmen . . .' In a racist, capitalist social formation, 'race' appears as the decisive social category of significance to most of the oppressed, as well as to their oppressors. The social movements for Black power in such societies must inevitably assume a racial form, and a political discourse that represents the cultural and social consciousness of national minorities or oppressed nations. But matters do not end there. For effective power is never exercised solely by a single race, but by a dominant social class. Thus Black political movements are simultaneously movements that seek to restructure or radically transform *class* relations. The purpose of this two-volume study is to explore the theory and practice of social class struggle and political change throughout the African Diaspora.

There are five chapters in each volume, and half of these chapters examine in some detail case-studies of Black political change. In the first volume, the primary focus is on the Afro-American political experience within the United States, although there is also much comparative data on the Caribbean and Africa. The three case-studies included here represent the most dynamic expressions of Afro-American political struggles in the first half of the 1980s: the 27 August 1983 March on Washington; the election of Harold Washington as mayor of Chicago in April 1983; and the presidential campaign of Jesse Jackson. Also included are two essays of historical interpretation which attempt to advance a general theory of Black politics and examine the evolution of Afro-American electoral politicians in the US from Reconstruction to the present. Thematically, all the chapters are concerned with several central issues: the relationship between racism and the capitalist state; the historical expressions or modes of resistance manifested by Afro-Americans and the strategies of their class opponents; the pivotal role of the Black petty bourgeoisie in political movements, and the dual tendencies towards accommodation and/or resistance that they manifest at different historical moments. The second volume will present case-studies of Ghana and Grenada, and will discuss the problems of theory and practice in the transition to socialism in the Black world.

Sections of some chapters have been published previously in an earlier form, and many of the major themes explored have been developed in other articles. Material from chapter two appears in the *Black Scholar*, vol. 14 (November-December 1983), the *Guardian* (US) (30 May 1984), and the *New Statesman*, vol. 107 (13 January 1984); from chapter four, in the *Journal of Intergroup Relations*, vol. 11 (Summer 1983); and from chapter five, in *Cross Currents*, vol. 34 (Spring 1984), the *New Statesman*, vol. 108 (6 July 1984), and the *Guardian* (US) (13 June 1984). Williams College gave me a month of solitude to complete the first drafts of several chapters in this volume during the cold winter of 1984. Once again, my thanks to professor David Smith of Williams for his support. Colgate University provided generous resources that assisted my research. My special thanks to my invaluable research assistant, Lisa Eiseman, and to Melanie Goldstein, Mary Smith and Thelma Mayer for their work on the manuscript. Neil Belton's editorial assistance and guidance was crucial in the final structure of this work, and I appreciated his constructive criticisms and suggestions. My deepest expression of gratitude goes, however, to my wife Hazel Ann and to my children, Malaika, Sojourner and Joshua, who have become too accustomed to my sixteen-hour workdays in my office. All theoretical work is the product of collective labour, and Hazel Ann consistently contributes more to my writing and research than Du Bois. Her personal courage and quiet dignity assume no small part in my interpretation of Afro-American social protest history.

Finally, a brief note about the origins of this study. Black radical social theory is unique because it has developed in the context of the two most fundamental questions which confront American bourgeois democracy — the existence of racial inequality, and the perpetuation of class exploitation. When Black political movements have expressed their own objective interests, they speak not only for the masses of Afro-Americans, but for all of the oppressed. This observation also applies, as I will discuss in Volume 2, to Black movements in both capitalist-colonial states and neo-colonial regimes. Hence the struggles of Black Americans cannot be studied or properly understood outside a Pan-African and international context. Capital's desperate struggle to maintain apartheid is indeed linked with the electoral machinations to suppress a Jesse Jackson or Harold Washington. Going beyond this boundary, we may now see the essential parallels between the struggles of labour against capital world-wide and the particular protests of Black, Latino and white workers in the US. Du Bois, Paul Robeson, C.L.R. James, Oliver C. Cox, St Clair Drake, Walter Rodney, Amilcar Cabral, all in their own special way, understood this. Racial equality and national liberation cannot be realized to their fullest extent beneath the weight of capital.

Manning Marable 15 January 1985

Dedication

C.L.R. James is the most creative and challenging Marxist intellectual of the mid twentieth century. Few of his many students and admirers have agreed with all of Nello's political affiliations or theoretical insights. But as a social historian of the African Diaspora, political strategist for West Indian independence, and for his total dedication to the self-conscious emancipation of labour and all of the world's oppressed peoples, he has no equal. James's greatness is his understanding that democracy and equality can be achieved only from the bottom up. His humanistic legacy shall be fulfilled as politically conscious women and men destroy all forms of exploitation, and create the institutions of accomplished democracy.

1

Historical Prologue
Towards a General Theory of Black Politics

The race question is subsidiary to the class question in politics, and to think of
imperialism in terms of race is disastrous. But to neglect the racial factor as merely
incidental is an error only less grave than to make it fundamental.

C.L.R. James

I

At the heart of Black politics is a series of crimes: the brutal
exploitation of the human and natural resources of the African
continent; the perpetuation of chattel slavery and the transatlantic
slave-trade for nearly four centuries; the sexual abuse, rape and
physical oppression of Black women; the lynching, assassination
and castration of Black men; the denial of basic human rights and
simple dignity which have been given to others without question;
the imposition of educational institutions which fetter the mind and
crush the spirit; the confiscation of billions of hours' worth of
unpaid or low-paid labour-power in the process of capitalist production; the attempted obliteration or distortion of indigenous
cultural, religious and social institutions among African people; the
expropriation of our land and economic institutions. Politics for
those in the historical crucible of exploitation and destruction
becomes both a means of human affirmation and a mode of resistance to the excruciating apparatuses of systemic violence in which
people of the African Diaspora find themselves. Thus Black
political movements in the Caribbean, Africa and the United States
have expressed several common objectives: the ultimate abolition
of racism and all forms of economic, political and cultural exploitation; liberation from national oppression; and the maximization of
'power', or 'the capacity of a social class to realize its specific
objective interests.'[1] The conscious, collective expression of power
represents the 'articulation of social conflict and particularly of class
conflict.' This 'pervasive and ubiquitous conflict' which circum-
scribes the modern history of the Black world is defined here as
'politics'.[2] This study will examine the theory and the historical

1

practice of Black politics: the racial politics of class struggle, the pursuit of power in monopoly capitalist and colonial capitalist societies.

Two central concepts employed throughout this text are 'race' and 'power'. Race has always been difficult to define: to rephrase Rosa Luxemburg's caustic comment about nationalism, race is nothing but 'an empty husk', into which 'class relations pour their special material content'.[3] For well over a century, anthropologists, sociologists and psychologists debated the rationales for the division of humanity into any number from three to over thirty distinct categories. The attempt to identify racial differences between social groups has until recent decades focused, at least in the US, on the question of 'the Black man's lack of success in America', which was attributed to 'some distinctly racial peculiarity or limitation, some defect in his biological equipment, [which] had rendered him incapable of maintaining himself on a level with his fellow Americans.'[4] Gradually, first in the field of anthropology and somewhat later in psychology, the bogus notions that obvious inherited differences in physical characteristics, such as skin colour and hair texture, were accompanied by distinctions in mental capacity were debunked.[5] But the necessity to provide some 'objective' concept of race persists, despite the fact that scientists themselves continue to be at odds as to the relative weight allotted to biological or cultural criteria. In the *Dictionary of Sociology*, Henry Pratt Fairchild asserts that race is unquestionably 'a biological subdivision based upon similarity of ancestry and consequent physical kinship . . . The ideal race is a group of organisms all descended from a single ancestor . . .'[6] Yet British zoologist Anthony Smith observes that 'race' is still a scientific unknown: 'Geneticists believe anthropologists know what a race is, ethnologists assume their racial classifications are backed up by genetics, and politicians believe that their prejudices have the sanction of both genetics and anthropology.'[7] The quest for race is at root an attempt to explain the pervasiveness of racial inequality, which in the capitalist West is usually regarded 'as something inevitable and ineradicable, like "original sin" ', writes political economist Victor Perlo. The bulk of racial research frequently places 'the main blame' for racism 'on the victims, on the alleged "shortcomings" of the Black people themselves.'[8] As Ira Katznelson notes, 'by themselves, the physical facts of race are of little or no analytical significance to the social scientist. Racial physical characteristics only assume social meaning when they become criteria of stratification.'[9]

Put another way, 'race' as a social category exists only within a social formation divided into classes.

Perhaps the best examination of race in social science literature was provided by Oliver C. Cox in his seminal work *Caste, Class and Race*. 'It should be made patently clear that the laboratory classi-fication of races, which began among anthropologists about a hundred years ago, has no necessary relationship with the problem of race relations as sociological phenomena.' Race is properly understood only in a 'social' context, not in terms of biological theories. For Cox, 'race' was not a thing, but a relationship between social aggregates. 'Race relations' was 'that behaviour which develops among peoples who are aware of each other's actual or imputed physical difference', such as skin colour. Hypothetically, if two individuals 'were to meet and deal with each other . . . without preoccupation with a social definition of each other's race — then it might be said that race here is of no sociological significance.' Race in the modern, capitalist sense of the term would not exist. 'But if their behaviour tended to be fashioned by ethnic attitudes toward each other's actual or purported physical differences, then the situation' could be viewed 'as race relations'. 'Race' as a social concept is, relatively speaking, historically new. It does not originate from some vague 'social instinct of antipathy' between peoples, nor was 'race' ever part of the cultural or political discourse or the pattern of social relations in antiquity.[10] There are, of course, numerous parallels between the oppression of social groups on the basis of caste within many societies and the socio-economic and political experiences of Black people under slavery, colonialism and modern capitalism. There are obvious similarities between India's Harijans (untouchables) and Afro-Americans, in terms of the systemic denial of their economic, political and social rights.[11] Similarly, the oppressed Burakumin caste of Japan, referred to by the majority as '*Eta*' [full of filth] have been regarded for centuries as 'mentally inferior,' 'incapable of high moral behaviour', and subjected to vigilante violence and physical segregation. Yet in the case of the Burakumin and most other oppressed castes, no racial or physical marks determine their subordinate status.[12] Despite the convergences, the essential social dynamics of caste and racial exploitation remain fundamentally different.

The Western notion of race, as it has evolved in the past four centuries, is dialectically related to slavery: or as Marxist anthro-pologist Bernard Magubane observes, 'the history of colonialism and imperialism is the history of the development of cultural institutions and of ideas of class and/or racial inequality in the newly created societies.'[13] Even before the transatlantic slave-trade began, however, two factors existed which prefigured the subsequent rise of white racism. First, from antiquity right up to the dawn of the Renaissance, Europeans believed in the inherent inequality of slaves. In classical Greece, slaves were usually termed *andrapoda* — man-footed beings. The enslaved were sometimes branded like animals; they were frequently subjected to sexual abuse, and instances of slave prostitution were hardly rare. In the field of medicine, Plato reports, there were 'two sorts of doctors', those who comforted freemen, and poorly trained, slave assistants who treated slaves. Aristophanes, noting that male slaves of any age were sometimes termed *pais* [boy], jokingly in his play *The Wasps* described slaves using the word *paiein* — the verb 'to beat'.[14] Intellectuals for two thousand years had few qualms about the necessity to enslave human beings. As historian David Brion Davis relates, Plato 'took for granted' the permanent inferiority of slaves in 'his ideal Republic'. He even proposed the right of any free man 'to judge and punish a slave for certain crimes', and denied slaves any 'friendly intimacy with the master class'. Aristotle did claim that a slave could surpass a master in virtue, yet this did nothing to abolish a slave's earthly bondage. 'From the hour of their birth,' Aristotle observed, 'some are marked out for subjection, others for rule.' For Saint Thomas Aquinas, the subordination of slaves to masters was 'part of the governing pattern of nature', in concert with God's will. Centuries later, Sir Thomas More's *Utopia* created a place for slaves in the perfect society. Given the weight of theological and philosophical justifications of human inequality and natural slavery, it is hardly surprising that European Protestants and Catholics alike had no difficulty in perceiving the need for human bondage in the New World.[15]

The second factor, more complex yet decisive, was the cultural and ideological orientation of Europeans to perceive 'Blacks' as inferiors. 'Black' in this instance is relative, a function of both ethnocentrism and the perception of colour. Ethnocentrism is 'a social attitude which expresses a community of feeling in any group — the "we" feeling as over and against the "others".' 'This attitude', Cox notes, 'seems to be a function of group solidarity, which is not necessarily a racial phenomenon.'[16] Ethnicity is a manifestation of cultural patterns in language, religion, family and community life, mediated by the character of the productive process. The belief in the singularly 'unique' character of such cultural phenomena, and a recognition of difference from the cultural norms and institutions of other social groups, is ethnocentrism. Thus we might describe the behaviour of the Chinese during the T'ang dynasty, who termed Indonesian and Persian outsiders as 'blacks', as ethnocentric.[17] Western Europeans were similarly preconditioned to identify aliens as 'black'. The word itself was by the fifteenth century linked with 'sin, damnation, death, despair, ugliness and evil'. The devil was the 'Black Prince'; to become black was gradually transformed from being merely 'soiled' and 'dirty' to a state of malignancy. As historian C. Vann Woodward observed, 'long before Jamestown was founded the English had associated slavery with blackness, heathens, captivity and Biblical injunction.'[18] The rapid transition from ethnocentrism to institutional racism occurred with the expansion of the slave-trade, the extermination of Native American populations in the Caribbean and the Americas, and the development of overseas plantations. A black skin, the cultural, Biblical and psychological symbol of sin and inferiority, became identified with the permanent economic and political condition of Black slavery. Without debate, therefore, Maryland issued a law in 1663 determining that 'all negroes shall serve *durante vita*; and all children born of any negro or other slave shall be slaves as their fathers were for the term of their lives.'[19] Saint Thomas once argued that 'the woman's womb had the same relation to a man's seed as a plot of land to a sower; hence the owner of the woman, like the owner of land, had claim to all produce.'[20] In 1796, a South Carolina newspaper advertisement offering Afro-American slaves for sale echoed the same argument: 'They were purchased for stock and breeding . . . and to any planter who particularly wanted them for that purpose, they are a very choice and desirable gang.'[21]

Racism, then, is a historically specific concept, which coincided with the unequal racial division of labour within the expansion of capitalist social formations, and, more generally, with the capitalist mode of production as dominant within the West. As Magubane relates, 'capitalism required an expansionist policy of conquest and exploitation which set off a cumulative process that produced its own ideology: this ideology in turn became a force capable of orienting choices and determining decisions.' Racism, 'fed by the expansionist and exploitative socio-economic relations of capitalist imperialism, became a permanent stimulus for the ordering of unequal and exploitative relations of production along "racial" lines, and further demanded justification of these relations.'[22] The social inequality of a racist social formation is, in the first instance, the unequal distribution of material resources and the super-exploitation of a social fraction, Blacks or other 'people of colour,' at the point of production. In a capitalist society, the chief bene-ficiaries of racism, as Perlo suggests, are 'those in positions of control over the corporate economy, who inspire and deliberately perpetuate inequality, and especially economic discrimination . . . The motive is clear — billions of dollars in profits.'[23]

But the racial division of labour is only part of the problem. Racism or racial inequality is no 'simple or mechanical reflection' of the conditions and restrictions of Black labour.[24] The guiding prin-ciple of inequality directs the patterns of political, cultural, social and ideological life. Such social patterns also involve the 'systemic isolation, exclusion and (in many cases) extermination' of Blacks; the perpetuation of the racist ideology in 'the universities, schools, media, theatre and all creative arts, religion, civic associations and political parties'; the use of racist coercive measures by 'the police, armed forces, prisons, the criminal justice system, and white vigilante hate-groups'; the social psychological positioning of Blacks in the lowest, most vulgar sexual and bestial terms.[25] In every sphere — political, economic and cultural — racism is not simply 'a "body of ideas", but distorted and inverted structures in which such ideas operate and become an active force.' After several centuries, Magubane notes, racist ideologies were so 'widely dis-seminated' in the various capitalist social formations that they 'tended to take on a life of their own . . . Racism, though it certainly falsifies reality . . . has become a real force and the "true" consciousness of a large majority of whites in capitalist societies.'[26] To be Black in a racist society, as Melville Herskovits once sug-gested, is to be perceived as a person 'without a past'.[27] Frantz Fanon expressed this as a process of being 'overdetermined from without'. Blackness exists not of itself, but only 'in relation to the white man'.[28] Thus from the point of view of the exploited, class struggle in a racist social formation is inextricably linked with the anti-racist struggle: the battle to affirm one's humanity and to abolish racist culture, racist political institutions and racist exploit-ation in the productive processes is a manifestation of class struggle.

The definition of 'power' cited above, suggested by Nicos Poulantzas, must be qualified and expanded. Any social class or social fraction — a combination of classes which develops cultural, economic and political cohesiveness as a historical unit — mani-fests 'specific objective interests' in four interdependent spheres:

cultural, economic, political and ideological.[29] 'Power is located at the level of the *various* class practices, in so far as there are class interests concerning the economic, the political and the ideological.' A class within a capitalist social formation may struggle for 'economic power, political power, ideological power and so on, according to the capacity of a class to realize its relatively autonomous interests at each level.'[30] Thus a social class may express itself as an economic power, but fail to assert cultural or political power. These 'centres' of power, arenas of class conflict, are not autonomous spheres. 'The separation between the political, economic, social and cultural parts of the social whole is artificial and arbitrary', Ralph Miliband notes. '. . . The notion of "economics" as free from "politics" is an ideological abstraction and distortion. There is no such thing as "economics" — only "political economy", in which the "political" element is an ever-present component.' The mechanistic idea of 'economic determination' is as ridiculous as the metaphysical notion of ideologies that exist outside their social and material context. Of these four interdependent spheres, the 'economic base' can be said to be decisive 'as a matter of the *first* instance', the factor which *roughly* sets the range of possibilities within a social formation.[31] As Karl Marx observed in *Grundrisse,* any specific mode of production is only 'a general illumination which bathes all the other colours and modifies their particularity. It is a particular ether which determines the specific gravity of every being which has materialized within it.'[32]

Power in a given social formation is not like a game of power — a 'zero sum game'. Poulantzas quite correctly criticizes sociologist C. Wright Mills on this score. 'A reduction of this capacity of a class' to assert its specific interests 'is not automatically translated into an increase in the capacity of another class . . . for example, the loss of power by the bourgeoisie does not mean that this power is added to the power of the working class.' In the context of class struggle in specific states, the 'loss of power at the economic level, a reduction of a class's capacity to realize its *specific* economic interests, is not translated directly into a loss of political or ideological power or vice versa. On the other hand, an increase of a class's economic power does not directly entail an increase in its political or ideological power.'[33] The conscious, organized struggle for power, therefore, also presumes as given another basic fact: that in all societies divided by classes, conflict is permanent and inevitable. A class-stratified social formation is, in essence, one in which a 'more or less veiled civil war [rages] within existing society, up to the point where that war breaks out into open revolution . . .'[34] Thus in a racially stratified class society, Black protest in a variety of modes of resistance is an omnipresent fact of political life. In the days of slavery, wherein various capitalist ruling classes reverted to a distinctly pre-capitalist mode of production in the exploitation of Black labour, the immediate object of the oppressed was 'freedom' — not merely emancipation from the institution of chattel slavery, but freedom from other general forms of racist oppression promoted by capitalism. In late capitalist social formations, the attack against racism is grounded in the demand for 'human equality' in all economic, cultural and political relations. Every positive step towards racial equality, directly or indirectly, increases the 'power' of the Black 'social fraction' vis-à-vis the capitalist class. W.E.B. Du Bois characterized this world-wide struggle against the colour line as 'fighting for universal equality . . . not to become white men . . . but to become ourselves and to hold ourselves the equal of any.'[35]

II

In *Black Skin, White Masks* Fanon briefly relates an encounter between a disabled war veteran, who is white, and a Black man. The amputee says: 'Resign yourself to your colour the way I got used to my stump; we're both victims.' Fanon responds: 'Nevertheless with all my strength I refuse to accept that amputation. I feel in myself a soul as immense as the world, truly a soul as deep as the deepest of rivers, my chest has the power to expand without limit.'[36] Fanon's statement reveals the living essence of history: human beings, through their conscious creativity, their hopes, their aspirations, create the possibilities for the historical process. All social class conflict, 'politics', arises from the conscious decision by some group of human beings to intervene in some sphere of the social formation, and to alter it according to their expressed cultural, political, ideological and economic desires. A structuralist analysis cannot express the inherently ephemeral nature of human societies. Social contradictions are temporarily resolved; and inevitably, others emerge to alter the dynamics of society's ever-changing structure. Jean-Paul Sartre expressed this dialectical dynamic best: 'History is not order. It is disorder: a rational disorder. At the very moment when it maintains order, that is, structure, history is already on the way to undoing it.'[37] There is an inevitable tension here, an uneven mixture of wills and institutions, of human values and the productive process. The structures of the productive process, in concert with the political/cultural/ideological structures, create an unsteady combination of force and fraud, coercion and consensus to create a 'stable' social formation. The ideological and cultural hegemony of the ruling class has a tremendous impact upon the class consciousness of the oppressed: thus it is not surprising to learn that thousands of early members of the African National Congress in South Africa holding anti-pass demonstrations would mix speeches 'about their defiance of injustice with songs of Britannica, with cheers for England's King and for President Wilson, only to have their meetings roughly dispersed by the police.'[38] But mass 'consciousness', the internalized kernel of the myriad patterns of class and national culture, is not so easily manipulated. As historian E.P. Thompson asserts, people 'handle their feelings within their culture as norms, familial and kinship obligations and reciprocities, as values within art or religious values.' Culture does not arise *outside* the historical process, but in conflict and/or in harmony with political and economic structures. Thus Thompson states that 'every contradiction is a conflict of value as well as a conflict of interest; that inside every "need" there is an affect, or "want", on its way to becoming an "ought" (and vice versa); that every class struggle is at the same time a struggle over values.'[39] Political history is thus simultaneously determined by structures and 'undermined' by the independent choices of human beings who, for an endless variety of reasons, interject themselves into the dialectic. The conscious will bends and breaks structure, only for a new order to arise, in turn to be transformed at some distant point.

Consequently no 'politics' are possible unless a class or social fraction is first *conscious* of its economic exploitation or political and cultural oppression: that is, all manifestations of Black politics assume a particular point of view which is antithetical to the prevailing cultural, political, ideological and economic order. We might well examine this thesis from the balcony of a great plantation-house on a hot afternoon in St Domingue in 1789; or from a plantation outside Charleston, South Carolina in 1822; or at a sugar plantation on Jamaica's north coast in 1831. The typical racist would view his complete hegemony as a permanent fact of life. The slave was less than human; the rape of a young Black girl was not a crime against a 'woman', but a ritual act of coercion upon an 'object,' a piece of property. Such perceptions reinforced the class interests of the plantation-owners, and helped to perpetuate the particular social formation of slavery. But let us descend from the balcony into the fields. The slaves are aware, better than any outside observer, of the coercive structure that manipulates them and extracts their labour power. But the political economy of exploitation, brutal as it is, does allow for a social space — even if only *mental* space. And inevitably, human will, the consciousness of the oppressed, expresses itself in ways that no master class can predict, or even comprehend. The material contradiction sparks a conflict of values, which is manifested in diverse forms of resistance and class struggle. What St Domingue master could read the mind of a grey-haired slave, Toussaint, as he nourished the aspiration of freedom for himself and other salves?[40] Did the brutal overseer who lashed the bloodied back of a common Black labourer, Jacques Dessalines, have any idea that his victim would become the first emperor of Haiti? Could he believe that this same slave would break up the plantations and order the execution of every white on the island? The South Carolina aristocracy would have shaken their heads in bewilderment and fear, had they been told that behind their backs a Black Charleston carpenter, Denmark Vesey, was plotting their extermination. The slave conspiracy once broken led to 139 arrests and 47 executions; but an estimated nine thousand slaves had been involved in the plan, including hundreds of trusted 'house Negroes'.[41] Jamaica planters may have first learned of Samuel Sharpe's uprising from the bittersweet smell of burning sugar-cane fields.[42]

In each instance, the intense contradictions of slavery created a different point of view for the slaves, as they sought to develop families and communities under extremely harsh conditions. Their perceptions were at times half hidden from themselves, only to be acted out in the political act of revolt when the structures of society least expected it. Men's and women's perceptions are grounded in their understanding of the past, and are made concrete in the form of specific behavioural modes as their vision of the future becomes clear. In its most elementary form, the ultimate struggle of a class begins when the individual member is transformed; and this process is frequently precipitated by the most coercive conditions. C.L.R. James observes that Gandhi, Nehru, Nkrumah and Nyerere 'didn't learn about democracy in British schools; they learnt it in the gaols into which the British had put them; and from those gaols they taught the population . . . what were the realities of independence.' When George Jackson was imprisoned in California at the age of eighteen, he was a 'juvenile delinquent'. Ten years later, over half that sentence having been spent in solitary confinement, James notes, Jackson was able to write 'the most remarkable political documents that have appeared inside or outside the United States since the death of Lenin.' Jackson 'arrived at the profound conclusion that the only way of life possible' for Black America 'is the complete intellectual, physical, moral commitment to the revolutionary struggle against capitalism.'[43] Politics is a conscious, historical act: the decision to create a new history from one's point of view within a class.

A common denominator of all racist social formations — and here I include societies with pre-capitalist modes of production (slavery) as well as all colonial regimes that suppress Black nations — is the omnipresence of systemic violence or coercion to facilitate Black labour-exploitation. A social formation with a racial division of labour and a civil society whose guiding star is 'inequality' cannot take for granted the accommodationist tendencies of the oppressed. The coercive apparatuses that secure domestic order permeate the entire character of social relations, even at the level of individual interaction. Gilberto Freyre, the Brazilian sociologist, writes candidly of the Portuguese planters' rapes of young Black boys as a normal 'social condition' brought about by 'all-powerful masters and passive slaves'. Brazilian 'lords of the manor' would think nothing of 'having pregnant slave girls burned alive in the plantation ovens, the unborn offspring crackling in the heat of the flames . . . There are tales of *sinhámoças* who had the eyes of pretty *mucamas* [slave girls] gouged out and then had them served to their husbands for dessert, in a jelly-dish, floating in blood that was still fresh. There were others who kicked out the teeth of their women slaves with their boots, or who had their breasts cut off, their nails drawn, or their faces and ears burnt.' Freyre speaks only of Brazil, but recounts a scene which recurred thousands of times during slavery, colonialism and racial segregation across the Diaspora. 'Not infrequently the young mistress, who has been brought up to rub against the sturdy slave lads, yields herself to them when her nerves give way to her irrepressible desires. Then it is that paternal morality intervenes; the Negro or mulatto is castrated with a dull knife, the wound is sprinkled with salt, and he is then buried alive.'[44] Every form of slavery was based upon the use of such violence.[45] Black politics in the first instance begins when individuals within a subordinated social class transcend their fear of the master class and the daily coercion that buttresses its authority: Black political movements begin at the historical

The Masters and the Slaves – Gilberto Freyre

moment when groups of such individuals find a common strategy, social vehicle or mode of resistance that contradicts the dominant coercive apparatuses. More simply, one could say that Black politics began in the New World when those first nameless slaves raised their hoes and, with calm deliberation, smashed them across their overseers' heads. As Frederick Douglass observed, he himself ceased to be a slave psychologically when he defeated his white overseer in a bloody, two-hour fist fight. 'This battle . . . was the turning point of my career as a slave. [It] rekindled the few expiring embers of freedom, and revived within me a sense of my own manhood.'[46]

The study of Black politics cannot limit its field of subjects solely to those delineated by 'race' or oppressed national categories. Capitalism is international in character: the patterns of political protest, which articulate class conflict, are never confined to a particular geographical area, or to a single social formation. The slave-trade, plantation economies, the development of bourgeois democracies in the West and their subsequent imposition of colonial and later neo-colonial regimes over Africa were international phenomena. The North American plantation finds its approximate duplicates across the Black world; Black miners extracted minerals from the earth in West Virginia, Jamaica, Brazil, Katanga and the Transvaal. Black Caribbean activists directly influenced the patterns of Black US resistance organizations, from Toussaint to Stokely Carmichael and Walter Rodney; Kwame Nkrumah's Pan-African consciousness was formed largely by Blacks in the US and in England; 'Black Power' in the US during the 1960s became, under different structural conditions, 'Black Consciousness' among Soweto's youth in the mid 1970s. Thus Black politics in the US, understood as a series of resistance modes, cannot be viewed outside the political sociology of the entire African Diaspora. And by extension, the entire process of human oppression, capital accumulation and cultural genocide experienced by the Black world must be viewed properly against modern world history, and particularly the history of the world proletariat.

If one cuts across the geographical boundaries and diverse cultural, social and political patterns found in the African Diaspora, focusing deliberately on the 'patterns' of historical modes of class resistance or social class conflict, one can observe three *general* tendencies that frequently recur. These three general typologies form the basis for this study: Black social movements; Black 'electoral' politics; and revolutionary or Marxist politics.

Between these broad categories there is a tremendous amount of overlapping. Alexander Bustamante of Jamaica, for example, was leader of a strong trade-union mobilization, a social movement, and was subsequently drawn into electoral politics although he had never run for public office. Nevertheless, there are clear differences which separate each typology. A social movement is a series or combination of different historical modes of class struggle. This social class conflict, the struggle to assert and to achieve greater power, can be within the economy, within political institutions, in social and cultural relations, in the ideological sphere, or in all spheres simultaneously. These modes of protest are exerted against the existing structures of society, including both the mode of production and the state apparatus. Any social protest movement attacks the power, the prestige and the excesses of the ruling class; they are by nature 'oppositional' in that they criticize clearly identifiable structures of exploitation and oppression. The various modes of social insurgency may be trade-union organizing, religious protests, the development of all-Black communities, and so on. What they all have in common is their spontaneity and effluence. No people live, after all, in a constant state of collective rage. Social movements rise and fall, only to emerge with vigour at various stages of history when they are least anticipated. They usually expand the necessary social space to maintain Black workers' cultural and social institutions. Frequently, especially in capitalist social formations where Blacks comprise a distinct national minority (for example in the United States), social movements successfully expand bourgeois democratic rights to include Blacks. Desegregation marches, pickets, demonstrations and economic boycotts represent different tactics of social protest, but all have a single focus, the destruction of Jim Crow laws and the coordinated assault against the social principal of racial inequality. Social movements may improve the material conditions of the life of an oppressed class (trade unionism, for example), but they do not overturn the basic dictatorship of capital over labour, and they do not end the racial division of labour across the society. Social movements may be generated by a single class; but within the Black Diaspora, given the ideological and political weight of both white racism and national oppression, almost all Black social movements have a multiclass constituency (for example, petty bourgeoisie, workers, and so forth).

Social movements of Black social fractions and national liberation movements (in the bourgeois democratic context) may also assume an electoral form. Two recent examples of this in the United States were the 1983 mayoral race of Harold Washington in Chicago, and the 1984 Presidential campaign of Jesse Jackson. In Black nations under European colonial oppression, electoral phenomena under the constraints of bourgeois democracy merge with the broader national liberation movement, as in the instance of Nkrumah's Convention People's Party in the Gold Coast during the late 1940s. Bourgeois democratic or 'electoral' political struggle has a general goal the expansion of Black representation in the existing state apparatus. The political practice of most Black leaders within this process indicates an explicit or implicit acceptance of the legitimacy of bourgeois democratic rule, and hence, of the continuation of the capitalist mode of production. In capitalist colonial nations, the usual aim of Black politicians is to occupy the political apparatus completely, without *first* overthrowing the state power of the ruling class and the colonialists' ownership of the means of production.

Finally, revolutionary political struggles are those in which a political agent or social vehicle, drawn from the exploited social classes, attempts to seize state power. In the colonial social formations of Africa and the Caribbean, such agents (for example, parties, national liberation fronts) may or may not be 'Marxist' in orientation: nevertheless, the general rubric of 'national liberation' is essentially a manifestation of class struggle in a national context of foreign oppression.

These three overlapping typologies of Black class conflict could be viewed as variants of what Immanuel Wallerstein characterizes as 'antisystemic' struggles waged against world capital.[47] But the central factor of racism in the evolution of capitalist social formations, the racial division of labour, has created basic divergencies between all-Black political movements and those involving white workers alone. Cox recognized that 'although both race relations and the struggle of the white proletariat with the bourgeoisie are parts of a single social phenomenon, race relations involve a significant variation':

> In the case of race relations the tendency of the bourgeoisie is to proletarianize a whole people — that is to say, the whole people is looked upon as a class — whereas white proletarianization involves only a section of the white people. The concept "bourgeois" and "white people" sometimes seems to mean the same thing for, with respect to the coloured peoples of the world, it is almost always through a white bourgeoisie that capitalism has been introduced. The early capitalist

settlers among the coloured peoples were disposed to look upon the latter and their natural resources as factors of production to be manipulated impersonally with "white capital" in the interest of profits. It is this need to impersonalize whole peoples which introduces into the class struggle the complicating factors known as race problems . . . The Europeans have overthrown more or less completely the social system among every coloured people with whom they have come into contact. The stability of colour and inertness of culture, together with effective control over firearms, subsequently made it possible for whites to achieve a more or less separate and dominant position even in the homeland of coloured peoples.[48]

III

A class-divided social formation is a society in permanent civil war. Frequently one can observe 'comparatively peaceful epochs' which seem to be 'filled with nothing but peace and harmony', noted Nikolai Bukharin. 'It merely signifies that the class struggle is proceeding in a concealed or incipient form . . . Such is the case with the oppressed classes. As for the ruling classes, they are waging the class struggle unceasingly.'[49] Despite the formidable weapons the ruling class has at its disposal, the exploited classes inevitably question the 'legitimacy' of the established order. As Frances Fox Piven and Richard Cloward observe, a legitimacy crisis first occurs when 'large numbers of men and women who ordinarily accept the authority of their rulers and the legitimacy of institutional arrangements come to believe that these rulers and arrangements are unjust and wrong.' People who were fatalistic yesterday, who doubted their ability to address political issues, suddenly become opinionated. They recognize immediate, perceptible grievances, and they begin to assert their 'rights' which in turn imply demands for basic change. Covert discussions culminate ultimately in public debates and assemblies devised by the masses themselves. 'People who ordinarily consider themselves helpless come to believe that they have some capacity to alter' the social hierarchy and class relationships. Piven, Cloward and political scientist John Q. Wilson describe this process as a 'social movement', which is 'a conscious, collective, organized attempt to bring about or resist large-scale change in the social order by non-institutional means.'[50] I would expand this definition somewhat: a social movement is the most common social manifestation of class struggle. Such movements are collective efforts made by a class, a social fraction or an oppressed nation to increase its class power, whether culturally, ideologically, economically or politically. A social movement represents the primary struggle for power of an oppressed class: other expressions of collective struggle, such as electoral campaigns of Blacks in bourgeois democracies, or revolutionary struggles, invariably begin as social movements, and are extensions of them.

Let us examine six rather different examples of Black social protest: the establishment in 1895 of the National Federation of Afro-American Women, with Margaret Murray Washington as its president, and the following year, the creation in Washington DC, of the National League of Coloured Women, led by Mary Church Terrell; the outbreak of Black violence among sugar-cane labourers and dock workers in Guyana in November-December 1905; the first public meeting of the Brotherhood of Sleeping-Car Porters, led by socialist editor A. Philip Randolph, and held at St Luke's Hall in Harlem on 25 August 1925; the first gathering of the *Frente Negra Brasileira*, held in Saõ Paulo, Brazil on 16 September 1931; the beginning of the 'Campaign for the Defiance of Unjust Laws' in Johannesburg and Port Elizabeth, South Africa, on 26 June 1952; and the incident on late Monday afternoon, 1 February 1960, in Greensboro, North Carolina, when four Black students — Joseph McNeil, Izell Blair, David Richmond and Franklin McClain — 'ignited one of the largest of all Afro-American protest movements', the 'sit-ins'.[51] What do these manifestations of Black social class protest have in common?

Social movements always focus on immediate, perceptible grievances, problems which affect an entire class or social fraction. In the development of the Afro-American women's organizations, activists were conscious 'of the need to challenge racism', as Angela Y. Davis writes. Negro women's clubs held mass public meetings to condemn lynchings, police brutality and political disfranchisement; more specifically, they denounced the racism of Susan B. Anthony, Elizabeth Cady Stanton and other white petty-bourgeois suffragists. One Black woman activist who was excluded from a white women's club, Fannie Barrier Williams, explained that the Afro-American women's 'club movement reaches into the sub-condition of the entire race . . . [It is] the struggle of an enlightened conscience against the whole brood of social miseries, born out of the stress and pain of a hated past.'[52] The 1905 riots in Guyana began on the sugar estates along the Demerara River, but the insurgency was most decisive among Georgetown's stevedores. Dockworkers demanded sixteen cents an hour for their normal ten-and-a-half-hour day; the going rate at the time was sixty-four cents a day. When management refused, work stopped; strikers 'roamed the business centre, and some looting took place at pawnbrokers' and jewellers'.' Militants threatened recalcitrant workers in other firms in efforts to make them leave their posts, and 'domestics were dragged out of private private houses.'[53] In the case of the Afro-American porters, low wages were only part of the problem. Historian William H. Harris notes that 'for their salary of /367.50 per month, Pullman porters were expected to perform 400 hours of service. These hours did not include the time porters spent in preparing their cars for the receipt of passengers or in making cars ready for storage', time that esentially represented 'millions of dollars that porters donated to the company annually'. Porters had 'no guarantee of time off to sleep', and for their first ten years on the job had to buy their own uniforms.[54]

For Black Brazilians during the 1920s and 1930s, the issues were more complex. Florestan Fernandes states that Blacks comprised 'the undifferentiated masses of the working classes, kept strictly in their place'. They were expelled from public establishments; 'if a Black person applied for a job, he was offered manual labour; if he took over a new [professional] position, he was mistaken for a servant or janitor; it was considered legitimate to . . . order him to do "nigger work"'. The bitterness and dissatisfaction among Blacks led to the spontaneous development of social movements representing the Negro's growing awareness of his situation . . . '[55] In South Africa, non-white militancy deepened with the election of the ultra-racist Nationalist Party in 1948, and the passing of a series of fascist laws between 1948 and 1952. Some aspects of apartheid legislation included: the removal of Indian representation in Parliament; the 1949 'Prohibition of Mixed Marriages Act'; the 1949 'Unemployment Insurance Amendment Act' which excluded from all benefits all migratory labourers and the majority of African workers; the 1950 'Population Registration Act' which required that everyone carry 'an identity card on which his race would be indelibly stamped'; the 1950 'Suppression of Communism Act' which banned the Communist Party; and the 1952 'Criminal Sentences Amendment Act', which increased 'whippings' for criminals. Brian Bunting noted that between 1942 and 1962 about one million 'strokes were administered to 180,000 offenders; and 850,000 of these strokes were administered after the 1952 Act was passed.'[56] The 'sit-ins' were based on Black youth opposition to racial segregation in public accommodation. On 2 February, about thirty students joined the Greensboro protest; within ten days, sit-ins were repeated by hundreds of Black and white students in five other North Carolina cities. 'Without an organizational structure and without a coherent set of ideas to guide their actions', Clayborne Carson writes, the students 'were determined to break with the past . . . In the beginning, they only spoke of modest desire: to drink a cup of coffee, sitting down.'[57]

All social movements encourage the oppressed to articulate their grievances, and to forge some plan of collective action. The initial confrontations educate the masses and give rise to a sense of purpose, a greater clarity of action. Confrontations of this type, whether they at first succeed or not, increase class or social fraction consciousness and thus increase class power. For Brazilian Blacks, increased expressions of 'race' consciousness were viewed as a necessary tactic in the battle for racial equality. The manifesto of the *Frente Negra Brasileira* urged Afro-Brazilians to become 'racially nationalistic': 'Let us unite Negro Associations, as a social force, as a moral force, as an economic force, as a Political Force to help the Brazilian Powers be Brazilian and to solve our problem . . .'[58] The Defiance Campaign was 'directed against the national motto of white South Africa, EUROPEANS ONLY, which is found across the length and breadth of the country', wrote African National Congress (ANC) president Albert Luthuli. Volunteers challenged 'separate but unequal' public facilities at train stations, post offices and waiting rooms. 'Our whole protest and resistance is based on our claim to human dignity.'[59] In the southern US, the initial sit-ins quickly sparked student resistance across the region. By mid April 1960, roughly fifty thousand demonstrators had joined the sit-in movement. At first, the level of political development among student desegregation activists was exceedingly low. Diane Nash, one of the earliest sit-in leaders, explicitly connected the student movement with the struggle against communism, declaring that once Blacks obtained equal educational opportunities, 'maybe some day a Negro will invent one of our missiles.' Yet non-violent confrontations against Jim Crow, 'when accompanied by a rationale based on Christian principles, offered Black students an appealing combination of rewards: a sense of moral superiority, an emotional release through militancy, and a possibility of achieving desegregation.'[60] As Vincent Harding notes, 'no one expected much in the way of social or political action' from these college students. But soon the young Afro-Americans 'were filled with vitality and passion, with belief and cascading hope . . . They were believers. When they sang in gaol, in mass meetings, in front of policemen and state troopers, "We Shall Overcome", they meant it. Few were certain about details, but they *would* overcome.'[61]

Such struggles for class power are waged, to a great extent, in the various spheres of the social milieu: economic, cultural-social, political. There is seldom a concerted struggle for political power — such as for the elimination of Jim Crow laws — without a concomitant effort to increase cultural and economic power. The sit-in movement rapidly created a new youth formation, the Student Non-violent Coordinating Committee (SNCC); but it also sparked within Black civil society many new protest elements. The SNCC's 'Freedom Singers', formed in 1962 largely of veterans from the desegregation campaign in Albany, Georgia, popularized the goals of the movement. Marchers and demonstrators sang as they protested:

> Ain't gonna let nobody turn me 'round,
>   turn me 'round, turn me 'round,
> Ain't gonna let nobody turn me 'round,
> I'm gonna keep on walkin', keep on a-talkin',
> Marching up to freedom land.[62]

Humour for the oppressed is invariably political. One popular joke among Blacks in the early 1960s was the following: 'A waitress told a pair of sitters-in, "I'm sorry but we don't serve Negroes here." "Oh, we don't eat them either," came the reply.'[63] A class struggle for political power is almost always translated into economic struggles. Within two weeks of the first sit-in, the Congress of Racial Equality (CORE) held solidarity demonstrations at 'dime stores' in northern states. Woolworth and other national chain stores which held Jim Crow lunch-counters in the South reported sharp declines in sales. Facing economic losses, corporate leaders were now willing to negotiate: within six months, firms in ninety cities in eleven southern states had desegregated.[64] And the process may be just the reverse — what begins as a cultural struggle may develop into a class struggle for political and economic power. The foundations of the *Frente Negra Brasileira* were formed in January 1924 with the emergence of *O Clarim da Alvorada,* a race-conscious publication 'with purely literary purposes'. The cultural nationalism of the small mulatto and Afro-Brazilian intelligentsia established the basic direction of the *Frente Negra,* which registered as a distinct political party in 1936.[65]

Social movements are rarely based within a single class or gender division in the Black Diaspora. Previously suggested were two factors: that in pre-capitalist and colonial environments, distinctly proletarian movements seldom develop; and that within advanced capitalist social formations with a racial division of labour, oppressed Blacks frequently express their 'class' outrage in distinctly 'racial' terms. The racism of white workers makes it difficult to proclaim proletarian unity as an immediate political and social programme. Thus Rodney observes that in the 1905 Guyana uprising, a cross section of the people were involved, and not merely workers. 'Members of the middle class expressed sympathy; and much of the cutting-edge of physical confrontation was provided by social elements on the fringe of the working class', the so-called 'centipedes' or 'quasi-criminal segment of hustlers' and 'urban youth gangs'.[66] Despite the emphasis laid by social historians and sociologists on the male leadership of such movements, the core group of militants are quite frequently women. Repeatedly, Black women have engaged in confrontationist tactics that many men would be reluctant to attempt. In the case of Guyana, Rodney notes that 41 of the 105 persons 'convicted in the Georgetown Magistrates' Court as a consequence of the riots were female.' Women in particular 'were said to have resorted to stone-throwing, and a band of women attacked' one police station. Dorothy Rice, a sugar-cane cutter who earned only six to seven shillings a week on a Ruimveldt plantation, was a spokesperson for all rural wage labourers. 'Her counterparts in the urban settings of Georgetown would have been washerwomen, seamstresses, street vendors, and, above all, domestics in private employment.'[67] In South Africa, after the Defiance campaign, African women continued 'a stubborn and militant struggle to frustrate the extension of the hated pass laws to themselves.'[68] On 9 August 1956, over twenty thousand African women demonstrated in Pretoria, carrying petitions, which called for an end to all pass laws, into the office of Prime Minister J.G. Strijdom, a noxious racist. When he prudently refused to meet the outraged women, they sang out loudly: 'Strijdom, you have touched the women, you have struck a rock, you have dislodged a boulder, you will be crushed!'[69]

The leadership of Black social movements both in advanced capitalist states and in colonial regimes are frequently drawn from the small intelligentsia; technicians, clergy, teachers, physicians, writers and other petty-bourgeois elements. Many of these women and men have undergone a process of cultural and ideological assimilation. They comprehend the specific strengths and weaknesses of the dominant classes, and represent an elite which is both inside the exploited and oppressed group and outside it. This ambiguity in their cultural and ideological composition creates an equally vascillating political posture, particularly in periods of crisis. The petty bourgeoisie become ataxic: former progressives may become reactionaries; and others, in Cabral's words, may commit 'class suicide' by voluntarily relinquishing their marginal prerequisites and participating in mass struggles.[70] In Guyana, the petty bourgeoisie oscillated between the masses and the state. Former 'radical' D.M. Hutson, past chairman of the Reform Association, 'accepted a brief from the police to watch over their interests during the inquest into the deaths of persons shot during the riots.' Conversely, A.A. Thorne, director of a Georgetown private secondary school, physician J.M. Rohlehr and attorney Patrick Dargan were 'well known for their militancy, [and] the strikers sought them out.' Dargan founded a newspaper which 'hammered the colonial administration over the riots and killings', and he served 'as an advocate in court on behalf of relatives of those killed . . .'[71]

The leaders of the Afro-American women's club movement were not proletarians. As Angela Davis comments, 'Josephine St Pierre Ruffin, for example, was the wife of a Massachusetts judge.' One Midwestern leader, a 'Mrs John Jones', was the spouse of 'the wealthiest coloured man in Chicago at that time'. The articulate and urbane Mary Church Terrell was the daughter of a wealthy Black entrepreneur from Memphis and was educated at Oberlin College, Ohio and in Europe. She was married to a powerful Black politician; and she 'became the first Black woman appointed to the Board of Education in the District of Columbia.' Davis writes: 'Had she sought personal wealth and fulfilment through a political or academic career, she would undoubtedly have succeeded. But her concern for the collective liberation of her people led her to devote her entire adult life to the struggle for Black liberation.'[72] In the southern desegregation movement, many Black student activists came from working-class or rural poor backgrounds, but were themselves class products of the universities or graduate schools. In the SNCC, John Lewis was one of the few Black students in Nashville's American Baptist Theological Seminary; Marion Barry — later to be elected mayor of Washington DC — was in 1960 a graduate student working for a master's degree in Chemistry at Fisk University; Diane Nash was also a Fisk University student; the SNCC's chief theoretician, James Forman, had been president of the student body at Roosevelt University in Chicago, and much later would earn a master's degree at Cornell University. Some SNCC leaders were second or even third generation Black middle class: Julian Bond, named by Forman as the SNCC's director of communications, was the son of the Dean of Atlanta University's School of Education.[73] The social significance of this group's class composition lies in the fact that only 7 per cent of all Black women and men between the ages of eighteen and twenty-four were enrolled in US colleges in 1960; in the South, only 15 per cent of all adult Afro-Americans had completed high school, and barely 3 per cent had college degrees.[74]

Social movements are usually initiated by a set of organizations or leaders who, in the process of class struggle, are replaced or supplanted by other leaders and formations. In other words, class struggles generate new class leadership, frequently from the working class, but also from the radical petty bourgeoisie who commit 'class suicide'. Individuals with hidden talents or abilities tend to be pushed forward, sometimes voluntarily, sometimes not. The Brotherhood of Sleeping-Car Porters provides some excellent examples. Randolph was the best-known figure in the Brotherhood: loyal members called him the 'chief ', and he won widespread support for the union, making it 'a movement for racial equality and not just a small union consisting of the few thousand porters who worked for the Pullman Company', as Harris relates. But the workers knew that the 'mundane' tasks of union organizing were not done by Randolph. Inside the union, others had far more influence in the actual day-to-day conflicts with management and dealt with the gritty local and regional recruitment of new members. A Black liberal Republican, Milton P. Webster, was the chief Brotherhood organizer in Chicago; Benjamin Smith was leader in Pittsburgh and Detroit; Morris 'Dad' Moore and the pugnacious C.L. Dellums emerged as the California leaders; and it was long-time porters Ashley L. Totten, Roy Lancaster and William H. Des Verney who were the real 'nucleus of this union movement', not Randolph.[75] From the SNCC's brief but radical history, one can follow the emergence of a truly talented Black woman, Ruby Doris Robinson. As a student at Spelman College in Atlanta, she volunteered to be arrested deliberately in order to support Blacks already gaoled in Rock Hill, North Carolina, in early February 1961. At the SNCC's 27-29 April 1962 general conference, she was elected an at-large member of the organization's Executive Committee. By early 1964, Robinson was pushing her co-workers to the left, insisting that civil rights legislation was meaningless unless Blacks won 'the basic necessities of life'. The SNCC needed to 'define its ideology' and to 'establish specific goals' beyond isolated protest campaigns. With the legendary Fannie Lou Hamer, Bond, Forman and others, she toured Africa in September-October 1964, and was encouraged by Guinean President Sekou Touré to 'take a broad view of the goals of their struggle', and to link their domestic issues with African liberation. In 1965, she was elected SNCC Executive Secretary, replacing Forman. As the SNCC's leader, she took 'a strong [Black] nationalist line', but refused to berate progressive white allies; she chastised SNCC chairman Stokely Carmichael for advocating 'the destruction of Western civilization'. By the spring of 1967, Robinson would probably have replaced Carmichael as chair and chief spokesperson of the SNCC, but a rare form of cancer ended her short life. Robinson's death ended a process of political development that surely would have culminated in the making of yet another Sojourner Truth or an Ida B. Wells.[76]

Finally, social movements focus on direct confrontations with those who dominate the political and economic institutions of a society. The type of confrontations varies: armed or unarmed: violence or passive resistance; strikes, public demonstrations, massive group relocations from one geographical area to another, and so on. Consequently, the organizational *forms* generated by social movements are *usually* transitory. They are born at a historical point to address basic grievances, and the structures are created to serve the process of mobilization. Usually, organizations of class power disappear or disintegrate before the social contradiction which forced their development is resolved. More often, new formations will rise from the ashes of older organizations, addressing the identical issues, but in a slightly different way. Social protest groups may splinter over strategic differences, and some organizations may be transformed from vehicles of class and social-fraction protest into agencies of class accommodation. The fundamental point here is that all Black social movements, sporadic outbursts of class violence, and protest organizations created within such movements, represent immediate or potential threats to the continued hegemony of capital, and to the perpetuation of a capitalist mode of production — whether the participants and leaders of these Black mobilizations realize it or not. There is no such thing as a one-sided class war. The capitalist class, especially in a racist social formation, takes every small manifestation of class consciousness and militant protest among Blacks with a seriousness that is sometimes missing among Black leaders.

IV

The history of Black politics is the history of class struggle, in a variety of social expressions. The initial historical mode of resistance, the struggle to assert power, occurred with slavery. Even before the encroachment of Europe along the African coast, Black societies had manifested sharp revolts against enslavement. Captive African slaves staged a major uprising in Mesopotamia in the year 696; there were slave rebellions by East Africans who were workers in the saltpetre mines along the Euphrates in the ninth century, and slave revolts 'were a threat to sixteenth-century Songhay.'[77] With the expansion of Western capital across the globe, political struggles were waged between African feudal and semi-feudal states to retard the slave-trade. For example, a leader of the Baga people, Tomba, in the region now known as the Republic of Guinea, organized an alliance among local indigenous groups to halt the slave-trade in the 1720s. Only a united front of 'local European resident traders, mulattos and other slave-trading Africans' defeated Tomba's coalition.[78] In 1724, the powerful king of Dahomey, Agaja Trudo, sent his soldiers to seize the coastal slave-dealing states with the objective of bringing 'the slave-trade to a halt'. For two years, he 'looted and burned European forts and slave-camps; and he reduced the trade from the "Slave Coast" to a mere trickle, by blocking the paths leading to sources of supply in the interior.'[79] In subsequent years, the area of struggle shifted to indigenous opposition to the spread of European settler regimes and the imposition of white colonial rule. Some of the earliest wars of colonial resistance were fought between the Xhosa and the Boer expansionists. From 1779 to 1857 there were nine separate wars, culminating in the direct annexation of the Xhosa people's territory, which the white conquerors contemptuously termed 'British Kaffraria', or 'niggerland'.

The general pattern of African resistance was similar across the continent. In Tanganyika, German troops destroyed the Unyanymbe in 1893 in order to control lucrative trade routes. The Unyanymbe leader, Isike, 'blew himself up in his powder magazine to avoid capture.'[80] After four years of intense guerrilla war, the Germans finally conquered the Hehe people, but their chief, Mkwawa, committed suicide rather than face the humiliation of surrender. In the Gold Coast, when the British crushed the Ashanti kingdom in 1896, their machine-guns met little organized resistance. But four years later, when the British governor, 'intent on asserting British paramountcy, visited Kumasi and demanded the surrender of the Golden Stool, the most sacred object in the *asantehene*'s regalia', a bitter revolt erupted which 'took the British several months of hard fighting to suppress.'[81] In Nigeria, British demands to enter Benin City in 1897, in an attempt to control its trade, were ignored by the Oba of Benin. When the Oba's soldiers repulsed British overtures, a well-armed British regiment invaded the city and carried off its ancient art treasures. In Mozambique, Portuguese slave-traders sent over a hundred thousand captives between 1817 and 1843 to Brazil alone. After the 1880s, intent upon establishing an overseas colony, Portugal poured thousands of troops armed with heavy artillery into Mozambique. Over a forty-year period of exhaustive military campaigns, the regime defeated the Massangano, Hanga, Angoche, Makua, Quitanghona, Barue and Gaza peoples and nations. The Germans seized control of Namibia by first crushing the Herero in early 1904, at a cost of fifty thousand African lives, and later ruthlessly suppressing the Nama Rising of 1904-1907. In South Africa, the Zulu nation offered the most unyielding resistance to British and Boer imperialism. At the battle of Isandhlwana on 22 January 1879, the Zulu army showed 'tremendous courage and great tactical skill' in nearly exterminating 950 British soldiers and 850 Black contingent troops, in the worst military defeat suffered by the British in the late nineteenth century.[82] The Basuto kingdom successfully defended itself against white Cape Colony troops during the 'War of the Guns' in 1880. The most devastating defeat of the imperialists occurred in Ethiopia, however, when King Menelik's troops overwhelmed three Italian brigades in the battle of Adowa on 1 March 1896. Italian efforts to seize Ethiopia would be buried for another forty years. But despite these stunning victories, the sheer superiority of European weapons and the capitalist West's ability to divide African nations by exploiting traditional rivalries and religious differences ultimately led to the defeat of the national resistance forces. African nations were unable to devise a common strategy which could successfully defeat the ever-tightening grip of European economic and political hegemony. Conversely, even before the age of late nineteenth-century imperialism, European theorists understood exactly what was at stake in the struggle to suppress African resistance movements. Malchy Postlethwayt, author of the 1746 tract *The National and Private Advantages of the African Trade,* argued that the slave-trade was just 'the mere skimming' of Africa's economic potential. Direct political control meant that Africans would become consumers of European goods; their social institutions would be destroyed and they would be forced to 'live something in the European way'.[83]

The second historical mode of resistance was found in the Caribbean and the Americas. The economic products of slavery were sugar, cotton, tobacco and other commodities; the political 'product' was Black revolt. In no slavery society have the slaves willingly accommodated themselves to oppression. Usually, the most prominent form of resistance was a conscious yet covert effort to disrupt the normal routine of production. This included the destruction of farm implements, the burning of crops and the killing of livestock. More generally, these normal resistance efforts, in which the great majority of slaves took part at one point or another, did not culminate in a well-planned insurrection against large groups of slave-holders. What is surprising, given the institutional constraints that severely checked slaves' day-to-day behaviour, is that so many slave revolts and unsuccessful conspiracies *did* occur. In Barbados, well-organized slave uprisings erupted in 1675, 1686, 1692 and 1702.[84] The Coramantee revolt in Jamaica in 1760 was led by an articulate rebel named Tackey, who called upon his fellow slaves to murder every white on the island. In 1733, Blacks on the Danish island of St John plotted a rebellion which very nearly succeeded. Seizing control of a major garrison, 'they raised the flag and fired three shots from the cannon, the signal for a general uprising on all the plantations on the island.' One of the first whites to be executed was the leading Danish magistrate. 'With flintlocks, pistols, and cane-knives the Negroes went about the bloody business of murdering all the whites they could find. Only after several days of terror was the uprising brought under control by the captain of the militia.'[85] In Bahia, Brazil's sugar-plantation region, African slaves staged nine revolts or attempted revolts in the first three decades of the nineteenth century. Even the free mulattos or coloureds, the offspring of the white colonists' rapes of African women, could not be trusted. Vincent Ogé, a free coloured living in Paris, organized plans to mount a revolt in St Domingue. With the financial assistance of British abolitionist Thomas Clarkson, Ogé bought guns and ammunition in the US, and dropped his cargo on St Domingue's north coast in October 1790. Ogé, his two brothers and another ally, Marc Chavannes, were unable to spark resistance among the island's coloured population. A planter militia soon defeated the small band of idealists. Ogé, Chavannes and the others had their arms, legs, thighs and backbones broken with clubs. Then, barely still alive, they were fastened to large wheels so that their faces glared into the noonday sun. At death, their heads were chopped off and displayed on poles in the major city, Cap François.

Two of the most fascinating revolts ended in failure, but pre-figured Black struggles to come. François Mackandal, a St Domingue slave, devised an ingenious method to eliminate the whites in 1757. Cap François's water supply would be poisoned with arsenic, and when the whites were incapacitated, the Africans would take command. The myth of Mackandal states that, at the last minute, the jealous husband of his lover betrayed him and other conspirators. Chained and beaten, Mackandal was burnt alive. But before he was engulfed by the flames, he vowed that 'one day' he would 'return more terrible than before'. The slaves claimed that 'he had escaped the flames by changing into a mosquito and flying away'. Years later, many Africans and not a few whites believed that the great Black general, Toussaint L'Ouverture, was the mystical reincarnation of that earlier Black Messiah, Mackandal. On 21 August 1831, Nat Turner, a 31-year-old Baptist slave preacher, convinced a band of Virginia slaves to revolt against their masters. Fifty-seven whites were killed within two days. State and federal troops suppressed the insurrection, torturing and lynching several hundred slaves in the process. Seventeen of the conspirators were hanged; Turner eluded his pursuers for two months, but was finally captured and lynched. The corpse was given to local doctors for dissection, and evidence suggests that souvenir purses were made from his skin. Moments before his death, a white journalist asked Turner whether he had repented of his sins. Turner smiled, 'Was not Christ crucified?'[86] Like Malcolm X a century later, Nat Turner became more powerful in death than in life. White slave-holders and racists in the United States who had argued that the African slave was inherently docile could never rest comfortably again in the presence of Blacks. Conversely, the militant message of resistance embodied in Nat Turner's uprising influenced US Black radicalism well into the late twentieth century.[87]

Whenever circumstances permitted, free Blacks fought against slavery by organizing abolitionist groups. The racism and pater-nalism within abolitionist circles, from England's Committee for the Abolition of the Slave-Trade, started in 1787, to the American Anti-Slavery Society, founded in December 1833, meant that few Blacks would be invited to play policy-making roles within these liberal circles. Only three well-to-do Blacks were invited to co-sign the American Anti-Slavery Society's original Declaration of Sentiments drafted by William Lloyd Garrison, and there were no Black officers in the group. Free Blacks in the 1830s formed 'vigilance committees' led by David Ruggles, a New York printer, Robert Purvis, a wealthy Black Philadelphia merchant, and others. The committees agitated publicly for abolition, and privately assisted runaway slaves by providing clothing, food, shelter and transport. New Black leaders emerged during the 1840s and 1850s: the Reverend Henry Highland Garnet of Troy, New York, who urged Afro-Americans to 'let your motto be resistance!'; the Reverend Alexander Crummell, who encouraged African emigration; the Reverend Theodore Holly, who counselled that Blacks come to Haiti; H. Ford Douglas, a fiery abolitionist speaker; polemicist Charles H. Langston; orator Henry Bibb, editor of the *Voice of the Fugitive;* and Frances Ellen Watkins Harper, antislavery lecturer, poet and political organizer. The three major spokespersons for Black equality in the North and for emancipation in the South were Frederick Douglass, a former slave who was the chief editor and orator of his generation and the leader of Black Republicans for three decades; Sojourner Truth, abolitionist orator and organizer of social-work efforts for ex-slave 'contraband' in Washington DC; and Martin R. Delany, a physician, a militant newspaper editor, and during the Civil War a major in the Union army. There were, to be sure, ideological differences among the Black abolitionists, despite their united opposition to slavery and institutional racism. One indication was provided by the different 'mottoes' of Delany's newspaper *The Mystery,* and Douglass's *North Star.* The banner of *The Mystery* declared: 'Hereditary Bondsmen! Know Ye Not Who Would Be Free, Themselves Must Strike the First Blow?' Douglass's paper read: 'Right is of no Sex, Truth is of no Colour, God is the Father of us all, and we are all Brethren.' Summing up his political feud with Delany, Douglass once commented: 'Every morning [I am] satisfied to thank God for making me a man simply; but Delany always thanks him for making him a Black man.'[88]

In Brazil, the abolitionist organizations tended to be far more 'colour-blind' than in the US. José Carlos de Patrocinio, a Black journalist, was the nation's most articulate polemicist for manumission. Another Black leader, André Rebouças, was a major organizer of pro-abolitionist clubs and a prominent public speaker on behalf of Black Brazilians' rights. The 'Frederick Douglass of Brazil', however, was the former slave Luis Gonzaga de Pinto Gama. A prominent attorney, Pinto Gama challenged slaveholders in the court-room and freed over five hundred slaves in the process. No advocate of non-violence, he championed 'the right to insurrection. Every slave who kills his master, no matter what the circumstances may be, kills in self-defence.' Pinto Gama also emphasized racial pride; one of his better-known poems begins with the lines 'My loves are beautiful, the colour of night.' Other non-white abolitionist leaders include two mulattos, Gonçalves Dias and Castro Alves, who 'wrote some of the most beautiful poetry produced in Brazil in the nineteenth century.' Alves 'depicted the plight of the slave with such moving verses that he awoke the social conscience of his readers to the injustices inflicted on the Negroes.'[89]

The slaves in every country followed the public debates over abolition, and devised their own means of speeding the process forward. In 1816, rumours about emancipation sparked slave disturbances in Barbados on Easter Sunday, as dozens of sugar-cane fields were torched. Seven years later, similar rumours provoked an uprising of thirteen thousand slaves in Demerara, British Guyana. British troops shot over one hundred Blacks, lynched forty-eight others, and flogged many more. In December 1831, Samuel Sharpe, a slave Baptist deacon in Jamaica, urged slaves to carry out a non-violent general strike which would put pressure on slave-holders to accept emancipation. Beginning in St James, hundreds of slaves non-violently refused to return to the fields. When outraged planters retaliated, slaves burnt the huge sugarworks in St James. In the end between four and five hundred slaves were murdered, and Sharpe and one hundred supporters were executed. In the United States, the national debates over abolition were among the factors that prompted many slaves to flee to the North, or to Canada. Abolitionists, Black and white, established an informal network, the 'Underground Railroad', which aided thousands of fugitive Blacks to gain freedom. Prominent Black activists in the Underground Railroad included John Henson, a former runaway slave who returned repeatedly to the South to help others escape. From 1850 to 1855, fugitive slave John Mason brought over one thousand slaves out of the upper South. At one point Mason was arrested and sold into slavery, but within months he had escaped again. He was finally captured in Kentucky, and died in a state prison in 1857. The most successful, and certainly the most fearless activist in this area of antislavery resistance was Harriet Tubman. Travelling deep into the South nineteen times, she brought over three hundred slaves to the North without losing a single 'passenger'. Always armed, she cautioned would-be fugitives that she would shoot personally any slave who expressed a desire to turn back.

Another approach to the problem was the development of autonomous African enclaves or separate communities. In this fourth historical pattern of social protest, the slaves withdrew their labour-power from the production process and left the plantations, with the desire to develop alternative societies under their own hegemony. This represented, first, an assertion of the Black oppressed class's economic power, the right to withhold labour, and secondly, a political and cultural rejection of the existing social formation. These communities, 'maroons', as they were termed in the West Indies, originated as early as 1519 when Africans ran off from their Spanish masters in Hispaniola and created their own indigenous communities. The maroons (called *palenques* in Spanish colonies, *quilombos* in Brazil) existed wherever geographical conditions permitted runaway Africans adequate space to build their alternative settlements outside the slavery system. *Palenques* developed outside Veracruz, Mexico, where they destroyed colonists' crops and burnt down houses. The local leader of an Indian and African *palenque*, Yanga, defeated several military efforts by troops to seize his village in 1609-1610. In the Spanish Audiencia of Caracas (Venezuela), an African runaway named Guillermo led a dissident community of ex-slaves which was suppressed only after a fifteen-year campaign in the 1760s-1770s. On the coast of Colombia, Domingo Bioho and other African fugitives defeated a series of Spanish troop assaults on their communities in 1619. In Martinique, about four to five hundred slaves led by the charismatic Francisque Fabulé organized a maroon which terrorized white planters. The desperate French governor agreed to negotiate with the rebels. Fabulé received one thousand pounds of tobacco for turning himself in, and obtained a job working in the governor's mansion. Still a subversive at heart, he 'convinced' his lover, a young Black woman, 'to stab her master'. Whipped for his part in the crime, Fabulé escaped and soon organized another new maroon with fifty Africans. After committing a series of 'robberies, thefts, and even a few murders and assassinations', Fabulé was finally captured in 1671 and 'condemned to the galleys for life'.[90] More successful than Fabulé was a Cayenne slave named Gabriel, who organized a band of maroon communities consisting of Indians and Africans. His followers, snubbing their noses at authority, called their leader *'Monsieur le Gouverneur'*. In 1725, sixty or more maroons were discovered in tiny Grenada, and the following year four groups of maroons, composed of two to six hundred Blacks each, terrorized the white settlers of Guadeloupe. The most astonishing maroon achievement, to be sure, was great Palmares, a *quilombo* kingdom of city-states set deep in the Brazilian interior. From 1605 until its fall in 1694, Palmares frustrated repeated efforts by Portuguese and Dutch troops to conquer the runaways. In 1676, Palmares consisted of ten principal cities, and altogether measured 240 miles in circumference. Large stores of food crops were produced by the residents, and Africans and mulattos worked in the cities.

The white response to the maroons was twofold: military conquest and, if this was unsuccessful, political accommodation into the colonial system. The Spanish established the latter pattern in 1533 when they agreed to sign a treaty with the Hispaniola maroons. The Spanish granted the free Africans a large preserve of land on the island, and they in turn promised to return all new fugitives to their masters. Almost a century later, in 1610, the Spanish authorities in Mexico made similar terms with Yanga's *palenque*. The African and Indian town was given a justice of the peace, and all persons who had been inside the group since 1608 would be free; other more recent arrivals were to be returned. Yanga stipulated that no other Spaniards would be permitted to live in his village, called San Lorenzo de los Negros, and outsiders could visit only on market-days. The Spanish in turn received the promise that Yanga's troops would help defend the state in the event of an attack. In 1731, Cuban mine workers rebelled and created Poblado del Cobre in Oriente Province. By 1781, the *palenque*'s African population had reached 1,065, and the local government finally agreed to grant it free status that year. The British were slightly more stubborn than the Spanish. From 1673 to 1739, English troops periodically fought against the Jamaican maroons with little success. Finally, the two sides agreed to peaceful coexistence within the colonial apparatus. Each maroon community was given a tract of land, and was permitted to set its own laws and to choose its own leaders. In return, the maroons agreed to halt their regular raids on isolated plantations, to return new runaways and to send troops to help the whites suppress slave uprisings. The Dutch in Surinam signed almost identical treaties with the two extensive maroon communities in the southern sections of their territory in 1761 and 1767. American whites, on the other hand, found it difficult to negotiate with Blacks or with Indians, if military genocide could resolve the contradiction. There were at least fifty small maroon communities that developed in the US South between 1672 and

1864 in the forests and swamp-land regions. In September 1733, the South Carolina governor offered rewards of £20 alive and £10 dead for each captured maroon Black. Major military expeditions against South Carolina, Georgia and Florida maroons occurred in 1816, 1819 and 1822. The leaders of one especially troublesome maroon group were captured and executed in South Carolina in 1823. One leader was decapitated; 'his head was stuck on a pole' and publicly displayed as 'a warning to vicious slaves'.[91]

After emancipation, the maroon impulse, the desire to construct separate Black communities outside the socio-economic boundaries of direct white control, continued to be attractive to many Afro-Americans. Disfranchised North Carolina Blacks journeyed to Whitesboro, New Jersey, to establish an all-Black city. Southern Blacks built twenty-five separate towns in Oklahoma between 1890 and 1914. The former slave of Confederate President Jefferson Davis's brother, Isaiah T. Montgomery, established an all-Black village, Mound Bayou, in the Delta of the Mississippi in 1887. Within several decades, the town boasted of its 'self-government in its Negro officials, its $150,000 high school, its cement sidewalks and attractive residences, its Masonic temple, its electric-light plant and waterworks, and its eighty-two business concerns, including a bank, three cotton gins and a telephone system'.[92] Of course, the survival of a Mound Bayou during the age of lynching and Jim Crow depended upon a subtle accommodation to the system of white supremacy. Like Yanga and Jamaica's maroon leaders centuries before, Montgomery recognized that the price of limited autonomy was subservience to the racist state. Thus as the only Black member of the Mississippi Constitutional Convention of 1890, he urged his white colleagues to disfranchise thousands of Black voters by means of literacy and property restrictions. Despite Montgomery's capitulation, other Blacks continued to advocate separate societies based on race. In 1913, an Afro-American writer, Arthur A. Anderson, drafted a polemic, *'Prophetic Liberator of the Coloured Race'*, calling for the creation of a separate, all-Black state within the continental US. The new nation, to be called Moderna, would be financed by reparations which totalled $600 million, to be paid by the US government for 'slavery, for the trail of blood sacrificed in human lives', and for 'the years of tyranny and oppression that followed and continues until today upon the ex-slaves and their offspring.'[93] A generation later, the concept was revived by the Nation of Islam. Muslim leader Elijah Muhammad called repeatedly for 'a separate nation for ourselves, right here in America . . .

To integrate with evil is to be destroyed with evil. Justice for us,'
Muhammad declared, 'is to be set apart.' Control of three to six
southern states would allow Black people 'to become self-
sufficient'.[94] In the late 1960s the militant Black nationalist group,
the Republic of New Africa, called for the creation of an all-Black
state in the southern US.[95]

A fifth historical mode of resistance was the insurgence of rural
Black farmers or peasants. With the demise of slavery, independent
Black farmers often developed political and economic organizations to fight for their right to own land and to destroy systems of
debt peonage. The largest social movement of this type in the Black
Diaspora was the Coloured Farmers' Alliance. Founded in Texas in
1886, the group was allied with white small farmers who organized
the Southern Alliance. The Coloured Farmers' Alliance established
hundreds of farmers' cooperatives across the South, and lobbied
vigorously for the passage of the Lodge Federal Elections Bill in
1890, which would have guaranteed Blacks' voting rights. In conjunction with white farmers, the Alliance seized control of several
state governments, passing legislation that expanded educational
expenditure, elevated Blacks to state and local offices, cut interest
rates and democratized the taxation system. With the merger of the
rival National Coloured Alliance, which had a quarter of a million
members in 1890, the Coloured Farmers' Alliance became the
largest single Black formation in US history. In early 1891 the
Alliance 'had organizations in twenty states and nearly one and a
quarter million members, of whom 750,000 were adult males,
300,000 females and 150,000 males under twenty-one years of
age.'[96] The collapse of the Alliance occurred with the initiation of a
mass cotton-pickers' strike in Texas. Some Black farmers' groups
and most whites did not support the strike, and the subsequent
political dissension split the national organization. Other Black
farmers and farm workers left the organization because a small
number of whites held key administrative posts in the Alliance's
state structures and in its cooperative stores. Still other militant
Black Alliance leaders, influenced by the radical antimonopoly
capitalist ideas within the organization's literature, were subjected
to vicious repression by racists and local white authorities. A similar
protest movement emerged among Black, white and mulatto
peasants in north-east Brazil in the late 1950s. Lawyer Francisco
Julião organized a racially integrated union of poor farmers called
the Peasants' League. Like the Alliance, the Peasants' League's
leaders blamed their economic troubles on large plantation-owners

and the corporations. Julião urged Brazilian peasants to call rural strikes and to 'utilize unity against your cruel enemy, which is the latifundia.' Frightened rural oligarchs denounced the League as a Communist conspiracy. In March 1964, the military overthrew the democratic government of João Goulart; one of its first acts was to outlaw the Peasants' League, burn their propaganda and arrest its key leaders.[97]

As illustrated previously, Blacks' class struggles for political and economic power may be initiated by the struggle to assert ideological, cultural and social power. The basic manifestation of cultural struggle found in all Black societies is the development of various forms of Black religious institutions and belief systems. In Africa prior to European imperialist colonialism, traditional African religions frequently provided an ideological framework to unite the masses, and generated an idealist rationale for anti-European protest. For subsequent generations, African Christianity and its spokespersons created the institutional space for expressing anticolonial and nationalist ideas. By 1938, there were over 380 African separatist churches in Mozambique. Church leaders like Samuel Belize of the AME Church and Sebastião Piedade de Sousa espoused a militant creed of racial pride and ultimate salvation from the Portuguese oppressors. Politics and religion were often inseparable. For John Chilembwe, a Nyasaland Baptist preacher, salvation for his people was equated with a righteous opposition to imperialism. But his short-lived uprising in 1915 was brutally suppressed, and Chilembwe was killed. In Northern and Southern Rhodesia as well as in Nyasaland, Chilembwe's work was carried on by African members of the Jehovah's Witnesses. Leader Eliot Kamwana promised his followers the destruction of British hegemony: 'We shall make our own ships, make our own powder, make or import our own guns.'[98] Although Kamwana was eventually arrested and deported, his church established in a spiritual context the rationale for independent and eventually revolutionary nationalist movements. In Haiti, a synthesis of the Voduns, or gods, of the Dahomey people with French Catholicism created the Voodoo religion. Priests met regularly and transmitted vital political information from one plantation to the next. Voodoo played a decisive ideological role in creating the alternative consciousness necessary for generating a popular Black social revolution against the planter regime. In Trinidad during the Great Depression, Pentecostal church leader Tubal Uriah 'Buzz' Butler combined Black religion with trade-union militancy. Butler's British Empire Workers' and Citizens' Home Rule Party, formed in 1936, was both an evangelical crusade and an organized force for Black working-class power.

Black faith was crucially important for Black social protest movements in the US. First, racial segregation and the imposition of racist constraints in electoral politics meant that the majority of politically conscious, aggressive Black males often went into the clergy as a means of expressing their activism. The Black minister was one of the few members of the Afro-American community whose income was not directly controlled by whites. As a consequence of his financial independence, he had the opportunity to articulate the political and economic concerns of his 'constituents' in an unambiguous manner. Secondly, with the growth of the Afro-American community, the Church itself became a major institutional powerbase from which racial inequality could be attacked. By the end of World War II, the thirty-four all-Black denominations had five and a half million dues-paying members, over thirty-five thousand churches and property worth almost $200 million. Thirdly, with the outbreak of the modern Civil Rights Movement, the ministers who suddenly became prominent — Martin Luther King Jr, Andrew Young, Ralph D. Abernathy, Fred Shuttlesworth, Jesse Jackson and Wyatt T. Walker — were prepared to fight segregation as an 'expression' of Black faith. This is to say that the affirmation of one's Christianity, one's faith in God, was the political willingness to break 'unjust laws'. Moreover, leaders such as King were effective in projecting the political aspirations of their social fraction to a larger white audience. King's 'use of religious phraseology and the Judaeo-Christian symbols of love and non-resistance' were critical in creating a democratic majority supporting the death of Jim Crow.[99]

A seventh historical mode of Black social resistance was the organized labour movement. The development of Black unionism began only a little more than a century ago in the US, as Black share-croppers and debt peons left the South and travelled with little more than their labour-power to the dirty industrial centres of the North. As early as 1850, Black artisans in New York City created the American League of Coloured Labourers, with Frederick Douglass acting as vice-president. Eight years later, the Association of Black Caulkers was formed in Baltimore; this was in response to race-riots and attacks by German and Irish caulkers who had attempted to ban Afro-American labourers from the docks. The real growth of Black unionism took place during Reconstruction. Black brickmakers in Philadelphia struck unsuccessfully for higher wages in July 1868, but their mobilization sparked organizing efforts by other Black labourers. Historian Philip S. Foner notes that by the fall of 1868 'there was not only an active Coloured Brickmakers' Association, but a large Hod Carriers' and Labourers' Association and a Working-men's Union built by Negroes in Philadelphia.'[100] A Black ship-caulker from Baltimore, Isaac Myers, was instrumental in starting the Coloured National Labour Union in December 1869, in Washington DC, with Black representatives from eighteen states. In the 1870s and 1880s, about sixty thousand Black workers joined the progressive Knights of Labour. Unlike the craft-oriented AFL, the Knights actively recruited Black labourers, and pursued a policy of labour solidarity across the colour line until the late 1880s. 'In 1886 Black workers constituted half of Virginia's 10,000 to 15,000 members; half of the 3,000 Arkansas and 4,000 North Carolina Knights, and a high percentage of the membership in Alabama, Florida, Georgia, Kentucky, Tennessee and Louisiana. Even South Carolina and Mississippi, with fewer than 2,000 Knights, included Blacks in the order.'[101] Black workers took the lead in championing the eight-hour day, which sparked a nation-wide demonstration of 340,000 workers on 1 May 1886 — the first 'May Day' or proletarian holiday in history. The multiracial unions created the potential — devastating to capital's interests — to forge a Black-white proletarian and agricultural workers' united front. In 1907, for example, a general strike involving ten thousand white and Black longshoremen, teamsters, freight handlers and coal-wheelers shook New Orleans. With the decline of the Knights of Labour and the institutionalization of the AFL by 1900, however, instances of Black-white labour cooperation became infrequent.[102]

In the Caribbean the organized labour movement began in the late 1890s. Alfred Richards, a Trinidadian druggist, founded the Trinidad Working-men's Association (TWA) in 1897, which was later associated with the British Labour Party. British Guyana dockworkers organized their own association under the leadership of Hubert Nathaniel Critchlow. After World War I, a new core of militant Black labour activists emerged in almost every Caribbean nation. Given the slower spread of the capitalist mode of production into Africa, the growth of trade unionism there was retarded. Yet by the early 1900s, Black workers' formations were set up, and they soon became an integral component of general anticolonialist struggles. In 1911, Francisco Domingos Campos, Alfredo de

Oliveira Guimares and Agostinho José Mathias attempted to form the *União Africano* (African Union) among the African labourers of Lorenço Marques, Mozambique. In their appeals to the new urban workers, they called for an end to tribal and class distinctions. 'In order to avoid capitalist exploitation it is necessary that we all unite . . . from the humblest porter to the ordinary worker to the civil servant.'[103] Strong opposition from the Portuguese colonial regime destroyed the *União Africano,* but within several years, its advocacy of class struggle resounded in the Lorenço Marques tram- workers' strike of 1917, the African railroad technicians' strike of 1918, the domestic workers' strike of 1916-1918 and the bitter Quinhenta port workers' strike of 1933. In South Africa, the union movement was sparked by the fiery energy of a young Nyasaland clerk, Clements Kadalie. Creating the Industrial and Commercial Workers' Union in 1920, Kadalie and his associates recruited over two hundred thousand African workers within eight years. In Nairobi, African nationalist Harry Thuku organized local domestic workers and clerical workers into the Young Kikuyu Association. When Thuku was arrested in 1922, colonial police fired on a pro- Thuku demonstration and murdered more than two dozen workers. In 1939, dockworkers in Mombasa, Kenya and Dar es Salaam organized an unsuccessful strike; but a second strike in Dar es Salaam in 1943 achieved sizeable pay rises for Black dockworkers. In Southern Rhodesia (Zimbabwe), branches of Kadalie's Indus- trial and Commercial Workers' Union began to form by the late 1920s. In April 1948, Bulawayo, Southern Rhodesia's second largest town, was 'paralysed by a general strike of African workers'. One frightened white journalist in Bulawayo noted that 'hundreds of natives armed with knobkerries, sticks, hatchets, lead piping, bicycle chains, etc.' were involved in the demonstration, and that they 'proceeded through the streets yelling, shrieking and beating up any natives who appeared to be going to work.'[104] The most successful African trade-union leader to emerge after World War II was Sekou Touré. Born in Guinea in 1922, Touré was influenced by the French Communist Party's *Confédération Générale du Travail* (CGT). A skilful politician, Touré became Secretary General of the *Parti Démocratique de Guinée* (PDG) in 1952; and a year later, as leader of the CGT in Guinea, he led a successful two-month-long strike in the capital city of Conakry. With its working-class base secure, the PDG won fifty-four out of sixty seats in the 1957 ter- ritorial elections. In 1958, the break with France was complete, and Touré became the leader of an independent and 'socialist' Guinea.

The chief impediment to the development of multiracial trade unions was the persistent racism among the majority of white workers, especially in South Africa and the United States. As historian George M. Frederickson relates, 'in South Africa there was never any prospect that employers would displace the entrenched immigrant labour aristocracy that engrossed the most highly skilled occupations in the mines. But there was a grey area of semi-skilled work that became a battleground between owners and white workers.' Being capitalists, the owners often attempted to cut labour costs by hiring African workers in these positions. White urban and industrial workers 'were at a competitive disadvantage in relation to the Africans because they refused to do "kaffir work" or accept "kaffir pay". The crisis generated by the conflict between the demands of newly augmented and insecure white working class and the established policy of capitalistic reliance on ultra-cheap African labour led to a violent confrontation between capital and white labour.'[105] The racism of white labour was made manifestly clear in April 1924, when the all-white Labour Party joined the ultra-racist Afrikaner Nationalist Party in the Pact Ministry headed by former Boer general J.B.M. Hertzog. From 1924 to 1929, white labour leaders and Hertzog established the economic foundations of modern apartheid within industry. Africans and Indians were prohibited from skilled mining jobs by the Mines and Works Amendment Act of 1927. Unorganized labourers — Black, Asian, coloured and European — were barred from striking, and the Native Administration Act of 1927 sanctioned the imprisonment of non-white labour organizers. The AFL also tried to construct a 'labour aristocracy' within the skilled, white working class, as outlined previously. Black workers' formations that were militantly anticapitalist, such as the National Negro Labour Council of the 1950s, were 'redbaited' and attacked by white union bureaucrats. Few unions, other than the liberal United Packing-house Workers, District 65, New York City's Local 1199 and a few United Auto Worker locals, actively supported the 1955-56 Montgomery Bus Boycott, led by Martin Luther King Jr. The rigid racial hierarchy within organized labour was a social reproduction of the racial division of labour within every modern industry or plant. Commenting on a typical automobile plant in Detroit in the late 1960s, Dan Georgakas and Marvin Surkin noted:

The exploitation experienced by all workers was compounded for Black workers by the institutional racism which pervaded every aspect of factory life. Dodge Main was typical: 99 per cent of all general foremen were white, 95 per cent of all foremen were white, 100 per cent of all superintendents were white, 90 per cent of all skilled tradesmen were white, and 90 per cent of all skilled apprentices were white. All the better jobs were overwhelmingly dominated by whites, and when whites did have difficult jobs, there were often two workers assigned to a task that a Black worker was expected to do alone.[106]

The institutionalization of racism in industrial labour insulated many if not all white workers from the worst aspects of capitalist production. In Detroit's Dodge Main plant, most of the white workers were first or second generation Polish-Americans who 'had acquired negrophobia as part of their Americanization. The Polish-Americans did not like the working conditions at Dodge Main any better than the Blacks did, but they had a power-base in the union and in the local government that made them concerned with the prosperity of Chrysler as well.' As for other white workers in still lower income groups, such as the white Appalachians, 'factory conditions were not much better for them than for Blacks', noted Georgakas and Surkin, 'but racist feelings kept the two groups effectively divided most of the time'.[107] The net result of racial stratification and the political backwardness of most white American workers has been that the organized Black labour movement has had to battle against capital and the national trade-union leadership simultaneously. Separate Black labour formations, from the socialist-oriented League of Revolutionary Black Workers to the more moderate Coalition of Black Trade Unionists, have represented the 'left possibilities' of the entire American working class.[108]

Historical modes of Black political struggle have generally. cut across generational lines. Yet special note must be taken regarding the pivotal role of young people as catalysts for social movements in virtually every part of the African Diaspora. The SNCC assumed a central role in the desegregation campaigns of the 1960s, but its ideological predecessor was the Southern Negro Youth Congress, founded over two decades earlier by radical journalist Louis E. Burnham, and organized by Black Communist James E. Jackson who worked as its educational director in Birmingham. The Congress militantly fought racial segregation, and in 1944 formed an 'Association of Young Writers and Artists' to promote Black cultural development. Du Bois spoke before the organization at its convention in Charleston, South Carolina in October 1946, and applauded its political efforts.[109] In Africa, youth networks and

40

organizations were often the nucleus of anticolonial and anti-
apartheid struggles. In Mozambique, the foundations of FRELIMO
(Front for the Liberation of Mozambique) were established in the
1950s with the creation of NESAM (Nucleus of African Secondary
Students of Mozambique). 'Under the guise of promoting social
and cultural activities, NESAM members — including Eduardo
Mondlane, Joaquim Chissano and Mariano Matsinhe, all future
leaders of the liberation struggle — clandestinely began to organize
politically "to spread the idea of national independence and
encourage resistance to the cultural subjection which the Portuguese imposed".'[110] African students were an important anticolonialist force within Nkrumah's Convention Peoples' Party in
the Gold Coast; Ethiopian students' protests were partially responsible for the collapse of Haile Selassie's corrupt monarchy in 1974.
The Youth Wing of the African National Congress, led in the late
1940s by Nelson Mandela, Walter Sisulu and Oliver Tambo, pushed
the organization beyond a limited legalistic strategy against
apartheid into the Defiance Campaign of 1952. And in Kenya,
when the Mau Mau rebellion erupted, 'one of the first things the
British government did was to close' 184 Kikuyu schools. 'They
were considered "training-grounds for rebellion",' writes Rodney.
'Europeans knew well enough that if they did not control the minds
of Africans, they would soon cease to control the people physically
and politically.'[111]

Within nearly every phase of all Black social movements, whites
also participated in the cause of Black equality and national liberation. Within racially pluralistic social formations, even in rigidly
racist South Africa, many whites have chosen to commit 'race
suicide', as it were, although not in sufficient numbers in most cases
to create an indelibly progressive tradition. Blacks, of course, in
racist social formations have repeatedly participated in all types of
movements led and controlled by whites; the reverse is not always
true. One can think of several prominent cases where Black activists, transplanted in a different cultural and political setting, have
made decisive contributions to other oppressed peoples' struggles.
The outstanding example here is Frantz Fanon: born in Martinique,
educated in France, he became a leading militant in the war for the
national liberation of Algeria.[112] Nevertheless, examples of white
support for Black social-class rebelliousness have long existed. In
colonial North Carolina and Virginia, sympathetic whites sheltered
runaway slaves and protected them from their masters.[113]
Thousands of whites, for reasons of religious principle or because of

their racially egalitarian views, fought openly against the African slave-trade, slavery, and other forms of racist exploitation. Political parties, notably the Communists in both South Africa and the United States, have played a critical role in democratic struggles against racism and against the apartheid regime.[114] There have been thousands of others who risked or gave their lives in the cause of Black liberation. In the United States, the deeply religious abolitionist John Brown towers above all others. As Du Bois remarked, 'John Brown never read the *Communist Manifesto* and knew little of the rise of Socialism. But he did realize that a suppressed and exploited part of the labouring class in America — the Negroes — had been deprived by capitalists and land monopolists of the freedom to earn a living and to direct their lives . . . He espoused therefore the freedom of the slaves knowing well that freedom alone was not the settlement of the Negro problem . . .'[115] After taking part in the political struggles to keep slavery out of Kansas, in October 1859 he led an unsuccessful raid on Harper's Ferry, Virginia, in an attempt to spark a general slave rebellion. He was executed on 2 December 1859. In Trinidad, Brown's counterpart was Captain A.A. Cipriani. Born of a white French Creole family in 1875, Cipriani served as an officer of the British West Indian Regiment during World War I. An articulate defender of Black soldiers against the military authorities, he was elected president of the Soldiers' and Sailors' Union in 1919. Four years later he was named president of the Trinidad Working-men's Association (TWA) and in 1925 was elected with an overwhelming majority to serve as legislative representative for Port of Spain. Cipriani was 'extremely popular, he had outstanding gifts of oratory and personal magnetism', and was 'a sincere advocate of all TWA's industrial demands'. In the council, 'Cipriani formed an almost one-man opposition to the government', and served to voice the grievances of Indians and Blacks.[116] Brown, Cipriani and thousands of other white anti-racists were an integral part of Blacks' class struggles. They were able to transcend the weight of white supremacy and capitalist ideology to embrace the humanity of those behind the omnipresent colour line.

V

In a racist social formation, 'race' becomes the heuristic principle that organizes cultural, ideological, political and economic relations for both the dominant and the subordinate 'races'. A consequence of this primacy of race is often the 'reduction' of the notions of class and gender divisions within the consciousness of many non-whites. Yet the reality of gender, and specifically the superexploitation of women of colour, has created the material and social foundations for a fundamentally different political experience. Theoretically, women's oppression, or what Sheila Rowbotham terms 'patriarchal authority', is rooted in men's 'control over the woman's productive capacity, and over her person. This control existed before the development of capitalist commodity production', in societies 'in which the persons of human beings were owned by others'.[117] Within both capitalist and pre-capitalist social formations, women's oppression assumes a distinct set of socio-economic and political features. Males control or own nearly all private property, land, and productive resources. In cash economies they receive greater wages for the expenditure of their labour-power than women for comparable work. Women have few if any legal or political rights, and are under-represented in or entirely absent from any social, economic or political positions of authority. Sexual rights, such as personal decisions concerning human reproduction, are largely determined by males. The 'coercive glue' that binds these male-dominated relations into a coherent pattern of gender inequality is systemic violence — rape, sterilization, and all forms of psychological and physical coercion.[118] The direct impact of women's oppression upon its victims frequently creates a sense of non-existence. Rowbotham expresses this eloquently: 'We encounter ourselves in men's culture as "by the way" and peripheral. According to all the reflections we are not really there. This puzzles us and means it is harder for us to begin to experience our own identity as a group. This gives female consciousness an elusive and disintegrating feeling. We are the negative of their positive. We are oppressed by an overwhelming sense of not being there.'[119]

As Marxist historian Bettina Aptheker has observed, 'the subjugation of woman is the oldest form of human oppression, with origins that date back to several thousand years before Christ. It was, in essence, the first class division in society, for woman's oppression is rooted in the fact that she was made the property of man and reduced in a literal sense for centuries to the status of a slave.' In all capitalist social formations, women's oppression 'is embedded in law, theology, work, and in assumptions about marriage, the family, sexuality, and procreative capacity.'[120] Thus the actual conditions of material, social and cultural life were never identical for Black women and Black men within any racist, capitalist society. Under slavery, both Black women and Black men were all expected to work to their full capacities; and as Angela Davis comments, 'where work was concerned, strength and productivity under the threat of the whip outweighed considerations of sex. In this sense, the oppression of women was identical to the oppression of men.' But women were oppressed in other ways that African men did not experience. 'Since slave women were classified as "breeders" as opposed to "mothers", their infant children could be sold away from them like calves from cows . . . As females, slave women were inherently vulnerable to all forms of sexual coercion.' The Black male who offered resistance could be lashed or castrated, but the rebellious female was not only flogged, but raped as well. Moreover, a sexual division of labour was also found within slave communities. 'Slave men executed important domestic responsibilities', but usually 'did the gardening and hunting', while slave women assumed primary responsibility for nurturing infants, cooking and sewing.[121] After slavery, Afro-American women had little choice but to seek employment outside their homes to help support their families. Invariably, their jobs, ranging from custodial to semi-skilled factory employment, were given the lowest wages. In the workplace, they frequently experienced rape and sexual exploitation by their white bosses. Those fortunate enough to obtain technical skills and college training discovered that white women, even those with fewer vocational abilities and poorer academic backgrounds, received higher wages and were able to advance to managerial positions much more rapidly than they could.[122] The sexist behaviour they encountered in their Black fathers, husbands or lovers was often viewed within an overall context of racist domination and class exploitation in which almost all members of the Black community were victims. As sociologist Joyce A. Ladner explains, the ordeal of history created millions of Black women who mastered their oppression, and who instilled a sense of worth and humanity in their children, and by extension, in the entire Black community:

> Black women became the object of the most debased sexual passions of white men . . . their very *femininity* and *humanity* were denied them because they were considered to be neither feminine nor human. In all of this suffering, Black women bore a remarkable and perhaps unprecedented courage, not to be paralleled in human history. They adjusted to all of these conditions, fought them with vigour and emerged with fewer scars than seems normal. All of these devastating influences

actually caused them to become stronger, and to transmit the art of survival to subsequent generations . . . Instead of becoming resigned to her fate, [the Black woman] has always sought creative solutions to her problems. Perhaps more than in any other way, the Black woman has suffered from the institutional racist impact upon her role in, and relationship to, her family. It has been within the family that much of her strength has developed because it was here that she was forced to accept obligations and responsibilities for not only the care and protection of her own life, but for that of her offspring as well. Still, under the most rugged conditions she has managed to survive and to offer substantial contribitions to the society as well.[123]

The historical experience of US Black women also diverges from that of most white women in their relationship with the capitalist state, and particularly, with the criminal justice system. Black women are more frequently raped, harassed and arrested by police than white women. About 50 per cent of all women currently in federal and state prisons are Black. As prisoners they are humiliated by frequent pelvic examinations conducted without consent; are paid 15 to 80 cents an hour for prison labour; and are forced to take psychotropic drugs at a rate three to eighteen times that of male convicts.[124] Outside prison gates, the typical Black woman experiences rape at a rate 1.7 times that of a white woman. 'Some 20 per cent of married Black women of childbearing age are sterilized, many without knowing the facts of the procedure, some without even knowing that the operation has taken place.'[125] White middle-class women have recognized the superexploitation of Afro-American women for over a century, yet their ingrained racism as well as their petty-bourgeois class identity has prohibited most of them from engaging in an honest dialogue with their sisters of colour. There are all too many examples which could be cited, but that of Susan B. Anthony is typical. At the turn of the century, Anthony's National American Woman Suffrage Assocation (NAWSA) made overtly racist appeals for the extension of the right to vote to women. In 1893, the NAWSA reminded white men that there were 'more white women who can read and write than all negro voters . . . the enfranchisement of such women would settle the vexed question of rule by illiteracy . . .' When Black women led by Lottie Wilson Jackson appealed to the NAWSA convention of 1899 to pass a resolution denouncing racially segregated railroad passenger cars, Anthony curtly replied 'We [white] women are a helpless disenfranchised class. Our hands are tied. While we are in this condition, it is not for us to go passing resolutions against railroad corporations or anybody else.'[126]

Afro-American males, as a rule, have been blind to the particularity of Black women's oppression. There have been important exceptions, notably Frederick Douglass and W.E.B. Du Bois, who took the question of women's rights as seriously as they acknowledged the necessity to mobilize social movements against white racism. But in general, Black civil society reflected male hegemony in the leadership of cultural, social, educational and political organizations. Within the Black Church, the central cultural structure in Afro-American life, women were commonly expected to perform the bulk of the hard organizational work, but were seldom among the clergy or deacons of particular denominations. In Black nationalist and Black evangelical cult formations, the Black woman was oppressed by being placed upon the 'pedestal', a familiar device employed also by white males. Within Nobel Drew Ali's Moorish Science Temple movement, which attracted perhaps thirty thousand Black followers in the urban North during the Depression, 'great emphasis' was placed upon 'the husband's responsibility as protector and provider of his family'. Women members were ordered 'to be good homemakers and to obey their husbands'. The Nation of Islam defined sexual morality in 'ultra-puritanical terms', noted social philosopher C. Eric Lincoln. 'No Muslim woman may be alone in a room with any man except her husband; and provocative or revealing dress, including cosmetics, is absolutely forbidden. Muslim males are expected to be constantly alert for any show of interest in a Muslim woman on the part of a white man, for whom sex is alleged to be a degraded obsession.' Muslim women were 'taught how to sew, cook, keep house, rear their children, care for their husbands, and how to behave at home and abroad.'[127] Ironically, Muhammad 'fathered' at least four children by a succession of his personal secretaries. Malcolm X wrote, 'They were brought before Muslim courts and charged with adultery', and after confessing, Muhammad's secretaries 'received sentences of from one to five years of "isolation" '.[128]

The Black left was hardly better. Black Panther Party leader Huey P. Newton argued in 1968 that white man was 'very envious' of Blacks: 'he doesn't have a penis, he psychologically wants to castrate the Black man'. The Black male had to 'recapture his balls, then he will lose all fear and will be free to determine his destiny. This is what is happening at this time with the rebellion of the world's oppressed people against the controller.' Panther women sometimes upheld this pathetic position. In the 4 January 1969 issue of the Black Panther newspaper, Evette Pearson warned men that 'genocide' was 'Planned Parenthood', 'Birth Control' and 'Venereal Disease'. 'Educate your woman to stop taking those pills. You and your woman — replenish the earth with healthy Black warriors. You and your woman can build the Black Liberation Army . . .'[129] Within the League of Revolutionary Black Workers, according to Georgakas and Surkin, a 'strong woman leader' was never allowed 'to emerge. Most of the women in the League had strong personalities and were hard workers; but they invariably found themselves under male supervision . . . Most of the male cadre proudly expressed chauvinistic attitudes, and some members . . . were charged with physically abusing women. The League considered women's liberation as it was then being discussed a divisive issue; and although at times there were women's committees, the League never drew up a programme for women.'[130] Much of the Afro-American left placed the issue of women's exploitation under the subcategory of 'The Woman Question': an important yet clearly secondary subject to be discussed in study-group circles after the major topics had been satisfactorily resolved. If pressed on this, many Black male Marxists might have suggested that once the socialist revolution occurred, women's oppression would disappear. Rigidly following Engels, they would argue that the creation of the socialist state constituted 'the first condition for the liberation of the wife . . .'[131]

The social impact of racism and women's oppression has perpetuated the conditions for triple exploitation on the basis of class, gender and race. As literary critic Barbara Christian comments, Black women 'by their very existence were deviants of the society — female in that they had breasts, vaginas and wombs, but non-women according to the mores of American society, which defined women as non-workers, asexual and fair.'[132] Yet despite their subordinate socio-economic and political status, Black women have participated in or helped to lead virtually every Black social movement previously discussed. Afro-American women were involved in slave uprisings across the Caribbean and the US; they built maroon communities with runaway males; they were an integral factor in the abolitionist movement and the Underground Railroad.[133] And at every level of political involvement, they have had to battle simultaneously against all forms of gender/race/class oppression. Black women leaders consistently raised the issue of gender inequality as an integrally related factor in the overall oppression and exploitation of Black humanity. Mary Ann Shadd

Cary, for example, was a noted abolitionist and one of the first women in North America to publish her own weekly newspaper, the *Provincial Freeman*, in 1853. But Cary was also a vigorous advocate of women's suffrage and other feminist issues. The development of the National Association of Coloured Women in 1896 provided a vehicle for politically active Black women to address public policy issues which, within a sexist social formation, were generally perceived as the province of males alone. During the early decades of the social movement to abolish Jim Crow, Black women leaders such as Mary McLeod Bethune, Ida B. Wells and Mary Church Terrell continued to enrich the social protest tradition established by Sojourner Truth and Mary Ann Shadd Cary.[134]

In the trade-union movement, a similar situation emerged. During the founding of the Congress of Industrial Organizations (CIO) in the Great Depression and the war years, Black women leaders and noted activists included Dora Jones of the Domestic Workers' Union, Floretta Andres of the New York Teachers' Union, and Miranda Smith and Velma Hopkins of the Food, Tobacco, Agricultural and Allied Workers' Union. With the rise of the National Negro Labour Council during the Cold War, North Carolina tobacco worker Estelle Holloway provided local union leadership, as well as serving as an officer of the Winston-Salem branch of the NAACP. In 1968, Black women labour leaders in Local 1199B led the entire Black working-class community in the struggle for economic rights and desegregation in Charleston, South Carolina. Six hundred South Carolina state troopers and US National Guardsmen led mass arrests of striking Black hospital workers. From her gaol cell, Mary Ann Moultrie, the 27-year-old president of the Black hospital workers, was able to draw from the state's brutal repression of Black women the broader class dimensions of her struggle: The government spends 'billions to kill people on the other side of the world . . . we are sending [astronauts] to the moon while children in Charleston go hungry.'[135] Yet with rare exceptions, few of these articulate and politically committed Black women ever won a place within the national leadership of the Black trade-union movement.

Within the modern desegregation movement, most of those who went to gaol or who mobilized communities were Afro-American women. Two important examples in the Congress of Racial Equality (CORE) were Ruth Turner and Gladys Harrington. Turner was a Black Cleveland schoolteacher who dropped out of Harvard University Graduate School and 'gave up her job to devote herself

full-time to [CORE's] Cleveland chapter' in 1961. As the chairwoman of Cleveland CORE, Turner led civil rights sit-ins at the Ohio
Statehouse in Columbus, and in April 1965 — over one year before
the Black Power upsurge — unsuccessfully moved to 'bar all whites
from staff positions' in CORE. A year later, 'with Ruth Turner
having effectively laid the groundwork', Black Power proponent
Floyd McKissick was elected national director to replace James
Farmer.[136] Harrington was a Black social worker who had been a
leader of the bus boycott in Tallahassee, Florida. Moving to
Harlem, she rose to become chairwoman of Harlem CORE. By early
1962, Harrington argued that all civil rights organizations 'should
basically be run by Negroes'. And three years before King and the
SCLC had begun to mobilize Blacks in the North for desegregation
efforts, Harrington was calling for such a shift in national strategy.
When policemen rode their horses over passive Black demonstrators in Manhattan during the summer of 1963, Harrington drew
the logical political conclusion: 'Horses in New York are no different from police dogs in Birmingham.'[137] Yet the majority of the
male Black Power advocates in CORE did not take women's
grievances seriously, nor did they encourage women's leadership.
McKissick equated Black Power with the process by which 'we left
our imposed status of Negroes and became *Black Men* . . . Black
men [who] realized their full worth in society — their dignity and
their beauty — and their power . . .' McKissick's 'macho' successor, Roy Innis, was even more explicitly chauvinistic. When
Innis was elected Harlem CORE chairman in November, 1965, a
'Black male caucus' was named 'the group's chief policy-making
body'.[138] Sadly, the identical pattern is found throughout the Third
World. As Fanon 'quickly came to understand, women's liberation
was a fine topic for Algerian militants except when it came to
liberating their own sisters or wives.'[139]

A related aspect of social oppression that cuts across race and
class categories is the problem of homophobia. Like the vast
majority of white Americans, most Blacks refused to acknowledge
the presence of lesbians and gay males within their communities.
Homosexual political leaders, entrepreneurs and ministers generally attempted to conceal their sexual preferences from neighbours,
constituencies and congregations. Lesbian and gay intellectuals —
including writer Alice Dunbar-Nelson, poets Langston Hughes and
Countee Cullen, literary critic Alain Locke and noted biologist
George Washington Carver — were reluctant to raise the issue of
Black homophobia. Black nationalist and radical writers con-

demned homosexuality in unambiguous terms. Le Roi Jones (Amiri Baraka) asserted that 'most American men are trained to be fags . . . so white women become men-things, a weird combination . . .'; Eldridge Cleaver argued that homosexuality is 'a sickness, just as are baby-rape or wanting to become the head of General Motors . . . Many Negro homosexuals are outraged and frustrated because they are unable to have a baby by a white man.'[140] As author Cheryl Clarke observes, 'Black gay men and lesbians have always been viable contributors to our communities, [and] it is exceedingly painful for us to face public denunciation from Black folk — the very group who should be championing our liberation.' Western capitalist culture demands that lesbians remain hidden away, and the majority of the Afro-American social fraction applaud this homophobic repression. 'Thus, when public denunciations of our life-styles are made by other Black people, we remain silent in the face of their hostility and ignorance', Clarke relates. 'The toll taken on us because we repress our rage and hurt makes us distrustful of all people when we cannot identify as lesbian or gay.'[141] For lesbians of colour, the levels of race/class/gender combine with homophobia to assault their sense of humanity. '[The] woman of colour is invisible both in the white male mainstream world and in the white feminist world, though in the latter this is gradually changing', writes Gloria Anzaldúa. 'The *lesbian* of colour is not only invisible, she doesn't even exist. Our speech, too, is inaudible. We speak in tongues like the outcast and the insane. Because white eyes do not want to know us, they do not bother to learn our language, the language which reflects us, our culture, our spirit.'[142]

In recent decades, Black feminist and gay/lesbian activists' organizations have assumed increased political significance.[143] In the 1950s, for example, one Black activist, 'Ernestine Eckstein', became a national leader of the Daughters of Bilitis, the first national lesbian political formation.[144] In the following years, hundreds of national and local feminist and gay/lesbian political organizations have been formed — from Boston's Combahee River Collective to Sapphire Sapphos, a Black lesbian group. The existence of such formations indicates not merely the continued prevalence of sexism and homophobia among Afro-Americans, but more generally, the inability to expand the concept of political resistance to express solidarity with all members of the community who experience multiple forms of oppression. Thus new social movements against intolerance and women's subordinate status must be waged within the context of larger social movements. And this development of movements-within-movements is not confined to the US. Throughout the world, women of colour are actively, consciously seeking power — the power to eradicate all forms of oppression. In Belize, 'women are the backbone of both [political] parties', argue activists Zoila Ellis and Cynthia Ellis Higinio. Yet none obtain 'any glory', and none are 'fully integrated into the Party structure and the decision-making process'. Belizean women are currently waging a political campaign against 'on-the-job sexual harassment', noting that 'this behaviour is common among male employers . . .'[145] In England, West Indian and Asian women confront a gender/race/class system of oppression remarkably similar to that in the US. They receive the worst-paid jobs; they are racially stereotyped as either inherently submissive (Asians) or as Black 'Matriarchs' who 'taunt and even bully their menfolk'; they are subjected to enforced sterilizations; and they are generally viewed as peripheral to the social and cultural 'norms' of British society.[146] But here, too, women of colour forcefully assert their power. Hazel V. Carby points out that 'strong female support networks continue in both West Indian and Asian sex/gender systems', which create the semi-liberated social space essential for developing 'new survival strategies'. However, Carby argues convincingly that the political and social oppression of *Black* women differs qualitatively from that of *white* females in Britain and that the struggle against male domination is not specifically or solely an attack on the 'family'. 'We would not wish to deny that the family can be a source of oppression for us but we also wish to examine how the Black family has functioned as a prime source of resistance to oppression.' Carby comments: 'the way the gender of Black women is constructed differs from constructions of white femininity because it is also subject to racism . . . Black women do not want to be grafted onto "feminism" in a tokenistic manner as colourful diversions from "real" problems. Feminism has to be transformed if it is to address us.'[147] Here, as elsewhere, Black women have come to the realization that social class equality cannot exist for anyone, so long as any fraction of a social group is coerced to submit to oppression.

VI

Nothing has perplexed Marxists more than the issue of Black nationalism. Lenin thought Afro-Americans 'should be classed as an oppressed nation, for the equality won in the Civil War of 1861-65 and guaranteed by the Constitution of the republic was in many respects increasingly curtailed in the chief Negro areas [the South] in connection with the transition from the progressive, pre-monopoly capitalism to the reactionary monopoly capitalism [imperialism] of the new era . . .' Under Stalin, the Communist International passed two resolutions on the 'Negro Question' in October 1928 and October 1930, which defined Afro-Americans in the South specifically as 'an oppressed nation'. The Comintern's 1930 document emphasized that it was referring to Blacks living and working in the 'Black Belt' region, which cut across the South from Virginia's Tidewater to eastern Texas, and which constituted the territory of this nation. 'Communists in the Black Belt will and must try to win over all working elements of the Negroes . . . to their side and to convince them not only that they must win the right of self-determination but also that they must make use of this right in accordance with the Communist Party.' The Comintern cautioned party members that in the event of a socialist revolution in the US, Communist Negroes must 'come out not for but *against* separation of the Negro Republic from federation with the United States. But the *right* of the Negroes to governmental separation will be *unconditionally realized* by the Communist Party; it will unconditionally give the Negro population of the Black Belt freedom of choice even on this question.'[148] White American Communists did not actively promulgate the self-determination slogan in the Black community, and focused largely on developing programmes that attacked Jim Crow, discrimination inside the trade-union movement, and racist violence. Consequently the Party's Black membership increased from 1500 in early 1930 to approximately 10,000 eight years later.[149] Black Communists never forgot the theoretical commitment of the Party to Black self-determination, but as they were increasingly pulled into labour-organizing and antiracist social movements, they too tended to ignore the full implications of the Party's formal position on nationalism. Only in the mid 1950s, with the development of the Montgomery bus boycott and widespread desegregation campaigns did the Party formally drop its 'Black Belt self-determination theses' under pressure from Black Marxist James Jackson. A few Black Communists, notably Harry Haywood, left the Party over the issue, but most accepted the theoretical shift.[150] Indeed, by the early 1970s, Jackson argued that 'exhuming the corpse of a variant of the old slogan of self-determination for the oppressed Black nation in America is self defeating.' Afro-

Americans were not a nation, but an 'oppressed nationality'. Blacks had none of the basic characteristics of a nation — no common territory, unique language, common 'psychological make-up', and so forth. Any nationalist separatist orientation 'is disorienting to the Black freedom movement and is confusing to the antimonopoly allies in the struggle.'[151]

The Trotskyist position on Afro-American nationalism was set decades ago by Trotsky himself. From exile, Trotsky criticized the Comintern's 1928 position on Afro-American nationalism; in principle, he believed that the 'Negroes are a race and not a nation.' Marxists should not 'obligate the Negroes to become a nation; if they are, then that is a question of their consciousness, that is, what they desire and what they strive for.' As in all political matters, the question of Black America was subsumed in the larger issue of Trotsky's theory of 'permanent revolution'. Negroes are 'convoked by the historic development to become a vanguard of the working class', Trotsky suggested in 1939. 'The most oppressed and discriminated are the most dynamic milieu of the working class.' He urged American Trotskyists to build a 'base' inside the 'Negro movement', and to defend the right of Black self-determination if Blacks themselves demanded it. If Trotskyists 'are not able to find the road to this stratum, then we are not worthy at all. The permanent revolution and all the rest would be only a lie.' In his ruminations on Afro-American nationalism, Trotsky made at least four critical errors, both tactical and strategic. First, he grossly underestimated the political importance of the Black petty bourgeoisie: in 1933 he argued that the Afro-American middle strata 'will take up the demand for "social, political and economic equality" . . . but prove absolutely incapable in the struggle; the Negro proletariat will march over the petty bourgeoisie in the direction of the proletarian revolution.' Secondly, Trotsky overestimated the racism of white workers, and thus pre-empted the possibility of effective social class protest movements with multiracial constituencies: '99.9 per cent of the [white] American workers are chauvinists; in relation to the Negroes they are hangmen and they are so also towards the Chinese. It is necessary to teach the American beasts . . . to make them understand that the American state is not their state and that they do not have to be the guardians of this state.' Thirdly, at times Trotsky advanced political tactics for Blacks that in the context of the segregated South would have produced widespread racist vigilante violence. In 1940, he urged American Trotskyists to 'approach [Negroes] everywhere by advocating that for every lynching [by whites] they should lynch ten or twenty lynchers.'[152]

However, Trotsky's greatest shortcoming was his dogmatic belief that the overwhelming majority of Black workers and farmers supported, or in the near future would advocate, Black nationalism and the right to self-determination. When confronted with evidence that the bulk of the Afro-American population did not advocate self-determination, Trotsky replied: 'The Negro has not yet got it into his poor black head that he dares to carve out for himself a piece of the great and mighty states.' In Coyoacan, Mexico, C.L.R. James impressed upon Trotsky the 'reactionary' aspects of the demand for self-determination. In his conversation of 4 April 1939, James argued that 'no one denies the Negroes' right to self-determination. It is a question of whether we should advocate it.' In Africa and the West Indies, 'the great masses of the people look upon self-determination as a restoration of their independence.' Consequently, the rise of nationalism was 'progressive' and 'puts the workers in a position to make great progress toward socialism.' In the US, James noted, the 'Negro desperately wants to be an American citizen.' Moreover, there was a distinct danger that 'injecting a policy of self-determination' would be 'the surest way to divide and confuse the workers in the South'. Trotsky refused to budge, since his thesis on the Negro was bound to his faith in the permanent revolution theory. James again cautioned that 'the idea of separating' could be 'a step backward so far as a socialist society is concerned', and observed that 'if white workers extend a hand to the Negro, he will not want self-determination . . . You seem to think that there is a greater possibility of the Negroes' wanting self-determination than I think is probable.' The founder of the Red Army dismissed James's views as 'abstract'. 'To fight for the possibility of realizing an independent state is a sign of great moral and political awakening', Trotsky concluded. 'It would be a tremendously revolutionary step.' Ill-equipped to judge the contours of Afro-American social history, paralysed by his theory of social transformation, Trotsky's bequest to US Trotskyists was an analysis which had little relevance or applicability to the class and racial struggles in America. Unfortunately, his epigones rigidly maintain his edicts on Black nationalism to this day, at an isolated distance from the Black working class.[153]

The question of the relationship between Black nationalism and the evolution of social class struggles for power in the US must be predicated upon a definition of 'nation'. Cox provides a sketchy terminology that is helpful but hardly complete: 'a nation . . . may be thought of as a tribal group conscious of cultural unity.'[154] More precise is the formulation of Horace B. Davis: 'a nation' is a social entity that 'always has (1) a specified territory; (2) a certain minimum size; (3) some integration (centralization, interdependence); and (4) a consciousness of itself as a nation. The first and fourth points are the key ones: a specified territory and national consciousness.' 'Nations' usually emerge in one of three ways. They 'may be formed from states'; 'in struggle against foreign oppression'; or 'by attaining first cultural solidarity and then political expression of that solidarity'.[155] A common language is an important but not essential characteristic of a nation: Canada has two official languages, as well as the Native American languages indigenous to North America; Switzerland has five languages; Nigeria has numerous commonly used local lanuages in addition to the recent language of colonialism, English. A population does not have to have local control or 'home rule' for it to be considered a nation; Cuba and the United States are prominent examples of places where local nationalist revolts or revolutions occurred prior to the assumption of state power by a local dominant social class. Nor does any 'state apparatus' have to exist for a national identity to develop: As Davis notes, 'were the Poles not a nationality during the long period when there was no Polish state?'[156] Thus 'nationalism' is 'a process, an implement . . . a political system of action', definitions that are inherently contradictory. Nationalism may mean 'the effort to advance the fortunes of one's own nation, especially at the expense of others', which can culminate in 'chauvinism' or 'jingoism'. Or nationalism 'may be used in the sense of working for the welfare of the collectivity [the nation]'.[157]

The social reality of nationalism coincided with the emergence of capitalist social formations, and accelerated with the development of capitalist states and the idea of bourgeois democracy. But there is no direct correlation between the advocacy of 'democracy' and 'nationalism'. The Chinese leader Sun Yat-sen was a radical democrat and nationalist; so too were the great Cuban revolutionists José Marti and Antonio Maceo. But the chauvinistic side of nationalism is utterly contemptuous of bourgeois democracy: Hitler, Mussolini and Peron were also nationalists. Even the 'nationalism' of bourgeois democracies, viewed from their colonial territories, is tyranny of the extremest degree. Cox argues that the most 'offensive nationalism has been most thoroughly developed among the British . . . The idea of white supremacy hangs over the world like a great mist, and former attempts to lift it have resulted only in its condensation over the intractable area. In this Great Britain has set the ultimate pattern of intrigue, subtlety, and force in dealings with peoples of colour; she is the great modern stabilizer of world white dominance.'[158] This apparent paradox of nationalism, its ever-present constructive and destructive elements, can be resolved by viewing this process through the historical evolution of either subordinated or dominant classes. In short, any judgement of nationalism must be made depending upon which social fraction or class advocates it, and under what set of conditions. Nationalism among Kenyans under British colonial rule in the 1950s must be seen as objectively progressive; the nationalism of Hitler, under the conditions of the Weimar republic of the early 1930s, was the ultimate chauvinism. Portuguese nationalism and fascism in a colonial context produced massive human atrocities in Angola, Mozambique and Guinea-Bissau; but the revolutionary national-ism of a Ho Chi Minh, Amilcar Cabral and Fidel Castro was in each case a decisive factor in a successful socialist revolution. Lenin was the first Marxist seriously to comprehend that class struggles in colonial nations would assume a 'bourgeois democratic form', and that Marxists must support revolutionary nationalist movements consisting primarily of peasants.[159]

Lenin also understood two more things: that 'there could be no question of a purely proletarian movement in a pre-capitalist environment', and that at the root of nationalist movements was the material reality of capitalist exploitation in colonial areas.[160] In the field of Black politics, we may also add several other observations. In a racially-stratified social formation, the nationalism of Black workers and the petty bourgeoisie is closely linked with their struggle against racism. Black nationalism may be the product of the historical struggle to overthrow a white colonial regime: as I shall discuss in Volume II, the 'nationalism' of Kwame Nkrumah and his Convention People's Party of the late 1940s must be traced back to the bourgeois nationalism of a John Mansah Sabrah or J.E. Casely-Hayford, who criticized British policies in the Gold Coast half a century before. In the Americas and the Caribbean, Black-nationalism assumes two basic forms. In the Caribbean's Black-majority islands, in the first case, the class struggle between Black slaves and their white masters generated a new sense of nationality and a 'desire for liberty; the ridding oneself of the particular burden which is the special inheritance of a Black skin', as James comments. Slave rebellions, labour-union unrest, and all forms of political violence were motivated by a social reality of both inequality and national oppression: by the fact that any 'white man, whatever his limitations, was a free subject, a man able to do what he could in the community', and that any Black person 'was made a slave'.[161] The cultural solidarity among slaves and, later, among agricultural workers, labourers and elements of the coloured petty bourgeoisie created an explicit sense of Caribbean nationalism, which expressed itself in regional revolts against colonial rule. In most islands, the features of this struggle were notably oriented more towards a nationalism that transcends imposed racial categories. Racism existed in the Caribbean, obviously. But a white Cuban former slave-holder, Carlos Manuel De Cespedes, in the context of a Cuban/Caribbean struggle for national independence, could draft the *grito de Yara* which linked nationalism with general Black emancipation, and could fight beside Maceo and other Black former slaves in a spirit of solidarity and anti-racism.[162] In the southern United States, the existence of any white leader remotely comparable to De Cespedes in the mid nineteenth century would have been inconceivable.

Black Americans in the US also developed a separate and distinct national culture which drew simultaneously upon their African origins and on their concrete development within slavery and the segregated South. Afro-Americans never found themselves being 'suspended between a lost African culture and a forbidden European one'.[163] The Afro-American, as Du Bois asserted in his famous passage, was *both* 'an American [and] a Negro; two souls, two thoughts, two unreconciled strivings; two warring ideals in one dark body, whose dogged strength alone keeps it from being torn asunder.'[164] This 'double consciousness' was the basis of the struggle to attack institutional racism, racial segregation and all forms of inequality, as well as of that internal collective effort to engender cultural and social structures specific to the Afro-American experience. Class struggle, or more specifically, the conscious struggle for power, is historically for Black America a dual dynamic: it has been both antiracist and nationalistic; it has attacked racial segregation, yet affirmed the cultural and social integrity of Afro-American people. Since the Afro-American population has never made up more than a fraction of the total US population, and because of the more intensely racist ideology promoted by the US ruling class and absorbed by many white workers, Black nationalism has always tended to assume the relative permanence and centrality of racial categories, over and above social class. Yet Black nationalist thought has not been hegemonic among Afro-Americans except during distinct and rather brief historical periods — the 1850s, 1880s, 1920s and 1960s.

To a great extent, a kind of 'fragmented nationalist' tradition exists within Black America: a social movement that retains deep roots within the cultural and social arena of Black life, yet acquires prominence only under certain historical conjunctures. The reasons for this fragmented tradition are many. With the prominent exception of the Black ghetto entrepreneurs, who employed nationalist rhetoric to control and expand their share of the Black consumer market, the majority of the Negro petty bourgeoisie have never been overtly nationalistic. As Du Bois observed in *Dusk of Dawn*:

> From the eighteenth century down, the Negro intelligentsia has regarded segregation as the visible badge of their servitude and as the object of their unceasing attack. The upper-class Negro has almost never been nationalistic. He has never planned or thought of a Negro state or a Negro church or a Negro school. This solution has always been a thought upsurging from the mass, because of pressure which they could not withstand and which compelled a racial institution or chaos. Continually such institutions were founded and developed, but this took place against the advice and best thought of the intelligentsia.[165]

The majority of Afro-American social institutions, from the Black churches to civic associations, were led by Blacks who were at best neutral, and more often than not positively hostile towards any form of racial separatism, whether imposed from without or created within their communities. Black workers created separate unions, but most labour leaders looked forward to a time when the colour line would not be drawn by the AFL. Black nationalist social movements tended to germinate and flourish during periods when several common political and economic factors converged: first, during phases of American capitalist economic expansion, in which Black workers' wages and job opportunities still lagged significantly behind those of white workers; secondly, when white politicians and the capitalist ruling class they represent turned sharply against Blacks' civil rights, and actively promoted racist vigilante violence; and thirdly, when the existing Negro petty-bourgeois leadership and organizations were incapable of articulating the demands of the Black oppressed masses in the form of new policies and programmes. All three conditions existed in the early 1850s: economic expansion; the adoption of both the Compromise of 1850, which strengthened the Fugitive Slave Act, and the Kansas-Nebraska Act of 1854 extending slavery into the western plains territories; and the failure of Frederick Douglass and other integrationist abolitionists to meet the nationalistic political challenge represented by Delany and H. Ford Douglas. Seven decades later, a similar conjuncture took place: the 'Red Summer' of 1919, the mushrooming of the Ku Klux Klan, the retreat of both capitalist parties from the principle of biracial democracy, and the inability of Du Bois, James Weldon Johnson and other NAACP leaders to express the aspirations of the Black urban working class and farmers. The result was the phenomenon of Garveyism, and the recruitment of millions of Afro-Americans into the Universal Negro Improvement Association (UNIA).

Radical nationalist movements outside the African Diaspora have frequently served to inspire and promote the development of similar movements among Blacks. The cases of Ireland and India are illustrative. Three years after the Irish Republican Brotherhood organized the Irish Easter Week Rising of 1916, a similar formation based on Black nationalism and radical socialist ideas was developed in the US, the secret African Blood Brotherhood for African Liberation and Redemption (ABB). Black nationalists, such as Harlem's charismatic orator Hubert H. Harrison, urged Blacks to 'rise against the government just as the Irish against England unless they get their rights.'[166] Du Bois frequently drew political parallels between British oppression in Ireland and white racism against Blacks. 'The recent Irish revolt may have been foolish,' he noted in August 1916, 'but would to God some of us had sense enough to be fools!' Du Bois praised the words of Irish Republican Terence MacSwiney in February 1921: 'Not those who inflict most, but those who suffer most are the conquerors.'[167] Marcus Garvey was particularly influenced by Ireland's example. Garvey's Black Star Line of steamships may have followed the lead of Sinn Fein, which a decade before had called for 'the re-establishment of an Irish mercantile Marine'. In its November 1905 convention, Sinn Fein proposed 'the establishment of an Irish consular service abroad'; Garvey enunciated the same idea in 1914 'for the protection of all Negroes, irrespective of nationality'. For decades, Garvey viewed himself as a Negro counterpart to Irish republican leader Eamon de Valera. The cry for an Irish Free State, 'Ireland for the Irish', was again echoed in Garvey's slogan, 'Africa for the Africans'. Even at Garvey's August 1920 convention of the UNIA, a huge banner above the multitude declared: 'President for Ireland;

Why Not One for Africa?' The US Military Intelligence Division was convinced that the Friends of Irish Freedom was helping Garvey's Black Star Line, with the purpose of '[carrying] arms to Africa'. Even Du Bois, a critic of Garveyism, commented that the UNIA was 'allied with the Bolsheviks and the Sinn Feiners in their world revolution'.[168]

Indian nationalism presents even closer parallels. Initial political and economic connections between Indians and Black workers were established in the nineteenth century, in both South Africa and the Caribbean. By 1897, Indians in Trinidad had founded the East Indian National Association, and Indians gradually began to work with Blacks in labour associations and to take part in early anticolonialist activities.[169] Even earlier in Guyana, during the 1880s, sugar-planters were complaining of Indian 'troublemakers' who were 'sowing the seeds of discontent and insubordination' among other non-white workers. Militant Indian labourers 'used their tools as weapons', and as Walter Rodney noted, 'such attacks represented an extremely rudimentary stage of class struggle.'[170] But as the emergence of the modern Indian nationalist movement against British domination took shape, hundreds of Afro-American and Afro-Caribbean leaders drew the similarities between their respective peoples' political conditions. No one did so more than Du Bois; indeed, Indian nationalism was for Du Bois what Irish nationalism was for Garvey — a model of resistance to racist exploitation and national oppression. As early as May 1915, Du Bois argued that colonialism and world war were creating the basis for a new generation of 'awakening leaders' in both India and Africa.[171] Two years later he joined Indian nationalist leader Lajpat Rai in speeches before a socialist group, and called for Indian independence.[172] In the 1930s he emphasized in a series of essays that the 'coloured peoples' of India and Black America were actually 'one in oppression' and exploitation.[173] Du Bois was most impressed by the political leadership of Mohandas K. Gandhi. In March 1922, Du Bois declared that the Indian nationalist was 'a man [of] sheer impeccability of character, extraordinary personality' who possessed an 'originality of doctrine and ideas'.[174] If anything, his admiration increased over the decades. In 1947 Du Bois proclaimed India's independence as 'the greatest historical date of the nineteenth and twentieth centuries', and hailed Gandhi as perhaps 'the greatest man in the world'.[175] Of course, the political example of *satyagraha* and non-violent resistance to oppression, which Gandhi first developed in South Africa and used with dramatic success in India, profoundly affected Martin Luther King Jr, who was hardly an Afro-American nationalist. But years before King, other Black intellectuals had perceived the necessity to journey 'to India to discuss with Gandhi the application of his technique' to the US. In 1929, Gandhi told Howard University president Mordecai Johnson that 'perhaps it will be through the Negro that the unadulterated message of non-violence will be delivered to the world.'[176]

One distinct expression of nationalist sentiment that has constantly resurfaced is Black emigrationism. Like the maroon impulse, advocates of emigration have concluded that the US is permanently racist, and that the sole hope for Black self-determination lies in a constructive disengagement from the white supremacist state. Yet there is something more here than a desire to reject the capitalist-racist social formation and the inferior position of Black people within it. Culturally and indeed psychologically, the image of the African continent as the geographical, political and economic future for the entire African Diaspora has informed the organizational evolution of emigrationist groups. Ever since 1789, when the Free African Society of Newport, Rhode Island, expressed support for Black American colonization of Africa, the ideological concept has continued to attract some level of Black support. In 1815 an affluent Black ship-owner, Paul Cuffee, paid for the transit of thirty-eight free Blacks from the US to Sierra Leone. The first Black newspaper editor in the US, John Russwurm, left for Africa in 1829. In 1859, Delany organized an expedition to what is today western Nigeria, and obtained a grant of land from the Yoruba which would have become the site for an Afro-American colony. After the demise of Reconstruction, a number of Black leaders spoke favourably of African emigration, including Virginia Congressman J. Mercer Langston, AME Bishop W.H. Heard of South Carolina and noted Professor W.S. Scarborough of Wilberforce University. Two hundred South Carolina Blacks left the US for Liberia in 1878. The principal nineteenth-century advocate of emigration was AME Bishop Henry M. Turner, the first Black army chaplain and a Georgia state legislator after the Civil War. Writing from Liberia in 1892, he proclaimed, 'One thing the Black man has here, that is manhood, freedom, and the fullest liberty; and feels as a lord and walks the same way.' Turner attacked those Blacks who criticized colonization, writing that 'a man who loves a country that hates him is a human dog and not a man'.[177] Although the popularity of emigration diminished after the 1920s among most Afro-

Americans, Turner's appeal still carries an emotional message for many: 'Gaols are broken open, and we are taken out and burnt, shot, hanged, unjointed and murdered in every way. Our civil rights are taken from us by force; our political rights are a farce. Can't the fool Negro see that there is no future in this country for him? If he cannot, then he should return to slavery.'[178]

Somewhat related to emigrationism is the much richer and more varied social protest movement tradition, Pan-Africanism.[179] Definitions of the concept vary, although the ideas of two central proponents of Pan-Africanism provide a necessary framework. Du Bois represents one tendency of Pan-Africanism, one that was an outgrowth of his 'double consciousness' theory. The fundamental struggle for power among Black Americans, Du Bois always insisted, was against racism. In the US special formation, this implied both a social movement to abolish racial segregation and a bourgeois democratic political movement to increase Black power in all levels of the existing political apparatus. But given the African cultural and social heritage of Afro-Americans, Du Bois reasoned, part of the political agenda must be to make connections with ongoing Caribbean and African social movements. 'All people of African descent', he argued, 'have common interests and should work together in the struggle for their freedom.' Du Bois was the first Western scholar 'to describe the great medieval kingdoms of West Africa; and he was among the first to regard the non-literate peoples of sub-Saharan Africa as possessing complex and sophisticated cultures.'[180] Sociologically and culturally, people of colour in the Caribbean and the US were tied to Africa. Therefore any effort to combat colonialism and racism of necessity had to be an anti-capitalist and Pan-Africanist struggle. Walter Rodney suggests that the development of Pan-Africanist ideology was as a response to world white supremacy, which 'has become part of the super-structure of the white capitalist world.' Throughout every colonial educational system, whites denigrated the cultural and political contributions of Africans to world civilization. 'We were told to forget slavery, forget Africa, and forget that we were Africans.' Rodney noted:

> What critics fail to realize is that there are fundamental political realities which draw the conscious Black man in the New World towards the African continent . . . Any Black man fighting against white oppression in his particular locality would sooner or later realize that all Africans 'at home and abroad' were caught up in the same predicament. Pan-Africanism is not simply a unity of colour, it is also a unity of common

> condition and one that retains its validity because the dominant group in
> the international political economy continue to define things in racist
> terms for their own convenience. For their own convenience, to be sure,
> but then they are playing with revolution.[181]

Many early Afro-American intellectuals and activists were 'Africa-conscious'. John Henry Smyth, a Black attorney and Reconstruction-era official, was appointed as Minister Resident and Consul General to Liberia in 1879. Smyth urged Black Americans to 'awaken [their] interest and sincere desire for the well-being of Africa and her races, for our people, and for accurate information concerning that most ancient and most mysterious of lands.'[182] Edward Wilmot Blyden, an emigrant from the Virgin Islands, travelled to Liberia for training as a teacher and minister. Blyden eventually became president of Liberia College, and later served as Liberia's ambassador to Great Britain. In a series of widely read books and essays, he propounded an early ideological perspective of race pride and racial solidarity which was essential for subsequent Pan-Africanists.[183] Trinidadian Jacob J. Thomas, while teaching at a public school in Grenada, wrote the influential tract *Froudacity* in 1888. Not only was *Froudacity* a polemic against British racism and the repressive colonial governments in the West Indies, but also it projected the concept of international Black political unity. A man who built upon Blyden's and Thomas's writings and ideas was Trinidadian educator and lawyer, Henry Sylvester Williams. After studying law in Canada, Williams travelled to London. In 1897 he founded the African Association, with the goal of creating a permanent political forum for Africans and Americans of African descent. Williams called together the first Pan-African Conference which met in London three years later. Williams, Du Bois and the others attending the meeting projected an international network of Blacks which would build African solidarity. Branches of Williams's group, called the Pan-African Association, were developed in Jamaica and Trinidad. Williams's death in 1911 cut short the development of this organization.[184] However, Williams's Pan-Africanist ideology was continued in the journalistic work of Duse Mohammed Ali, editor of the London-based *African Times and Oriental Review*, and in the 1920s by Trinidadian activist F.E.M. Hercules's *African Telegraph*. Across the Caribbean, political organizers began to develop race-conscious groups that were oriented favourably towards Pan-Africanism. James B. Yearwood toured Central American countries to build the Universal Loyal Negro Association among emigrant West Indian labourers. The

Negro Progress Convention of British Guyana emerged under the guidance of Randolph Smith. Du Bois also returned to Europe in 1919, 1921 and 1923 to convene another series of Pan-African Congresses. The 1921 Congress, which included forty-one delegates from Africa, thirty-five Blacks from the US and seven West Indians, issued a challenge to white colonialism. 'The absolute equality of races, physical, political and social is the founding-stone of world and human advancement', the delegates declared.[185]

The second major current of Pan-Africanism is best represented by the seminal Black nationalist of the twentieth century, Marcus M. Garvey. Born in August 1887 in St Ann's Bay, Jamaica, Garvey began his life as a printer and itinerant publisher. After travelling throughout the Caribbean, Central America and England, Garvey came to the US in March 1916. Embarking on a year-long lecture tour, Garvey visited thirty-eight states and established political contacts and local groups of supporters. He had originally intended to use the money collected during his tour to return to Jamaica and establish a trades school, based roughly on Booker T. Washington's Tuskegee Institute. But with the eruption of post-war racist violence, and the concomitant failure of the NAACP and the Negro petty bourgeoisie generally to express the political demands of the Black masses, the historical conditions were ripe for a militant Black nationalist agenda. Standing on Harlem street corners, the young Jamaican mesmerized audiences with his bold assertions of Black nationalism, Black armed self-defence and Black power. He quickly became the voice of the unemployed, the semi-skilled and impoverished workers, and poor Black share-croppers across the Deep South. Drawing from the organizing work of an earlier Black Harlem radical, Hubert H. Harrison, Garvey championed the slogan 'Race First'. Reversing its earlier lukewarm stance against politics, the UNIA now embraced a revolutionary nationalistic creed. 'It will be a terrible day when the Blacks draw the sword to fight for their liberty', Garvey warned in October, 1919. 'I call upon you four hundred million Blacks to give the blood you have shed for the white man to make Africa a republic for the Negro.' Unlike Du Bois, Garvey viewed the clash between races as the fundamental factor in world politics.

UNIA organizers quickly established all-Black groceries, laundries, a doll factory, printing establishments and a hotel. Thousands of poor Blacks poured their meagre savings into Garvey's Black Star Line, and hundreds of young women joined his Black Cross nurses. Garvey linked the struggle for Black liberation

with all other dynamic nationalist campaigns in India, Ireland and
China, while constantly reinforcing a self-confidence and determination to succeed against all odds. 'Up you mighty race,' he declared,
'you can accomplish what you will!' The foundation of Garvey's
support was within the poor and working-class Black communities
of the Caribbean, Canada, Central America and the United States.
But Garvey could not have created this powerful Black nationalist
organization without the assistance of a number of gifted Black
ministers, lawyers and skilled journalists. Garvey scholar Robert
Hill illustrates that Garvey recruited a substantial array of militant
Black middle-class intellectuals, who were able to administrate and
to expand the UNIA. Hubert Harrison worked for Garvey in 1920-21
as UNIA Commissioner of Education. Wilfred A. Domingo, the
articulate Jamaican socialist, was the first editor of the UNIA's
popular newspaper, the *Negro World.* Noted scholar Arthur A.
Schomburg, whose collection of rare works on Africa later became
the Schomburg Collection of the New York Public Library, was also
a Garvey supporter. John A. Bruce, called 'the prince of Afro-
American correspondents', wrote a regular column in the *Negro
World* and was knighted by the UNIA as 'the Duke of Uganda' in
1921. Militant anti-lynching crusader Ida B. Wells entertained
Garvey in her Chicago home. But Garvey's principal success came
from recruiting dynamic Black ministers into his organization. The
Reverend Egbert Ethelred Brown, a Unitarian minister and
spokesman for Jamaican striking workers during that country's
labour unrest in 1918-19, was an early Garvey supporter. Bishop
George A. McGuire came to the US from Antigua to establish the
African Orthodox Church, which projected Garvey's vision of a
Black Christ. Undoubtedly the chief UNIA leader, second only to
Garvey, was an AME Zion minister James Walker Hood Eason.
Breaking with the NAACP, Eason served as the first UNIA chaplain-
general, and in 1920 was elected to the post of 'Leader of American
Negroes' in the UNIA. With the support of Black nationalist-
oriented petty-bourgeois elites, Garvey successfully established
almost a thousand chapters and divisions of the UNIA in over forty
nations, with an international membership of four to six million.
For Garvey, national liberation of his native Jamaica, or the Afro-
American 'nation' in the US, depended upon the unification and
liberation of the continent of Africa.

The meteoric rise of Garveyism in the early 1920s was quickly
followed by its crushing collapse. Prominent Afro-Americans,
particularly the leaders of the NAACP, denounced the UNIA's

business ventures as a gigantic swindle. When the mercurial Garvey met with white supremacists and agreed with the principle of strict racial separation, Du Bois denounced Garvey as 'the most dangerous enemy of the Negro race in America and the world . . . either a lunatic or a traitor.' One group of leading civil rights activists, who included Robert S. Abbott, editor of the *Chicago Defender* and William Pickens of the NAACP, petitioned US Attorney General Harry M. Daughterty to 'use his full influence completely to disband and extirpate this vicious movement and speedily push the government's case against Marcus Garvey for using the mails to defraud.' In 1926, Black sociologist E. Franklin Frazier characterized the UNIA as 'the Black Klan of America'. Even for his devoted followers, Garvey's statements were sometimes difficult to comprehend. 'We were the first fascists', Garvey declared in the late 1930s. 'Mussolini copied fascism from me. What the Negro needs is a Hitler.' After Garvey's imprisonment in 1925 and deportation from the US to Jamaica in 1927, the UNIA splintered and rapidly began to disappear. In 1935 he moved to London, where he resided until his death in 1940. After Garveyism's demise, however, even its Black critics found something positive about the mass movement. A. Philip Randolph praised Garvey for destroying 'the slave psychology which throttles and strangles Negro initiative'. James Weldon Johnson wrote that Garvey 'had energy, daring and the Napoleonic personality . . . that draws masses.' E. Franklin Frazier declared that 'as a leader of a mass movement among Negroes, Garvey has no equal.' The most articulate assessment of Garvey and the UNIA was given by James. 'Garvey never set foot in Africa. He spoke no African language. But Garvey managed to convey to Negroes everywhere his passionate belief that Africa was the home of a civilization which had once been great and would be great again', James writes. 'When you bear in mind the slenderness of his resources, the vast material forces and the pervading social conceptions which automatically sought to destroy him, his achievement remains one of the propagandistic miracles of this century.'[186]

After the decline of Garveyism, the centre of the Pan-Africanist movement moved to London, focusing around a West Indian intellectual, George Padmore.[187] Born Malcolm Nurse in Trinidad, Padmore acquired his *nom de guerre* as a Black leader of the Communist Party in the 1920s. Breaking with the Communists during the Great Depression, Padmore established the International African Service Bureau in London as the centre for anticolonialist activities. In his small home, he regularly gathered together young African students (including Jomo Kenyatta and Nkrumah) who would eventually succeed in ending colonial rule. In Manchester in 1945, Padmore, Nkrumah and Du Bois held the fifth Pan-African Congress, which initiated the process of decolonization. Padmore's major book, *Pan-Africanism or Communism*, became the political 'bible' for the Pan-African Congress (PAC), a revolutionary nationalist formation in South Africa. Working closely with Padmore in the 1930s was C.L.R. James. The son of a Black Trinidadian school teacher and grandson of slaves, James promptly became involved in radical politics. His interests were catholic: sports, sociology, labour history, West Indian literature and political theory. Although affiliated with British Trotskyists, he developed close ties with Padmore and Black American artist/ activist Paul Robeson. James served briefly as editor of the *International African Opinion*, Padmore's journal. Throughout his subsequent career, James was chiefly responsible for integrating the insights of Marxism-Leninism into a critical analytic frame which advanced the African social revolution. As Rodney was to observe, James was among the first to comprehend the significance of 'classes forming within African society'. James understood that fundamentally problematic for Pan-Africanism was the 'reconciliation between the African and the World Revolution, as it were, and a plotting of the coordinates of race and class'.[188] Nkrumah was the first African intellectual to apply Padmore's Pan-Africanist concepts to the practical democratic struggle to challenge British colonial rule in his native Gold Coast. Three decades later, Rodney would apply his version of revolutionary socialism and Pan-Africanism against the neo-colonial regime of Forbes Burnham, the dictatorial prime minister of Guyana. The hosting of a sixth Pan-African Congress by Tanzanian president Julius Nyerere in 1974 is indicative that Pan-Africanism retains its central vitality as an international and militant tradition of social change throughout the African Diaspora.

On balance, Black nationalism and Pan-Africanism are logical manifestations of the political, ideological, cultural and economic development of the peoples of African descent. The fundamental struggle for power expressed by the oppressed Afro-American national minority inside the US had been, and remains to this day, the demand for complete social class equality. Black Americans are not in the fullest sense a 'nation', and Black nationalism has not been the central focus of Black political practice and social thought.

In contrast, for peoples of African descent in the Caribbean and for those of the African continent itself, nationalism is the element at the core of modern politics, if by nationalism one refers to the movements to eliminate colonial political rule and the cultural, social and economic hegemony of the West. In Africa and the Caribbean, liberation movements necessarily involve a systemic assault against racism, as in the US; but unlike the United States, a white majority does not exist. Thus for most Afro-Americans in most historical periods, the struggle for equality and full democracy has taken precedence over the nationalist protest tradition. However, the extensive linkages formed over two centuries — by Delany, Turner, Du Bois, Garvey and Padmore — between Africa and the peoples of African descent in the West guarantee that both Black nationalism and Pan-Africanism will continue to remain powerful and dynamic factors in the future evolution of Black politics.[189]

VII

The diverse historical examples of Black social movements cited by no means exhaust the range of past and present social forces, strategies and oppositional currents throughout the African Diaspora. Yet certain material and social factors within each specific social formation can largely dictate the mode and degree of protest that any oppressed community is likely to generate over time. Geography is under certain circumstances an important factor for consideration. Maroons or *quilombos* could develop in the Caribbean and in Latin America because the initial pattern of European colonization was along the coastline. White planters in the Caribbean often lived in the towns, and plantations were often adjacent to vast stretches of wilderness. Slaves in the United States usually worked in smaller units, and were usually located in close proximity to white population centres. It was difficult for runaway slaves to locate any wilderness regions in the South after 1820 where large-scale maroons could exist. The relative density of the white population, and the comparatively small size of the slave community, were other important factors in limiting North American slave revolts. In Jamaica in 1774, there were 205,000 Blacks and only 18,400 whites, most of whom lived in Kingston or one of several other towns. Before the 1780s, the Spanish colony of Trinidad had only a few hundred whites. Even by 1800, its population consisted of over 10,000 slaves, 2,000 Europeans and 4,000 coloureds. The demographic situation for white colonists in Africa was similar. The white population in South Africa immediately after the Boer War was 1.1 million, compared with over 4 million non-Europeans; by the year 2000 South Africa's projected population will be 42 million, of whom only 7 million will be whites. The entire dynamics of organizing an oppressed national minority to fight for political power are fundamentally different from mobilizing a majority of society to overthrow a minority racist regime.

Another factor in the evolution of social movements was the relative cultural, political and economic cohesion of Black communities/nations prior to their contact with or domination by slavery and/or colonial capitalism. In Africa, traditional rivalries were exploited by European slave-traders and colonial officials to divide-and-conquer. The British pitted the Fante against the more powerful Ashanti kingdom in the Gold Coast; the Germans divided the Herero and Nama in Namibia, using Nama soldiers to destroy the Herero, and then turned their gatling-guns on the Nama. In South Africa, the Khama assisted imperialist Cecil Rhodes to crush their old foes, the Ndebele. In July 1876, an army of 2,500 Swazi and 200 Transvaal Boers attacked the Bapedi. This pattern of exploiting African subnationalist rivalries has continued into the twentieth century. The creation of Bantustans and the emphasis on 'tribal origins' among the African working class is an effort to divide the Black enemy and to reduce the possibility of an anti-apartheid united front. Quislings like Hastings Banda of Malawi and the states of Lesotho and Swaziland maintain close relations with the apartheid regime. In both the West Indies and South Africa, the coloured population was often used to divide non-Europeans into bickering factions. During Caribbean slavery, many coloureds even owned slaves: one Jamaican coloured planter owned a large sugar-plantation with 217 slaves. During the San Domingue revolution, most coloured leaders vehemently opposed African emancipation. Under the leadership of Alexander Pétion they established their own coloured armies and unsuccessfully resisted the forces of Toussaint L'Ouverture in a brutal war. Colour divisions were never as severe in the US among Blacks as elsewhere. But colour distinctions were often apparent within the social and cultural institutions established by Blacks for themselves. In almost every instance, religious, caste, and ethnic distinctions among Africans or Americans of African descent were manipulated to oppress the entire community.

More fundamental are certain strategic questions: Why do most social movements fail? Poulantzas defines this as a question of 'the *capacity* of a class to realize specific objective interests . . . [The] presence of a class as *social force* in fact presupposes a certain organizational *threshold,* in the broadest sense of the term.' Open, unqualified class struggle around cultural, economic or political grievances 'indicates that a social force has its "own" political *power* and that it is normally associated with its organization as a distinct and autonomous party.'[190] If we follow Gramsci's rather broad definition of a 'party', then given the historical constraints, the Negro Convention Movement of the 1840s-1850s in the US, the SNCC, the *Frente Negro Brasiliera,* the African National Congress, the UNIA and Padmore's International African Service Bureau are or were all Black or multiracial political 'parties'.[191] As agents of an oppressed class, social fraction or nation, they attempted to increase the power of their 'constituencies' within their respective social formations. But the precise *structure* of each 'party' may take a form which does not maximize the struggle for power to its full potential. Some Black organizations tend to evolve as tightly grouped conspiracies. For example, Cyril V. Briggs's African Blood Brotherhood (ABB) 'not only practised an initiation ritual for new members, but also divided its membership on the basis of "seven degrees, the first being given upon entry, the next five for educational progress, the last and Seventh for Superlative Service." ' The ABB at its peak in 1923 had seven thousand members in the West Indies and the US, and a number of radical Garveyites left the UNIA to join it. The ABB's Black nationalist and socialist orientation could have generated mass support, but its secretive, cadre structure and Masonic organizational style were not suited to reaching urban Black workers.[192] The NAACP, throughout its history, has been plagued by an opposite problem. Anyone can join the NAACP; it makes no coherent demands of its members beyond a vague commitment to racial equality. The constant fluidity of its membership base, and the lack of ideological training, has led to the concentration of decision-making power in the hands of a very small core of Black petty-bourgeois professionals.[193] This process was begun under the direction of Walter White, executive secretary of the Association from 1930 to 1955. When Du Bois returned to work for the NAACP in 1944 after a ten-year absence, he was shocked to find that 'almost every vestige of democratic method and control had disappeared from the organization . . . The branches of their officials [had] no scientifically planned programme except to raise money and defend cases of injustice or discrimination in courts . . .

All meetings and programmes are "fixed".[194] Du Bois complained directly to White that the NAACP was not 'a democratic organization', and that it should not regard 'the demand of regions and branches for increased autonomy as revolt against the New York headquarters'.[195] Not surprisingly, Du Bois was subsequently fired from the organization he himself had founded.

The example of the NAACP should also serve as a warning: sometimes social classes may develop organizations or 'parties' that *outlive* their historical utility. Inherent in all social structure is the problem of bureaucracy, which for the oppressed is generally a petty-bourgeois elite that assumes certain political functions of the movement as a whole. Radical Black intellectuals may in theory commit 'class suicide', but they are socialized within the cultural hegemony of capitalism, and therefore tend to replicate the political procedures of the corporation within the process of their own social movement. In practice, this means a refusal to learn from the masses, and a tendency to 'dictate' to them; a psychological tendency that assumes that poor people or workers require an 'intermediary' who can best represent their grievances before the capitalists and political authorities. Another related problem is one of 'intervention', the specific strategy of the insurgent organizations within a social formation. The procedure for making and implementing political decisions is vitally important. If an organization draws its basic information from limited sources, or fails to conduct extensive discussions within its membership prior to the implementation of some collective social protest action, or if it does not have a strategy 'appropriate' to the temporal convergence of material and social conditions, the social movement as a whole will suffer, and it may be crushed.

Any successful political, cultural or economic struggle for power must begin with a concrete analysis of one's social forces, their strengths, contradictions and previous history. A strategy for protest must relate in a very intimate way to the actual material conditions of the oppressed, beginning with grievances that occur on a daily basis. As James explains, 'Workers are at their very best in collective action in the circumstances of their daily activity or crises arising from it.' Frances Fox Piven and Richard Cloward concur. 'If there is a genius in organizing, it is the capacity to sense what it is possible for people to do under given conditions, and to then help them to do it . . . . Most organizing ventures ask that people do what they cannot do, and the result is failure. People cannot defy institutions to which they have no access, and to which they make no contribution.'[196] Thus sugar-cane workers in Samuel Sharpe's general strike smashed the sugarworks and burnt the cane; the very elements of production became the immediate targets of their anger. Factory workers protest by going out on strike because their common working experience is the factory setting; unemployed Black youth of Miami experience police brutality and the ghetto merchants' exorbitant prices, and during urban uprisings these become the targets of mass grievances. Organizers of social protest who advance strategies of resistance that have little practical relevancy to the daily life of Black workers are unable to sustain social movements. Basic institutional realities of the social formation — the mode of production, the civil society and hegemonic ideology, and the political composition and character of the state, and the place of Blacks within this complex social framework — will in the last analysis dictate what type of resistance movement will fail or succeed. The task of the agent of social change is to make practical and yet visionary demands upon the oppressed classes, demands that will disrupt the established order with the broadest possible participation of the oppressed classes or social fractions.

Finally, there is the basic issue of one's class opposition, or the 'strategy of the opponent'.[197] Piven and Cloward suggest that the ruling classes have 'three rather obvious options when an institutional disruption occurs. They may ignore it; they may employ punitive measures against the disruptors; or they may attempt to conciliate them.' Each option has its drawbacks, and none is mutually exclusive of the others. 'Politically unstable conditions make the use of force risky, since the reactions of other aroused groups cannot be safely predicted.'[198] Weaker colonial regimes in Africa and the newly developed plantation states in the Caribbean and Brazil in the seventeenth and eighteenth centuries could not afford to make any serious concessions to the Black peasants or slaves. The dreaded corvée system of forced labour in the Congo, and chattel slavery in the New World rested fundamentally on naked, unambiguous coercion. Conversely, in more advanced colonial-capitalist states, European colonists were able to employ a more judicious combination of threats and paternalistic concessions. For example, the French were confronted at the end of World War II with a broadly based independence movement in the Ivory Coast. The leader of the *Parti Democratique de la Côte d'Ivoire* was a wealthy Catholic plantation-owner and populist demagogue, Felix Houphouêt-Boigny. The nationalist forces had a strong trade union and left wing which was influenced to a degree by the French

Communist Party. The authorities began to break up trade-union meetings in 1948, arresting and imprisoning hundreds of African Marxists. Simultaneously, they made Houphouêt-Boigny understand that the French government was prepared to accept nominal African petty-bourgeois rule of the Ivory Coast, so long as the exploitation of the nation's wealth remained under external control. Houphouêt-Boigny agreed, banishing the remnants of the left from his party, preparing the way to establish a pro-capitalist neocolonial regime by 1960. The Trinidadian labour movement of the 1930s provides a different example. In 1933, Cipriani cancelled an oil workers' demonstration when the British promised to adopt a minimum wage level. The government passed the bill, but for four years the governor refused to implement the provisions. Cipriani had been convinced that legal pressure, not demonstrations, would eventually force the governor to comply. Militants led by 'Buzz' Butler vigorously dissented, and after being expelled from the Trinidad Labour Party, formed their own party. After the Butler-inspired oilfield riots and England's entrance into war, the Trinidad government promptly imprisoned Butler on the grounds that he was a threat to national security. By shrewdly pitting East Indians against Blacks, Hindus against Catholics and labour radicals against more 'responsible' labour leaders, the government retarded the development of any single working-class party right up to the late 1940s.

Every social movement always contains the seeds of a future political revolution, but generally does not give rise to an immediate restructuring of the state apparatus and the basic power relations within a given society. A revolutionary situation exists only when the old order, the ruling class, is unable to respond to mounting class contradictions and to social challenges that periodically occur. Theda Skocpol differentiates rebellious social movements from social revolutions by positing the existence of two factors in the latter: 'the coincidence of societal structural change with class upheaval; and the coincidence of political with social transformation. In contrast, rebellions, even when successful, may involve the revolt of subordinate classes — but they do not eventuate in structural change.'[199] Lenin makes a similar point, but in a slightly different manner: 'For a revolution to break out it is not enough for the "lower classes to refuse" to live in the old way; it is necessary also that the "upper classes should be unable" to live in the old way.'[200] Most Black social movements neither made the existing state apparatus a target for fundamental change, nor created the conditions necessary for the ruling class to be 'unable to live in the old way'. But social revolutions are impossible without pre-revolutionary modes of social class struggle which set the historical stage. As Rodney notes, 'So long as people can be mobilized to use weapons, and so long as society has the opportunity to define its own ideology, culture, etc., then the people of that society have some control over their own destinies.' The subsequent social revolution is the culmination of the myriad of previous protests, simply 'the most dramatic appearance of a conscious people or class on the stage of history'.[201]

2

Marches on Washington, 1941, 1963, 1983

The Social Movement for Racial Equality

> It is but human experience to find that the complete suppression of a race is impossible . . . This the American Black man knows: his fight here is a fight to the finish. Either he dies or wins . . . He will enter modern civilization here in America as a Black man on terms of perfect and unlimited equality with any white man, or he will enter not at all. Either extermination root and branch, or absolute equality. There can be no compromise. This is the last great battle of the West.
>
> W.E.B. Du Bois

I

To be Black in America is to live within a fundamental contradiction, which rests between the promise of democracy and the harsh reality of racial inequality. During slavery, the dominant expressions of Black class struggle included slave conspiracies and revolts, the creation of maroons and abolitionist agitation. The goal of this ceaseless struggle was the abolition of slavery; reduced still further to its most elementary dynamic, this meant the achievement of 'freedom'. Yet within this quest the Black abolitionists understood something more. The continued existence of racial inequality abrogated the central principles of democracy, revealing to Afro-Americans the abscess of hypocrisy upon which the state was grounded. 'What to the American slave is your Fourth of July?' asked Frederick Douglass before a group of liberal whites in 1852. 'I answer, a day that reveals to him more than all other days of the year, the gross injustice and cruelty of which he is the constant victim. To him your celebration is a sham; your boasted liberty an unholy licence; your national greatness, swelling vanity; your sounds of rejoicing are empty and heartless; your denunciation of tyrants, brass-fronted impudence; your shouts of liberty and equality, hollow mockery; your prayers and hymns, your sermons and thanksgivings, with all your religious parade and solemnity, are to him bombast, fraud, deception, impiety, and hypocrisy — a thin veil to cover up crimes . . . The great principles of political freedom and of natural justice, embodied in that Declaration of Independence', Douglass observed, are not 'extended to us'.[1] A century later, Paul Robeson issued a similar challenge to modern capitalist America. 'Who built this great land of ours? Who have been the guarantors of our historic democratic tradition of freedom and equality?' Robeson declared. 'Our nation, born in a bloody battle for freedom against imperialist tyranny, has itself become the first enemy of freedom and the chief tyrant . . . We demand the same approximation of the American democracy we have helped to build.'[2] The peculiar subordinate status of Afro-Americans permitted us to raise 'some of the insistent and radically effective questions', as Vincent Harding observes. 'We were the local bearers of the challenge to Western cultural, political and economic hegemony.'[3] But despite our petitions and demonstrations, that critique of the *status quo* was all too often ignored. In a racist social formation, as Cox reminds us, a Black person may eventually acquire wealth, education and social influence. 'Yet Negroes and whites will still be unequal, obviously in colour. For a person born white could never have the privilege of becoming black.'[4] Slavery had been destroyed, but American society, especially after 1890, descended into a depth of race hatred that was without precedent. Even white racists in South Africa stood in awe of the US's plunge into terror and bigotry, and patterned their own route to apartheid along the rigid lines of race suggested in the American South.[5]

The American social formation had always been racist — built around a rigid racial division of labour, with the political apparatuses, ideology and cultural institutions that rationalized and perpetuated white supremacy. But at the dawn of the twentieth century, 'Jim Crow' came to represent something qualitatively new in the socio-economic and political relations between whites and Blacks. The *basic* social approach to the Afro-American was now dictated by brute coercion. White racists at the time also recognized the radical change in the social position of Blacks. In his 1914 polemic, *Race Orthodoxy in the South*, Thomas P. Bailey asked: 'Is not the South being *encouraged* to treat the negroes *as aliens* by the growing discrimination against the negro in the North, a discrimination that is social as well as economic? Does not the South perceive that all the fire has gone out of the northern philanthropic fight for the rights of man? *The North has surrendered!*'[6] Politicians throughout the South agreed. Tom Watson, once a Populist Party candidate for the presidency and a noted advocate of racial harmony, now advocated 'the superiority of the Aryan' and attacked the 'hideous, ominous, national menace' of the Negro. South Carolina Senator Ben Tillman declared that Afro-Americans were 'akin to the monkey' and an 'ignorant and debased and debauched race'.[7] This racist position was manifested at virtually every institutional level of society, North and South. In the southern criminal 'justice' system, as sociologists Allison Davis, Mary R. Gardner and Burleigh B. Gardner observed, 'the Negro is, from the very beginning, in a position subordinate to both the police and the court. His testimony will not be accepted if contradictory to that of the police. His witnesses carry little weight with the court, and he can wield no political influence.'[8] In the decisions involving civil rights made by the US Supreme Court between 1868 and 1936, Blacks 'won only two of fourteen cases in which they claimed the right to use the same facilities as whites in common carriers, public places, and schools or housing.' Sociologist Monroe Berger also noted that during the same period, Blacks lost six out of sixteen cases 'in which they sought federal protection of their right to vote, or of other rights which they claimed were attributes of federal citizenship'.[9] State and local laws were modified to perpetuate white supremacy. As historian C. Vann Woodward comments, 'between 1900 and 1911 ten southern states elaborated their laws requiring separation of races in transportation facilities, all of them including laws for street railways, and some for ferries and steamboats.' By 1908, Atlanta had racially segregated elevators.[10] Jim Crow taxicabs were required state-wide in Mississippi in 1922; in Jacksonville, Florida in 1929; and in Birmingham, Alabama in 1930. Atlanta 'prohibited amateur baseball clubs of different races from playing within two blocks of each other' in 1932. A Birmingham ordinance of 1930 even made it illegal for Blacks and whites 'to play together or in company with each other' at checkers or dominoes.[11]

Jim Crow was rather different from classical caste systems in that it was dynamic and aggressive. No matter how miserable or oppressed the Afro-American was, the system would soon require a new low in racial subordination. As John Hope Franklin observes, 'in 1900 for every $2 spent for the education of Negroes in the South, $3 was spent on whites; but in 1930 $7 was spent for whites to every $2 spent for Negroes.' By 1935-36, 'expenditures per Negro pupil averaged $13.09, slightly more than one sixth as much as for all schools of the United States.'[12] The Black prison population continued to increase alarmingly: Black incarceration rates mounted from 256 per 100,000 in 1904 to 1,079 per 100,000 in 1910.[13] But the central social element of Jim Crow was the omni-presence of 'lynching', which meant any form of random racial violence. Lynchings 'may appear to have a high degree of spon-taneity', writes Cox, but they are a logical 'overt threat' which 'functions to maintain white dominance. They provide, in fine, the socio-psychological matrix of the power relationship between the races.' Lynching had nothing to do with punishing criminals. 'It is an attack principally against all Negroes in some community rather than against some individual Negro. Ordinarily, therefore, when a lynching is indicated, the destruction of almost any Negro will serve the purpose as well as that of some particular one.' The primary political utility of lynching was self-evident: to destroy any pos-sibility of the development of a coherent Black social movement which sought to undermine Jim Crow. As Cox observes, 'during a lynching all Negroes are driven under cover. They are terrified and intimidated . . . few will dare even to disagree with white persons on any account whatsoever. The man who does so is not considered a hero by the majority of Negroes; rather he earns their censure.'[14] Throughout the 1920s, southern lynchings horrified the world. Writing in *La Correspondance Internationale* in 1924, a young Viet-namese Marxist — who would later assume the name Ho Chi Minh — declared that 'the Black race is the most oppressed and most exploited of the human family . . . After sixty-five years of so-called emancipation, American Negroes still endure atrocious moral and material sufferings, of which the most cruel and horrible is the custom of lynching.'[15]

But there was a second function of the racist terror inherent in Jim Crow. As long as white workers perceived Blacks as their permanent enemies, no genuine working-class social movements that transcended racial barriers could take hold. The Populist Party and the widespread agrarian movements of the late nineteenth century had illustrated to the ruling classes the vast political poten-tial of biracial cooperation among workers and poor farmers. The development of capitalist production in the South depended largely upon the propagation of white supremacist ideology, at every level of society. Cox observes:

> The Southern agricultural capitalists initiated a counter-revolution and re-established a high degree of control over their labour supply. To do this they had to marshal every force, including the emotional power of

the masses of poor whites, in a fanatical campaign of race hatred, with sexual passion as the emotional core . . . All sympathetic contact between the races was scrupulously ruled out by a studied system of segregation . . . The guardians of the racial system in the South control or spend millions of dollars to maintain segregation devices — the most powerful illusory contrivance for keeping poor whites and Negroes antagonized — and to spread anti-colour propaganda all over the nation and the world. For this expenditure they expect a return more or less calculable in dollars and cents. Today it is of vital consequence that Black labour and white labour in the South be kept glaring at each other, for if they were permitted to come together in force and to identify their interests as workers, the difficulty of exploiting them would be increased beyond calculation. Indeed, the persistence of the whole system of worker exploitation in the United States depends pivotally upon the maintenance of an active race hatred between white and Black workers in the South.[16]

The problem of developing a democratic social movement against Jim Crow, therefore, was part of a broader class question. Put another way, the exploitation of labour by capital was facilitated in the context of American cultural and social relations by Jim Crow. The fight for racial equality was in essence in the objective, material interests of all workers, Black, Latino and white. Trade-union movements that accepted the legitimacy of racial segregation would ultimately be unsuccessful, or would achieve only marginal gains from capital.

In the last half-century, the social movement to abolish racism has experienced several profound shifts, each of which may be categorized as marking a specific phase of related struggles: the period of Jim Crow's declining hegemony, 1930-1955, in which the collapse of southern agriculture and the rise of the first generation of Black industrial workers occurred; the period of legal segregation's collapse, 1955-1970, a collapse that was forced by the successful mobilization of millions of Blacks and their white liberal allies both inside the bourgeois democratic political apparatus and, more decisively, outside it; and the period of political reaction and transition, from 1970 to the present, in which limited socio-economic and electoral political gains by segments of the Black social fraction have been compromised by a national trend towards political conservatism and the destruction of civil rights reforms. The particular protest tactics of Black leaders varied from period to period, depending in part upon the degree of cohesion and organizational development of the democratic forces for racial reform, the level of militancy found among Black working-class and poor people, and the receptivity to certain types of political reform expressed by white politicians and capital at both national and regional levels. Yet there is also a basic continuity within the Black social movement for equality. In each historical period, political events outside the United States have shaped the strategies of both Black reformers and the US state in the context of desegregation struggles. In every period, the Black social movement has been characterized by intra-group conflict, partially rooted in personality and parochial organizational jealousies, but more basically provoked by radically different political definitions as to what constitutes 'freedom' and 'equality' for the Black social fraction, and as to the relationship between the quest for freedom and the structures of American monopoly capitalism and bourgeois democracy. Finally, each phase of struggle has witnessed the call for a national demonstration in Washington DC, which has included various programmatic demands in the larger democratic struggle to realize Black equality.

In the light of Black social history, the 1983 March on Washington represented both the past and the future promise of militant democratic reform. The recent mobilization's slogan, 'Jobs, Peace and Freedom', meant little in isolation from an analysis of both the 1963 march and the abortive March on Washington in 1941, led by A. Philip Randolph. The attempt here is to place the recent protest within the context of the Black social movements of the past, identifying the unique strengths and weaknesses of these prior mobilizations, and addressing the parallels and discontinuities between the former and the more recent efforts. All of the marches, as specific tactics of American social protest, were limited, as we shall observe, by the theoretical and programmatic outlook of their originators, as well as by the social class forces in which they identified the promise of fundamental social reform and Black equality.

II

The context of the democratic movement against US racial segregation in the 1930s and 1940s was largely determined by four factors: the election of Franklin D. Roosevelt as president in 1932, and the subsequent shift in the Afro-Americans' electoral allegiance from the Republican to the Democratic party; the unprecedented crisis in the domestic and world capitalist economies, the Great Depression;

the rise of fascism and the outbreak of the Second World war; and domestically, the rise of militant trade unionism and the emergence of the CIO. By previous standards, Roosevelt was the most liberal chief executive in American history in regard to the civil rights of national minorities. The number of Black Federal employees was increased from fifty thousand in 1933 to two hundred thousand by 1946. Roosevelt had selected a small group of prominent middle-class Blacks, including lawyers Robert C. Weaver and William H. Hastie, journalist Robert L. Vann and educator Mary McLeod Bethune, to hold administrative posts. However, government agencies in the 'New Deal' administration of Roosevelt were organized on strictly segregated lines. Youth who worked in the Civilian Conservation Corps camps were segregated by race; provisions in the Public Works Administration were often denied to Black rural farmers through fraud and outright corruption. Key elements of New Deal reform legislation simply extended the colour line. One blatant example was the passage of the National Labour Relations Act in 1935, which gave American workers the right to vote for unions and banned gross anti-union activities by capital. Blacks demanded that a clause outlawing racial discrimination by unions should be added to the act. But white AFL leaders 'let it be known that, if the antidiscrimination clause were incorporated into the proposed bill, the federation would prefer to see the entire measure defeated.'[17] Roosevelt sided with white labour, and the antidiscrimination clause was defeated. In the South, 'New Deal agricultural policies paid plantation-owners general subsidies to take land out of production', thereby forcing hundreds of thousands of poor Black tenant farmers off white-owned property. Consistently, as Piven and Cloward observe, 'Roosevelt chose to avoid head-on clashes with the South over the race issue (by refusing support to anti-lynching legislation, for example).' The New Deal 'submerged the civil rights issue in order to maintain greater party unity' in the South, and in doing so, perpetuated the authoritarian structures of Jim Crow.[18]

To complicate matters there was a growing collaboration between capital, white political leaders and the leadership of the fragile Black middle class — Black newspaper editors, clergy, entrepreneurs, civil leaders — which often presented a serious obstacle to the building of desegregation movements. During the late 1920s and 1930s, a number of Black newspapers parroted the view that Blacks had to 'align themselves with the wealthier classes in America'. When the Brotherhood of Sleeping-Car Porters attempted to mobilize Black workers, most Black publishers rallied behind the interest of capital. The St Louis *Argus* ran a series of editorials that denounced the Brotherhood and Randolph as 'reds'. Much of the Black press, including the *Chicago Defender* and the Pittsburgh *Courier*, was subsidized by the Pullman Company 'to launch an all-out offensive against the union'.[19] Several years later, during the initial formation of the CIO, many influential Blacks charged that the organization was being financed by 'Moscow Gold', and declared that Afro-Americans should be at best neutral towards unionization. 'The leaders of many local NAACP branches had formed close alliances with employers' during the Depression and 'were opposed to all unions'. National Urban League leader Lester Granger warned Blacks against 'jubilantly rushing towards what they assume to be a new day for labour and a new organization to take the place of the AF of L'. [20] In reaction to the accom- modationism of the traditional Black leadership, Black workers and radical intellectuals organized by Randolph founded the National Negro Congress (NNC). At its initial session on 14 February 1936, the NNC had attracted the support of 585 Black and integrated groups with a combined Black membership of 1.2 million. The focus of the organization, which operated essentially as both a Black united front and a more progressive alternative to the NAACP, was, in Randolph's words, to 'seek to broaden and intensify the move- ment to draw Negro workers into labour organizations and break down the colour bar in the trade unions that now have it.' The unity between such diverse factions as Black liberal Republicans and Black Marxist-Leninists, however, was all too brief. The NNC initiated local and national campaigns which smashed Jim Crow restrictions within the House of Labour, and NNC leader John P. Davis was a critical figure in organizing Black workers behind the United Auto Workers during its bloody strike against Ford Motor Company in 1941. But Randolph, Black intellectual Ralph Bunche and other more moderate Blacks resigned from the NNC as the Communist Party's influence inside the front became dominant. Thus on the eve of World War II, no single progressive formation (if one excludes the NAACP) embraced a broad spectrum of Afro- American working-class and middle-class opinion.[21]

By 1940, the situation of Black labour was still critical. Over a quarter of the Black force was jobless, despite the plethora of public programmes. Increasingly, Blacks' grievances focused on defence- related industries. Already suffering twice the unemployment rate experienced by whites, Black workers found it nearly impossible to obtain jobs in defence plants. From January to March 1941, tor example, 1,066 employees were hired in electrical equipment firms that held federal government contracts. Of these new workers, only five were Black. In the same period, aircraft industries with war department contracts hired 8,769 workers, and all but thirteen were white. During the presidential election of 1940, a number of civil rights and liberal organizations — the NAACP, the Allied Committees on National Defence, and the Committee for Participation of Negroes in the National Defence — began to criticize the Roosevelt Administration's failure to pressure these corporations to hire Blacks. In September 1940, a group of middle-class Black leaders met with Roosevelt personally in an effort to obtain concessions, but came away empty-handed. Even NAACP leader Walter White, no paragon of Black militancy, was deeply angered by an unproductive meeting with Roosevelt in November 1940. In White's words, 'Bitterness [was growing] at an alarming rate throughout the country.'[22]

This is hardly to suggest that unemployed Black workers remained docile throughout this period. Black workers were involved in the mid to late 1930s in a series of bloody union-organizing efforts, especially in heavy industry. Throughout the Depression, common poverty and hunger brought a new militancy to Black and white unemployed workers alike. Across the country, as Piven and Cloward note, thousands of relief and unemployment marches and public demonstrations erupted spontaneously. When unemployed workers were killed in a job riot by police in Dearborn, Michigan in March 1932, 'sixty thousand Detroit workers marched behind the coffins to the tune of the Internationale' two days after the shootings. Also that year, when Chicago's 'relief funds were cut 50 per cent by a financially strangled city administration, some twenty-five thousand of the unemployed marched . . . in a cold, driving rain. The authorities quickly managed to borrow funds from the Reconstruction Finance Corporation, and the cut was rescinded.' In St Louis, Missouri, three thousand jobless women and men mobbed City Hall, and forced politicians to ratify local relief legislation. In August 1933, seven thousand unemployed workers marched on the state capital in Colombus, Ohio. 'In Colorado, when the federal relief funds were discontinued in the winter of 1934 . . . mobs of the unemployed rioted in relief centres, looted food stores, and stormed the state legislature, driving the frightened senators from the chamber. Two weeks later, the General Assembly sent a relief bill to the governor, and federal funding was resumed.' In late 1935, when Kansas City, Kansas reduced relief funds, 'Two thousand of the unemployed assembled in front of the court-house where they remained and prayed and sang hymns until a new relief appropriation was voted.'[23] Most of these demonstrations had few visible 'leaders', lacked prior co-ordination, and tended to focus their energies on symbols of bourgeois democratic authority, such as a city hall or state assembly building. In a number of instances, these mass mobilizations secured some basic material concessions, yet they did not overturn the hegemony of capital. These unemployed workers' demonstrations were in some respects similar to those of pre-revolutionary Russia. As Lenin observed, spontaneous revolts are 'simply the resistance of the oppressed'. Well-coordinated trade-union demonstrations and strikes 'represent the class struggle in embryo, but only in embryo.' The former type of militant workers' revolts can paralyse the capitalist state, but only briefly, because spontaneous demonstrations, 'the movement along the line of least resistance', do not usually produce an explicitly anticapitalist consciousness among the participants. All social movements that culminate in decisive class struggles must emphasize 'the conscious element', as Lenin suggested.[24] Demonstrations and spontaneous acts of class protest without political education and conscious direction that develop into newer, more advanced workers' political formations can achieve reforms, but not systemic change.

As a socialist and trade-union leader, Randolph was fully aware of the character and form of these recent spontaneous workers' and trade unions' mobilizations. With the decline of the NNC and the failure of the NAACP to initiate any mass mobilizations similar to those of labour, Randolph and the leaders of Brotherhood proposed their own solution to the problem of racial hiring policies in defence plants: a national march on Washington DC, which would be staged on 1 July 1941. Randolph's challenge to the Roosevelt Administration departed sharply from the legalistic and non-confrontational tactics of White's NAACP. In the Black press, he justified the necessity for Black workers to surround the White House. 'Only power can effect the enforcement and adoption of a given policy', he declared. 'Power is the active principle of only the organized masses, the masses united for a definite purpose. We loyal Negro-American citizens demand the right to work and fight for our country.' Randolph issued the march's ambitious demands: an executive order forbidding government contracts to be awarded to any firm that practised racial discrimination in hiring; an executive order abolishing segregation in the armed forces; an executive order abolishing racial discrimination in government defence training courses; an executive order requiring the US Employment Service to supply workers without regard to race; an executive order abolishing Jim Crow in every department of the Federal government; and a formal request from Roosevelt to the Congress to pass legislation forbidding any benefits of the National Labour Relations Act to be given to unions denying membership to Blacks. The demands represented something qualitatively new in Black desegregationist strategy: the active pursuit of executive intervention to overturn the major pillars of Jim Crow.[25] Individually, none of the demands was revolutionary; taken together, they comprised a set of militant reforms that could simultaneously capture the political imagination and popular support of the Black working class, and force the Roosevelt Administration to choose between the growing northern Black electorate and the solidly racist South. Even if every demand were granted, Jim Crow would still exist, but the system's foundations within the capitalist state would be seriously weakened, perhaps beyond the point of repair.

Historians August Meier and Elliott Rudwick correctly noted that Randolph's 'March on Washington Movement clearly foreshadowed the goals, tactics and strategy of the mid-twentieth-century civil rights movement . . . Unlike the older Negro movements, the [march] had captured the imagination of the masses.'[26] From the beginning, Randolph decided that the mobilization should include only Blacks. Some Black leftists, civil rights leaders and white liberals criticized Randolph in this regard, reminding him of his bitter opposition to the Black nationalist efforts of Marcus Garvey two decades before. How could the Black trade unionist fight for integration while mobilizing Blacks separately? His critics forgot, or perhaps did not know, that Randolph had developed a close alliance with Garvey's UNIA from 1916 to 1919, in opposition to Du Bois and the NAACP. His break with Garvey's leadership did not represent a strategic repudiation of all-Black organizations. 'We believe that Negroes need an all-Negro movement, just as the Jews had a Zionist movement', Randolph replied. 'We believe that Negroes should supply the money and pay the price, make the sacrifices, to break down the barriers to a realization of full citizenship rights of America.'[27] White progressives could offer material and political support, he suggested, but they could not participate in the march itself. Randolph's uncompromising response evoked even greater support among thousands of Black trade unionists and the unemployed, many of whom had been members of the UNIA or sympathetic to militant Black nationalism. By April 1941, the Negro March on Washington Movement had fifty thousand members who had each paid one dollar or more toward the campaign. All-Black rallies and demonstrations in churches, schools and union halls occurred across the country. At the core of the social movement stood the members of the Brotherhood. In every American city with a substantial population, they lobbied extensively in churches, tenements and barber shops. They succeeded in forcing Black newspaper publishers and most Black conservatives to accept their leadership and publicly to endorse the march. The union's newspaper, *The Black Worker*, was the primary vehicle of propaganda used in the campaign. One broadside, published in May 1941, expressed the workers' militancy:

> We call upon you to fight for jobs in National Defence. We call upon you to struggle for the integration of Negroes in the armed forces . . . of the Nation. We call upon you to demonstrate for the abolition of Jim-Crowism in all Government departments and defence employment . . . While billions of the taxpayers' money are being spent for war weapons, Negro workers are being turned away from the gates of factories, mines and mills — being flatly told, "NOTHING DOING . . ." The Federal Government cannot with clear conscience call upon private industry and labour unions to abolish discrimination based upon race and colour so long as it practises discrimination itself against Negro Americans.[28]

By late spring, the Roosevelt Administration had clearly begun to panic. The spectre of an estimated fifty thousand Black workers surrounding the White House grounds at a time when Nazi Germany was winning its war against Britain caused considerable anxiety. Eleanor Roosevelt, the President's principal instrument of liaison with civil rights leaders, visited Randolph in New York City and urged him to call off the demonstration. He bluntly refused. Subsequently, on 18 June, Roosevelt summoned Randolph to the White House. With both the Secretary of War and the Secretary of the Navy, Roosevelt demanded that the campaign be discontinued. At this moment, Randolph made a tactical blunder. He suggested that he would halt the march if Roosevelt agreed to only one demand: an executive order to end racial discrimination in federally funded war production factories. Roosevelt refused. Randolph then announced that the march would bring a hundred thousand Afro-Americans to Washington, making the demonstration the largest in US history at that time. With less than a week to go before the march, a mood of near-terror paralysed white neighbourhoods in the District of Columbia. Civic leaders in this racially segregated city warned of bloody racial violence in the streets. Finally, on 24 June, a compromise was reached. For Randolph's cancelling the march, the President agreed to sign Executive Order 8802 which would outlaw racist hiring policies inside war production plants. The next day, Roosevelt announced that it would be 'the duty of employers and of labour organizations . . . to provide for the full and equitable participation of all workers in defence industries, without discrimination because of race, creed, colour or national origin . . . All contracting agencies of the Government of the United States shall include in all defence contracts hereafter negotiated by them a provision obligating the contractor not to discriminate against any worker . . .'[29]

Historians continue to debate whether the Negro March on Washington should have been held. Many Blacks once again bitterly accused Randolph of political opportunism, citing the unfulfilled list of demands that Roosevelt had refused to grant.[30] Jim Crow would have received a devastating blow had the original set of militant reforms been enacted. Over three million Black men would ultimately register for the armed services, and half a million Blacks stationed in the Pacific, Africa and Europe would fight World War II in racially segregated units. The nation's capital would remain Jim-Crowed for over another decade. Always an astute politician, Roosevelt turned the compromise into a publicity *coup*. Civil rights historian Herbert Garfinkel observed that the white 'press hailed the Executive Order as further demonstration of America's love of democracy, but continued to ignore the role of the "march" in applying pressure on the administration.'[31] The President thus presented himself before the Black public as its benevolent saviour, while at the same time privately fighting behind closed doors to keep angry Black workers off the capital's streets. Southern segregationists comprehended that the Executive Order was a necessary accommodation to ensure Blacks' loyalty in the war that loomed ahead; and on balance, the compromise left the larger national commitment to white supremacy unchallenged. Finally, Roosevelt's continued staunch defence of American apartheid perpetuated a political culture of race hatred which would have devastating consequences during the war against fascism. For example, between March and June 1943, a series of 'hate strikes' against the upgrading of Blacks in industries contributed to a total one hundred thousand man-days lost. Philadelphia street-car workers refused to work with Blacks in 1944, and Roosevelt was forced to order five thousand federal troops into the city to restore order.

Conversely, the Negro March on Washington Movement of 1941 set into motion a variety of protest currents which would be manifested fifteen years later in the 'Second Reconstruction'. The movement's activities, which included 'organizing local coalitions, soliciting thousands of endorsers, adopting resolutions, distributing hundreds of thousands of leaflets [and] releasing news stories to the Black press, forced the issue of job discrimination to the centre of the nation's life.'[32] In July 1941, Roosevelt was forced to set up the Fair Employment Practices Committee (FEPC), which included Brotherhood leader Milton Webster, NAACP activist Earl B. Dickerson and Black newspaper publisher Mark Ethridge. Despite inadequate funding, the FEPC pressured war industries to move towards at least token compliance with the law.[33] The proportion of Blacks employed in war-related industries increased from 2.5 to 3 per cent in March 1942 to above 8 per cent by November 1944. The new spirit of Black militancy during these years directly benefited the NAACP; from 50,600 members and 355 branches in 1940, the NAACP grew to almost 450,000 members and 1,073 branches in six years. The March on Washington organization continued to exist after 1941, challenging the racist policies of Roosevelt and the Democratic Party. New civil rights agencies, such as the Congress of Racial Equality (CORE) were formed in the wake of the mobilization.

Randolph's abortive march was only one factor in the desegregation efforts of the early 1940s. Without question, however, the campaign for racial justice and the public policy trend against Jim Crow would not have assumed such a decisive character had the mobilization not taken place. Before 1940, few outside the Black community criticized the legitimacy of Jim Crow; by 1945, it was obvious to many white Americans that the system of racial segregation would have to be radically modified, if not entirely destroyed.[34]

III

The social and political situation that created the second March on Washington in August 1963 differed sharply from the one that had produced the earlier mobilization. At least four critical factors were at work. The first factor was the rise of new civil rights agencies, more in the radical reformist tradition of the National Negro

Congress than in that of the NAACP. The Montgomery County Bus Boycott of 1955-56 represented the successful adaptation of Gandhian non-violence to suit the Black desegregation movement.[35] The boycott campaign created a new charismatic leader, the Reverend Martin Luther King Jr, and a year later generated the Southern Christian Leadership Conference (SCLC), an alliance of activist Black clergy. The SNCC emerged in the spring of 1960, as thousands of Black and white youth demonstrated across the South. And after a decade of organizational malaise, the CORE and its new leader James Farmer captured national headlines by starting the Freedom Rides, a series of sojourns by Black and white groups challenging illegal segregationist restrictions on public buses. With the emergence of these groups, the NAACP and White's successor, Roy Wilkins, suffered a loss of prestige and support within the national Black community. An uneasy Black United Front existed, with the NAACP and Urban League on the right wing, the SCLC in the ideological centre, and the CORE and the SNCC on the left. Wilkins complained frequently in public that these new desegregation groups generate 'the noise and get the publicity while the NAACP furnishes the manpower and pays the bills.'[36] Conversely, for many SNCC leaders, Wilkins and Urban League Director Whitney Young were only a little more advanced than proverbial 'Uncle Toms'. What kept this front together for a half dozen critical years was its common dedication to the eradication of Jim Crow, root and branch. All tactics of protest, from mass arrests to legal manoeuvres before the US Supreme Court were part of the overall strategy to destroy legal segregation.

A second factor was the changing international climate brought about after the end of World War II. The intense geopolitical opposition of the US to the Soviet Union and the determination of world capital to halt the spread of Marxism produced the Cold War. Republican and Democratic presidents alike after 1945 attempted to contain the military and political advances of Communism, even to the point of overthrowing legitimate governments (for example, in Iran and Guatemala, under Eisenhower), and assassinating political opponents. The non-white non-aligned states in Africa and Asia could scarcely view America as a democracy, however, when it doggedly clung to a system of race relations only a notch superior to South African apartheid. In United Nations negotiations and in Third World diplomacy, Jim Crow had become a major liability to the American pursuit of Cold War objectives. Thirdly, the period of domestic capitalist expansion after the war consolidated and extended national corporations across the country. Wall Street and larger corporations viewed segregated facilities as an unnecessary drain on the overall resources of both fixed and variable capital. Racial confrontations in the streets and public demonstrations created a poor investment climate, and lowered sales and profits. While southern-based capital maintained Jim Crow, large capital placed increasing pressure on its agents in the public sector to provide a peaceful solution to the crisis — while simultaneously keeping institutional racism. Finally, the election of John F. Kennedy to the presidency in 1960 accelerated the destruction of Roosevelt's New Deal coalition, which had embraced both Blacks and the racist South. Personally, the northern liberal had little sympathy with the plight of the Blacks under the segregationist regime. As Clay Carson notes, 'Soon after taking office, Kennedy had decided against asking for new civil rights legislation or using the power of the federal government to achieve desegregation of public facilities. Rather, he intended to concentrate on the investigation of white interference with Black voting rights, believing that such a course would not alienate white southerners . . .'[37] The president elevated white supremacists to federal judgeships; used the Federal Bureau of Investigation to wire-tap civil rights leaders; and did little to protect the lives of desegregationist demonstrators. But after the Birmingham, Alabama desegregation campaign of April-May 1963, led by King and the SCLC, the administration increasingly used its influence to support the more moderate demands of the civil rights front, and cut most of its public ties with the segregationists. Pragmatically, Kennedy had concluded that the national Democratic Party needed the support of the Black electorate and white northern liberals more than it did the support of southern 'Dixiecrats'.

All these factors converged during the year 1963, the climax of the Second Reconstruction. Besides Birmingham, hundreds of cities and small towns were the sites of dramatic civil rights confrontations that year. On 31 May over five hundred demonstrators were arrested in Jackson, Mississippi. Marches of Black schoolchildren, a few as young as six years old, resulted in another six hundred arrests in that city several weeks later. Thomas Gentile observes that 'the week commencing June 7 1963 saw some of the most widespread demonstrations that the country had ever experienced.'[38] One thousand Blacks in Greensboro, North Carolina demonstrated for an end to Jim Crow public facilities; other marches and pickets that week occurred in Sarasota, Florida, Tallahassee, Florida, Nashville, Atlanta, St Louis, Charlestown, South Carolina, Savannah, Georgia, Gadsden, Alabama, Ocean City, Maryland and Danville, Virginia. These mass democratic movements sparked simultaneous protests outside the South. On 7 June, the CORE 'picketed the Beverly Hilton over hiring bias'; on 10 June, seven hundred Black prisoners 'at the Rahway, New Jersey prison farm reported on sick call in what officials declared was a demonstration stemming from racial tensions'; in Colombus, Ohio and Providence, Rhode Island, hundreds of Blacks and progressive whites demonstrated at their state legislatures for the passage of 'fair housing' bills; in New York City 'at a construction site of a Harlem hospital, police battled demonstrators protesting alleged job discrimination.'[39] The Southern Regional Council of Atlanta later estimated that 'during 1963, 930 public protest demonstrations took place in at least 115 cities in 11 southern states. Over twenty thousand persons were arrested during these protests, compared with about 3600 arrests in the period of non-violent protests prior to the fall of 1961. In 1963, ten persons died in circumstances directly related to racial protests, and at least thirty-five bombings occurred.'[40] This unprecedented civil unrest forced President Kennedy to call for the passage of a comprehensive civil rights act. Kennedy admitted privately to civil rights leaders that 'the demonstrations in the streets had brought results, they had made the executive branch act faster and were now forcing Congress to entertain legislation which a few weeks before would have had no chance.'[41]

Months before Kennedy announced his decision to obtain a new civil rights act, however, Randolph proposed organizing a second March on Washington DC, both as a means of dramatizing the campaign for desegregation and as a method by which to place 'additional pressure on the Kennedy administration to support equal employment legislation'.[42] In December 1962, Randolph asked Bayard Rustin to draft a memo 'outlining the possibilities and tentative plans for such a march'.[43] The selection of Rustin was not accidental. A pacifist and long-time social democrat, the 52-year-old organizer had served over two years in prison as a draft protester during World War II. He had volunteered to help Randolph in the 1941 march, and had been bitterly disappointed when that demonstration was cancelled. In 1947 he had organized the CORE's first Freedom Rides, then called the Journeys of Reconciliation. In 1955-56 Rustin assisted King during the Montgomery Bus Boycott, and in 1960 he 'led a march across the Sahara Desert in an attempt to stop the first French nuclear test explosion.'[44] Although a close disciple of Randolph, Rustin had acquired the reputation of being a radical and rather dangerous socialist. In October 1960, Rustin's invitation to attend an SNCC conference in Atlanta 'was withdrawn when a union sponsoring the conference objected to [his] radical reputation.'[45] Rustin in turn recruited two other aides to help draft the march memo — Tom Kahn, the leader of the League for Industrial Democracy, and Norman Hill, a CORE activist. By late February 1963, the draft was given to Randolph, and the labour leader announced the plans publicly on 7 March. The response within the civil rights front was at best mixed. The CORE's national steering committee 'eagerly agreed to act as a co-sponsor.'[46] SNCC leaders, particularly chairman John Lewis, and theoretician James Forman, viewed the march as an opportunity to stage demonstrations at the US Justice Department against its abysmal failure to protect civil rights workers' lives. SCLC leaders Clarence Jones and Reverend George Lawrence projected 'massive, militant, monumental sit-ins on Congress . . . We will tie up public transportation by laying our bodies prostrate on runways of airports, across railroad tracks, and in bus depots.' Such rhetoric threw a chill into the NAACP and Urban League bureaucrats. After learning that Kennedy objected to the march, Wilkins contemptuously dismissed the mobilization before reporters, stating, 'That little baby does not belong to me.'[47] By late June, however, the call for a second march had acquired a life of its own, and it was too late for Randolph, Wilkins or anyone else to cancel it.

It was at this point that both the march and the entire civil rights movement took a decisive shift to the right. As SCLC leader Walter Fauntroy, the CORE's Julius Hobson and NAACP organizer Edward Hailes drafted the actual logistics of the demonstration, a meeting of all civil rights power-brokers was called on 25 June. Wilkins laid his reservations before King, Farmer, Young, Randolph and John Lewis. First, no disruptive modes of protest would be acceptable to the NAACP. No civil disobedience could occur, and the Kennedy administration had to be consulted at every stage. Finally, Wilkins demanded that Rustin, who was the chairman of the march, be removed. Rustin was simply 'too controversial, too radical', a proven 'draft dodger' and a suspected 'homosexual'.[48] Thus Randolph was given the title of chairman, while Rustin was expected to do the actual work as his nominal deputy; on every major point, Wilkins had his way. Suddenly, large amounts of money were made available to the march and related desegregation activities. Steven Currier of the Taconic Foundation raised over $800,000, giving the bulk of the money to more conservative Black groups. The SNCC, for instance, received a paltry $15,000 of the amount. The Kennedy Administration stepped in, encouraging 'officals and liberal supporters to work with the planners of the march'. The President came to understand that a symbolic protest would act as a necessary safety-valve for Black discontent. As Randolph himself told Kennedy, Blacks were now in the streets and it was 'very likely impossible to get them off. If they are bound to be in the streets in any case, is it not better that they be led by organizations dedicated to civil rights and disciplined by struggle rather than to leave them to other leaders who care neither about civil rights nor about non-violence?'[49] The movement's radicals watched with dismay and disgust as their visions of a militant demonstration were shattered. SNCC activist Stokely Carmichael rejected invitations by Rustin and Kahn to work on the march, declaring that the 'struggle for voting rights in Mississippi was more important than a showy display in Washington.'[50] The CORE's enthusiasm quickly disappeared, and Farmer did not even attend the march: he was in gaol in Louisiana. Even King was affected by the rightward shift. The SCLC leader fired a close aide, Jack O'Dell, when the FBI charged that he was a former Communist. Every effort was made to distance the march from any leftist tinge. When the Chinese Communist government cabled their endorsement, Wilkins bluntly attacked that nation's criticism of the Kennedy Administration within their original statement. With an uncharacteristic flourish, Wilkins added, 'We await the opportunity to send our felicitations to the Chinese citizens gathered in a huge demonstration in your nation's capital to protest living conditions under your government, and welcomed there by your heads of state.'[51]

It would be incorrect to assume that the moderation of the march in any way silenced its critics. The media attacked the proposed march throughout the summer. The Washington *Star* described the plans as 'misguided pressure . . . capped by climatic idiocy'. The New York *Herald Tribune* ran a lengthy editorial declaring 'The March Should Be Stopped.' The owner of the Washington *Post* and *Newsweek* magazine, Agnes Meyer, warned that there would be 'catastrophic outbreaks of violence, bloodshed, and property damage'.[52] In the Senate, Democrat segregationist Strom Thurmond made Rustin a target for special abuse, and declared that the Kennedy Administration was trying 'to whitewash the question of communist influence or involvement in these Negro demonstrations'. Senator John Stennis of Mississippi gleefully predicted that the march 'was going to help defeat' the civil rights bill. And Georgia Senator Richard Russell advanced the view that most Negroes did not desire equal public accommodations with whites: 'There are Negro restaurants in every town in the South . . . and it is not at all unusual to send down to get some of their barbecue and some of their other specialities. They are very fine cooks.'[53] The bulk of the white labour leadership shared Russell's views. AFL-CIO head George Meany bitterly opposed the march from the first moment he heard of it. Despite the support of liberal union-leaders Walter Reuther and James Carey, the AFL-CIO Executive Council, under Meany's prodding, refused to endorse the march. Meany's threats had little effect on the more liberal unions, as financial and membership support for the mobilization came from the United Auto Workers, the Hotel and Restaurant Employees and Bartenders International, the Electrical Workers, the American Federation of State, County and Municipal Employees (AFSCME), the Brotherhood of Sleeping-Car Porters and the International Ladies' Garment Workers' Union (ILGWU). A Black trade unionist, Cleveland Robinson of District 65, served as treasurer for the march, and for a time Robinson's union also paid Rustin's salary. Despite the criticisms, the march continued to gather momentum in the summer.

The results of the months of planning and energy came together on the morning of 28 August 1963, as 250,000 Americans came to the Lincoln Memorial in the capital to demonstrate for civil rights. The biracial audience was perhaps 20 per cent white, and 'an estimated total of forty thousand were union members, the largest [single] mobilization of trade unionists in American labour history.'[54] A series of writers, folk-singers and entertainers was on hand to rally the crowd: the SNCC's 'Freedom Singers' Cordell Hull Reagan, Bernice Johnson, Chuck Neblett and Ruth Harris; blues artist Josh White; folk-artists Odetta (Filious), Bob Dylan, Joan Baez and the group Peter, Paul and Mary; actors Marlon Brando, Harry Belafonte, Charlton Heston, Ossie Davis and Ruby Dee; novelist James Baldwin, gospel great Mahalia Jackson, the legendary artist Josephine Baker and comedian Dick Gregory. In the early afternoon a series of speeches was delivered by the civil rights leadership, most of which were fairly repetitious. Randolph emphasized the need to link desegregation with economic justice, noting that 'we have no future in a society in which six million Black and white people are unemployed and millions more live in poverty.' The Black trade unionist also attacked the critics of the march. 'Those who deplore our militancy, who exalt patience in the name of a false peace are in fact supporting segregation and exploitation. They would have social peace at the expense of social and racial justice', Randolph argued. Walter Reuther declared that he shared 'the view that the struggle for civil rights and the struggle for equal opportunity is not the struggle of Negro Americans, but the struggle for every American to join in.' CORE Chairman Floyd McKissick read a prepared statement from Farmer, which warned that Afro-Americans would not 'come off the streets until we can work at any job befitting our skills any place in the land . . . until our kids have enough to eat and their minds can study and range wide without being cramped in Jim Crow schools.' Whitney Young delivered a brief but surprisingly sharp critique of 'those who would make deals, water down civil rights legislation, or take cowardly refuge in technical details around elementary human rights.' Wilkins focused on the necessity of ratifying the civil rights bill and insisted that Kennedy's 'proposals represent so moderate an approach, the remainder will be little more than sugar-water.' The high point of the rally was, of course, Martin Luther King's eloquent 'I Have A Dream' speech. Stamped on public memory, there is no need to recount it fully here. The rolling, soaring rhetoric of King at that moment caught the spirit of the entire audience, and of his generation:

> We cannot turn back. There are those who are asking . . . "when will you be satisfied?" We can never be satisfied as long as the Negro is the victim of the unspeakable horrors of police brutality. We can never be satisfied as long as our bodies, heavy with the fatigue of travel, cannot gain lodging in the motels of the highways and the hotels of the cities . . . We can never be satisfied as long as our children are stripped of their selfhood and robbed of their dignity by signs reading "For Whites Only". We can never be satisfied as long as a Negro in Mississippi cannot vote . . .[55]

The entire day passed without public incident, and as smooth as clockwork. At 4.15 p.m., Morehouse College President Benjamin Mays gave the benediction. The crowd left almost immediately afterwards; in fact, by sundown 'the city seemed strangely deserted'.[56] The major leaders caucused with the President at 5.00 p.m. sharp. Kennedy was pleased that they had managed the entire affair without embarrassing the administration and compromising its new-found commitment to desegregation. Indeed the only serious controversy that had taken place that day had been behind the scenes. With Forman's assistance, Lewis had drafted a fiery speech which was seriously at odds with the more conciliatory tone of the other presentations. The day before the demonstration, the Catholic archbishop of Washington let it be known that he would boycott the podium unless Lewis's hot remarks were cut. Fresh from the Deep South, and after having experienced dozens of beatings and arrests, young Lewis was in no mood to compromise. But Martin took Lewis aside, softly chiding him: 'I think I know you well. I don't think this sounds like you.' Rustin initially supported Lewis, but Eugene Carson Blake of the National Council of Churches was 'vociferous in his criticisms'. Randolph pleaded, 'John, for the sake of unity, we've come this far. For the sake of unity, change it.' In a room inside the Lincoln Memorial, Forman rewrote the speech quickly, and the revisions finally met with general approval. But even in its censored form, Lewis's speech rocked the audience. The message expressed the fighting militancy of the SNCC, and was a warning of Black radicalism on the political horizon:

> We come here today with a great sense of misgiving . . . It is true that we support the administration's Civil Rights Bill in the Congress. We support it with great reservations, however . . . In its present form this Bill will not protect the citizens of Danville, Virginia who must live in constant fear of a police state. It will not protect the hundreds and thousands of people who have been arrested upon trumped charges . . . It will not help the citizens of Mississippi, of Alabama and Georgia who are qualified to vote but lack a sixth grade education . . . We must have legislation that will protect the Mississippi share-cropper who is put off his farm because he dares to register to vote. We need a bill that will provide for the homeless and starving people of this nation . . . My friends, let us not forget that we are involved in a serious social revolution . . . Where is our party? Where is the political party that will make it unnecessary to march on Washington? Where is the political party that will make it unnecessary to march in the streets of Birmingham?[57]

What was the lasting impact of the second march on Washington? The absence of any display of civil disobedience and militancy on the part of activists brought more liberal-to-moderate white trade unionists into the civil rights coalition. The AFL-CIO Executive Council 'called upon all affiliates to join energetically in the fight to achieve passage' of the 1964 Civil Rights Bill. 'The Alabama, Mississippi, Texas, and Oklahoma AFL-CIO councils defied segregationist forces within their affiliates and came out in favour of the House-approved version of the bill.' By June 1964, the toughest desegregation act in US history was passed. As Foner notes, 'the new law covered voting, public accommodations, public facilities, education and fair employment practices. It established a federal Employment Opportunity Commission and extended the life of the Commission on Civil Rights to January 1968. Title VII of the law prohibited unions and employers of more than a hundred workers from discriminating in employment, membership, apprenticeship or promotion "against any individual because of his race, colour, religion, sex or national origin".' Soon after its passage, leaders of the 1963 march met again and drafted preliminary plans for another peaceful demonstration in the capital, this time to force Congress to enact strict legislation protecting Blacks' voting rights. But subsequent desegregation campaigns across the South in 1964 and in early 1965 quickly led to the collapse of national segregationist resistance. The Voting Rights Act of 1965, pushed through Congress by the administration of Lyndon Johnson, appointed 'federal examiners to conduct registration and observe voting in states and counties where patterns of discrimination existed and suspended all literacy tests and other disfranchising devices in states and counties where fewer than 50 per cent of the adults had voted in 1964.'[58]

Unquestionably, the second march on Washington movement had accelerated the passage of desegregation legislation at both national and state levels. It forced the Kennedy administration, and later, the Johnson administration, to align themselves closely behind the moderate civil rights leadership. It elevated the charismatic figure of Martin Luther King Jr, to international prominence as a symbol of democratic rights and equality. But in the long run, it also brought about a major shift within the desegregationist united front, which ultimately tore the coalition apart. Johnson's support for the civil rights agenda did not come cheaply. In an unspoken *quid pro quo* relationship, King and other civil rights moderates tried to halt desegregation demonstrations in the summer and fall of 1964, in a shabby effort not to embarrass Johnson during the presidential campaign. The president expected Black leaders to support every public policy of his administration, both foreign and domestic. Thus the 'alliance' between Johnson and leaders like King, Randolph, Wilkins, Young and others was no alliance at all; it simply muzzled the Negro moderates and effectively curtailed their non-electoral political activities. Moreover, within the Black movement itself, the strain between the moderates and the militants that existed during the March mobilization rapidly became an ideological chasm. Even the more progressive proponents of non-violent confrontation — John Lewis, Bayard Rustin and James Farmer — were quickly superseded by newer, stronger, uncompromising leaders — Stokely Carmichael, H. 'Rap' Brown, Floyd McKissick, Roy Innis, Huey P. Newton and, above all, Malcolm X. The rise of Black Power in the summer of 1966, and the growing dissension over the Vietnam War broke apart the Black united front, and led to the rapid resurgence of modern Black nationalism. The march's relative conservatism was in part responsible for the breakdown within the Black leadership several years later. It probably did more to divide and to retard the Black Freedom Movement than any other single mobilization between 1960 and 1966.

IV

The decade that followed the second March on Washington movement was, by almost any criteria, equivalent to a Second Reconstruction period for Black America. Legal desegregation had not only forced down the 'whites only' signs at lunch-counters and hotels, but permitted millions of Afro-Americans new opportunities for economic and social advancement. Affirmative action/ equal opportunity provisions in the private sector created new jobs for Black workers. Despite continued opposition to school desegregation, almost all public-school systems were compelled to extend some measure of educational equality to Black youth. In the colleges and universities, Afro-American enrolments soared from about 75,000 in 1950 to 666,000 by 1976.[59] In the private sector, there was solid growth promoted by Black entrepreneurial capitalism. Between 1970 and 1975, twenty-four Black-owned banks were established; the number of Black-owned businesses jumped from 163,000 in 1969 to over 231,000 in 1975; the estimated gross expenditures of Black consumers in the US increased from $30 billion in 1960 to over $145 billion in 1983. Concomitant with the entrepreneurial explosion was the establishment of a small but economically secure Black petty-bourgeois stratum. In 1940, barely 4 per cent of all Afro-Americans held occupations in professional, technical or managerial capacities. By 1975, about 15 per cent of all Blacks were in these fields. If one includes craftsmen, foremen, and all white-collar employees under the rubric of 'middle class', the percentage of Blacks in the middle class had moved from 9.6 per cent in 1940 to 35.4 per cent in 1970.[60] Most striking perhaps was the sharp increase in Black elected officials. In 1964, there were only 103 Blacks holding elective office in the entire country, including five in Congress. By 1983, the number of Black officials exceeded 5,600, and twenty-one Afro-Americans held Congressional seats. Blacks had won mayoral races in Los Angeles, Newark, New Orleans, Charlotte, Richmond and over two hundred other cities. In many respects, the leading activists of both the civil rights and the Black Power movements, having reached middle age, found themselves ensconced in higher education, government and trade-union leadership. The examples are many and varied. In September 1968, Andrew Young was arrested for blocking sanitation trucks during a strike of Black garbage workers: after serving two terms in Congress, and a stormy tenure as United Nations ambassador, Young is currently the mayor of Atlanta. Marion Barry, former SNCC leader, is now mayor of Washington DC; Howard Fuller, former Maoist and leader of the revolutionary Malcolm X College in North Carolina, is currently a cabinet member and leading Black administrator to the Democratic governor of Wisconsin; SNCC leader John Lewis served in the Carter administration, and is currently a member of the Atlanta City Council.

Yet there are flaws in this Horatio Alger story: depending upon one's class position, the movement forwards could be viewed as a retreat. Motivating the political practice of this recent generation of Black leaders, both in government and in the private sector, was the perception that racial equality could be achieved within the basic structures of the existing US political economy. Few doubted the necessity for continued reforms — increased federally funded programmes in education, public housing, health services and jobs. But with the decline of national demonstrations and mass mobilizations of the mid 1960s, and after the rise and precipitous decline of Black Power, most leaders acknowledged the necessity to push for social and economic equality through the existing state apparatuses. With this decision came an unconscious shift in political style and demeanour. The desire to 'deliver' goods and services to a particular constituency took precedence over the inner urge to articulate the deep bitterness and frustrations of the Black unemployed; the necessity to conform to the routine political discourse of bourgeois democracy, to play within the established boundaries, implicitly meant a repudiation of the activist tradition. The new Black courtiers were not cowled, yet they were limited by the fact of their electoral advancement.

Even more disturbing was the near-universal tendency of the Black petty bourgeoisie to equate 'integration' with the incremental achievement of racial equality. The philosophical foundations of the modern integrationist position can be traced to Supreme Court Justice John Marshall Harlan's famous dissent in the *Plessy v. Ferguson* decision in 1896. While a majority of justices supported the 'separate but equal' doctrine that validated Jim Crow, Harlan insisted that the Thirteenth, Fourteenth and Fifteenth Amendments had 'removed the race line from our governmental systems . . . The law in the states' should be exactly the same 'for the black as for the white'. Harlan observed that 'in view of the Constitution, in the eye of the law, there is in this country no superior, dominant, ruling class of citizens. There is no caste here. Our Constitution is colour-blind, and neither knows nor tolerates classes among citizens.' During the next half-century and more, Harlan's dissent formed the 'colour-blind' ideology of integrationist educators and civil rights activists. In the briefs submitted by the NAACP during the *Brown v. Board of Education* decision in the 1950s, Black social scientists who testified claimed that 'if coloured children are denied the experience in school of associating with white children, who represent 90 per cent of our national society . . . then the coloured child's curriculum is being greatly curtailed.' The chief counsel for the Black plaintiffs in the Topeka case, attorney Robert Carter, argued that the constitutional rights granted by the Fourteenth Amendment were 'individual rights' and not 'group rights'. No state government could create or maintain racially identifiable educational institutions, since 'race and ancestry and colour are irrelevant differences and cannot form the basis for any legislative action.' The NAACP brief went even further than Carter. All racial distinction constituted 'a badge of inferiority'. Thurgood Marshall added in his oral arguments before the Court that racial barriers of any sort were 'odious', 'individious', 'suspect' and 'irrational'. The victory of the *Brown* decision decisively reinforced the 'colour-blind' orientation of Black leaders. As late as 1963, in his Congressional testimony on the pending Civil Rights Act, Wilkins attacked 'employment quotas as "evil" and predicted that they would be used to restrict the opportunities of Black workers'.[61] Neither Wilkins nor White before him could have predicted that 'racial quotas' would one day preserve Blacks' jobs.

Integrationists were convinced that 'social equality' meant the granting of full access to Blacks within the social, political and economic institutions of American society. This implied 'racial' or 'caste reform', the assimilation of Blacks as individuals within the structures of the larger society without regard to race. It also implied an acceptance of the class dynamics and power arrangements that existed in the capitalist social formation. Integrationists in the Walter White tradition opposed any and all forms of racial categorization, and the existence of all-Black neighbourhoods and institutions. In cultural terms, integration connoted aesthetic and social homogeneity as a major political objective. In conflict with this 'colour-blind' approach to Black politics is the position of cultural pluralism, best represented by Du Bois. Equality in the abstract meant to Du Bois the full and unfettered access of Blacks to political, economic and social institutions. But Blacks' 'full access' to such institutions could not be achieved without a systemic transformation for both whites and Blacks. In other words, if racial categories were non-existent in the US, or if race declined in social significance, the problem of social class inequality for working and poor people would still exist. For the cultural pluralist, *individual* socio-economic advancement is secondary to *group* welfare and achievement. In September 1933, Du Bois asked his NAACP colleagues, 'What are we really aiming at? The building of a new nation or the integration of a new group into an old nation?' Du Bois predicted that the 'next stage' of the struggle for racial equality would require 'group action. It involves the organization of intelligent and earnest people of Negro descent for their preservation and advancement in America, in the West Indies and in Africa; and no sentimental distaste for racial or national unity can be allowed to hold them back from a step which sheer necessity demands.'[62] Racial barriers within society, therefore, may be internal — protective, socially constructive and defensive — or external — imposed from outside, repressive, subordinating. When imposed by the dominant white society, as in the instance of Jim Crow, they must be fought. But when self-generated, under specific historical conditions — such as the creation of the Black Church — they are beneficial. The cultural pluralist sees the law as a product of the larger social order. If society is not 'colour-blind' in the allocation of unemployment, poverty, health care and education, one can assume that the criminal justice system and the legislative process will also perpetuate racial inequality. The construction of a biracial democracy required 'race-conscious solutions', such as affirmative action and race quotas in hiring. It also demanded all-Black or Black-initiated political, economic and social protest movements and institutions.

The full implications of the philosophical debate between cultural pluralists and integrationists did not become apparent until the early 1970s. The petty bourgeois integrationist position would dictate the ultimate transformation of historically Black academic institutions into the non-racially based, cultural 'mainstream'. If racial assimilation is to be realized, Black colleges must acquire majority-white student bodies, white faculties, white administrators and white presidents. Kenneth Clark, former president of the American Psychological Association and member of the Board of Trustees at Howard University, carries the integrationist goal to its logical conclusion:

> I am not in favour of Black colleges, white colleges, or colleges for those who are five feet eight inches tall. You can only have Black colleges if you accept that certainty of racism . . . I happen to take education seriously. I think its purpose is to broaden people away from the institutionalization of racism. Education is much more important than baseball. We did something about Black leagues — we now have major leagues. Why can't we do the same with education? The question is — Is Howard a good university? Does it stimulate creativity?[63]

Du Bois would have shuddered at such logic. Desegregation ended *de jure* segregation, but it did not abolish institutional racism. Moreover, Clark and other liberal integrationists obscure the cultural and pedagogical distinctiveness of white and Black institutions of higher learning. As Du Bois asserted in April 1960, if desegregation were to be carried out in full in public universities, 'certain things will inevitably follow. Negro teachers will become rarer and in many cases will disappear.' Black students will be 'taught under unpleasant if not discouraging circumstances' and 'fewer will go to college. Theoretically, Negro universities will disappear.' The challenge of racial equality in the post-Jim Crow era, Du Bois predicted, will be the preservation of Afro-American 'cultural patterns', and the maintenance of all-Black educational and social institutions. 'American Negroes must remember that voluntary organization for great ends is far different from compulsory segregation for evil purposes.'[64]

Du Bois's predictions and warnings concerning the implicit dangers of desegregation-from-above, mandated by a capitalist state apparatus that is still systematically racist, rapidly assumed reality as the 'paradox of desegregation'. Students from Black elite backgrounds, whose parents had been the products of historically Black colleges and who could afford to pay full tuition, now enrolled in 'Ivy League' and large, predominately white state universities. Black colleges found it increasingly difficult to compete with white institutions for students, administrators and faculty. As the Carnegie Commission on Higher Education Report of 1971 observed, the basic 'rules' of American education for Blacks had radically changed, to the detriment of historically Black institutions. 'Colleges founded for Negroes must now compete with predominantly white institutions for financial support from government agencies and from foundations . . .' Competition for the Black student, Black faculty and financial resources 'centres less on what these colleges have achieved for Black Americans during the past century and more on their quality in the present as compared to white institutions.'[65] As funds for private Black colleges diminished, administrators were forced to hike tuition fees and to exhaust their endowment funds to cover annual operating costs. Fisk University in Nashville, one of the elite Black institutions, experienced a decline in its endowment from $14 million in 1969 to barely $3.5 million a decade later. Its student body dropped from 1,569 in 1973 to less than 600 in 1984. State-supported Black universities encountered different problems. Title IV of the 1964 Civil Rights Act forced Black public institutions to merge with neighbouring all-white schools. By the early 1980s, Lincoln University of Missouri and the University of Maryland-Eastern Shore, both historically Black institutions, had majority-white student bodies. Delaware State, Kentucky State and Maryland's Bowie State had student populations of which one third to one half were whites. Federal courts did little or nothing about the continuation of segregation at white universities, while pressuring Black colleges to conform to desegregation guide-lines. On 20 July 1984, for example, one US district judge declared that Tennessee State University could no longer be allowed to keep its 'Black identity'. Any retention of a 'Predominately Black faculty and a Black president' was a 'situation which has got to change'.[66]

In short, the application of desegregation by the racist-capitalist state, in conjunction with the colour-blind philosophy of misguided petty-bourgeois Blacks, actually reduced educational opportunities for Afro-Americans. Between the academic years 1976-77 and 1980-81, Black college enrolment increased by 3.3 per cent, while the number of Black high school graduates jumped by 20 per cent during the same period. The number of Blacks awarded master's degrees actually fell 16 per cent, compared with a 4 per cent decline for whites. Thousands of Black students were shifted into two-year junior college programmes, which would decrease the probability of them competing for professional and managerial positions upon graduation. By the early 1970s, one third of all Afro-American college students were enrolled in junior colleges; ten years later, more than 51 per cent were attending two-year institutions, and the vast majority never graduated. The Reagan administration accelerated the demise of Black educational opportunity still further in 1982, by sharply curtailing student loans at many Black colleges. Consequently by October 1982, only 36 per cent of all Black high-school graduates were enrolling in any colleges, compared with 52 per cent of white high-school senior. Only five years before, 50 per cent of all Afro-American high-school graduates had gone on to college. Commenting on the 'erosion of higher education opportunities for Blacks', educator Marian Wright Edelman noted in 1984: 'Today, over 56,000 Black males aged 20 to 24 are inmates of correctional institutions, while only 44,000 in the same age group are living in college dormitories.'[67]

The rapid growth of an articulate Afro-American elite also obscured from view the absence of economic and social advancement for the vast majority of Black workers and the Black poor. In 1967, almost six out of every ten Afro-American families had two or more income-earners, and 16.7 per cent had three workers or more — a much higher rate than among white families. About 80 per cent of all Black males between the ages of sixteen and twenty-four who weren't attending school had jobs. Black families were shaken by periodic recessions, but were able to maintain a high degree of internal stability. Three quarters of all Black households in the mid 1960s had two parents, and only 21.6 per cent of all Afro-American children were born out of wedlock. With the structural crisis of US and world capitalism in the 1970s and 1980s, however, millions of Black families were pushed into marginal employment, joblessness and poverty. The subsequent economic impact upon Black households was in many respects as destructive as the Great Depression. By 1977, more than 17 per cent of all Afro-American families had no income-earners, while the average number of earners in each family dipped to 1.5, slightly below that of whites. By 1982, 20 per cent of all Black males of working age, about 2 million persons, were out of the labour force, a 300 per cent increase since 1960. Black young adults experienced official unemployment rates of about 50 per cent in 1982-1983, and unofficial rates of joblessness in many ghettos exceeded 80 per cent. The impact upon Black families was inevitable. The proportion of two-parent Black families dropped to 53 per cent; over half of all Afro-American children were born out of wedlock in the mid 1980s; since 1960, the number of Afro-American families headed by single, divorced or widowed women had increased by over 300 per cent, and more than 60 per cent of these families lived in poverty. Overall, Black median family income in 1983 had fallen to only 55 per cent of white family income — the largest wage gap recorded in a quarter of a century. More than half of all Black children under the age of three in 1983 were living in poverty.[68]

The Reagan administration did its best to expand human suffering within the Black community. In its first year in office, among other things, it eliminated the Comprehensive Employment and Training Act programme, originally funded at $3.1 billion, which ended 150,000 federally supported jobs; it cut by $1.7 billion the child nutrition programmes, designed to curtail urban hunger; it removed more than 400,000 families from the welfare rolls on 1 October 1981. Within twelve months, the median income of Afro-American families had fallen 5.2 per cent below the 1980 figure, and the number of Americans below the poverty level had increased by 2.2 million.[69] The capitalist state responded to the crisis of Afro-American social instability by attempting to impose its own 'structure' on the Black social fraction. This structure assumed myriad modes. Unemployed and low-income Blacks were far more likely to be determined 'mentally ill', for example, than were whites. Black male teenagers were admitted to state and county mental hospitals at a rate two-and-a-half times that of white male teenagers; for Black males aged 25-44, the rate of mental hospital admissions was almost three times higher than for white males in 1980. A second method of racial institutionalization was through the armed forces, presented to Blacks as the 'employer of last resort'. In 1972, Afro-American first-term re-enlistments in the US army were only 20.4 per cent. Ten years later, Black re-enlistments were 71 per cent, compared with 49.9 per cent for whites. The criminal justice system, and particularly the prisons, represented the capitalist state's principal structure for regulating Black family and community life. From the mid 1970s on, over 2.2. million arrests of Blacks were made every year. Approximately 300,000 Afro-Americans were incarcerated by 1983, most of whom were under thirty years of age.[70]

The Black elite's leaders could hardly ignore the ground-swell of anger from every Afro-American working-class neighbourhood. Desegregation had been achieved legally, yet Black unemployment rates had more than doubled in the past fifteen years. Equal opportunity had created gains for many, but millions more lived on the edge of or below the poverty line. In the name of 'integration', historically Black universities, public and private, were rapidly being destroyed. Even within the ranks of the Black petty bourgeoisie, there were disturbing indications of socio-economic decline. In 1980, nearly half of all Black women and 35 per cent of all Black men 'owed their jobs either directly or indirectly to government spending', notes Richard McGahey. '54 per cent of the Black male college graduates and fully 72 per cent of Black female college graduates' in 1980 held positions 'tied to this spending'. Elected with a mandate to reduce non-military-related federal expenditures, the Reagan administration promptly terminated thousands of public positions. 'Federal agencies dismissed minorities at a rate 50 per cent greater than whites during 1981, and the number of lay-offs doubled in 1982, hitting upper-level Black professionals the hardest.' Increased unemployment rates among the Black elite, according to McGahey, illustrated that 'the gains made by the emerging Black middle class were much more contingent than many believed.'[71]

The social and economic crisis of the 1980s forced many civil rights leaders and Black politicians to reassess their strategies. Years before, King had advanced an ambitious programme of domestic social reconstruction, which perceived that the root of poverty, war and racism was the capitalist system. As long as 'profit motives and property rights are considered more important than people', King declared in 1967, the 'triple evils' of 'racism', 'militarism' and 'economic exploitation . . . are incapable of being conquered.' As a devout Christian, King could not embrace the 'atheism' inherent in the Marxian critique of society, yet he could still praise Marx as a 'crusader for social justice'. He hoped that American capitalism could be structurally reformed without a social revolution that would displace the ruling class, and held up the example of Swedish social democracy.[72] In the optimistic context of the 1960s, most Black petty-bourgeois leaders were unwilling to tread in the direction of democratic socialism, much less of Marxism, as a means to eliminate racial inequality. Only with the paradox of desegregation and the steady erosion of Afro-Americans' socio-economic status in the 1970s and early 1980s were significant numbers of Black middle-class leaders prepared to advocate the basic reforms King had advanced in his last two years of life.

With new clarity and urgency, they began to perceive the central role of US militarism in the racial and social class exploitation of Black America. An analysis of US military spending during the period 1970 to 1978, by political economist Marion Anderson, indicated that every time the military budget went up by $1 billion, Blacks lost 1,300 jobs. During the period, Blacks received 84,000 jobs from military contracts, and another 290,000 Blacks were employed in the military. But over 483,000 jobs for Blacks would have been created for the same expenditure in 'durable and non-durable goods production, construction, services, state and local government'. Part of the problem was the capital-intensive character of military expenditures. In 1983, an investment of $1 billion in the production of guided missiles would have generated 20,700 direct and indirect jobs. The identical amount spent on iron and steel production, on average, would have created 34,700 jobs. One billion dollars allocated for public health facilities and hospitals in 1983 would have produced 54,260 direct and indirect jobs; for public schools, 71,500 jobs would have been the result. And even these statistics were misleadingly low. According to the US Bureau of Labour Statistics, only 28 per cent of all employees engaged in guided missile production were 'production workers'. In older industries, where the percentage of Black production line workers was high, 'production workers' made up 70 per cent or more of all employees. Most of the employees hired in defence plants by the 1980s were highly trained white-collar workers — scientists, computer analysts, engineers — job categories with very low Black representation. Black leaders now saw the wisdom of King's anti-militarism: as Martin had declared, 'Somehow we must transform the dynamics of the world power struggle from a negative nuclear arms race which no one can win, to a positive contest to harness [humanity's] creative genius for the purpose of making peace and prosperity a reality for all of the nations of the world.'[73]

Increasingly the political nexus between 'jobs' and 'peace' found support within the Black electorate. In November 1982, a series of public referenda calling for a nuclear freeze between the US and the USSR received a total of 11.6 million favourable votes. Significantly, in cities with sizeable Black populations or Black majorities, the nuclear freeze received its largest mandates. In Chicago, for example, the vote for the nuclear freeze was 404,173 to 135,325; in Washington DC, 77,521 votes were cast in favour of a freeze to only

23,369 against. In Congress, the Congressional Black Caucus (CBC) took the lead in advocating a national policy of military conversion to human needs programmes. The CBC 'Alternative Budget' of May 1982, which projected billions of dollars of cuts in nuclear and conventional weapons expenditures, was trounced in the Democratic-controlled House by a vote of 85 for, 322 against, and 24 not voting. The left wing of the CBC advanced even more progressive proposals. Congressman Ronald V. Dellums, a democratic socialist, introduced an alternative Appropriations Bill (HR-6696) which reduced by more than $50 billion the Reagan war budget, HR-6696 was also crushed in the House, receiving only 55 votes in favour. Several months later, Brooklyn Congressman Major R. Owens introduced a constitutional amendment which 'guaranteed' the 'right to employment' for 'each person by the United States'. What was striking about Owens's amendment was its 'transitional' character. That is, it could not be achieved without a fundamental transformation of the capitalist political economy, yet it was at face value a 'reasonable' legal demand which had the potential of winning majority support among Black, Latino and white voters.

Thus when the Reverend Joseph Lowery, now head of the SCLC, and Coretta Scott King decided independently in mid 1982 to issue a call for another March on Washington, the agenda of this new social mobilization had been largely predetermined from above and below. Martin's goal of a social democratic political economy could not be realized when the US government was allocating $1.6 trillion for military expenditures over the next five years. From above, the Reagan administration had placed lifelong reactionaries in the Office of Federal Contracts Compliance Programmes and in the Justice Department's Civil Rights Division. Reductions in federal jobs had weakened the Black middle class, and affirmative action was a dead letter. From below, the Black poor, unemployed, and working classes were experiencing unprecedented attacks, cuts in welfare, in public housing, in job training programmes, food stamps and other essential services. Pushed from below and pressured from above, the Black elite proposed a renaissance of social protest at the nation's capital. As in the 1963 mobilization, Lowery and King recognized the necessity to build the broadest possible united front of liberal to progressive constituencies. Technically, the demonstration was to be in honour of the twentieth anniversary of the 28 August 1963 march. But programmatically, the slogan of 'jobs, peace and freedom' spoke both the paradox of desegregation and the national retreat from the vision of the Second Reconstruction, as well as the role of US militarism in reinforcing Black poverty and unemployment.

Walter Fauntroy, the local Washington coordinator of the 1963 March, and currently Congressman from the District of Columbia, agreed to serve as national director of the 'Twentieth Anniversary March'. National co-chairs were selected to appeal to a multiracial constituency — Judy Goldsmith of the National Organization for Women, Asia Bennett of the American Friends' Service Committee, Black recording artist Stevie Wonder and NAACP director Benjamin Hooks. Other national convenors included: Clyde Bellecourt, a leader of the American Indian Movement; John Jacob of the National Urban League; Rabbi Alex Schindler, Union of American Hebrew Congregations; Richard Deats, Fellowship of Reconciliation; liberal feminist Bella Abzug; Puerto Rican Congressman Robert Garcia; civil rights leader Jesse Jackson; and Bishop James Armstrong of the National Council of Churches. The co-chairs, convenors, and a select group of 'individual endorsers' (for example, Washington DC mayor Marion Barry, former US Attorney General Ramsey Clark, Congressman Parren Mitchell, Congressman Harold Washington, Ralph Abernathy, Julian Bond, the Reverend Benjamin Chavis, Andrew Young, and DC Councilwoman Hilda Mason) were chosen to reflect the multinational, left to centre formation that was necessary to halt Reaganism. Fauntroy used his local resources to set up a small office for the mobilization. Donna Brazile, a 23-year-old progressive organizer and leader of the US Student Association, was chosen to coordinate nearly all of the day-to-day preparation to build for the march.[74]

V

On 19 October 1982, the efforts to build the third March on Washington Movement received a stunning blow from a curious source. Bayard Rustin and Norman Hill of the AFL-CIO-funded A. Philip Randolph Institute, sent a devastating memo to Coretta King, Lowery, and other major civil rights leaders. Rustin and Hill raised 'a number of questions regarding' the 'wisdom' of carrying out the new mobilization. First, in their view, the march would be too expensive. The 1963 March had spent about one million dollars, and Rustin and Hill did not believe that 'significant funds' could be obtained this time around. Secondly, 'the 80s are more complicated than the 60s.' The authors claimed that Afro-American leaders had made the new call for a march 'out of a sentimental appreciation' for the sixties 'and out of deep respect' for Martin Luther King. Many leaders may 'therefore approve such a march while not recognizing that they cannot arouse in their constituencies either the political and moral response, the financial commitment, or the energy to equal or surpass' the 1963 March. Rustin and Hill warned that the 'Black Leadership Forum', the NAACP and others in the civil rights community would be unable to attract masses of people to the demonstration. The 'failure to equal the quarter million mark will automatically be considered by the media as a failure of the movement.' It would also be a 'failure attributable to today's Black leadership', and 'civil rights forces will be seen not as gathering strength, but as withering on the political vine.' Part of what characterized Rustin and Hill's polemic was a deep pessimism about the current political period. '1963 was a period of great hopes', the authors declared, while the basic political tenor of this era was one of apathy and 'despair'. They doubted that Blacks and their allies could 'top' the 250,000 figure, and hinted that 'extreme political consequences' would occur if 'we did not succeed'.

But the most controversial statement in the Rustin-Hill memo focused on 'The Question of Order' and 'Programmatic Confusion'. The authors characterized the second March as an event of 'joy, camaraderie, and order. In fact, not a single arrest was made in all of Washington that day.' The decorum displayed by the marchers 'helped convince some in Congress who had opposed civil rights legislation to reverse their positions.' Now, Hill and Rustin cautioned, 'There is a serious question in our minds as to whether order can be maintained in Washington DC, on a hot summer afternoon in a period when Black youth are justifiably distraught and angry; when their rate of unemployment is far greater than that for the average adult even in the Great Depression; when training programmes have been curtailed; and when the loss of welfare and other benefits the government once provided has caused many Black youths to lose faith that there is a role for them in American society.' Given the level of anger against Reaganism and the economic crisis, the civil rights leaders should not 'shoulder the responsibility' for keeping Black youth under 'control'. Finally, Hill and Rustin sharply criticized the inclusion of 'peace and environmental' issues in the demonstration. 'The achievement of programmatic unity among ourselves becomes more difficult with the inclusion of peace, thereby making the success of the event even more problematic. Can such issues be separated out if the form of protest is a march in which it is patently impossible to control the material distributed, or the posters, banners, and other displays carried and sold [?]' The authors suggested that an 'indoor political meeting' be scheduled for 27 August, instead of a march, with the purpose of outlining 'a concrete, limited manifesto' for the poor, Blacks and other minorities. Instead of hundreds of thousands of marchers, a guest-list would include Congressional representatives, 'administration officials, and other prominent people'.[75]

The Rustin-Hill memo failed to derail the march mobilization. Yet two points must be noted here. Rustin's recollections of the 1963 March were, on balance, a distortion of the historical record. As discussed previously, Rustin was part of the 'emergency committee' that forced John Lewis to rewrite sections of his militant speech. Where was the 'sense of joy, camaraderie, and order' in this pre-emptive action?[76] Rustin's entire public career had emphasized the necessity for building multiracial coalitions — yet when the issue of 'peace' was introduced as an integral part of a more advanced civil rights agenda, Rustin's identification as an unreconstructed Cold Warrior and client of the AFL-CIO since the mid 1960s forced him to oppose such a mobilization. Rustin's and Hill's notion of coalition politics depended upon the acquiescence of the government and capital. What the majority of their former allies were proposing by the march, in effect, was to concretize political links with the most progressive newer currents of liberal and radical social reform which challenged Reaganism and the momentum toward war in a more effective manner.

During the first six months of 1983, the mobilization effort for the third March was not particularly effective. Given the relatively more advanced programmatic thrust of this march, a number of traditional liberal white supporters of the civil rights community refused to finance the effort. Rustin's objections were also echoed by several national Black leaders in the NAACP. In public, they embraced the new march but privately, they resorted to several scurrilous tactics to undermine it. A 'whisper campaign' of sorts was launched against the main organizer, Donna Brazile, which included assertions that she was 'too left'. Some members of staff on the Congressional Black Caucus complained that Brazile did not 'consult' adequately with the members. Some local NAACP leaders were not urged to mobilize their members to travel to Washington. A number of the prominent convenors provided little to no assistance to their own organizations in recruiting personnel to assist Brazile and her overworked staff. At the NAACP's July 1983 convention in New Orleans, Hooks 'damned' the march with faint praise. 'Let's be honest', he told reporters. 'People might not come because of a lack of money. Also, what we don't take into account is that hidden factor. People become discouraged.' Hooks concluded, 'Whether it's 1,000 or 1 million, we will be there.'[77] Even the leaders of the march itself seemed at times to be strangely divorced from the actual organizing campaign. One story told about Lowery illustrates the problem. In June 1983, Lowery was invited to speak at a plenary session of the World Peace Council, meeting in Prague, Czechoslovakia. The SCLC leader delivered a forthright, anti-imperialist speech. Yet he did not mention the importance of the forthcoming August 27 march in the context of the battle for world peace. One special delegate who knew about the march, and who later raised questions about Lowery's lapse, was Yasser Arafat, leader of the PLO![78]

A number of the more right-wing elements of the old desegregation united front of the 1960s were at best lukewarm towards the march. Conspicuous within the Black community in this regard was the quiet capitulation of the National Urban League. With the departure of former leader Vernon Jordan, the trajectory of the Urban League was towards the right, a return to its accommodationist philosophy during the decades when George Edmund Haynes, Charles S. Johnson and Eugene K. Jones determined policies.[79] New League director John E. Jacob advanced the rhetoric of anti-Reaganism with the political economy of the Booker T. Washington tradition. At the 31 July-3 August 1983 convention of the Urban League, for example, Jacob took pains publicly to vilify the Reaganites. 'Black people looked to Washington for fair play and for protection of our civil rights. Instead,' Jacob declared, 'we got Pac Man social policies and cave man civil rights policies.' The Black masses were 'driven to the margins of despair by the most hostile Administration in fifty years'. Simultaneously, however, David T. Kearns, chief executive officer and president of Xerox Corporation, was made the Urban League's new national Chairman. In an interesting *quid pro quo* arrangement, Kearns announced the gift of a five-million-dollar grant from Xerox to the League. Secretary of Transportation Elizabeth Dole spoke at a convention luncheon and announced that her department would give $325,000 to the League. Reagan's notorious Assistant Attorney General for Civil Rights, William Bradford Reynolds, claimed before the convention that the Administration's civil rights programme 'outshines that of any prior Administration of the past thirty years', and predicted that it will 'become the standard against which future Administrations are measured.'[80] Given the League's efforts to please corporate and Administration interests, it was no surprise that it took no organized role in the mobilization. Vernon Jordan and large numbers of Urban League affiliates did, however, take part in the march.

The Jewish community was also decidedly split over the march. The leftist New Jewish Agenda was enthusiastic in its support. The American Jewish Congress, after some internal debate, announced late in the summer that it would join the new Coalition of Conscience. In an open letter to Coretta King, the Congress's executive director Henry Siegman declared that he and his members 'will walk proudly beside you and your colleagues on August 27th, as we walked proudly with Martin Luther King twenty years ago.' The state of Israel marked the twentieth anniversary of King's 'I have A Dream' speech with the planting of additional trees in the forest that bears his name near Nazareth, in the hills of Galilee.[81] The Union of American Hebrew Congregations also agreed to participate; Rabbi Alex Schindler agreed to deliver 'a prayer for a world of jobs, peace and freedom' at the afternoon rally. Other Jewish groups, and especially conservative Zionist factions, bitterly rejected calls for unity. Although no representatives of the PLO were given the podium, the mere presence of former Senator James Abourezk, founder of the American Arab Anti-Discrimination Committee, as a march national convenor was intolerable. The newspaper *Jewish Week* openly redbaited the mobilization, declaring that the march was dominated by 'left-wing' elements.' One group, the Jewish War Veterans, at first endorsed the march but subsequently withdrew its endorsement. More fundamentally, right-wing Zionists were enraged by the Coalition's inclusion of the demand for 'peace'. Leaders of the American Jewish Committee and the Anti-Defamation League of B'nai B'rith took turns before the media to smear the mobilization. Typical of the calumny was the comment of Hyman Bookbinder, a Washington DC spokesperson of the American Jewish Committee: 'The organizers made a serious mistake when they moved away from the 1963 civil rights goals into complicated foreign policy questions.' Bookbinder objected to the march's original call, which stated opposition to 'the militarization of internal conflicts, often abetted and even encouraged by massive US arms exports, . . . in the Middle East and Central America.' Such statements, in Bookbinder's view, were 'too pro-Third World and anti-American'.[82] Such shrill protests were all too reminiscent of Lyndon Johnson's opposition to King, when the civil rights activist became a proponent of world peace and US disengagement in Vietnam. Unquestioned support for Israeli aggression abroad, subsidized by American taxpayers, was more important than achieving human needs at home. The failure of many traditionally 'liberal' American Jewish leaders to support the march created profound distrust between the American Black and Jewish social fractions, which would turn to bitter acrimony during the national presidential campaign of Jesse Jackson the following year.

Despite these political and financial problems, Brazile and her staff were able to disseminate information about the march to hundreds of communities across the nation. The Black Church was particularly decisive in this regard. Bishop John H. Adams of the Congress of National Black Churches was a convenor of the march; other prominent clergy who had endorsed the campaign included Chavis, Rev. Otis Moss, Bishop J. Clinton Hoggard, Rev. B. W. Smith, Rev. John R. Bryant and Rev. Ernest Gibson. Members of the National Planning Council of the march included Dr Charles Butler, President of the Progressive National Baptist Convention, Dr Charles Cobb, Executive Director of the Commission for Racial Justice of the United Church of Christ, Rev. Herbert Daughtry, leader of the National Black United Front (NBUF), Dr Emanuel McCall, head of Black Relations of the Southern Baptist Church, and Bishop Chester Kirkendall of the Christian Methodist Episcopal Church.[83] Many local organizing meetings for the march were staged in Black churches in dozens of towns and cities; nearly every local 'Coalition of Conscience' involved to some degree the Black clergy.

Even more decisive was the vital contribution of labour — Black, Latino and white. Kirkland's hostility to the march's demand for 'peace' was expressed in a cynical manoeuvre calling for unions to place their energies into local Labour Day marches, one week after 27 August. This not-so-subtle attempt by the ALF-CIO bureaucrats was largely ignored by the progressive and moderate tendencies of labour. Representatives of labour on the National Planning Council included Howard Samuel, President of the Industrial Union Department, AFL-CIO; Willie Felder of the United Auto Workers (UAW); Robert White, President of the National Alliance of Postal and Federal Employees; and Cleveland Robinson, Vice President of the Coalition of Black Trade Unionists.[84] Locally, union activists and leaders independently took the initiative to build towards 27 August. On 13 June, a major press conference for Mrs King was staged at the New York headquarters of District 65, UAW, which was supported by District 1199 of the Hospital workers union; DC 37, the American Federation of State, County and Municipal Employees (AFSCME); and the Amalgamated Clothing and Textile Workers. Henry Nicholas, the president of District 1199, donated $10,000 to the march, and pledged that his union would 'charter and fill 150 buses'. The union also promised to appoint staff in fifteen cities to assist the campaign.[85] By the end of June, progressive unionists were actively building support for the march at the grassroots level. One of hundreds of examples was the action of Earl Keihl, District 4 director of the United Furniture Workers of America. The York, Pennsylvania labour leader sent leaflets for plant bulletin boards, urging members to organize buses and carpools to get to Washington DC. The letter declared: 'The struggle for JOBS requires little explanation. There are millions of workers who through no fault of their own, have been thrown out on the street . . . The fight for PEACE is the ultimate struggle, for without peace, we will continue to suffer the social cuts and finally, we will perish in nuclear ashes . . . The fight for FREEDOM is as necessary today, if not more so than it was twenty years ago. Black unemployment is more than twice that of whites . . .'[86] The Communication Workers of America (CWA) endorsed the march at its June convention in Los Angeles; and the General Executive Board of the United Electric Workers (UE) called for 'the biggest possible UE participation in the march'. United Steel-Workers of America (USWA) Vice President for human affairs Leon Lynch drafted a letter to all USWA staff representatives, district leaders and local presidents, urging them to take part. Lynch stated, 'We are still in search of a discrimination-free, pluralistic society. Now more than ever we need jobs. The callous policies of the Reagan Administration have had a devastating impact on workers, minorities and poor people.' The March on Washington would 'dramatize' the fight against Reaganism.[87]

One rough index of the kinds of constituencies that took part in the march mobilization is the number of groups which reserved buses to Washington DC. One list obtained from march co-ordinators in New York City is quite revealing. In mid August, the number of confirmed buses in Brooklyn totalled 30; Queens, 23; Staten Island, 5; Long Island, 33; and Manhattan, 367. At least 78 per cent of Manhattan's buses were reserved by the labour movement, 285 in all. These included 54 buses for District 65, UAW. Over thirty New York-based union locals took part. The list also indicates a few interesting anomalies. For example, relatively few Black elected officials, apart from Brooklyn's progresssive Congressman Major Owens, organized buses for their constituents. Brooklyn's NAACP chapter reserved one bus, as did Harlem's NAACP branch. A large number of small Black churches each obtained a single bus for the demonstration, yet few Black denominations seemingly co-ordinated efforts or pooled their resources in order to obtain a maximum presence in Washington. However, Brooklyn's New Jewish Agenda obtained three buses; the predominately white Riverside Church Disarmament Programme reserved five buses.[88]

The march mobilization proceeded in quite different ways across the nation. In the smaller towns and communities, representatives of the Black Church and civil rights activists, Black and white, were largely free to determine the local character of the 'Jobs, Peace and Freedom' coalition. In Seattle, Washington, for example, the formation was pulled together by two liberal Black leaders, City Councilman Sam Smith and the Reverend Samuel McKinney. A small delegation from Seattle was organized to travel to Washington, and organizers planned a local rally on August 27. In Salem, Oregon, marchers planned to assemble on the steps of the state capitol building and scheduled presentations from multicultural groups.[89] In Charleston, South Carolina, local Black activist Jerome Small, a member of the CORE and spokesperson of the 'Charleston Progressive Coalition', organized several hundred marchers to go to Washington DC.[90]. In Greensboro, North Carolina, leadership was taken up by members of the Shiloh Baptist Church and that city's NAACP branch.[91] Many 27 August local coalitions became involved in various joint political activities before the march itself took place. In Newport News, Virginia, the local coalition passed a resolution in support of striking telephone workers. The resolution declared that King had 'stood for the right of working people to organize and defend themselves against those who would seek higher profits at the expense of human justice. It is in this spirit that this body — which represents a broad coalition of trade unions, civil rights, civic, religious leaders, and community activists — extends its solidarity.'[92]

In New Orleans, the key organizers who emerged were from the labour and civil rights movements. The Reverend Jerome Owens, president of the New Orleans A. Philip Randolph Institute, and S.L. Harvey, state president of the SCLC, called the first local committee meeting on 23 June. The overwhelming majority of participants were Black workers, mostly representing UAW local 1921; the CWA; the Oil, Chemical and Atomic Workers (OCAW)

Local 4-522; Local 277 of the Office of Professional Employees International Union; National Association of Letter Carriers Local 124; and the Cement Masons Local 567.[93] In the Philadelphia metropolitan area about sixty-four community organizations and union locals endorsed the march. Moderates responded to the mobilization there by obtaining a Philadelphia City Council resolution endorsing the march. Black mayoral candidate Wilson Goode endorsed the March, reserving five buses for his supporters; local unions reserved another eighty buses by early July. Further to the left, more militant march activists distributed three thousand posters which urged Philadelphians to 'March before one more plant closes, before one more person dies in Central America, before one more Klan demonstration.'[94] Throughout the country, centrist forces expressed a willingness to work with the left as never before. In St Louis, for instance, the 16 June conference of the Association for Non-violent Social Change brought religious leaders, peace, civil rights and Marxist activists together in support of 27 August. At a crowded press conference, Martin Luther King III and Grenadian ambassador to the Organization of American States Dessima Williams united by their joint presence the international and domestic agendas for democratic progressives. Williams applauded the march, reminding her audience that the Black movement had 'inspired the concept of freedom' in her nation and throughout the Third World.[95] Farmers' groups from the Midwest and the Black Farmers' Association made plans to bring members; prisoners in Leavenworth Penitentiary started a funds drive to help low-income people to travel to Washington; and organizations of disabled people in Chicago scheduled a caravan to DC.[96] A 'freedom train' was planned to bring demonstrators from the Deep South.[97]

The US left, with a few exceptions, and the more eclectic national peace community voiced nearly unanimous support for the march. A number of antinuclear, antiracist, peace and Marxist representatives could be found at every level of the march mobilization. On the National Planning Council, these forces included Leslie Cagan of the Mobilization for Survival; Anne Braden, the highly respected Co-Chairperson of the Southern Organizing Committee for Economic and Social Justice; the Reverend William Sloan Coffin; Anna Gyorgy of Critical Mass; Rafe Pomerance, President of Friends of the Earth; former King adviser Jack O'Dell; Randy Kehler of the Nuclear Weapons Freeze Campaign; and Frank Chapman, Associate Director of the National Alliance Against

Racist and Political Repression.[98] The left press, particularly the Communist Party's *Daily World*, gave generous coverage to the march's activities. Both the Nuclear Freeze campaign and Jobs with Peace endorsed the march, and circulated literature to members and supporters encouraging active participation. Various Marxist-Leninist parties and radical currents participated in local march meetings.[99] The two largest national organizations on the left, the Communist Party and the Democratic Socialists of America (DSA), were particularly closely involved. For the Communist Party, the march fell clearly in line with Party Chairman Henry Winston's call for 'an all-people's front against Reagan's policies at home and abroad'.[100] The DSA's Youth Section moved its 24-27 August national conference to Washington DC in order to maximize the organization's turn-out. Even left academic groups such as the Union of Radical Political Economics rescheduled their national meetings to Washington DC to promote participation in the march. The general view of Marxists and left peace activists was expressed by *Frontline* writer Frances M. Beal, who noted that the call for 'Jobs, Peace and Freedom' was politically 'more advanced than that of other recent efforts to unite civil rights, labour, liberal and progressive forces in common activity, such as the AFL-CIO-initiated Solidarity Day or the June 12 [1982] peace demonstration.' Perhaps even more importantly, 'activists from around the country' understood that 'if the mobilization is small' it could demonstrate 'the weakness of the broader Black liberation and antiracist movement . . .'[101]

Many Black and Latino nationalists, reformist and revolutionary alike, tended to view the march through the historical prism of 1963, and were initially reluctant to participate in the mobilization. Eventually, most of the independent Marxists, Third World solidarity groups and radical nationalists found the march worthy of support. The Coalition of Latin American Trade Unionists joined with the National Congress for Puerto Rican Rights to build a Puerto Rican contingent. Diana Caballero-Perez, the National Congress's chairwoman, criticized Lowery and King for being 'reluctant to grant Latinos a genuine voice and presence in August 27 activities', but still insisted that the march was a positive means of building Black-Latino unity. New York Black political activist Muntu Matsimela condemned the march as an attempt 'by the traditional Black petty-bourgeois leadership . . . to try to rustle to some degree some concessions from the Democratic Party'. Nevertheless, Matsimela agreed that 'as long as our people see an issue

that's important enough to bring them out, we have a responsibility as revolutionaries to merge ourselves into that mass
dynamic . . .'.[102] The example of Amiri Baraka (Le Roi Jones) is
also illuminating. Twenty years before, he had dismissed the 1963
March as 'a night-club act, and a "moral victory" for the middle
classes, with marines and plain-clothes men on the scene just to
make sure the audience liked the show they were going to put on'.[103]

Now, as a Marxist, Baraka viewed things somewhat differently.
'The August 27 March should be as significant as its predecessor',
he predicted in early August. It was true that the mobilization was
led by 'the Black bourgeoisie and petty bourgeosie'. However, the
focus of the march was 'around the continuing struggle of the
African-American Nation and people for democracy', as well as
around the struggles of women, other national minorities and 'the
whole multinational working class against exploitation and the use
of their resources to bully most of the world . . .', Baraka argued
that the mobilization was progressive in part because 'when the
Black masses move forward in any sharp and forceful manner, the
whole of society must feel the impact.'[104] Bob Brown of the All-
African People's Revolutionary Party, a Pan-Africanist formation
founded by Carmichael, was critical of the march leadership's
'attempt to revive the civil rights agenda of the 1960s with its
legislative solutions'. Nevertheless, like Baraka and Matsimela,
Brown was supportive of the effort, and A-APRP members made
plans to attend the march.[105]

There was one significant problem that the march coordinators
could not control. By mid morning on the twenty-seventh, the
temperature was just below 90 degrees, and by early afternoon the
high exceeded 95 degrees with about 70 per cent humidity — in
short, it was a hazy, hot and uncomfortable atmosphere. About six
hundred people were treated for heat exhaustion during the eleven-
hour-long demonstration, and over one hundred were hospitalized
for minor injuries. There were also the typical scheduling problems
that generally plague any large demonstration. Most chartered
buses were timed to arrive before 9.00 a.m., but only 314 had come
by 10.00. Many of the twenty-eight feeder marches from various
neighbourhoods in the district, which were supposed to move out at
8.00 a.m. for the Mall, were late.[106] Huge lines of people often had
to wait for what seemed an eternity to get sodas and other cool
drinks from vendors. Despite these and other normal setbacks, the
march was very well organized. People generally did not push on
the very crowded Metrorail trains; the DC police department's 3,600

officers were out in force, but nearly all were kept at a judicious distance from the demonstration. The presence of over three hundred portable toilets throughout the Mall provided many irritable marchers with some welcome relief. City officials found accommodation for hundreds of marchers who had missed their buses home. Only twenty-four arrests were made, and most of these involved street entrepreneurs charged with operating vending stands without licences. Participants were in good spirits; here and there civil rights and anti-war veterans would bump into old comrades-in-arms they hadn't seen in years. Even the police were impressed. As Metro Police Chief Angus MacLean commented, 'This is the best crowd I've ever seen.'[107]

At least three hundred thousand people had gathered together to attend the historic occasion.[108] What had they come to experience? In a sense, the official programme listed few genuine surprises. Scheduled speakers included both the moderate and the more progressive elements of the civil rights leadership. In the former category were Andrew Young, Ralph David Abernathy, Norman Hill, Benjamin Hooks and Dorothy Height, leader of the National Council of Negro Women; in the more progressive tendency were Joseph Lowery, former CORE leader James Farmer, Jesse Jackson, and John Lewis. What set 1983 above and apart from the 1963 March, however, were three historic 'openings' to other vital currents of American social protest. First, and most controversially, was the left — Marxist-Leninist, democratic socialist, and all shades of opinion in between. With their banners, posters and other political displays, the left was an open and unambiguous current within the rally. The Communist Party and the Democratic Socialists of America appeared to be the largest organized left-wing forces present. Secondly, other large anticorporate, if not explicitly socialist forces, were represented both in the crowd and at the podium. This diverse bloc included liberal feminist speakers (Bella Abzug and Judy Goldsmith of NOW), left to centre labour leaders (UAW leader Owen Beiber, AFSCME's William Lucy, Robert White of the National Alliance of Postal and Federal Workers, and Addie Wyatt of the United Food and Commercial Workers' Union), lesbian and gay community representative Audrey Lorde, and liberal religious groups (Cora Weiss of the Riverside Church Disarmament Programme and Richard Deats, Director of the Fellowship of Reconciliation). Some of these anti-Reagan and progressive forces had, as in the case of the gay and lesbian constituencies, been almost non-existent on the political landscape twenty years before.

Others, such as the unions, were being pushed to the left by the crude and criminal domestic policies of Reaganism. Two decades before some of these leaders would have been 'Cold War Liberals'; now they stood to applaud Reuben Zamora, a representative of the El Salvador Revolutionary Democratic Front, and anti-apartheid activist Alan Bosak.

The third 'opening' was the potential establishment of the basis for programmatic unity between the 'historic' currents of Black protest, integration and Black nationalism. Few nationalists possessed the charisma and fiery credentials of Louis Farrakhan, leader of the Nation of Islam. Yet Farrakhan was scheduled to speak, and delivered before a thoroughly integrated crowd (almost one third of the demonstrators were white) an articulate message of multiracial political unity. The image of this representative of Elijah Muhammad — whose organization had repeatedly attacked Martin Luther King for turning 'potential freedom-fighting Negroes into contented, docile slaves' — now standing beside Coretta King, Lowery and Hooks in a popular front, could hardly escape the notice of many movement veterans.[109] To a degree, given the noticeable presence of a number of revolutionary Black nationalist forces within the rally, the march symbolized the historic unity of the trajectories of Malcolm and Martin, cut short by their assassinations. Many felt that had these two men still been alive they would have been arm in arm at the podium on this day.

Most of the speeches were spirited but lacking in theoretical clarity. Speakers were warned that they would have only five minutes at the mike before the sound system was shut off. Typical of most of the addresses was the statement by Hooks. 'We are not here to live in the past and leave here simply singing that we shall overcome. We are here because we are committed to the elimination of Reaganism from the face of the earth', Hooks shouted. 'Reagan no more in 1984.' The NAACP leader described Reaganism as a 'virus of elitism cloaked in garments of fiscal austerity, and wrapped in trappings of patriotism'. The only cure for the virus was to meet it 'at the ballot box and cut it off'. What was interesting about the speech was what it did *not* say. Hooks did not dwell on the 'peace' component of the march's slogan, nor did he sketch a programme for uniting these broad social forces beyond the 1984 presidential election. Mrs King's speech was a disappointment. Gratified by the number of forces that had shown up, she basically gave a disjointed discourse in moral persuasion. 'We've made great progress since Martin Luther King Jr defined that struggle in the poetry of his dream . . . Let us go back to the Southland,' she declared, 'back to the Pacific, back to the prairies, back to New England, back to the thousands of cities and towns and farming communities we represent today. Let us resume that ministry . . . as servants of the poor and the dispossessed reaching out to the needy . . .'.[110]

There were some rhetorical exceptions, to be sure. Jesse Jackson's well-timed if somewhat hoarse speech brought thousands to their feet chanting 'Run, Jesse, Run!' — in obvious reference to his possible presidential bid. The speech combined a recognition that a new historic bloc of national minorities, women, and other suppressed sectors could be forged, with a militantly reformist faith in the decisive role of the bourgeois democratic electoral apparatus to transform society:

> We need not explode through riots, nor implode through drugs. We can have change through elections and not bloody revolution . . . We must now move as a nation from racial battleground to economic common ground. In 1980 Reagan won with a reverse coalition of the rich and the unregistered . . . Reagan won in Massachusetts by 2,500 votes. There were 64,000 unregistered Blacks . . . He won Mississippi by 11,000 votes. There were 153,000 unregistered Blacks . . . Black Americans, Hispanics, women, change your mind. Our day has come . . . We will rise never to fall again. From slaveship to championship, march on! From the out-house to the state-house to the court-house to the White House, we will march on.[111]

Other than the talk by Randall Forsberg, a leader of the Nuclear Freeze campaign, one of the few addresses that explicitly linked the march to global concerns of war and peace was made by Black actor Harry Belafonte. In a forceful appeal for world unity against racism and war, Belafonte declared:

> There are those who would have history believe that our presence here today is either the result of some massive communist conspiracy or that we represent malcontents who are perpetually dissatisfied in the face of progress and the supposed great strides being achieved by the vast majority of people all over this world who have watched the great dreams turn into a twilight zone . . . For the Black family of this nation, it has been more than 20 years. It has been 364 years. Racial injustice is still our crippling burden and America's shame.[112]

What did 27 August accomplish? From the beginning, key organizers emphasized their intention to create a permanent antiracist, anticorporate popular front. 'The aim and objective is that many coalitions will remain in place after the march, particularly at the local level', declared Carol Page, a staff member of the national office. 'The coalitions being built mark a watershed in terms of the number of progressive groups working for social change in this country who have come together.'[113] Yet there were many difficulties in the implementation of such a strategy. Each constituency had its own set of priorities, a host of fractious organizations, and a desire to project this new 'Coalition of Conscience' in its own image. Cultural and ideological differences of opinion nearly broke the Coalition several times. On 25 July, for example, Rev. Herbert Daughtry sent a letter to Fauntroy expressing his 'profound disappointment with the treatment' of the National Black United Front by the March Committee. On two separate occasions Fauntroy had 'brought delegations to New York, [but] calls have been placed to your office with no response from you.' Daughtry warned Fauntroy that he had 'excluded from the national leadership structure any organization that represents the masses of progressive Pan-Africanist people. This exclusion encompasses the enormous number of unemployed, mostly youthful, angry brothers and sisters and raises questions about the legitimacy of the entire programme.' As a result of Fauntroy's actions, the NBUF's national convention voted to hold 'in abeyance the endorsement of the march'.[114] Others angered by Fauntroy's political behaviour included lesbian and gay men's groups. The coordinators had decided just before the march that no lesbian or gay speakers would be permitted, stating privately that 'a gay speaker might give the appearance of advocating the gay life-style, which some members of the coalition would find objectionable.' According to one source, Fauntroy contemptuously dismissed homosexuals' demands, equating them with the call for 'penguins' rights'! On 24 August, outraged gay and lesbian activists held a peaceful two-and-a-half-hour sit-in in Fauntroy's office. Four homosexuals were arrested and charged with unlawful entry. At the last minute, room for a lesbian spokeswoman was made on Saturday's agenda.[115] It is difficult to build principled unity when homophobia and a distinct reluctance to deal openly with revolutionary Black nationalists dictates petty-bourgeois Black political practice.

For all its shortcomings, however, the march proved to be a qualitative advance on the 1963 effort, and attained a level of grassroots mobilization on a par with Randolph's earlier campaign. The abortive 1941 effort had dramatically raised the political consciousness of millions of Afro-American people, and created the social space for the creation of the CORE and a number of smaller political formations in the battle against Jim Crow. The 1963 march had represented the high point of the desegregation movement, to be followed by the radicalization of its most militant elements several years later. The 1983 mobilization, in retrospect, made the Jackson presidential campaign inevitable. It mobilized thousands of Blacks to register, and directly contributed towards successful Black mayoral candidacies, such as the 1983 triumph of Wilson Goode in Philadelphia. It also brought together thousands of white, Latino and Black trade unionists, many of whom for the first time recognized that the struggle for civil rights was in the material interest of all workers.

But a basic tactical problem in all three of these antiracist demonstrations was their domination by the progressive petty bourgeoisie. The full potential of militancy was checked, because each march represented a type of 'orchestrated spontaneity': orchestration of the Black liberal petty bourgeoisie, combined with some of the worst features of spontaneous workers' protests — the lack of a coherent radical programme, the dependence on established bourgeois political parties or the capitalist state to resolve their socio-economic problems, and so on. In each mobilization, the leaders exhibited a certain amount of *mauvaise foi*: Randolph may have never actually intended the 1941 March to take place; in both 1963 and 1983 'leaders' who had denigrated the mobilization effort were permitted to appear, jumping before the public limelight at the last possible minute to perform before a mass audience. Yet the ability of the liberal Black petty bourgeoisie to manage such staged demonstrations has declined over the decades. Randolph could call off the 1941 March at a moment's notice; Wilkins in 1963 could not. Wilkins could force the programmatic thrust of the 1963 March to the right; but in 1983, Rustin failed to accomplish this service for the bourgeoisie. Each democratic mobilization manifested a more complex programmatic set of public-policy objectives to attack racial inequality. But only in 1983 did a substantial number of march organizers realize that the racial division of labour in a capitalist political economy created the material foundations for US racism — and that genuine racial equality could not be completely achieved unless Blacks and all workers transformed the capitalist mode of production. The 1983 March may prove to represent a turning-point in the history of civil rights demonstrations. If a fourth March on Washington — when it occurs — completes the theoretical transition, and declares that the fight for racial equality is the fight against monopoly capitalism, the political aftermath of that mobilization will be radically different.

3

Black Politicians and Bourgeois Democracy

For some time now it has been apparent that the traditional leadership of the American Negro community — a leadership which has been largely middle-class in origin and orientation — is in danger of losing its claim to speak for the masses of Negroes. This group is being challenged by the pressure of events to produce more substantial and immediate results in the field of civil rights or renounce the position it has long held.

Julian Mayfield

I

The secular religion of the capitalist West is 'democracy'. Politicians and intellectuals, corporate executives and managers kneel before its altar and chant a familiar liturgy: the democratic idea, first fostered in Athenian society in antiquity, nurtured through the Enlightenment, and brought to full maturity in the United States and England, is the highest form of political organization developed by humankind. The democratic state, the republic, stands for human equality and human freedom. Each citizen is equal in his/her right to vote and to gain access to public decision-making. No single economic or social interest can dominate the entire state, because the rights of every individual are guaranteed in the constitution. The economic arrangements of society work in harmony with the maturation of the democratic idea. Supplicants submit before this estabished democratic dogma: 'In America the principle of the sovereignty of the people is neither barren nor concealed . . . it is recognized by customs and proclaimed by the laws; it spreads freely, and arrives without impediment at its most remote consequences.' To be sure, the high road to democracy has had many regrettable detours, slavery, high Black unemployment levels, Jim

Crow segregation and disfranchisement among them. But the general direction of democracy is profoundly egalitarian. As Alexis de Tocqueville continues, within democracies people 'are happy to relieve the grief of others when they can do so without much hurting themselves; they are not disinterested, but they are humane . . . In democracies servants are not only equal among themselves, but are, in some sort, the equals of their masters. Servants do not form a separate class, they have no habits, prejudices, or manners peculiar to themselves . . . they partake of the education, the opinions, the feelings, the virtues and the vices of their contemporaries . . .'[1]

From the terrain of Black social history, it is difficult to take such democratic dogma seriously. One is reminded of Mao's humorous criticism of those leftists who 'regard Marxism-Leninism as religious dogma' as promoting a social theory 'less useful than excrement'. At least excrement can 'fertilize the fields'.[2] Yet such is the ideological hegemony of bourgeois democracy that Black social movements within nearly all areas of the African Diaspora have attempted to increase their respective social classes' political power through participation in electoral phenomena. Within bourgeois democracies, such efforts to maximize power usually assume the form of electoral campaigns and the winning of public office. A critique of the electoral experiences of Afro-Americans must begin with a precise definition of the democratic state, its governing ideology, the composition and function of its political parties, and its relationship to capitalism. Theoretically, our concern should focus on the inherent contradiction between the idea of human equality, which is at the foundation of Afro-Americans' political struggles, and the philosophical notions of liberalism and liberty which provide the ideological framework for the practices and policies of bourgeois democracy. Our second point of inquiry is essentially anthropological: given the structures of bourgeois democracy, what types of Black politicians have emerged to participate in the state apparatuses? Here we must include a preliminary examination of the social class origins of such women and men, their educational and vocational training, and their involvement in Black social movements prior to their seeking elective office. Can we discern broad historical patterns of Black political strategies within electoral politics and if so, how do such manoeuvres address the domination of capital over the lives of working people and national minorities? Finally, there is the problem of the theory and practice of Black electoral political leaders. What theory of social reality and change do most Black politicians propose? What is their organizational capacity to increase the power of their constituents — within the structural confines of the bourgeois democratic state?

As in chapter one, it is essential to begin by defining our terms. A 'state', as Engels understood it, is a 'product of society at a certain stage of development; it is the admission that this society has become entangled in an insoluble contradiction with itself . . .' In order for the society to manage these 'antagonisms', it becomes necessary to have a power, seemingly standing above society, that would 'alleviate the conflict and keep it within the bounds of "order"; and this power arisen out of society but placing itself above it, and alienating itself more and more from it, is the state.'[3] The political form that this 'reconciliation' of 'irreconcilable class antagonisms' takes must, of course, be a form of dictatorship, or 'rule'. As Lenin notes, 'the state is an organ of class *rule*, an organ for the *oppression* of one class by another; it is the creation of "order", which legalizes and perpetuates this oppression by moderating the conflict between the classes.'[4] The character of all states is defined by their ability to control and exploit sectors of the society: 'state power' is the 'medium' through which the most dominant class maintains, expands and secures its 'political' or 'class' power. Domination includes the maintenance of certain coercive apparatuses, 'not merely of armed men,' Engels writes, 'but also of material adjuncts, prisons, and institutions of coercion of all kinds . . .'[5] But no state could survive on brute force alone. The state must, if it is to dominate classes, seek hegemony, an attempt to 'conform civil society to the economic structure', in the words of Gramsci. It must 'raise the great mass of the population to a particular cultural and moral level, a level that corresponds to the needs of the productive forces for development, and hence to the interests of the ruling class. The school as a positive educative function, and the courts as a repressive and negative educative function, are the most important State activities in this sense . . .'[6] The dominant or hegemonic ideology within the social formation must legitimate the existing state power and the political power relations between the classes.

All states are transitory, in that the social forces that culminated in their creation inevitably sow the seeds of their destruction. Since class antagonisms within society cannot be resolved by state power, new subordinated classes emerge which seek to seize the state, and wield it toward their own ends. 'At a certain point in their historical lives, social classes become detached from their traditional parties', notes Gramsci. The established powers are 'no longer recognized by their class as its expression. When such crises occur, the immediate situation becomes delicate and dangerous, because the field is open for violent solutions . . .' This 'crisis of authority' is in essence 'the crisis of hegemony, or general crisis of the State', because the old order now lacks legitimacy. As the 'great masses have become detached from their traditional ideologies, and no longer believe what they used to believe previously', the historical stage is set for a new class to destroy the old regime, and to construct for itself the particular modes of state power.[7] Thus every class in the state has 'class power', whose full potential may or may not be realized in part as 'state power'. As Miliband suggests, 'state power is the main and ultimate — but not the only — means whereby class power is assured and maintained.'[8] Thus a powerful class may lose state power, but, by virtue of its previous material and social advantages, maintain itself as a *political* power. It may even retake the state at some later point.[9] But the primary political goal of all classes is the control of the state. As Cox writes, 'different political factions may represent the same political class. Political factions may come into being, disappear, or regroup', but all classes are 'preoccupied with devices for controlling the state . . . The ideal of the attacking political class is neither utopian nor merely conflictive; it involves a rational plan for displacing the existing government.'[10]

Democracies are merely 'a form of the state, one of its varieties', as Lenin observes. 'Consequently, it, like every state, represents, on the one hand, the organized, systemic use of force against persons; but, on the other hand, it signifies the formal recognition of equality of citizens, the equal right of all to determine the structure of, and to administer, the state.'[11] Barrington Moore comments that most bourgeois democracies have acquired other recognizable features: 'the right to vote, representation in a legislature that makes the laws and hence is more than a rubber stamp for the executive, an objective system of law that at least in theory confers no special privileges on account of birth or inherited status, security for the rights of property and the elimination of barriers inherited from the past on its use, religious toleration, freedom of speech, and the right to peaceful assembly.' Moore summarizes the bourgeois democratic impulse as 'a long and certainly incomplete struggle to do three closely related things: 1) to check arbitrary rulers, 2) to replace arbitrary rules with just and rational ones, and 3) to obtain a share for the underlying population in the making of rules.'[12]

The emergence of modern democratic states was marked by the class conflict between declining feudal aristocracies and the landed gentry on the one hand, and the rising merchant and bougeois class and its allies on the other. As Erik Olin Wright notes, 'As capitalism expanded, the absolutist state increasingly became an obstacle to capital accumulation . . . This structure of the state gradually became non-reproductive of the emerging economic relations even though it still fell within the structural limits of variation.'[13] A crisis of hegemony occurred, as the bourgeoisie and its political and cultural representatives criticized the existing power relations within their respective societies; and in the end, they successfully wrested state power from the old order. It is crucial to observe that the transition from one ruling class to another, and one state apparatus to another, did not take place without violence. The bourgeoisie had no reservations about '[destroying] the freedom of the feudal nobility so that they themselves might be free', observes Cox.[14] In the name of 'democracy', they ruthlessly executed and exiled their opponents. In the name of freedom of the press, they silenced the polemicists of the aristocracy. This point must be emphasized, because liberal democratic ideologues often falsely oppose the peaceful, consensus model of Western democracy to socialist 'totalitarianism', usually embodied by the Soviet Union. As Theda Skocpol relates, 'the French Revolution culminated in the coexistence of a centralized, bureaucratic state with a private-propertied society and market economy.' The plight of the power-less peasantry and the urban sansculottes was not measurably different after the upheaval. The greatest revolutionary of the age, Robespierre, ruthlessly crushed the more radical left, the Hebertists, to suppress the militant social protest of the poor. 'Popular assemblies and bodies that had once been direct democracies were either discouraged from meeting or co-opted as subordinate organs of the dictatorship, with their leaders in many cases becoming paid government officials.' A decade later, Napoleon was able to create the 'modern state edifice' which was 'anything but democratic or liberal'.[15] Democracy was achieved by bloodshed, not by polite conversation and passive negotiations. No ruling class yields state power willingly. 'Political classes are never convinced merely by arguments at the round table. These groups match power, not wits.'[16]

The democratic state in a capitalist social formation functions in such a manner that the general interests of the ruling class *coincide* with the basic public policies of the state apparatus. Poulantzas explains that the 'state always has a direct economic role in the reproduction of the relations of production: direct insofar as it is not limited to simple cases of repression and ideological inculcation in the economic sphere. However, this economic role is not a technical or neutral function of the state; it is always governed by political class domination.'[17] Broadly defined, the state has 'two basic and often mutually contradictory functions — *accumulation* and *legitimization*', notes James O'Connor. 'This means that the state must try to maintain or create the conditions in which profitable capital accumulation is possible. However, the state also must try to maintain or create the conditions for social harmony. A capitalist state that openly uses its coercive forces to help one class accumulate capital at the expense of other classes loses its legitimacy and hence undermines the basis of its loyalty and support. But a state that ignores the necessity of assisting the process of capital accumulation risks drying up the source of its own power, the economy's surplus production capacity and the taxes drawn from this surplus (and other forms of capital).'[18] In mature capitalist social formations, hegemony, or the quest for ideological legitimization, becomes increasingly central to the continued viability of the state. Gramsci provides his famous formulation of the problem: 'the same thing happens in the art of politics as happens in military art: war of movement increasingly becomes war of position, and it can be said that a state will win a war in so far as it prepares for it minutely and technically in peace-time. The massive structures of the modern democracies, both as state organizations and as complexes of associations in civil society, constitute for the art of politics as it were the "trenches" and the permanent fortifications of the front in the war of position: they render merely "partial" the element of movement which before used to be "the whole" of war . . .'[19] Ideological institutions are not agencies of state power; they have a *relative* autonomy. The churches, public schools, universities, civic associations and the mass media are centres of public opinion where oppositional forces may develop bases in challenging the state power and class power of the hegemonic class. But the traditional intelligentsia and bureaucracies in civil society, in 'normal' periods, dominate the public discourse, justify and rationalize the existing state power, and 'rewrite' the histories of those who exert dominant power. 'Every social group', Gramsci notes, 'creates together with itself, organically, one or more strata of intellectuals which give it homogeneity and an awareness of its own function not only in the economic but also in the social and political fields.'[20]

Most political parties in bourgeois democracies share the gener-ally conflicting anatomy of civil society. Most are in the last analysis *capitalist* parties in that they support the capitalist state's legitimacy and defend the interests of various fractions or combinations of monopoly capital. Yet they are never monolithic in their social composition, nor can they be, if they wish to preserve the hegemony of the system. 'One should stress the importance and significance which, in the modern world, political parties have in the elaboration and diffusion of conceptions of the world, because essentially what they do is work out the ethics and the politics corresponding to these conceptions and act as it were as their historical "laboratory". The parties recruit individuals out of the working mass, and the selection is made on practical and theoretical criteria at the same time.'[21] It would be incorrect to assume that in the United States the differ-ences between the Republican and the Democratic Parties are meaningless. O'Connor and Victor Perlo describe the Democratic Party as a multiclass amalgam consisting of 'the corporate liberal wing of the monopoly capitalist class'; 'organized labour, including organized labour in the construction trades'; and 'unorganized competitive-sector workers, minorities, and the poor'. The 'shift of the Black vote from the Republicans to the Democrats in the 1930s coincided with the emergence of the new, militant industrial trade unions and the allegiance of these unions to the Democratic party.'[22] The social composition of the Republican Party differs 'in significant ways. The core of the Republican Party is middle-scale and large-scale capital in the traditional industries, small business, competitive-sector and professional and managerial strata. The Republicans also are the party of the hard-core military con-tractors.'[23] Moreover, the Republicans have recruited the bulk of the arch-segregationists and southern reactionaries who a gener-ation ago were the 'Dixiecrat' wing of the Democratic Party. They have also made substantial gains among evangelical and funda-mentalist Christians, and have expanded their electoral base among conservative Catholics who oppose state-funded abortions and social welfare legislation. Since the passage of the Voting Rights Act of 1965, most Americans are technically able to vote — subject to the 'normal' restrictions of most bourgeois democracies. But the state blocks the development of rival third parties that would raise the level of class consciousness among the workers, and ruthlessly persecutes those political fractions that raise fundamental questions about the reality of capitalist state power. Thus, paradoxically, the working class is usually disfranchised in its enfranchisement.[24]

The dominant ideological foundations of Western bourgeois democracy are various forms of 'liberalism'. Liberal political thought, best represented in the US by Thomas Jefferson and the *Federalist Papers*, and in a broader context by the utilitarian Jeremy Bentham and the philosopher John Stuart Mill, did admittedly represent a qualitative advance over absolutist thought. Benjamin Barber suggests different historical models of liberal representative democracy: 'authoritative', in which the executive branch is dominant, 'order' is the dominant social value, and the government is 'centralized' and actively involved in the economic sphere; 'juridical', in which citizens' rights are emphasized, the government is centralized but limited by checks and balances, and 'arbitration and adjudication' are the dominant 'political mode'; and 'pluralist', in which 'liberty' is equated with democracy, the legislature is dominant, and the private market is virtually free from government regulations. 'No actual regimes correspond perfectly with the types,' Barber notes, 'yet most actual regimes are composite and combine features from each type.'[25] We may well criticize Barber's failure to relate these liberal representative regime 'models' to the actual productive forces and class interests that produced them, but his insight here is basic: bourgeois democracies attempt to implement 'liberalism' of different kinds. On the side of 'pluralist' democracy, we find the high priest of capitalism, Milton Friedman, who concisely defines 'liberalism' as the belief in 'freedom as the ultimate goal and the individual as the ultimate entity in the society. It supported *laissez-faire* at home as a means of reducing the role of the state in the economic affairs and thereby enlarging the role of the individual; it supported free trade abroad as a means of linking the nations of the world together peacefully and democratically. In political matters, it supported the development of representative government and of parliamentary institutions . . .' During the early twentieth century, and more specifically with the world-wide emergence of trade unionism and labour movements, a second, more 'egalitarian' definition of liberalism came into use. Friedman writes, 'it came to be associated with a readiness to rely primarily on the state rather than on private voluntary arrangements to achieve objectives regarded as desirable. The catchwords became welfare and equality rather than freedom. The nineteenth-century liberal regarded an extension of freedom as the most effective way to promote welfare and equality; the twentieth-century liberal regards welfare and equality as either prerequisites of or alternatives to freedom.'[26] Friedman and contemporary 'conservatives' are, in fact, eighteenth and nineteenth-century liberals — philosophical dogmatists who perceive political economy from the past, rather than where it has evolved today.

On the left of the liberal spectrum, in what Barber refers to as 'authoritative representative democracy', is twentieth-century liberalism — Social Democracy. One articulate representative of this current was Evan Durbin of the British Labour Party. In *The Politics of Democratic Socialism,* Durbin insisted that 'the only conceivable route to a better social order lies in the pathway of democracy and the political method of democratic government is an essential principle, not an accidental accompaniment of any just society.' For Durbin, a 'political democracy' consisted in 'three characteristic habits or institutions': 'the ability of the people to choose a government; the freedom to oppose the government of the day; [and an agreement] between the parties contending for power not to persecute each other'.[27] The second and third points cannot be reconciled in a class-divided society, it would seem, unless Durbin's parties have an a priori understanding about state power itself. Friedman, at least, is quite frank about the relative harmony of purposes between the major feuding camps of liberal thought. Both groups favour 'parliamentary institutions, representative government, civil rights, and so on'. Both 'condemn out of hand the restrictions on individuals imposed by "totalitarian socialism" in Russia.'[28] Robert Heilbroner, a 'modern' liberal critic of Freidman, agrees. 'A Marxist, I very much fear', is totally unprepared 'to cope with the "contradictions" of individualism in a society of technologically imposed large-scale organization, or with the irrationalities and terrible dangers of the modern nation state.'[29] In short, both are committed to bourgeois democracy.

How does liberal representative government function in an institutionally racist and class-divided social formation? Speaking in broad terms, one can first observe that all bourgeois democracies have been rooted in class exploitation and racial oppression, of one kind or another, since their beginnings. For example, in writing the Declaration of Independence, Thomas Jefferson attacked the King of England for waging 'cruel war against human nature itself, violating its most sacred rights of life and liberty in the persons of a distant people who never offended him, captivating and carrying them into slavery in another hemisphere'. But the Continental Congress, packed with plantation-owners, quickly deleted this passage.[30] Eleven years later at the Constitutional Convention in Philadelphia, slavery was a major issue which divided the 'Founding

Fathers'. But the spirit of compromise among this ruling class prevailed. In Article I Section 2 of the Constitution, the so-called 'three fifths compromise', Afro-American slaves were judged to be 'three fifths of all other persons' in the determination of the apportionment of 'Representatives and direct Taxes'. Article II Section 9 permitted the infamous African slave-trade to last another twenty years. And Article IV Section 2 declared that free states had to return all fugitive slaves to their owners. Historian John Hope Franklin sums up the historic democratic convention this way: 'the slave-owners won sweeping constitutional recognition of slavery . . . The fathers of the Constitution were dedicated to the proposition that "government should rest upon the dominion of property". For the southern fathers this meant slaves, just as surely as it meant commerce and industry for the northern fathers . . . America's freedom was the means of giving slavery itself a longer life than it was to have in the British empire.'[31] On the other side of the Atlantic, advocates of bourgeois democracy toppled the French aristocracy, but held similar sentiments about slavery. David B. Davis notes that Caribbean coloureds, 'encouraged by the Declaration of the Rights of Man and by the subsequent republican rhetoric, appeared before the bar of the National Assembly on October 22 1789, petitioning to be seated as West Indian representatives.' They were supported by a small group of French liberals, the *Amis des noirs*. But they 'were shouted down, outmanoeuvred', and finally rejected. 'Moreau de Saint-Méry, the distinguished jurist from Martinique who had briefly governed Paris after the fall of the Bastille, bitterly attacked the *Amis des noirs* and warned that France must either renounce its commerce and wealth, or frankly declare that the Declaration of the Rights of Man did not apply to the colonies . . . Accordingly, until 1793 the slave-trade continued to receive an official subsidy.'[32] Slavery was not abolished in the French colonies until 1848.

Thus bourgeois democracy is always *relative* and *conditional*. The ability to exercise democratic rights is relative, depending upon one's location in the class structure, and also according to categories of race and gender. It is conditional in that the state establishes elaborate methods to limit the franchise: property qualifications, residence requirements, poll taxes and the like. Lenin aptly described the democratic dictatorship of the bourgeoisie as a type of 'class democracy'. 'Bourgeois democracy, although a great historical advance in comparison with medievalism, always remains, and under capitalism is bound to remain, restricted, truncated, false and hypocritical, a paradise for the rich and a snare and deception for the exploited, for the poor.'[33] Institutional racism, the oppression of women and the exploitation of the labour force are perpetuated, despite the liberal rhetoric of equality, freedom, and democratic rights. In Brazil, as historian Carl Degler observes, 'the overwhelming majority of the Blacks are at the bottom of the political as well as the economic scale. Negroes generally cannot vote [because] 'literacy is a requirement for suffrage.' But even if the Afro-Brazilian 'should organize to seek laws and benefits for his improvement,' Degler continues, 'he lacks . . . power at the ballot box.'[34] Even if progressive Black activists from social movements are elected, they sometimes run the risk of not being allowed to serve. The Georgia state legislature provides two examples. In 1874, white Democrats expelled twenty-seven Black legislators 'who were deemed ineligible because of their race'. From the house floor, Henry McNeal Turner denounced their expulsion as being simply part of the larger race/class war then raging in the Reconstruction-Era South: 'You have all the elements of superiority on your side; you have our money and your own; you have our education and your own; you have our land and your own, too. We [are] strangers in the land of our birth . . . [However] never, so help me God, shall I be a political slave . . .'[35] Almost a century later, Julian Bond 'was denied his seat in the Georgia legislature because he had backed SNCC's [anti-Vietnam War] stand.' Bond was denounced in newspapers across the state, and noted southern liberal Lillian Smith, 'who had once supported SNCC and had spoken at its meetings', suggested that Bond and the SNCC were controlled by Communists.[36]

Bourgeois democracy in every form — classical liberal, Keynesian liberal, Social Democratic — is a 'dictatorship' of capital over labour, Blacks, most women and the poor.[37] But it is absolutely crucial to view bourgeois democracy as only *one* particular form of class dictatorship. Lenin repeatedly criticized Marxists who insisted that bourgeois revolutions were 'advantageous only to the bourgeoisie':

> And yet nothing can be more erroneous than such an idea. A bourgeois revolution is a revolution that does not depart from the framework of the bourgeois, i.e. capitalist, socio-economic system . . . In countries like Russia the working class suffers not so much from capitalism as from the insufficient development of capitalism. The working class is, therefore, most certainly interested in the broadest, freest, and most rapid development of capitalism. The removal of all the remnants of the old order

which hamper the broad, free and rapid development of capitalism is of absolute advantage to the working class . . . That is why a *bourgeois* revolution is *in the highest degree advantageous to the proletariat* . . . The more complete, determined, and consistent the bourgeois revolution, the more assured will the proletariat's struggle be against the bourgeosie and for socialism . . [And] *in a certain sense,* a bourgeois revolution is *more advantageous* to the proletariat than to the bourgeoisie . . .[38]

Every expansion of democratic rights — universal suffrage, civil rights laws, labour-union legislation and so on — is of vital and immediate importance to the working class. It is crucial to note as well that bourgeois democracy is *only one form* of capitalist dictatorship. During periods of crisis, more authoritarian forms are possible. Two types that have been historically decisive are 'Bonapartism' and 'fascism'. Bonapartism, emerging in France in the wake of the revolution of 1848, was the dictatorship of the military and fractions of the bourgeoisie, represented by Louis Bonaparte. Its social base was the politically conservative rural peasantry.[39] Fascism, a product of twentieth-century capitalism, was 'the open terrorist dictatorship of the most reactionary, most chauvinistic, most imperialist elements of finance capital'.[40] Fascism maintained part of its social base among fractions of the petty bourgeoisie and the labour movement: Mussolini had been a leader of the Italian Socialist Party before World War I; and thousands of workers, especially in northern Germany in the late 1920s, were recruited to the National Socialism of Hitler by 'left' Nazis Gregor and Otto Strasser. Yet these were the necessary 'soldiers' for fascism's war against the liberal bourgeois democratic state. Clearly in command were the most racist, reactionary and imperialist sectors of the bourgeoisie. Both of these forms of capitalist state power are *qualitatively worse* — more brutal, more restrictive — than bourgeois democracy: there is 'a *real* differrence in the manner of operation between different forms of the capitalist state', and any confusion about this difference can produce 'catastrophic consequences'.[41]

A third authoritarian, antidemocratic form of the capitalist state is apartheid. Its basic political philosophy is simple: white supremacy. Ten full years before the Nationalist Party won its first national election, it declared in its Party Congress that it 'regards the dominant position of the White race in the spirit of guardianship as of vital importance . . . It declares therefore that it must be the earnest and determined struggle of that race to preserve its racial purity, to ensure the creation of a sound relationship between it and the non-White races, and also to avoid its economic destruction.' In short, as Nationalist leader D.F. Malan declared, 'We want to make sure that South Africa remains a White man's country.'[42] Unlike European fascism, apartheid does permit whites to vote for various parties, with the obvious exception of the Communists and other extremely liberal formations. Hitler's intolerance of the Jews led to mass extermination, whereas the Nationalists' racism culminated in the creation of Bantustans and the vicious suppression of the ANC. Conversely, there are some clear similarities between the Third Reich and the apartheid regime. Like the 'left-wing' Nazis, some early Nationalists applauded Bolshevism 'in their unceasing campaign against the British' in the early 1920s.[43] Brian Bunting notes that 'Jews had belonged to and played a prominent part in the Nationalist Party during the twenties, some of them holding official positions.' But Malan, as Minister of the Interior, pushed for a reduction in European Jewish immigration in May 1930. Years before he became Nationalist Prime Minister, H.F. Verwoerd called for a 'quota system for Jews in all occupations' in South Africa. Most of the South African sympathizers of Hitler's regime joined Malan's Nationalist Party in the 1940s, and many members of the explicitly fascist Greyshirts, the *Boerenasie* and the New Order cooperated with or became members of the Nationalists.[44] And again like fascism, apartheid serves the direct interests of capital. 'Apartheid is primarily an attempt to restructure the distribution of African labour for more effective exploitation and to cope with the often conflicting demands of the agricultural and mining industries and white workers', writes Magubane. To maintain the ruthless process of African labour-exploitation, apartheid must stimulate 'action towards a political state bordering on fascism. It makes those who believe in it both escapists and storm troopers.'[45]

But a caveat is also necessary. As illustrated previously, any bourgeois democracy may treat social fractions intolerably: anti-Semitism has long persisted in England, France and the US. In rigidly racist societies, such as in the American South particularly during Jim Crow, the legal, social and economic treatment of Blacks frequently approximated the material and social conditions of Africans under apartheid. What we are observing here are degrees or variations of capitalist and racist rule, *vis-à-vis* Africans and people of African descent, which have the explicit purpose of denying Blacks any genuine power. In a racist social formation, in other words, the rules of liberal bourgeois democracy may be extended *to whites only,* while Blacks and other national minorities are circumscribed by structures that differ not at all from apartheid or fascism. If *really* pressed, the liberal bourgeoisie will shed its ideals, its great liberal expressions of humanism, and will crush Black and proletarian social movements with every means at its disposal. In the wake of the 1973 Chilean coup, Miliband commented on 'the savagery of the repression unleashed' by the military junta. 'Had a left-wing government shown one tenth of the junta's ruthlessness, screaming headlines across the whole "civilized" world would have denounced it day in day out. As it is, the matter was quickly passed over and hardly a pip squeaked when a British Government rushed in, eleven days after the coup, to recognize the junta. But then so did most other freedom-loving Western governments.'[46] Historian Eric Hobsbawn reminds us, 'the left has generally underestimated the fear and hatred of the right, the ease with which well-dressed men and women acquire a taste for blood.'[47]

The singular strength of bourgeois democracy lies in the fact that it masks its terror so well for so many millions of citizens. Human freedom under liberal democracies is defined strictly as 'political freedom' within the confines of the capitalist state. The right to select candidates in caucuses or in primary elections, the right of any citizen to 'run for office', the right to choose between representatives of different parties in general elections, the right to petition one's representatives and the ability to recall one's officials, are seen as the ultimate expression of personal choice and free will. Yet at its roots, such freedom is actually the 'freedom of the market and of exploitation . . . the freedom of the few as over against freedom of the masses', as Cox asserts. 'Capitalism constricts the freedom of the people, so that they are more or less impotent to act in accordance with their own welfare. The people are not free when a relative few masters of industry could deny them the control of their resources. Under capitalist freedom the people may not eat or shelter themselves unless, in the production of food and shelter, some individual makes a profit.'[48] In electoral politics the identical logic applies. 'An abstract or formal posing of the problem of equality in general and national equality in particular is in the very nature of bourgeois democracy. Under the guise of the equality of the individual in general, bourgeois democracy proclaims the formal or legal equality of the property-owner and the proletarian, the exploiter and the exploited.'[49] But an examination of this 'formal equality' rveals the dynamics of the market. Workers and the poor do not generally possess adequate personal funds to 'run' for elective office; if they do so, they have few resources with which to 'advertise' their candidacies and their programme in the capitalist-owned press. To be 'credible' as candidates, they must run within one of the established capitalist parties — at least in the United States — and attempt to push their own class agenda or 'class power' within multiclass formations dominated by fractions of monopoly capital. If they are elected, but go beyond the consensus boundaries of 'accepted' legislative behaviour by articulating the interests of oppressed classes, they may be disciplined: corporate capital may aggressively finance candidates against them in either the subsequent primary or the general elections; they may be impeached and expelled from office; they may be charged by grand juries with imaginary crimes; and in rare instances, they may be assassinated, either by agents of the state, or by right-wing vigilante groups which function as a paralegal arm of the most chauvinist and reactionary fractions of monopoly capital in almost every western democracy.

Parliamentary democracies survive, to a great degree, because among vast numbers of workers, national minorities and the unemployed, they retain their 'legitimacy'. This particular mode of bourgeois rule, more than any other that history has evolved, has the greatest viability in preserving the dictatorship of capital; many leftists often forget this. As Lenin observed, 'Parliamentarianism [may be] "politically obsolete" . . . but we must *not* regard what is obsolete to *us* as something obsolete *to a class, to the masses* . . . [One] must *soberly* follow the *actual* state of the class consciousness and preparedness of the entire class (not only of its communist vanguard), and of all the *working people* (not only of their advanced elements) . . . Parliamentarianism . . . has *not yet* politically outlived itself, [and] participation in parliamentary elections and in the struggle on the parliamentary rostrum is *obligatory* on the party of the revolutionary proletariat . . .'[50] However, there are fundamental and structural limits to what bourgeois democratic states can and cannot provide for the majority of society. Every basic expansion of democratic rights creates a reaction within the ruling class. This reaction is manifested, in part, in the blatant hypocrisy of the political establishment *vis-à-vis* the actual condition and the political demands of the social majority. 'Hypocrisy is elemental to democracy', Cox charges, because there is a permanent contradiction separating the public rhetoric 'that every individual in the system is in fact equally free to achieve' and the cruel material reality of 'bourgeois society'.[51] A more advanced form of democracy, a democratic state ruled by the majority, is impossible

to achieve within the existing structure. 'Modern democracy, therefore, is antagonistic to capitalism; the greater the development of
democracy, the greater the limitations upon capitalist freedom and
the stronger the proletariat.'[52] Basic human rights that the majority
desire — universal free education from primary to postgraduate
level, free public medical care, full employment, low-cost or free
public housing for all, expanded social services for infants, children
and the elderly, the abolition of race and gender discrimination in
all aspects of civil and economic relations — can never be granted
in their entirety, because of the demands of monopoly capital upon
the state. Modern social democracy or egalitarian liberalism can
make notable advances along these lines, when contrasted with the
Draconian public measures of a Reagan or Thatcher. But even its
left wing cannot live up to its own rhetoric. As Marx stated in March
1850, 'the democratic petty bourgeois, far from wanting to transform the whole society . . . aspire only to a change in social conditions that will make the existing society as tolerable and as comfortable for themselves as possible . . . [they] want better wages
and security for the workers, and hope to achieve this by an extension of state employment and welfare measures; in short, they hope
to bribe the workers with a more or less disguised form of alms and
to break their revolutionary strength by temporarily rendering their
situation tolerable.'[53]

In every bourgeois democratic state there lurks a fear, sometimes
hidden to be sure, but nevertheless a recurring nightmare for the
ruling class. This suppressed fear draws its energy from the class
power of the working class, Blacks and other oppressed social
fractions of society. And this fear has been given a name: *equality*.
The capitalists and their bureaucratic and academic epigones
clearly understand what many workers do not: real democracy
means the abolition of classes. 'Democracy means equality', Lenin
commented. 'The great significance of the proletariat's struggle for
equality and of equality as a slogan will be clear if we correctly
interpret it as meaning the abolition of *classes*.'[54] Comprehending
the dangers of equality, the ruling class in liberal democracies
focuses on the *individual's* civil liberties. As Jane J. Mansbridge
describes the process, citizens in a democracy 'count each individual's interests equally, weighing them up, and choosing the
policy that accumulates the most weight (majority rule). The ideal
of equality . . . is quantitative, part of the weighing process, and
mandates that in a decision each individual's interests have equal
weight. When interests conflict, a secret ballot minimizes the cost to

individuals of pursuing their interests.' As the ideal appears in institutional form, the 'combination of electoral representation, majority rule, and one citizen one vote' is perceived as the only legitimate definition of 'democracy'.[55] The working embodiment of this ideal is Parliament for the British; the Congress, Supreme Court and the executive branch of government for Americans. For Mansbridge, there are some problems with this rather formal definition of equality. 'It replaces common interest with self-interest, the dignity of equal status with the baser motives of self-protection, and the communal moments of a face-to-face council with the isolation of a voting machine.'[56] In theory, the state is the neutral arbitrator of competing interests. The radical separation of private from public concerns, and the ideological emphasis on the near-sanctity of the individual, connote the reinforcement of individual liberty and personal choice without undue constraints imposed by the state. If farmers, or dentists, or multinational corporate executives have *individual* grievances, they all have an 'equal' vote at election time. The oppressed classes become convinced that their inputs, added together, really can direct the public policies of the state. And, within limits, in bourgeois democracies this is absolutely true. But the limits are set by capital *before* the elections take place, every time. The entire procedure feeds the illusion of equality, the illusion that the majority in bourgeois democracies actually rules, while in reality the dictatorship of capital continues.

You don't have to be a Marxist to recognize the inadequacies of this system, its preservation of the individualistic liberty (of capital to exploit) combined with the equal right to choose (whomever will exploit us). Black sociologist Charles S. Johnson was hardly a radical. But in 1943 he suggested that the basic and unresolved 'contradiction of democracy' was its dual commitment to both liberty and equality. 'Liberty is an individualistic notion which gained ascendancy when modern society superseded feudalism. Equality is something else; it is a notion, however, that is implicit in the concept of socialization — socialization of medicine, socialization of industry . . . [Socialization] seems to be a principle at once ethically sound and politically effective . . .' But within the social formation of monopoly capitalist production and institutional racism, how are these principles manifested in existing public policies? Johnson argued that racism is a type of racist's egalitarianism: as it were, a commitment to exclude the Negro from power in order to protect the limited expansion of equal rights to others:

From the beginning of our history two fundamental principles have been active in shaping American initiative, and racialism. In a virgin country with an unlimited frontier and vast natural resources our capitalistic economy, with its emphasis upon free competition and exploitation of both men and resources, seemed the most efficient and quickest method of developing the country. With the closing of the frontier and the "settling down" of the world, it became evident that unrestrained competition leads to excesses that have seemed to benefit a few but have worked hardships on vast numbers. In the logic of this system, freedom of opportunity meant eventually the freedom of the strong to survive at the expense of the weak. In the end the free play of individual and economic forces has come near to destroying the economic and political system it created, along with the individual freedom which it was designed to ensure.

Johnson stated that the evolution of capitalistic liberty, or 'free competition', was 'closely linked' with the systemic oppression of Blacks. 'The effects of the unrestrained operation of the principle of racialism are conceivably as dangerous to American society as the unrestricted play of free competition in the economic sphere.'[57] The implications of Johnson's assertions are fairly clear: racism as we know it cannot be uprooted within a political economy committed to 'unrestricted' and irresponsible capitalism. Moreover, the state apparatuses defined as democracy, always committed more to 'liberty' than to genuine equality, must within a biracial society tend towards institutional racism.

The larger point to be made is that this contradiction between the capitalist's individual right to exploit and the oppressed majority's desire for social equality can be balanced for only so long. Eventually, the question of equality must be resolved one way or another. A random reading from the scriptures of bourgeois democracy's champion, Tocqueville, is quite illuminating. 'In ages of equality every man naturally stands alone; he has no hereditary friends whose cooperation he may demand; he is easily got rid of, and he is trampled on with impunity . . . Equality', Tocqueville continued, 'sets men apart and weakens them . . . Private rights and interests are in constant danger if the judicial power does not grow more extensive and stronger to keep pace with the growing equality of conditions. Equality awakens in men several propensities extremely dangerous to freedom . . . [such as the tendency] to despise and undervalue the rights of private persons.'[58] The tension within bourgeois democracy between the larger social welfare — in essence, democracy as class equality — and the individual rights of 'private persons' who legally own the means of production increases over time. A perceptive, non-Marxist critic of capitalism, Josheph Schumpeter, suggested over forty years ago that 'there is inherent in the capitalist system a tendency towards self-destruction', and that sooner or later, liberal democracy and capitalism would come to a parting of the ways. Democracy cannot promise equality endlessly to all, if the society is to remain divided by classes.[59]

II

Electoral politics in the African Diaspora can be classified into three historical experiences. The first is found in the US, where a substantial social fraction of African descent has for over a century attempted to increase its power through the bourgeois democratic state. The second and third examples, which will be discussed in detail in Volume 2, are nationalist movements that assume an electoral party form within capitalist-colonial regimes, and Black electoral politics within post-colonial, semi-autonomous states that adhere to the Westminster model of parliamentary government. Focusing solely on the US, one may also discern three, or perhaps four, basic periods of Black electoral politics. The first coincided with the end of the American Civil War, the emancipation of the slaves, and the emergence of Black politicians throughout the states of the old Confederacy. Although the movement for biracial democracy was severely crippled by the Compromise of 1877 and the Supreme Court's 1883 repeal of the Civil Rights Act of 1875, twenty-two Afro-Americans secured election to the US Congress between 1869 and 1901. The first Reconstruction period was effectively ended by a combination of several factors, political and economic: the great economic depression of the 1890s; the collapse of the Populist Party and development of 'lily-white' Republicanism which excluded Black leaders; the disfranchisement of virtually all Afro-Americans and many poor whites through state constitutional conventions (beginning in Mississippi in 1890), and the use of poll taxes, literacy and property restrictions to determine voter eligibility; and the widespread use of lynching and racist violence to terrorize Black communities. The second period of Black electoral politics, which developed during the regime of Jim Crow segregation, may be subdivided by the Great Depression of the 1930s. During the initial phase of the Jim Crow era, Blacks were generally denied access to elective office. Thus Black politicians formed 'clientage' relationships, usually with the Republican Party on the national left, but occasionally with conservative Democrats in major cities (such as Cincinnati and Kansas City) and in some southern states. Black representation in the federal government was restricted to a few appointive positions. The second phase of the Jim Crow period, lasting up to the early 1960s, was characterized by the rapid growth of the Black urban working class; the creation of new civil rights formations (the CORE, SCLC, SNCC, and so on) and the increasing influence of the NAACP and other petty-bourgeois Black organizations upon the domestic policies of the federal government; and the development of a new clientage relationship between the Black electorate's representatives and the Democratic Party of Roosevelt. The third and shortest period of Black electoral politics coincides with the Second Reconstruction and the achievement of legal desegregation, from the early 1960s until the end of the Carter administration. This period of liberal reform was terminated, in part, by the economic recessions of 1974-75, 1980 and 1982-83; the ideological and programmatic repudiation of Cold War liberalism, characterized by both the Carter and the Reagan administrations; and the rise of an ultra-conservative mass base among millions of white Americans in support of anticommunism abroad and racial inequality at home. A possible fourth period, emerging in the 1980s, is characterized by Blacks' increasingly independent attitudes towards both of the major capitalist parties — exemplified by both the Harold Washington mayoral campaign in Chicago in 1982-1983 and the Jesse Jackson presidential campaign in 1984.

The initial period of Black electoral politics marked the first time in American history that the bourgeois democratic system had made any concession to even a remote possibility that Blacks might be able to govern themselves and others. This was not done out of some abstract commitment to humanism. With the prominent exception of a few radical abolitionists and white Republican leaders, most white politicians shared the racial convictions of President Andrew Johnson. 'This is a country for white men,' the president declared after the war, 'and by G-d, so long as I am President, it shall be a government for white men . . . [Blacks] have shown less capacity for government than any other race of people.'[60] Congressional Republicans who impeached Johnson, imposed federal troops upon the South, and extended suffrage to Black adult males were motivated not by antiracist ideals but by other considerations. First, the Republican Party was still a minority party. Lincoln had been elected to the presidency in a unique four-way race and had obtained only 39 per cent of the popular white male vote. Even with running a war hero, Ulysses S. Grant, as their presidential candidate in 1868, the Republicans received only 52.7 per cent of the popular vote. Elementary arithmetic showed that the addition to the electorate of Afro-Americans — who comprised substantial minorities throughout the South (and majorities in Mississippi and South Carolina) — would permit the Republican Party to control the federal government. Even more decisive were the interests of northern industrial capitalists and financiers, who had a stake in the South's future development. The small southern aristocracy had been crushed beneath the Union army — only 1,733 white families had owned more than a hundred slaves each before the war. Yet the best guarantee of cheap labour and cheap land, the immediate objectives of northern capital, was control over the region's electoral political apparatus. If allowing Black males the right to vote promoted their regional economic interests the capitalists had few qualms about breaking the colour line.

The vast majority of Afro-Americans who struggled and survived the ordeal of chattel slavery were an illiterate, largely propertyless people. Their courage and determination to exercise their newly won freedom was great, yet their allies were few. Viewed from the perspective of social class, those members of the Black social fraction who were best prepared to exercise leadership within the bourgeois democratic apparatus were a very small stratum of Black artisans, entrepreneurs, intellectuals, former abolitionists and small landholders. Even before the Civil War, there were a number of southern Blacks who had access to property and considerable privileges. A group of over eight hundred free Blacks in New Orleans possessed property and private businesses worth nearly $2.5 million in 1836, plus titles to a total of 620 slaves. By 1860, New Orleans's free Creole and Black elites were worth over $9 million. North Carolina free Blacks owned about one million dollars' worth of personal property and real estate in 1860, and Virginia's free Blacks controlled 60,000 acres of farm property. The majority of the southern free Black community, about 258,000 people in 1860, existed as labourers, porters, domestics or small farmers — but clearly a small elite of educated, skilled workmen, planters and professionals had been created. It was this small southern elite, along with a number of Black northern abolitionists who had come to the South with the Union army and a somewhat smaller group of ex-slaves, that composed the first generation of Afro-American public officials.[61]

Most of the major Black public leaders during the first Reconstruction period were members of this Negro elite, or, if born in slavery, rapidly rose to accumulate capital and social status within the Black petty bourgeoisie. Frederick Douglass, for example, is usually thought of as an abolitionist orator and crusading editor of the *North Star*. But despite his social origins as a slave, by the age of sixty Douglass had little in common economically or socially with those whose interests he advocated. After 1870, he was appointed to a series of government posts: Secretary to the Santo Domingo Commission (1871); Marshal of the District of Columbia (1877); Recorder of Deeds for the District of Columbia (1881); US Minister to Haiti (1889). Douglass's income was supplemented by rather high lecture fees — $125 per speech until 1888, and $150 until his death in 1895. He served briefly as president of the Freedman's Bank, was the first president of the Industrial Building and Savings Company, and was one of the major stockholders in the Black-owned and directed Alpha Life Insurance Company. By the 1880s Douglass owned houses in Rochester, New York and Baltimore, and held real estate in the District of Columbia. His Washington DC home, 'Cedar Hill', was a twenty-room mansion set on a fifteen-acre estate. Douglass's biographer Benjamin Quarles suggests that the Black leader was 'a wealthy man by Negro standards. During the last years of his life, his total resources probably amounted to $100,000.'[62] Douglass's accumulation of wealth was exceeded by that of Mississippi Senator Blanche K. Bruce. Born into slavery, he escaped and was able to start a small school for Blacks in Hannibal, Missouri, during the Civil War. Bruce arrived in Mississippi only in 1869, four years after the conflict, but was soon elected to the post of tax-collector. Rapidly moving up to become sheriff, then superintendent of schools, he was elected to the US Senate in 1874. Simultaneously Bruce purchased large amounts of real estate, and when he left office in 1881 had acquired a small fortune. Although the colour line prohibited Bruce from joining the ranks of the southern white bourgeosie, he had used public office to secure for himself and his family a position within the fragile Black elite. Bruce's son, Roscoe Conkling Bruce, was a graduate of Harvard University, and was later appointed assistant superintendent of Washington DC's public schools in 1907. In his later career, Bruce became a strong supporter of industrial and technical education for Negroes, and advocated the necessity for Blacks to develop strategies for 'material growth'. Having been appointed by Republican President William McKinley as Register of the Treasury and Recorder of Deeds, Bruce at his death in 1897 was worth over $200,000.[63]

Douglass and Bruce were hardly exceptional for their generation. Some of the Reconstruction era Black politicians, it is true, were self-educated and devoid of personal property. But as John Hope Franklin observes, 'What is surprising is that there were some — and no paltry number — who in 1867 were able to assume the responsibilities of citizens and leaders.' In North Carolina the Negro elite was led by such men as James H. Harris and James W. Hood. Born in North Carolina but educated in Ohio, Harris was the major Black figure at the state's 1868 constitutional convention. Harris was also a keynote speaker and convention president of the Coloured National Labour Union, formed in Washington DC in December 1869. The Reverend James Walker Hood had been educated in Pennsylvania, and became Assistant Superintendent of Public Instruction in the state.[64] Jonathan C. Gibbs, described by Du Bois as a 'born orator', was educated at Dartmouth College and had served in the North as a Presbyterian clergyman. Moving to Florida, Gibbs assumed the office of Superintendent of Public Instruction and 'virtually established the public schools of the state as an orderly system'. At this death in 1874, Gibbs was Florida's Secretary of State.[65] James T. Rapier, Congressman from Alabama in 1873-1875, had been sent to Canada by his white father before the war to receive an education. In Mississippi, Hiram Revels was selected to serve out the unexpired term of Jefferson Davis in the US Senate. Born in North Carolina and educated in Indiana, Revels became a minister in Baltimore. During the war he had organized two all-Black army regiments, and he had come to Mississippi as an official of the Freedman's Bureau.[66] These were all men of considerable talent, academic training and organizational experience — and hardly an illiterate, rural peasantry.

Let us examine the social class profile of Black officials in one state, South Carolina. This first generation of Afro-American politicians can be classified into two rather general tendencies. First there was a core of pre-war free Negroes who by their personal wealth, education or conservative social background, immediately assumed positions of leadership during Reconstruction. One prominent representative of this group was Francis L. Cardozo. Free-born of African, Native American and Jewish descent, Cardozo had been educated at the University of Glasgow and in London. Before the war he was a Presbyterian minister in New Haven, Connecticut. Before his entry into South Carolina politics, he was principal of the Avery Institute in Charleston. Cardozo was elected Secretary of State (1868-1872) and later State Treasurer (1872-1876).[67] Others in this group tended to be southern, free-born Blacks, or slave and free-born mulattos, the sons of the plantation-owners and house-servant class; and a small number of northern Blacks who had come to the state as soldiers in the Union army. In the subcategory of free Blacks and mulattos were William McKinlay, a free mulatto who had owned more than $25,000 in real estate before the Civil War; Joseph A. Sasportas, a free mulatto entrepreneur who had owned $6,700 worth of property and five slaves in 1860; free mulatto leader Robert C. De Large, who had 'earned a tidy sum while in the employ of the Confederate navy'; Richland State Representative Charles Wilder; and free Black leaders Joseph H. Rainey and Alonzo J. Ransier. Northern Blacks and mulattos aligned with this group included Dr Benjamin A. Bosemon of New York, who had served as an army surgeon; Landson S. Langley, a Vermont-born mulatto who had worked for the Freedman's Bureau; and Henry W. Purvis, the son of prominent Philadelphia abolitionist Robert Purvis. The second group, which tended to be linked more directly with the economic and political demands of rural former slaves, comprised free, northern-born Blacks with some direct involvement in abolitionist causes, a few free-born mulattos or free Blacks from the South who had vigorously resisted slavery, and some representatives of the Black field-hands and labouring classes. Some of these leaders were Robert B. Elliott, who had been educated in Edinburgh; AME minister Richard H. Cain; free mulatto Robert Smalls, a skilled artisan who had achieved considerable fame for capturing a Confederate ship and delivering it to the Union navy in 1862; and William Beverly Nash, an illiterate yet powerfully charismatic man who had once been a porter in a Columbia, South Carolina hotel. Most of these men achieved effective political power in the period 1867–1880. Some served in the US Congress — Rainey (1871–1879). De Large (1871-73), Elliott (1871-1875), Ransier (1871-73), Cain (1873-1875, 1877-1879) and Smalls (1875-1879, 1881-1887). Others held high positions in state government: Nash served with distinction as a South Carolina State Senator; Bosemon was a leader of Charleston coloured petty bourgeoisie in the state legislature.[68]

At first appearance what seemed to divide South Carolina's Reconstruction era politicians into antagonistic factions was the colour caste which distinguished mulattos and well-educated Blacks from the former field-hands. Certainly South Carolina's struggles are reminiscent of the warfare between Toussaint and the coloured generals Rigaud and Pétion. As early as 1790, Charleston's free mulattos had established a 'Brown Fellowship Society', designed to protect its members both from whites, 'the dominant race', and from 'the backward race' of slaves. Not only did the Carolina mulattos own slaves themselves, but in 1817 the Brown Fellowship Society even expelled one of its members for being involved in a slave uprising plot. During the war, Society members helped the Confederate cause by extinguishing fires started by federal artillery turned upon Charleston. As historian Thomas Holt comments, 'the ruling class was so certain of their loyalty that they were exempted from the ordinance requiring the presence of a white man in any meeting of more than six Negroes.'[69] During Reconstruction, Bosemon, De Large and McKinlay were all leaders of the Society; Wilder served as president of a similar group of free coloureds, the Friendly Union Society. These literate, affluent mulattos continued to distance themselves from the former slaves in cultural and social relations; marriage and business partners were usually selected on a skin-colour basis. McKinlay and Wilder, for instance, were both members of the board of directors of the South Carolina Bank and Trust Company in 1870. Some coloured aspirants to elective office campaigned on their caste credentials. In 1868, one mulatto candidate for the state constitutional convention boldly declared: 'I never ought to have been a slave, for my father was a gentleman . . . If ever there is a nigger government — an unmixed nigger government — established in South Carolina, I shall move.' During Rainey's successful 1870 race for Congress, his Black Republican opponent charged that Rainey 'cared nothing about the poor Blacks, looked down on them', and added that he had even 'tried to pass for white' during a recent trip. At times the Black ex-slaves protested that the mulatto elite was attempting to become the new ruling class. Senator Nash argued in 1873 that the coloureds were simply manipulating the Black electorate to benefit themselves: 'I know that my ancestors trod the burning sands of Africa, but why should men in whose veins run a great preponderance of white blood seek to specifically ally themselves with the Black man, prate of "our race", when they are simply mongrels?'[70] The colour-caste question was not confined to South Carolina politics. In Louisiana, Creole and mulatto leaders usually cooperated with Black former slaves, but most looked down upon them as illiterate and uncultured. Light-skinned, upper-class Negroes maintained their own social clubs, spent their vacations in Paris or New York, and tended to monopolize the key elective offices during Reconstruction.[71] And at the national level, despite his support for trade unionism and social reforms, Douglass also falls into this conservative-caste category. Late in life he attacked the notion of racial pride as 'mischievous', and denounced the idea that Blacks constituted 'a nation within a nation . . . There can be but one American nation, and we are Americans.' His personal decision to marry a white woman in 1884 was criticized by many Blacks, and was seen in part as an expression of his commitment to racial assimilation.[72]

Beneath this colour-caste division was in reality a struggle between representatives of antagonistic social classes. The fact of colour and the well-established privileges of a mulatto elite tended to obscure this class struggle even from its participants. In his informative study on South Carolina Black politics, Holt illustrates that the Black leaders who emerged at the state's 1868 constitution convention were hardly a 'penniless proletariat'. In 1860, the total number of free Blacks and slave or free mulattos made up less than one tenth of the state's non-white population. Yet at the 1868 convention, 44 per cent of all Black delegates had been free before the war. 14 per cent were college graduates; 44 per cent owned real estate, and within this group, about half held property valued at between $1,001 and $20,000. Vocationally, the majority of these would-be officials were lawyers, merchants, ministers, landlords, schoolteachers and tradesmen. A distinct minority were illiterate (18 per cent) or claimed to own no property (19 per cent). This social class pattern persisted throughout the Reconstruction period. As Holt notes, 'out of a total of 255 Negroes elected to state and federal offices between 1868 and 1876, approximately one in four had been free before the war, and one of every three was a mulatto. Almost one in three owned some real estate, and 46 per cent possessed some form of wealth, real or personal.'[73] Two thirds of all officials were literate, 10 per cent had attended universities, and 40 per cent were ministers, lawyers, teachers or farm owners. Only 15 per cent held no property, and out of the entire group, only nine (4 per cent) were labourers; the state's largest Black social class, the rural tenant farmers, had elevated only fifteen men (6 per cent) from its ranks to elective office. Conflicts over public policy were frequently fought out between on the one hand a mulatto and pre-war free Black professional-entrepreneurial elite, which favoured an accommodationist, pro-capitalist agenda, and on the other the less educated, poorer former slaves and their Black abolitionist allies from the North, who advocated more radical reforms.

The major issues at stake focused on voting rights, desegregation, land redistribution, and legislation protecting tenant farmers and Black labourers. All non-white Republican leaders favoured the expansion of male suffrage to Blacks, yet the accommodationists openly flirted with denying voting rights to the poor. At the 1868 convention, Langley and McKinlay urged delegates not to permit illiterates to have the ballot. Rainey even asserted: 'if a man could not raise one dollar a year poll-tax . . . they should look upon him as a pauper that has no right to vote.' Nash instantly recognized the danger of illiterate rural Blacks being disfranchised by the Negro elite. 'I believe, my friends and fellow-citizens, we are not prepared for this suffrage', he responded. 'But we can learn. Give a man tools and let him commence to use them, and in time he will learn a trade. So it is with voting. We may not understand it at the start, but in time we shall learn to do our duty.' Nash's speech, along with the support of Elliott and Cardozo, swung the majority of delegates to bury literacy and poll-tax requirements.[74] On civil rights and social relations, the majority of Black politicans in South Carolina and throughout the South 'conceded to the insistence of whites that they were a race apart; and they made little or no attempt to invade social privacies.'[75] During the convention's debate on integrated public schools, Cardozo advanced the thesis used nearly a century later by the NAACP — that 'the integration of schools might deter the growth of prejudice in future generations by encouraging children to associate before adult prejudices had been established.' Yet Cardozo refused to endorse a constitutional provision that would ban racially segregated schools. Alonzo J. Ransier, a conservative known chiefly for his 'outright timid' behaviour and failure to take 'a forthright position on any controversial issue', was the voice of Charleston's Black elite. Characteristically, he proposed a position which would later be embraced by Roy Wilkins — that the words 'race' and 'colour', had no place inside the constitution. School policies should be 'colour–blind.' Interestingly, the radicals in the convention were divided on the issue. Nash and former army chaplain Benjamin F. Randolph demanded a constitutional provision requiring integrated schools. Radicals who were inclined toward Black nationalism, such as Richard H. Cain and Robert B. Elliott, argued against racial integration.[76] Several years later, as a member of Congress, Cain again expressed his contempt for integration. 'Do you suppose I would introduce into my family a class of white men I see in this country?' Cain asked his colleagues. After surveying the floor of Congress, he added, 'No, sir.'[77]

Land redistribution across the South was the central political demand of the rural Black majority. Even before Reconstruction, some white military leaders and abolitionists within the Republican Party were urging some kind of compensation to be paid to former slaves. In July 1862, Union general Rufus Saxton had urged the War Department to allocate plantation properties to ex-slaves. General William T. Sherman's 'Order No. 15' of January 1865 seemed to be a justification for the seizure of plantations by Afro-Americans. In early 1867, Senator Charles Sumner fought unsuccessfully in Congress to secure a 'permanent policy of national aid to education and economic redress of the robbery of slavery'. In the House, Representative Thaddeus Stevens and other radicals had called for the seizure of the South's public lands and their redistribution to Afro-Americans: 'to each head of a family 40 acres; to each adult male, whether head of a family or not, 40 acres; to each widow, head of a family, 40 acres.'[78] Pressure also came from northern Black abolitionists. Douglass argued that the emancipation of Russian serfs in 1861 had been accompanied with some land tenure. Afro-American former slaves without property, by contrast, would be 'naked to their enemies . . . sent away empty-handed, without money, without a foot of land upon which to stand.'[79] From the countryside, a social movement to seize the land was already in process. Black freedmen understood with utter certainty that wage labour meant wages hardly better than none at all. Thousands of Mississippi Blacks in the Loyal Leagues took pledges not to pay more than $1.50 an acre rent, and not to work as wage labourers. Representatives of ex-slaves in Alabama called for former slave-owners 'to pay ex-slaves at least $10 a month for every month after the Emancipation Proclamation of January 1 1863, to May 20 1865.'[80]

The great failure of the first Black political elite was its unwillingness, or inability, to demand land and material compensation for the ex-slaves. In no southern state, according to John Hope Franklin, did 'any considerable number of Negroes seek to effect an economic revolution'. In Georgia, for example, Black nationalist minister Henry McNeal Turner 'did what he could to assist the whites in recovering their economic strength.' Turner obtained the passage of a bill that prevented the sale of properties whose owners had failed to pay back taxes, and another bill that 'provided for the relief of banks'.[81] In South Carolina, the story was the same. At the state constitutional convention, Joseph H. Rainey secured a resolution declaring that poor Blacks had to obtain property 'through their own private initiative'. William James Whipper, a northern Black, even dismissed the concept of government aid to the poor: 'There has already been too much holding out this idea whereby a poor man shall be a landowner without any help of his own.' The only measure of assistance to the rural peasantry adopted at the convention came from Richard H. Cain. He requested the delegation to petition the US Congress for a loan fund of one million dollars for the state to buy, divide and resell lands to Afro-Americans at reduced prices. The question of ensuring legal contracts for share-croppers and rural labour was extensively debated in the state legislature in 1868 and 1869. Nash pushed for a tough provision to safeguard workers' interests against the landlords. But under Whipper's judiciary committee, a bill was produced permitting any labourer to lose 'up to a month's wages for one day's unexcused absence'. Class interests, not race, bound a section of the rising coloured and Black petty bourgeoisie to northern capital and the defeated white aristocracy. Leaders like De Large and Langley boldly promoted a policy for 'a permanent halt to the confiscation of land and disfranchisement for political offences' of the southern white bourgeoisie. Cardozo concurred: the Black politicians had to 'demonstrate the absence of any desires for revenge on their part'.[82]

From a longer view, both tendencies of this Black and mulatto petty bourgeoisie held many interests in common. First among these was wealth: the reformers wanted to acquire it; the conservatives wanted to accumulate more. These Black politicians were reasonably honest men, when compared with their white predecessors, but most of them also comprehended that a public office was a means to greater personal wealth, the ownership of real estate, and social prestige. Richard H. Cain and Robert Smalls were among the leading radicals, men who consistently tried to represent the Black rural peasantry and workers. Cain even boasted that he had 'never [asked] for political patronage'. But after several years of public service, he found that his income from running a local newspaper and his funds from his AME congregation were not enough. In his private correspondence, Cain complained that he 'must look after something or . . . be left out in the cold.' Smalls was slightly better situated financially; he had received $1,500 for the captured Confederate ship, and had invested in real estate and several business ventures near Beaufort, South Carolina. Inspired by the construction of railroads by northern capitalists throughout the South, Cain, Smalls and a group of well-to-do Negro conservatives created the 'Enterprise Railroad', a Charleston streetcar service designed to transport goods from the harbour district. Cain became president of the company, and Smalls served on the board of directors. Their business colleagues, who quickly raised $13,000 for the venture, included William James Whipper, company vice-president, board members Joseph H. Rainey, Benjamin A. Bosemon, Thaddeus K. Sasportas (son of mulatto businessman and ex-slaveholder Joseph A. Sasportas) and Alonzo J. Ransier, company secretary. Major stockholders included the wives of Ransier and Bosemon, as well as William McKinlay. Holt observes that the rail line 'paid a handsome profit to its investors', but regrettably it threw 'the Black draymen out of work', labourers who made their wages by transporting dock cargo.[83] It was increasingly difficult for many Black radicals to take the side of the workers and peasantry, given their shifting social class status and material interests. In July 1876, the Black wage labourers in the coastal rice plantations staged a bloody uprising. Governor Daniel H. Chamberlain, fearful of a general revolt, sent Smalls to the centre of the rebellion to assess whether troops were needed to halt the resistance. Smalls reported that the workers had legitimate grievances, and that the state militia was not necessary. However, the key leaders of the strike were arrested and gaoled. Smalls's basic argument was a justification for capitalist economics: 'workers had a right to strike, but not to prevent others from working.' It was also in this spirit of labour-exploitation that many Black leaders briefly adopted a convict-leasing system, in which Black and poor white prisoners were leased to private companies in South Carolina.[84]

Overall, Du Bois's critique of the first generation of Black elected officials was probably too generous. This ascending Black elite 'was not at all clear in its economic thought. On the whole, it believed in the accumulation of wealth and the exploitation of labour as the normal method of economic development. But it also believed in the right to vote as the basis and defence of economic life', Du Bois added, and it 'wanted the Negro to have the right to work at a decent rate of wages . . .'[85] Recent historical evidence suggests that the Black elite was genuinely split over fiscal and civil rights policies, but that division did not occur because of a lack of clarity about what was at stake. Radical reformers and conservatives alike were committed to a capitalist political economy, and to their own advancement within the upper strata of the petty bourgeoisie and local bourgeoisie. The conservatives, partially for reasons of colour-caste, but more fundamentally owing to their

accumulation of wealth and property, tended to be openly accommodating to the ruling class. The radical Republicans, despite their
ideological commitment to the ex-slaves, the tenant farmers and
wage labourers, were often but not always compromised by their
own desires for social class upward mobility. What was missing from
this historical period was a political leadership that effectively
articulated the social class interests of the Black majority. Other
than Nash and Elliott, the one leader in South Carolina who could
have done this was Martin R. Delany. From 1865 to 1868 he had
been an agent for the Freedman's Bureau in the state. In this
position, he gave political lectures throughout rural districts, and in
1867 he made an extensive speaking tour across the South. Delany
encouraged Black tenant farmers and labourers to draft contracts
protecting their rights. He started a cotton press for Black farmers
which siphoned trade from white firms. Like many of his rural
supporters, Delany distrusted the mulatto-free Black elite, which
he criticized in May 1865 for playing the role of 'confidantes and
spies against the Blacks' during slavery. Like Garvey fifty years
later, Delany urged poor and working-class Blacks to create their
own leaders who were committed to racial solidarity and
nationalism. 'No people have become a great people who had not
their own leaders', Delany declared in 1870. He believed that a
Black third party was not possible, despite a Black majority in the
state. Nevertheless, he urged Blacks to demand a strict racial quota
of all state offices, and to defeat any white 'whom the coloured man
does not approve of '.[86] Given these sentiments, it is not surprising
that many Negro politicians treated Delany as a pariah. Delany, the
state's best-known and most articulate Black leader, was never
elected to public office during Reconstruction. With the election of
Wade Hampton as Democratic governor in 1876, the stage was
well-set for the white supremacist counter-revolution of the 1890s.
Delany and Cain, who in 1880 was named an AME bishop, now
concluded that biracial democracy in the US was impossible. In
creating the South Carolina Liberian Exodus Association, both
men returned to the 1850s strategy of emigration as the only realistic
solution to the race question.[87]

The case of South Carolina is instructive because it represents the
general social pattern of Black electoral politics in the US, from
Reconstruction to the present day. Most Black elected officials at
any one time belong to the same party (Republicans, pre-1940;
Democrats, post-1940); they are recruited from the Afro-American
petty bourgeoisie — lawyers, doctors, ministers, entrepreneurs,

teachers, landlords, administrators; they frequently use appointive and elective positions to improve their social class position and to accumulate capital; like their white counterparts, they tend to be ideologically pragmatic, voting not so much according to their constituents' interests or to national party dictates, as roughly according to their own perceived social class interests; they accept, generally, the legitimacy of bourgeois democracy, and approach electoral politics not so much to change the 'system' as to 'make it work' for Blacks and other allied social groups; they often advocate state intervention in the economy and society to assist Blacks (for example, in education, health, housing, jobs programmes, and so on), but stop short of circumscribing the broad prerogatives of capital over labour. The accommodationist tendency forms a clientage relationship with a national party and national (and local) capital, whereas the reformers tend to articulate the grievances of the majority of Black workers and the poor. The accommodationists perceive no connection between racism and capitalism, and glorify capital accumulation as the means for Black group advancement; the reformers tend to be much more critical of capitalism and to sympathize with the struggles of labour. Admittedly, this is an elementary sketch of a very complex and contradictory social dynamic. Most elected officials and political leaders fall into neither tendency precisely: accommodationists are sometimes reformers during phases of their public careers, and reformers may ultimately retreat into accommodationism. Looking at South Carolina again, we may note that Robert C. De Large, the affluent conservative, voted with Black radicals on crucial fiscal issues while serving as chairman of the ways and means committee in the state legislature in 1868-1869. Despite Whipper's call for poll-taxes, he usually voted with the radicals once he was elected. In the 1868 constitutional convention, radicals such as Elliott and Nash voted in favour of De Large's motion to protect the political and property rights of white southerners. Probably the most conciliatory speech by any Black representative was given by Nash, who championed the southern white man as 'the true friend of the Black man'. Anticipating Booker T. Washington, Nash proclaimed his ultimate goal as a vision of 'the white man and the Black man standing with their arms locked together, as the type of friendship and union that we desire.'[88] Even Delany, who by 1874 was politically alienated from the petty-bourgeois Republican hierarchy, ran unsuccessfully for lieutenant governor on a 'fusion ticket' with a white Democrat! Hampton rewarded Delany's 'independence' by appointing him as a trial judge in 1877. Black nationalists and integrationists alike can be accommodationists or reformers, depending on the conjuncture of political issues at a particular moment. Political and ideological inconsistency is the principal political trait of the petty bourgeoisie.

Radical Reconstruction's failure was not simply due to the ideological and political shortcomings or contradictions of the fragile Negro petty-bourgeois stratum. The possibility of biracial democracy was also forfeited by the decision of the national Republican party to jettison its Negro junior partners, a choice dictated by northern capital. Under the Grant Administration, federal expenditures in the South were miniscule. Between 1867 and 1873, the federal government had spent only $9.5 million in the former Confederate states, out of $103 million in domestic spending in all states. Out of $104 million allocated to subsidize private railroad construction, the South obtained only $4.4 million. With the Depression of 1873, hundreds of banks closed and investment capital was scarce. Despite the relative 'moderation' of Reconstruction governments — with the establishment of convict-leasing, the failure of land reform for Black farmers, region-wide low wage rates — northern capitalists with investment plans for the South concluded that the southern 'Conservatives' were more acceptable business partners.[89] When the Republican Party's presidential candidate Rutherford B. Hayes lost in 1876 to Democrat Samuel J. Tilden, a deal was struck. Hayes was given the presidency, and the Democrats were permitted narrow control of the House of Representatives. Hayes promised to obtain millions of dollars in federal subsidies through Congress to promote economic expansion, to withdraw all remaining federal troops from the South, and to give white Conservatives free control over their state governments. With the crucial support of white southern Democrats, Hayes was 'elected' president in 1877, and Reconstruction ended.[90] Black politicians witnessed this conjugal relationship between northern capital, the Republican Party and white racists in the South, but most were theoretically ill equipped to understand its dynamics. Ideologically, as members of the bourgeois democracy apparatus, they had also come to embrace nineteenth-century liberalism, Adam Smith's economics and the rule of capital over labour. The state had no responsibility to provide for the material welfare of its citizens: civil rights did not include the right not to starve, or the right to control the products of one's labour-power. Cain spoke for his social class in this manner: 'Let the laws of the country be just; that is all we ask . . . Place all citizens upon one broad platform; and if the Negro is not qualified to hoe his row in this contest of life, then let him go down.'[91]

The next two generations of Afro-American political leaders were forced to operate under the totalitarian constraints of Jim Crow. The vast majority of Blacks were disfranchised, and Black public officials nearly disappeared. The two dominant political tendencies of the Black petty bourgeoisie were represented by Booker T. Washington and Du Bois. Author of the infamous 'Atlanta Compromise' of 1895 which accepted white supremacy, and founder of the Tuskegee Institute in Alabama in 1881, Washington is frequently perceived as something of an 'Uncle Tom'. Nothing could be further from the truth. Like De Large and McKinlay before him, Washington represented the growing stratum of Black entrepreneurs, editors, lawyers and independent farmers. Accommodation for Washington was a political style, not a political philosophy. His immediate concern was to secure a pragmatic alliance between the Negro entrepreneurial elites, the white southern ruling class and the national Republican Party. His long-range goal was to create, via his National Negro Business League, racial parity within the political economy of capitalism. To ensure the success of this strategy, Washington publicly accepted racial segregation codes and political disfranchisement. Upon occasion, following the lead of his white philanthropic and capitalist benefactors, he also denounced trade unions and strikes. Many but not all of the politicians in the 'Tuskegee Machine' lacked the wealth and higher education of Charleston's mulatto elite. Many of them were businessmen or ministers without university training; quite a few were without a secondary-school level education. Typical of this latter group was Charles W. Anderson. Born in Ohio, Anderson made his way up the political bureaucracy in New York. Named to the state racing commission in 1898, he became Washington's chief Black Republican leader in the North-East. Through Washington's close clientage relationship with President Theodore Roosevelt, Anderson was named collector of internal revenue in New York (1905-1915). Other Black Republican politicians in Washington's orbit included J.C. Dancy, federal recorder of deeds, (1901–1910); R.L. Smith, founder of the Texas Farmers' Improvement Society, state representative in the Texas legislature (1894-1896) and later US Marshal for eastern Texas; H.A. Rucker, collector of internal revenue in Atlanta (1897-1910); and J.C. Napier, Nashville banker, leader of southern Black Republicanism and registrar of the US Treasury (1911-1913). Two of Washington's most effective but frequently independently minded operatives were attorney Robert H. Terrell, a Harvard graduate who served as magistrate in the District of Columbia and James Weldon Johnson, an Atlanta University graduate for whom Anderson obtained appointments to consular posts in Venezuela and Nicaragua. Also in the Tuskegeean's circle were several sons of prominent Reconstruction politicians — notably DC Schools assistant superintendent Roscoe Conkling Bruce, and Whitefield McKinlay, named collector of the port of Georgetown in 1910.[92]

The Tuskegee Machine during the Jim Crow period was more formidable than the Congressional Black Caucus is in the 1980s. As Du Bois remarked in his autobiography:

> Not only did presidents of the United States consult Booker T. Washington, but governors and congressmen; philanthropists conferred with him, scholars wrote to him. Tuskegee became a vast information bureau and centre of advice . . . After a time almost no Negro institution could collect funds without the recommendation or acquiescence of Mr Washington. Few political appointments of Negroes were made anywhere in the United States without his consent. Even the careers of rising young coloured men were very often determined by his advice and certainly his opposition was fatal.[93]

The first forces in opposition to accommodation emerged from New England's Black middle classes. George W. Forbes, an Amherst College graduate, and Harvard graduate William Monroe Trotter launched a fiercely anti-Tuskegee publication, the Boston *Guardian*. Connected with the 'Boston radicals' were attorney Clement Morgan, another Harvard graduate and member of the Cambridge, Massachusetts City Council (1896-1898) and Harvard Law School graduate Archibald H. Grimke, a former consul in Santo Domingo and leader of the Massachusetts Suffrage League. After the 1903 publication of *The Souls of Black Folk*, which criticized Washington's programme as 'practically [accepting] the alleged inferiority of the Negro races', Du Bois soon became the central leader of the radical reformers. Under the guidance of Trotter and Du Bois, the 'Niagara Movement' was created in 1905 to combat the Tuskegee Machine. Lasting but four years, the Niagara Movement never attracted more than four to five hundred active supporters and members. Within this group, however, came many leaders of the Negro intelligentsia and upper petty bourgeoisie: John Hope, president of Atlanta Baptist College; Kentucky State College president J.R.L. Diggs; AME minister and activist Reverdy Ransom; attorneys Clement Morgan of St Paul, Minnesota and George H. Jackson of Cincinnati; and leading clergymen such as J. Milton Waldron of Washington DC, George Freeman Bragg of Baltimore and Byron Gunner of Newport. With the prominent exception of Trotter, most of these highly educated petty-bourgeois reformers merged their energies with a core of white liberals to create the NAACP in 1909-1910. Ransom articulated the liberal Black intelligentsia's position in 1906: 'There are two views of the Negro question. One is that the Negro should stoop to conquer; that he should accept in silence the denial of his political rights . . . There are others who believe that the Negro owes this nation no apology for his presence . . . that he should refuse to be assigned to an inferior place by his fellow-countrymen.'[94]

The debates between the accommodationist politicians and the reformers were acrimonious. Washington used his patronage to have his Black enemies demoted or dismissed from their jobs; he pressured Black newspaper editors to attack the Niagara Movement. During these years, in his private correspondence to John Hope, Du Bois affirmed that 'Washington stands for Negro submission and slavery.'[95] However, half a century later, Du Bois reflected that he and Washington had not been irreconcilably at odds:

> I believed in the higher education of a Talented Tenth who through their knowledge of modern culture could guide the American Negro into a higher civilization . . . Mr Washington, on the other hand, believed that the Negro as an efficient worker could gain wealth and that eventually through his ownership of capital he would be able to achieve a recognized place in American culture and could then educate his children as he might wish and develop their possibilities . . . These two theories of Negro progress were not absolutely contradictory. Neither I nor Booker Washington understood the nature of capitalist exploitation of labour, and the necessity of a direct attack on the principle of exploitation as the beginning of labour uplift. I recognized the importance of the Negro gaining a foothold in trades and his encouragement in industry and common labour. Mr Washington was not absolutely opposed to college training and sent his own children to college . . .[96]

The parallels between the two leaders were more extensive than Du Bois suggests. When Washington's Atlanta Compromise speech was widely republished, the initial reaction of the Afro-American press was mixed. One Washington DC newspaper which later backed Washington commented that the speech 'suited the white prejudiced element of the country'.[97] Conversely, Du Bois promptly wrote Washington a note of congratulation for his 'phenomenal success at Atlanta — it was a word fitly spoken.'[98] Du Bois, not Washington, first proposed the development of the National Negro Business League. This Black chamber of commerce spawned a series of Black entrepreneurial groups generally allied with Washington, including the National Negro Bankers' Association in 1906 and the National Negro Retail Merchants' Association in 1913. And as historian Louis R. Harlan has illustrated, Washington never fully accepted racial disfranchisement and segregation, despite his accommodationist public platitudes. In 1899 he helped to finance a legal suit to reverse the disfranchisement of Louisiana Black voters. Washington and most of the Tuskegee Institute faculty were registered voters, and he wrote 'anonymous editorials in Black newspapers urging more Blacks to vote'. In 1906 Washington hired a former US Senator, Henry W. Blair of New Hampshire, to lobby for the defeat of a bill requiring racial segregation on railroads.[99]

The fact that Washington and Du Bois could agree on so many points indicates that they represented political tendencies within the same social class, the Negro petty bourgeoisie. Indeed, the majority of Black political leaders during the Jim Crow era simply cannot be categorized as Du Bois reformers or Washington accommodationists. Depending upon their geographical location, vocation and social base, they could move in almost any direction. Several prominent reformers in the 1880s and 1890s eventually supported Washington's policies. T. Thomas Fortune, militant editor of the New York *Age* and founder of the Afro-American League in 1890, had aligned himself with Washington by 1907. Black Georgia Republican leader William A. Pledger was a well-known opponent of racial segregation. But by 1900, he was urging those few Georgia Black voters still on the rolls to support an all-white Republican ticket. Four years later he was termed 'an ardent champion of Dr Washington'. Boston attorney William H. Lewis had started his public career as an ardent supporter of Trotter. After his 1901 election to the Massachusetts legislature, he began to make amends with the Tuskegee Machine. With Washington's backing, Lewis was appointed special attorney for naturalization affairs in 1907, and assistant US attorney general in 1911. Washington *Bee* editor Calvin Chase ridiculed Booker T. Washington for nearly a decade; but by 1910, Chase was 'lyrical' in his praises for Tuskegee and resorted to 'venomous' attacks against

Du Bois and the NAACP. For many erstwhile accommodationists, the process was reversed. Two major 'Bookerites', S. Laing Williams of Chicago and John Quincy Adams of St Paul, Minnesota, had defected to the NAACP by 1914. When Baptist minister J. Milton Waldron held a church in Jacksonville, Florida, he was one of the state's chief defenders of Washington's programmes. Safely relocated in Washington DC, he became the comrade of Du Bois and the local chapter president of the NAACP. The best example here is that of James Weldon Johnson. While part of the Tuskegee Machine, he classified the supporters of Du Bois as 'the enemy' and praised his patron as a 'first-class man'. In 1916, Johnson became national organizer for the NAACP, and during the 1920s served as National Secretary. With the wisdom of hindsight, Johnson then denounced Washington's Atlanta Compromise as 'illogical'. Black scholars were not immune to this type of theoretical and programmatic inconsistency. During the 1880s the president of Wilberforce University, W.S. Scarborough advocated a radical reformist position. In the years of Washington's rise to public prominence, Scarborough urged Blacks to accept the Tuskegeean's 'sound philosophy'. But by 1910, Scarborough had shifted course again and joined the NAACPs national advisory committee.[100]

What helps to distinguish reformers from accommodationists are their extreme wings, both on the right and on the left. Accommodationists genuinely tried to use the political apparatus to benefit themselves, their immediate social class, and, in general, the Black community as a whole. Their apologetics and benign behaviour had the inevitable tendency to create true 'conservatives' who simply capitulated to the racist-capitalist state. There were always politicians like William H. Councill and Thomas E. Miller. The leading Black Democrat in Alabama, Councill was notorious for his 'oily flattery' of whites. Even Washington privately admitted to associates that he did not want to appear on the same public platform as Councill. Miller was president of the all-Black state college in Orangeburg, South Carolina, and was widely praised for his 'obsequious' behaviour. Miller repeatedly urged Blacks to stop 'croaking and fault-finding, and whining and pining' against segregation.[101] No Millers or Councills could be found among the members of the Niagara Movement, or within the early NAACP. Conversely, the reformist critique of the Niagara Movement, which advocated the destruction of Jim Crow and the granting of full civil rights to Blacks, contributed to the development of a small but articulate Black left wing which supported the ideas of class struggle and socialism. The chief example of this is of course Du Bois, who considered himself a socialist by 1904 and who briefly joined the Socialist Party in 1911. In Du Bois's publication *Horizon,* in November 1909, he specifically called for Afro-Americans to 'make common cause with the oppressed and downtrodden of all races and peoples . . . and with the cause of the working classes everywhere.'[102] But there were other reformers who went a good deal further to the left than Du Bois. AME bishop Reverdy Ransom had embraced socialism by the mid 1890s. In one 1897 essay for a church journal, Ransom linked his Christian ideals with the cause of liberating the proletariat:

> Socialism places its chief value upon man. Socialism, like the inspired Carpenter of Nazareth, places more value upon man than it does upon riches. It believes that the rights of man are more sacred than the rights of property, believes indeed, that the only sacred thing on earth is a human being . . . The American Negro belongs almost wholly to the proletarian or industrial class. He constitutes a large and important factor in the development of this country and the production of its wealth . . . The battles of socialism are not to be fought by white men, for the benefit of white men. It is not, as we have said, a question of race, it is a question of man. So far as America is concerned, this question cannot be settled without the Negro's aid. The cause of labour, of the industrial army, is one. When millions of toilers are degraded, labour is degraded, man is degraded. That the Negro will enthusiastically espouse the cause of socialism we cannot doubt.[103]

Probably the most influential Black proponent of socialism during these years was the Reverend George Washington Woodbey, who explicitly denounced Booker T. Washington as 'a good servant of capitalism'. The activism of Woodbey and other early Black socialists established the foundations of modern Afro-American radicalism, later embodied by Randolph and the African Blood Brotherhood. The logical culmination of militant reform was in some variety of socialism — for example, the social democracy of Randolph, the Christian socialism of Woodbey and Ransom, or the Marxism-Leninism of Cyril Briggs.

During the second phase of the Jim Crow period, the number of Black appointed and elected officials began to increase, but not to the levels of the Reconstruction era. Between 1933 and 1941 Roosevelt appointed 163 Afro-Americans to advisory and administrative posts. The colour line was still maintained, however, in a number of

key federal departments: for example, only three Blacks held positions in the diplomatic and consular service in 1941, compared with
eleven Blacks in the service in 1908. In elective positions at the state
and federal level, Black politicians were successful primarily in the
north-eastern and mid-western states. In 1940, a total of twenty-
three Blacks were elected to various state legislatures: six won state
representatives posts in Pennsylvania, five in Illinois, three in New
York, and the remainder in Indiana, Michigan, Nebraska, Kansas,
California, New Jersey and West Virginia. Most of the members of
this third generation of Black office-holders had a social class
identity with the Negro petty bourgeoisie. As physicians, entrepreneurs, lawyers and educators, they usually held nominal
membership in the NAACP, but most were not civil rights activists or
militants. Although the Black electorate by World War II was
strongly oriented towards the Democratic Party, its official representatives tended to be more equally divided between the two
capitalist parties. For example, an analysis of the party affiliations of
the thirty-nine Black state senators, state representatives, county
commissioners, city councilpersons, magistrates and constables
elected in 1946 indicates that twenty-five (64.1 per cent) were
members of the Republican Party.[104] Black Republicans tended to
espouse an updated version of nineteenth-century liberalism; Black
Democrats, particularly those elected from urban political
machines, were frequently accommodationists. With the prominent
exception of Communist Party leader Benjamin J. Davis Jr, who sat
on the New York City Council, most Negro politicians had much in
common ideologically with South Carolina's mulatto elite of the
1860s. Du Bois recognized the trend towards accommodation
within the NAACP and the Negro elite generally, and attempted to
combat it during the Great Depression. In an April 1933 essay in the
NAACP journal, *Crisis*, he urged the Black middle class to
recognize the limits of bourgeois liberalism and clientage with the
major parties. 'We must have power; we must learn the secret of
economic organization', he argued.[105] Two months later, Du Bois
linked the use of electoral politics with the necessity to uproot the
capitalist system. 'The problem, therefore, is how democratic
government is going to be restored in the South through Negro
votes, and how the votes of white and Black workers are to be used
for the advancement and development of the nation.'[106] As committed integrationists and political liberals, other NAACP leaders
and most Black politicians could readily concur with Du Bois's first
proposition, but could not accept the second point. They presumed

the long-term existence of the capitalist political economy ,and, unlike Du Bois, saw no structural relationship between institutional racism and capitalism. As Matthew Holden observes, the NAACP 'has never given the economic problems of Blacks sustained attention comparable to its attention to the question of segregation *per se* . . . [they] never faced seriously the question of capital accumulation.'[107]

The fourth generation of Black politicians surfaced within the powerful social movement for racial equality during the 1960s. Perhaps the most interesting dimension of these women and men was the impact of their initial organizational affiliation upon their subsequent political development. As previously noted, many of the SNCC's activists had social class origins in the Negro elite; but a good number of those who later entered elective office did not. Marion Barry, for example, grew up on a farm in Itta Bena, Mississippi, and John Lewis was one of ten children, raised in a tenant farmer's home outside Troy, Alabama. Charles Sherrod, who served as the SNCC's first field secretary and was later elected city commissioner in Albany, Georgia, was the oldest of six children from an impoverished home in Petersburg, Virginia. Years before his civil rights activities, Sherrod had shone shoes and worked odd jobs to support his family and to pay for his education at Virginia Union University.[108] Also striking is the fact that Blacks from middle-class backgrounds involved in the SNCC often tended to move further to the left in later years than those SNCC recruits from social class origins of extreme poverty. One example, of course, is that of Julian Bond — a graduate of the elite high-school academy, The George School of Pennsylvania, who later became a prominent democratic socialist. In 1968 Bond received forty-eight and a half votes for the Democratic Party's vice-presidential nomination, although he was legally too young to serve in that office.[109] Further to Bond's left are SNCC veterans Angela Y. Davis and Stokely Carmichael. Davis was born in a Black middle and working-class neighbourhood in Birmingham in 1944. Her mother was a college graduate and had been extensively involved in antiracist work with the Communist Party; her father was the proprietor of a gasoline service station. Davis's marginal interest in the left was sparked during her undergraduate studies at Brandeis, where she was the pupil of Herbert Marcuse. Her graduate studies were in Frankfurt, where she attended lectures by Jurgen Habermas and Theodor Adorno. But Davis's real involvement in domestic political struggles began in 1968, when she was a member of the SNCC's Los

Angeles chapter. Joining the Communist Party the following year, she ran as her party's vice-presidential candidate in 1980 and 1984.[110] Carmichael attended the highly competitive Bronx High School of Science in the late 1950s. There he became friends with Gene Dennis, whose father was General Secretary of the Communist Party. Attending college at Howard University, Carmichael next came under the influence of Rustin, through his involvement in the Non-violent Action Group (NAG). Carmichael's relationship with the SNCC came about through his NAG activities, but he did not become a full-time SNCC worker until after his graduation from Howard in 1964. Since the 1970s, Carmichael's involvement in politics has been non-electoral, but his All-African People's Revolutionary Party adheres to a type of socialist analysis.[111] Perry Anderson's observation that the social origins of many western Marxist intellectuals lie in the petty bourgeoisie also seems applicable to Black politics in the US.[112]

The CORE tended to develop politicians with a flair for entrepreneurialism and accommodation with the political establishment. James Farmer, the son of a college professor, had become active in civil rights work from his background in religious training at Howard University. In 1969, after leaving the CORE, he accepted a cabinet position in the Nixon Administration.[113] Attorney Floyd McKissick, who had helped to organize the initial sit-ins in North Carolina and later became the CORE's national director endorsed Richard Nixon for re-election in 1972. The *quid pro quo* for McKissick was Nixon's promise to help finance 'Soul City', an all-Black planned town in rural North Carolina.[114] Another member of the CORE was Kenneth A. Gibson. Like McKissick, Gibson's primary interest was in the area of economic development. As director of Newark, New Jersey's Business and Industry Coordinating Council, Gibson attempted with mixed results to increase jobs and to promote entrepreneurial activity for Blacks. Using his base in the CORE, the NA'ACP and the Council, he ran unsuccessfully for mayor of Newark in 1966. With the critical support of Black nationalists led by Imamu Baraka, Gibson was elected mayor in 1970 — although he later broke with Baraka's militant constituency.[115] Slightly different was the political career of St Louis CORE activist William Clay. Known throughout inner-city districts as a 'Black people's Black man', Clay was frequently arrested in local civil rights demonstrations. In the aftermath of one 1963 protest, Clay served nearly four months in gaol. Clay's election to Congress in 1968 came about not solely from his involvement in the CORE, but from the common perception that he 'had always done everything within his power to help any Black person' regardless of the person's 'economic or social status'.[116]

The Southern Christian Leadership Conference was the starting-point for a much more eclectic group of politicians. When the central political issue under discussion was the destruction of Jim Crow, all of the leaders of the SCLC were quite prepared to lead non-violent street demonstrations. But in the absence of Martin's leadership, and without any ideological orientation save the desire to achieve racial equality, SCLC veterans moved in various directions. The Reverend Walter Fauntroy, director of the SCLC's Washington DC bureau, went to Congress as the District of Columbia's representative. Andrew Young had first joined King's staff as the administrator of a Field Foundation grant of $40,000 via the United Church of Christ in 1961. Martin came to value Young's contributions to the movement, but affectionately called him 'Tom' because of his 'frequent readiness to conciliate'.[117] Perhaps King sensed Young's desire to mediate the demands of a social movement with the interests of those exercising state power — which has been a constant theme of Young's whole career, especially at the United Nations and during the Democratic presidential primaries in both 1976 and 1984. Particularly tragic were the subsequent careers of Hosea Williams and Ralph David Abernathy, two of King's closest associates who, to an extent, followed the accommodationist footsteps of earlier Black Georgia politician William A. Pledger. Williams first emerged as the charismatic leader of the SCLC in Savannah, Georgia. Abernathy, born in the rural Black belt of Alabama, had been pastor of Montgomery's First Baptist Church in 1955 when the bus boycott began, and was beside King at virtually every desegregation campaign right up to 1968. Williams won a seat in the Georgia state legislature, but in 1977 Abernathy failed to gain election to Congress as a Democrat. In 1980, both men endorsed Ronald Reagan for president.[118] Even more striking was the strange evolution of James Bevel, who was the most radical leader inside the SCLC during the early 1960s. By 1984 Bevel had joined the Republican Party and had run unsuccessfully for a Chicago Congressional seat on a platform clearly to the right of Booker T. Washington.

So many different leaders have held membership in the NAACP, from Marxist-Leninists to Republicans, that it is impossible to summarize their political behaviour. Although Benjamin Hooks is not currently an elected official, his evolution is of some interest, since he represents a 'type' of leader that first came into power during the first Reconstruction. Although an attorney by training, Hooks first developed his political constituency in Memphis as pastor of a large baptist church. In the 1950s and 1960s, while many Black leaders were leading demonstrations, Hooks was busy cultivating his business and electoral political affairs. He was co-founder and vice-president of the Mutual Federal Savings and Loan Association in Memphis; concurrently he was elected as a criminal court judge in Shelby County, Tennessee. In 1972 the Nixon Administration appointed Hooks to the Federal Communications Commission, and five years later he became executive director of the NAACP.[119] Another NAACP veteran who retains characteristics of earlier Creole/mulatto politicians from the Reconstruction period is Ernest 'Dutch' Morial, mayor of New Orleans since 1978. A product of the city's Creole elite, Morial was the first Black since Reconstruction to be elected to the Louisiana state legislature, and later to the state court of appeals. Morial's political base was formed during the 1960s when he was head of the New Orleans branch of the NAACP. Deliberately projecting himself as an ideological 'maverick' who could nevertheless work with the corporate establishment, Morial won a position on Tulane University's formerly all-white board of trustees. Significantly, when Morial ran for mayor, none of the city's major Black political groups endorsed him, and he won only 58 per cent of the Afro-American vote.[120]

Although a large number of Black politicians have emerged from particular national organizations, the majority have not. In some instances, clusters of activist-oriented, petty-bourgeois Blacks created their own local formations, and politicians used such groups as their base from which to contest for public office. In others, Black leaders were involved in two or more national groups, and picked up certain ideological characteristics from each of them as they matured. Gary, Indiana mayor Richard Hatcher illustrates the first example. He arrived in Gary in 1960 after receiving a law degree at Valparaiso University. He quickly joined the NAACP, becoming counsellor of the chapter's youth members, and he was the leader of Gary's 120-member group attending the March on Washington. But he began to rise in local electoral politics as president and co-founder of 'Muigwithania', a 'Black man's organization committed to community uplift'. The term was taken from the title of Jomo Kenyatta's newspaper in Kenya. Muigwithania had no roots in Gary's large Black industrial working class, but was tightly led by a small number of Black professionals. Muigwithania successfully backed Hatcher, who won election to Gary's city council in 1963, and subsequently became mayor in 1967.[121] Jesse Jackson initiated his political career in the CORE. As president of North Carolina Agricultural and Technical College's student body, Jackson, together with CORE activist Ike Reynolds, led 850 protestors in a mass demonstration in Greensboro on 5 June 1963, resulting in nearly three hundred arrests.[122] At the age of twenty-three, Jackson served briefly as the CORE's field director of south-eastern operations. Only in 1966, after graduate studies at Chicago Theological Seminary, did Jackson join the SCLC staff and work closely with King. But Jackson's activism still retained an entrepreneurial focus so typical of McKissick, Roy Innis and other CORE leaders. Young Jackson was named director of the SCLCs 'Operation Breadbasket', and in this capacity he negotiated agreements with large corporations to hire local Blacks and to invest in the ghetto.[123]

A substantial group of Blacks who won elective offices came from social origins of rural and urban poverty. It is ironic, therefore, that a number of such 'first-generation' middle-class Blacks who also lacked any direct or intimate involvement in desegregation formations were among the most conservative of all Black public officials. Los Angeles mayor Thomas Bradley is surely the most outstanding example in this regard. Born into a Texas share-cropper's family, Bradley spent over two decades as an officer in the Los Angeles Police Department. After being elected to the City Council, Bradley won the city's mayoral race on his second attempt in 1972. As mayor, he 'rarely took strong stands on issues that were racial', and took special care to cater to corporate interests. As one newspaper writer observed, Bradley was 'the kind of Black that [white] people feel comfortable with'.[124] Wilson Goode was the son of a southern share-cropper; as mayor of Philadelphia, he has advocated public policies favourable to downtown business interests. One caustic critic of Goode's clientage with the Democratic Party's leaders has suggested that 'perhaps the home mentality of the early environment of Mayor Goode still lingers.'[125] Less accommodating, although hardly a radical reformer, is Louis Stokes. Born in Cleveland, Stokes shone shoes as a child, then worked as a clerk in an Army-Navy surplus store. After a stint in the army, he obtained a law degree and began to practise in Cleveland. Stokes's brother Carl, also an attorney, rapidly moved to a succession of appointments — assistant police prosecutor in 1958, Ohio state representative in 1962, and finally the first Black mayor of Cleveland in 1967. Louis Stokes hardly considered himself 'a political man', but he did provide free legal services for some Black nationalists and community leaders. And although Louis Stokes was admittedly 'not an advocate of [Black] militancy', he sought and won election to Congress in 1968, largely on the strength of his ties with his brother.[126]

The rough polarization between accommodationists and reformers that characterized Black political culture during Reconstruction continues into the current period, although the ideological axis around which the two groups are formed has shifted. Contemporary accommodationists now generally accept twentieth-century liberalism, which advocates the continued existence of the capitalist economy. Usually they are moderate integrationists of the NAACP variety, but frequently they are bourgeois Black nationalists of the CORE type who support a Booker T. Washington strategy of coalitions with the Republican Party and conservative corporations. The reformers tend to espouse social democratic solutions to the crisis of race and class, and support insurgent efforts outside established political channels to obtain concessions for their constituents. In many instances, local reformers and activists have tried to recruit accommodationist, petty-bourgeois Blacks without genuine ties to social movements to run as their representatives for elective office. Usually this strategy does not work particularly well. A classic example is provided by Oakland, California mayor Lionel Wilson. In 1973, Black Panther Party co-founder Bobby Seale ran for mayor essentially on a left social democratic programme of city-wide rent controls, community control of the police and the creation of public jobs for city residents. Running against a millionaire businessman incumbent, Seale received 36 per cent of the vote. Four years later, the Black Panthers, the United Farm Workers and other leftists backed Wilson, a middle-class judge, for the mayoral race. Although Wilson won, primarily with the Panther's assistance in working-class precincts, he actually received fewer votes than Seale had in 1973. Once in office, 'Wilson turned out to be acceptable to the downtown corporate interests, and indeed came to identify himself as the political representative of all the people, a centrist who could talk to the corporate leadership . . .'[127]

The most significant ideological shift within the ranks of Black political reformers over the past two generations has been an undisguised advocacy of socialism within certain quarters of the left. Within the Congressional Black Caucus, Ronald V. Dellums of Berkeley-Oakland and John Conyers of Detroit have maintained deep relationships with the organized US left. In cities with large numbers of Black industrial workers, the tendency for Black reformers to identify with the left is very strong. Three prime examples from Detroit are Coleman Young, George Crockett and Kenneth Cockrel. In the 1940s Young had been director of organization of the Wayne County, Michigan CIO Council, and in 1950 he was elected Executive Secretary of the National Labour Conference for Negro Rights. This militant formation of Black labour activists, also led by Cleveland Robinson of the Distributive, Processing and Office Workers' Union and William R. Hood of the United Auto Workers, became the progressive National Negro Labour Council in October 1951. During its short but stormy existence in the Cold War, it fought against racism within the corporations and the white-led labour movement. Hounded by charges that it was merely a 'Communist front', Council leaders were investigated by the House Committee on Un-American Activities (HUAC). In the February 1952 HUAC hearings in Detroit, Young seized the offensive, ending his vigorous testimony with a memorable statement:

> I am a part of the Negro people. I fought in the last war and I would unhesitatingly take up arms against anybody that attacks this country. In the same manner I am now in process of fighting against what I consider to be attacks and discrimination against my people. I am fighting against un-American activities such as lynchings and denial of the vote. I am dedicated to that fight, and I don't think I have to apologize or explain it to anybody, my position on that.[128]

Young's close friend George Crockett had been one of the defence attorneys for the Communist Party in the Smith Act trials of 1948 and 1949, during which he had been sentenced to serve four months in a federal prison on contempt of court charges. In the HUAC harassment of the National Negro Labour Council, Crockett served as Young's attorney. Only during the renaissance of the civil rights movement in the following decade could these Black radicals seek public office: Young was elected to the Michigan state legislature in 1964, and Crockett became judge of the Recorder's Court in Wayne County in 1966. A decade later, Young narrowly defeated right-wing Detroit Police Commissioner John Nichols to become the city's first Black mayor, and several years later Crockett won a Congressional seat. Although Crockett is still a strong leftist, Young has moved to the ideological centre during his tenure as Detroit's mayor.[129]

Cockrel was a product of Black working-class radicalism during the late 1960s. Like thousands of others, his parents had migrated to Detroit from the rural South during World War II. An orphan by the age of twelve, Cockrel left high school before graduation and eventually joined the air force. Admitted into Wayne State University as a 'conditional adult student', Cockrel finally earned his BA degree in 1964, and obtained a law degree three years later. Cockrel's interest in elective office predated his involvement in radical political work. In 1966, as a third-year law student living in the city's public housing projects, he ran for state representative in the Democratic primary, finishing in third place. But Cockrel's real development occurred within the context of the Dodge Revolutionary Union Movement (DRUM), formed by General Baker, Mike Hamlin and Ron March in 1968, and with the subsequent formation of the League of Revolutionary Black Workers. Cockrel successfully defended League members in numerous criminal and civic actions, and was perceived by many as the League's 'intellectual in residence'. In the 1970s Cockrel organized DARE (Detroit Alliance for a Rational Economy), a multiracial, explicitly left force which fought against Young's plans to give major tax abatements to large auto corporations. Now a long-time Marxist, Cockrel announced his decision in 1977 to seek a seat on the Detroit City Council. Something of a popular front was created to keep Cockrel out of public office, and this included Young, UAW leaders, and the local Democratic Party bureaucrats. Even Conyers, a long-time associate of Cockrel's, refused to endorse him. But by mobilizing over a thousand volunteers at a block-by-block level, Cockrel won the Council race. Some observers of Detroit politics now predict that Cockrel may become mayor after Young's retirement.[130]

It would be premature to suggest that the strategy of clientage and accommodation to one of the major capitalist parties has in any way been replaced by attempts to circumvent the two-party system. Neither the radicalized petty bourgeoisie (such as Bond, Conyers) nor the working-class radicals (such as Cockrel) are representative of the majority of Black politicians now within US bourgeois democracy. The central fact about Black political culture from 1865 to 1985 is that only a small segment of the Afro-American social fraction, the petty bourgeoisie, has dominated the electoral machinery and patronage positions that regulate Black life and perpetuate the exploitation of Black labour. This buffer stratum has historically focused its energies on non-economic issues, such as the abolition of legal segregation; and when it has developed explicitly economic agendas, more frequently than not it presumes the hegemony of capital over labour. Even during periods of Black working-class insurgency within electoral politics, the Negro petty bourgeoisie tend to surface on the crest of such movements. A social class profile of the Black delegates at the 1984 Democratic Party National Convention is illustrative. 56 per cent were between thirty and forty-nine years old, and 37 per cent held some office within the Democratic Party. 10 per cent were lawyers, 4 per cent union officials, 8 per cent public officials, and 32 per cent college professors or other professionals. Compared with white delegates, Blacks were slightly better educated. 13 per cent of the white delegates had only a high-school or lower level education, compared with only 8 per cent of the Black delegates. 73 per cent of the Black Democrats possessed a college education, compared with 60 per cent for whites; and 55 per cent of the Black delegates had either masters', doctoral, or professional degrees. But less than 13 per cent of all Afro-Americans between the ages of twenty-five and thirty-four in 1978 — which would fall within the age range of these delegates — had completed four years or more of college.[131] More significant are the figures for family income. Only 17 per cent of the Black Democratic Party delegates reported annual household incomes under \$25,000. 37 per cent earned \$25,000-\$50,000 annually; 34 per cent made \$50,000-\$100,000; and another 7 per cent earned \$100,000 or more.[132] In 1982, the median family income of Black Americans was \$13,598, or about 55 per cent of the white median family income of \$24,603.[133] According to US Bureau of the Census statistics in 1979, only 61,000 Black families reported incomes exceeding \$50,000, and barely 14,000 households had family incomes exceeding \$75,000.[134] It seems apparent that this small Black petty-bourgeois elite was well represented at the San Francisco convention — despite the thousands of low-income and working-class Blacks who were active inside the Jesse Jackson presidential campaign.

The profile of Afro-American politicians is strikingly similar to that of other political leaders throughout the African Diaspora. In the Caribbean, Norman Manley had been a Rhodes scholar at Oxford University, and became a member of the king's council in 1932. Years before his entry into electoral politics, he earned the hostility of Jamaican Black nationalists by representing both the Kingston and St Andrew Corporation Council and private citizens in legal suits against Marcus Garvey.[135] Grantley Adams received a scholarship to read law at Oxford; Eric Williams was a product of

Queen's Royal College in Trinidad, studied history at Oxford, and became a noted historian of slavery well before he was named deputy chairman of the Caribbean Research Council of the Caribbean Commission in 1948. Aime Césaire was of course an internationally known poet of *négritude* before his election as deputy to the French National Assembly and his subsequent establishment of the *Parti Progressiste de la Martinique*. In West Africa, a similar profile emerges. Among the earlier nationalist politicians, J.E. Casely-Hayford, the son of an affluent Gold Coast family, studied law at Cambridge and London, and authored the pioneering nationalist tract *Ethiopia Unbound*; Dr Milton Margai, leader of the Sierra Leone People's Party, was the first African in his nation to become a physician, and had spent decades as a colonial bureaucrat; Senegalese *citoyen* Lamine Gueye was an affluent Dakar lawyer before forming his local social democratic party in the 1930s; Nigeria's Nnamdi Azikiwe was educated in the United States, and was a successful newspaper publisher and businessman before becoming secretary general of the National Council of Nigeria and the Cameroons in the 1940s. As in the Black American political experience, organic leaders of the Black working class were slow to emerge in nationalist social movements, and when they did, they were frequently hostile to socialism. Sékou Touré of Guinea represents one type of leader with strong links with the Black working class, but other examples less favourable to the left include Tom Mboya, a Luo trade unionist in Nairobi who rose to political power under a neo-colonial state and Eric Gairy of Grenada, who first organized Aruba oilworkers in the late 1940s before mobilizing the Manual and Mental Workers' Union in his own state. In summary, the history of Black electoral politics is the history of the class-conscious Black petty bourgeoisie, seeking to influence the bourgeois democratic or colonial-capitalist state for its own purposes. Such political interventions, whether in a clientage or reform protest mode, may or may not serve the social class interests of the Black majority.

III

Why have Black politicians, as a social group, usually failed to increase significantly the capacity of Black Americans to realize their specific objective interests — that is, to maximize their power? I have discussed the structural limitations and contradictions of bourgeois democratic states in general, and those of the

United States in particular, and how they negate the historic social class interests of Afro-Americans. A few comments must be added on the specific failures both in theory and in practice of Black petty-bourgeois politicians. For the purpose of this brief critique I will delete Black political activists and those few elected officials who have committed class suicide, and who are an integral part of the struggle for an American socialism. I shall also ignore the group I have previously termed 'Black Reaganites': conservative economist Thomas Sowell; Samuel Pierce, Reagan's Secretary of Housing and Urban Development; Art Fletcher, a Labour Department officer under the Nixon Administration; Gloria E.A. Toote, millionaire Republican real-estate developer; and Black nationalist-turned-neo-conservative journalist Tony Brown, among others. This tiny coterie of corporate directors and administrative bureaucrats is reminiscent of W.H. Councill and Thomas E. Miller in that it exercises no effective independent power, and provides marginal ideological cover for the modern white supremacy movement that Reagan embodies. The Black Reaganites are 'true conservatives', not accommodationists of the Booker T. Washington tradition.[136] Our focus here is principally on the reformists and accommodationists.

Several general theoretical points can be made. First, it must be apparent that the vast majority of Black politicians lack a social theory that explains the essential dynamics of the political economy of capitalism, and the utility of racism in the process of capital accumulation. This failure to reflect critically upon the concrete reality of Black life and labour is manifested in several different attitudes of the Negro elite and its representatives. There is of course a widespread contempt for theory in general, which is so typical of the American petty bourgeoisie. Richard Hatcher's 1970 statement on electoral political power could be repeated verbatim by other Black officials. 'We need not waste our time on subtle word–distinctions between "reform" and "revolution" or between working "in" or "out" of the system', Hatcher argued. 'What we need is not polemics but a viable politics for Black survival; that is, we need a political strategy that speaks to a condition and not to a theory.'[137] Hatcher's theoretical poverty is shared by many Black political scientists. Charles V. Hamilton, co-author of *Black Power,* warned leaders to avoid getting 'bogged down in repetitious internecine debates — debates whose boundaries and terms have usually been determined by others . . .' Blacks should be 'dealing with a condition not a theory . . . not debating the efficacy of Marx and contemplating the cosmos.'[138] As modern Black nationalism's chief theoretician Maulana Karenga has noted, 'the ideological deficiency of Black middle-class leadership is clearest in its lack of a grand strategy, a theory of social reality and social change which gives at the minimum a clear socio-political identity, purpose and direction . . . This is not to say Black middle-class leadership lacks views, opinions, ideas and strategies, but rather that these ideological assertions are neither coherent nor grand, though often grandiose.'[139] Hence there is a marked inclination among such leaders to substitute form for substance, to emphasize rhetoric and style at the expense of a critical analysis of their constituents' material interests.

This historic inability to link theory to practical political endeavours contributes to the Black elite's failure to advance a systemic criticism of US capitalism. The labour theory of value is alien to the accommodationists and to most reformers. They do not comprehend that the masses of working people create all wealth, and that employers are not doing Blacks or other workers any real favours by creating jobs. Thus the failure of Black Reconstruction-era politicians to demand wholesale land seizures and financial compensation for enslavement, and the anti-trade union policies of Booker T. Washington, reveal a basic sympathy towards the fundamental prerogatives of capital over labour. With the rise of social democratic ideology among Black reformers over the past three decades, the inclination to promote *laissez-faire* capitalism has been curtailed. But at best, most reformers promote only the idea that Blacks should receive a larger 'piece of the pie', and inclusion in 'the organization and structure of power in the public and private sectors'.[140] Congresswoman Shirley Chisholm, for example, writes of the need for Blacks to acquire their 'fair or equitable share of economic and political power'; that for too long, Afro-Americans, women, Latinos and others have been denied 'strong voices within the decision-making process.'[141] Chisholm's statement indicates no awareness of the systematic class inequalities that are part of the bourgeois democratic state. There is the unquestioned belief that the general 'decision-making process' can be made equitable simply by the addition of Black leaders. Thus the 'leaders', not the masses, are the key actors on the historical stage — a traditional role which the petty bourgeoisie always like to assume for themselves. Given the theoretical vacuity of such leaders, plus their cultivated emphasis on matters of style and rhetoric, it is not surprising that many have come to believe that they know better than their constituents what socio-economic problems must be addressed. It is only a minor step from this argument to the position of paternalistic reform — the masses of working-class and poor people should have no decisive input on liberal public-policy decisions made by 'their' leaders. Political scientist Leonard A. Cole's study of Black and white politicians in New Jersey confirms the pervasiveness of such paternalism. Words like 'will of the people' and 'power to the people' were frequently spouted by Black elected officials. But when asked what position a leader would take 'when your personal conviction differs from that of the people you represented', only 7 per cent of the Black public servants replied that they would 'always go with the people's convictions'; 45 per cent would 'usually' go with their personal convictions, and another 23 per cent would 'always' follow their own instincts. Black politicians in New Jersey were even less likely to 'take the position of the people' who had elected them than white leaders, according to public opinion polls.[142]

The lack of any social theory or awareness of capitalism's perpetuation of institutional racism therefore negates any efforts by reformers and accommodationists to suggest a viable theory of the state, and to accept as given the political apparatus as it exists. Consequently most Black politicians do not in any real sense 'govern' — they merely seek to participate in the system as marginal adjuncts to a long-standing political process. Historically, Black office-holders have viewed electoral politics as 'the main strategy for Black liberation . . . the key instrument or form of struggle for gaining political power to resolve the social problems confronting Black people', according to William E. Nelson and Philip J. Meranto. This strategy not only ignores 'the historic and continued tension between the Black middle class (those most likely to run for elected posts) and the Black working and underclass', but it does little to 'ensure that Black people will gain community control over their own economic, political and socio-cultural environment.'[143] Even in the 1960s, when many Black officials identified themselves with the slogan 'Black Power', they were usually quick to explain that the phrase did not mean that Blacks should 'try to take over the country or overthrow the government'. Cole observed that most Afro-American officials integrated Black Power into their basically 'liberal philosophy'. The phrase only gave 'direction to an assumption that government can actively respond to the needs of its citizens'.[144]

The lack of theory is also directly related to Black politicians' misconceptions about nationalism, ethnicity and gender. Since many elected officials from the Great Depression to the present have been integrationists, there is often an attempt to downplay race as a significant social category within American politics — in short, a regrettable detour to avoid facing reality. Officials inclined toward a more cultural pluralistic approach usually argue the ethnic-interest group model: Blacks, as an ethnic bloc, must seek to increase their power at the expense of other ethnic groups. This method underestimates the role of social class which frequently cuts across ethnic social behaviour and politics, and it also grossly misinterprets the Afro-American experience within the US. As Nelson and Meranto suggest, 'implicit in the ethnic analogy is the assumption that America is a democratic and pluralist society open to effective competition by all groups who wish to use the political process as a lever to social and economic progress. But this assumption does not take into account the unique position of Blacks in the American social order', and it also 'de-emphasizes race as a fundamental factor in the distribution and exercise of power in American politics.'[145] Afro-Americans are, and are not, Americans: the essential characteristics of our socio-economic and political evolution have been our utility to generate profits for capitalism, our marginality to the cultural and social centres of state power, and the ability of our people to form an alternative, counter-hegemonic consciousness and cultural patterns of resistance. Manifestations of Black nationalism within electoral politics, rather than the colour-blind approach, may be 'useful for mobilizing masses of Blacks — especially those characterized by lower socio-economic life conditions', as political theorist James Jennings argues. 'But progressive Black nationalism is not an end; ultimately it is a means by which to encourage people to question the distribution of wealth and power in American society. Because of this, Black nationalism becomes — albeit indirectly — a useful tool by which to discourage racism among white working-class sectors; in the long run, Black nationalism can help to raise the political and social consciousness of white ethnics in American cities.'[146] There are parallels between the failure of most Black leaders to comprehend the protest-potential of the national minority consciousness and cultural traditions of Afro-Americans and the reluctance to examine the issue of gender-exploitation. Most Black elected officials have been and continue to be males. The majority of Black women who gain public office tend to be placed on school boards and in city council posts and lack effective representation within both civil rights organizations and most Black electoral political formations.[147] The theoretical and practical nexus between gender oppression and racism is seldom raised, even by some Black women politicians, who argue that feminism has little place in the Black movement.[148]

Why do these ideological blinders still hinder the social vision of the Black politician? We may look to the burden of our history for the answers. The objective of anti-slavery agitation, slave rebellions and conspiracies was the removal of our shackles, the end of the lash and of the sale of our spouses and children. Freedom meant the absence of slavery. But from Reconstruction through the next century, freedom became identified with equal opportunity and the demise of Jim Crow: representation within the electoral political apparatus, access to educational facilities, employment within existing economic enterprises, the right to own property, the ability to obtain investment capital from banks. The accommodationists, looking upwards perceived the possibility of freedom via capitalism and clientage coalitions with the ruling class; the reformers, listening more closely to the masses, tried earnestly to advocate freedom as an equal opportunity for all. The critical theoretical distance that separates the militant Black reformer from the Black progressive is quite small, but crucial. As Jack O'Dell remarks, the liberal reformist tradition 'stands for minimal change and a kind of patchwork approach to the problems of the country', while the 'progressive trend stands for fundamental change.' The antisegregationist liberal desires 'the implementation of civil rights laws'. The progressive has made the leap from a civil rights agenda to a 'struggle for civil equality'.[149]

The problems of Black political practice stem from the inadequacies of theory. First, there is a dual tendency for Black officials either to overemphasize the importance of electoral participation, or to subordinate it to the process of petty capital accumulation. Liberal integrationists tend to fall into the first category. Benjamin Hooks, in a rare excursion into the realm of theory, once claimed to 'have read and studied Frantz Fanon. There are a lot of ways an oppressed people can rise . . . [and] the concept of rising against oppression through physical contact is stupid and self-defeating.' Hooks urged instead that Afro-Americans 'become a political commodity . . . voting our own self-interests as other ethnic groups do . . .'[150] Black political scientist Chuck Stone got to the heart of the matter: 'The age of demonstrations has passed, and the age of the ballot box is upon the Black man. It is the tool of survival . . .'[151] Accommodationists have urged Blacks to vote, but frequently view electoral phenomena as a product of Black economic development within capitalism. The classic representative of this position is Booker T. Washington. 'Too much stress had been placed upon the mere matter of voting and holding political office' during Reconstruction, Washington noted, 'rather than upon the preparation for the highest citizenship . . . I believe it is the duty of the Negro to deport himself modestly in regard to political claims, depending upon the slow but sure influences that proceed from the possession of property, intelligence and high character for the full recognition of his political rights.'[152] Few Black middle-class representatives went so far as to deny the utility of voting. But in the 1960s and 1970s, many Black officials accepted much of Washington's gradualistic, 'self-help' philosophy. In 1970, Newark mayor Kenneth Gibson insisted that 'you do not achieve economic power by winning an election . . . You have to understand that nobody is going to take care of you. Nobody is going to deal with our problems but us.'[153] National Urban League leader Whitney Young urged Blacks to study the 'works' of Booker T. Washington, as well as those of other more militant Afro-Americans.[154] Even Martin Luther King frequently quoted from Booker T. Washington, and once suggested that in 'Du Bois's outlook there was no room for the whole people'.[155]

Secondly, Black political leaders have a rather mediocre track record on forming effective coalitions and alliances with other social movements and political organizations. Accommodationists usually extend their support to sections of the ruling class that inevitably pursue policies that are detrimental to Blacks' material, social and political interests. For example, in 1901 Washington actively lobbied for the appointment of former Alabama governor Thomas G. Jones as federal district judge for northern Alabama. Washington wrote to Theodore Roosevelt that Jones was 'a clean, pure man in every respect', opposed lynching and supported 'the education of both races'. Jones, a descendant of an old slave-holding family who perceived 'the negro race' as being 'under' whites, got the job. Once on the bench, Jones's rulings supported the interests of railroads and corporations, checked the growth of labour unions, crushed strikes, and nearly abolished Black suffrage.[156] Latter-day accommodationist endorsements, such as Abernathy's and Williams's support for Reagan in 1980, have yielded similar results. Conversely, liberal reformers tend to advocate coalitions simply for their own sake, whether or not they produce tangible assets for the Afro-American electorate. The worst offender in this regard since 1960 has been Bayard Rustin. His 1966 essay in *Commentary*, 'Black Power and Coalition Politics', urged Blacks to 'stay in the Democratic Party . . . the party of progress', without providing any serious critique of the major short-comings of Democratic administrations or of the party as a whole with respect to Blacks' needs and demands.[157] Following Rustin's questionable path in 1980 were Coretta Scott King and most of the Congressional Black Caucus. After nearly four years of attacking the Carter Administration's policies towards Blacks and the poor, the Black elite gave a ringing endorsement for the southern white Democrat. As King told reporters: 'the White House [under Carter] belongs to us. We are here in large numbers and staying as long as we want.' Nowhere was there any concept of 'critical support', or the demand for major concessions from the admini-stration in order to receive the electoral backing of Afro-Americans.[158] Many Black local and state-elected officials operate in exactly the same manner. As Cole's study noted, most Black politicians do not 'define' their 'aims and expectations' while seeking election, and they 'rarely enter office on a platform of specific programmes'. Black officials usually join coalitions even before their programmatic objectives have been developed.[159]

Other Black politicians and political scientists, recognizing the inadequacies of their associates' positions on coalitions, have advocated a 'no permanent interests' thesis to guide electoral prac-tice. One of the earliest proponents of this view was NAACP official Henry Lee Moon, who in 1948 argued that the Negro electorate was the 'balance of power' between the Republican and Democratic Parties.[160] Moon's thesis has led to two rather different conclusions. Some leaders have taken the balance of power concept to mean that Blacks 'have no permanent friends or permanent parties, only permanent interests', as Congressman William Clay argues.[161] Black leaders who have been the direct beneficiaries of Republican administrations, such as Benjamin Hooks, imply that Blacks should abandon their fifty-year association with the Democratic Party. 'The Democratic candidates . . . take the Black vote for granted', Hooks complained in 1981, and the Republicans 'don't see any advantage to be gained in seeking votes where there are none . . . Down the road we'll have to figure out a way to prevent candidates from ignoring us.'[162] Others who hold some affinities with Black nationalism interpret the balance of power thesis to mean that coalitions of almost any sort are questionable. Hatcher insisted in 1970 that he did 'not feel very much hope in coalitions . . . it is not possible to develop really meaningful relationships with others.'[163] Stokely Carmichael and Charles V. Hamilton presented a slightly less pessimistic perspective in *Black Power*. After asserting that racial integration was 'a subterfuge for the maintenance of white supremacy', the authors dismissed Black alliances with traditional white liberals and organized labour, which had 'cast its lot with the big businesses of exploitation . . .' Coalitions could only make sense between Blacks and poor whites, even though 'poor white people are becoming more hostile — not less — towards Black people.'[164] The poverty of political practice in this instance is, again, a poverty of theory and historical observation. Historically, Black voters have been overwhelmingly represented in one capitalist party or another since 1865. Black workers and poor people tend to vote for parties that, on the basis of practical experience, are likely to favour their material, social and political interests; the Black petty-bourgeois accommodationists tend to support the political party that represents the dominant sectors of capital; and reformers are oriented towards the party that provides tangible benefits (jobs, housing, schools, civil rights laws) to Blacks. Afro-Americans did not support the Republican Party in the nineteenth century simply because Lincoln signed the Emancipation Proclamation. Nor did Blacks vote for Roosevelt just because he signed Executive Order 8802. Various fractions of capital dominate both parties, and different social blocs are represented within the parties, which can under certain circumstances produce sharply divergent public policies. The question of coalitions is, at root, an issue of common social class interests, which may result in a joint electoral manoeuvre between two or more groups. It is clear, for example, that white workers and poor people gain materially from antiracist coalition politics: in 1979, 63 per cent of all household recipients of food-stamps were white, as well as 59 per cent of all families in public housing and 68 per cent of all Medicaid recipients.[165] Ethnocentrism and white supremacy are quite consciously manipulated by capital and by both major parties to frustrate and divide the working class. But the inability of many Black petty-bourgeois politicians to contemplate strategies that employ the ultimate centrality of social class in political and power struggles often renders them incapable of building effective electoral coalitions.

A third area of Black electoral political practice which is not frequently explored is the problem of corruption. Probably the most prevalent social characteristic of all bourgeois democracies is the omnipresence of corruption. Michael Parenti's *Democracy for the Few* lists only a small number of examples from the US in the 1970s. First, there is the normal petty graft that accompanies any position of authority. Parenti notes that about one third of the Illinois state legislature was estimated by a Republican member as accepting 'pay-offs'. In some states such as Louisiana 'scandals are so prolific that exposure of them has absolutely no impact.' During his 1976 Presidential campaign, Carter 'made a plea for honesty in government at a $100-a-plate dinner in Miami while beside him on the dais sat a mayor recently imprisoned for tax evasion, a couple of Florida state senators who had just pleaded guilty to conflict of interest, a commissioner facing trial for bribery, and three other commissioners charged with fraud.' Secondly, there is meritorious graft, for service beyond the call of duty. Between 1957 and 1974, for instance, New York Governor Nelson Rockefeller 'admitted to having given nearly $1.8 million in gifts and loans to eighteen public officials, including $50,000 to Henry Kissinger (who had worked for Rockefeller for fifteen years) three days before Kissinger became special adviser to President Nixon.' One reason that corruption has become endemic is the longevity of the public careers of officials. Parenti observes that 'from 1924 to 1956, 90 per cent of the Congressmen who stood for re-election were victorious.' In 1970, '94 per cent of those seeking re-election to the House were returned' to office, and 10 per cent had no opponents in either their primary or the general elections. The electorate has, as we have seen, little accountability over its own 'representatives', while corporate interests legally or illegally funnel monies to those who support their projects. Minor parties that might upset the system are discouraged by state laws that require them 'to gather a large number of signatures on nominating petitions', or by laws that demand 'exorbitant filing fees and observe exacting deadlines when collecting and filing nominating petitions.' In any event, 'when change threatens to rule, then the rules are changed.' Under more democratic circumstances, the graft and corruption the electoral system promotes might be checked by rigorous law enforcement. But as Parenti also notes, 'in New York City alone half the Police Department was reported by the Knapp Commission (in 1974) to be accepting pay-offs. In 1974 widespread corruption was found in the police forces of Chicago, Philadelphia, Indianapolis, Cleveland, Houston, Denver and New York, involving gambling, prostitution, narcotics and stolen goods.'[166]

In racist social formations, racists have historically used corruption as a means to co-opt Black leaders and to minimize dissatis-

184

faction among the oppressed masses. A Black woman or man who refused to steal, who rejected petty graft, was not to be trusted. Richard Wright explains:

> Pretending to conform to the laws of the whites, grinning, bowing, [Negroes] let their fingers stick to what they could touch. And the whites seemed to like it. But I, who stole nothing, who wanted to look them straight in the face, who wanted to talk and act like a man, inspired fear in them. The southern whites would rather have had Negroes who stole, work for them than Negroes who knew, however dimly, the worth of their own humanity. Hence, whites placed a premium upon Black deceit; they encouraged irresponsibility; and their rewards were bestowed upon us Blacks in the degree that we could make them feel safe and superior.[167]

Few elected officials are immune to the perquisites of power. More consistently than many of their white counterparts, Black state legislators or Congressional representatives, when re-elected once, usually have very little difficulty in securing their seats. As Black elected officials acquire seniority, deals made to secure legislation beneficial to their constituents may involve some minor, if technically illegal, trade-offs. The white conservative politician may commit gross public fraud, but little is said: Black politicians' minor peccadillos may be used to guarantee their loyalty to the party or to the state apparatus. When reformers attempt to use the system effectively, some then become quite vulnerable to attack. Harlem leader Adam Clayton Powell, elected to Congress in 1944 with the support of the Communist Party and Black activist organizations, was an early proponent of Black Power. By 1961, Powell had risen in seniority to chair the important House Committee on Education and Labour, from which he secured the passage of liberal legislation. His personal weakness for luxuries at government expense permitted hypocritical House leaders to remove him from his seat. A decade later, Michigan Congressman Charles Diggs had replaced Powell as the Blacks' chief spokesperson in the House, ranking fourteenth in overall seniority in the chamber. Diggs established the Congressional Black Caucus and was active as a leader in the National Black Political Convention of March 1972. In the mid 1970s he chaired both the House subcommittee on African Affairs and the House Committee on the District of Columbia. Suddenly he was charged and later 'convicted of pay-roll fraud and finally gaoled.' Diggs's undignified removal 'tainted' the entire CBC, which left 'the organization slipping ever deeper into political chaos'.[169]

When co-optation fails, the option of coercion always exists. Most Black reformist leaders and community leaders with histories of involvement in social protest movements fall under local police scrutiny years before they seek public office. In most US metropolitan areas, the police department maintains its own intelligence units to track such leaders. By 1968, the Detroit Police Department had 75 officers in such a unit; Boston had 40; New York had 90 with 55 additional undercover; and by 1970 Los Angeles had 167 agents.[170] The Washington DC police department's political surveillance unit focused on a number of local Black groups in the early 1970s, including the 'Howard University Committee to Free Angela Davis', DC Statehood Party', 'Black People's Party', RAP Inc' (a local drug rehabilitation centre), 'Tenants' Rights Workshop', and the 'People's Coalition for Peace and Justice', as well as individual Black political leaders.[171] The US bourgeois democratic state has quietly developed an internal police state apparatus, which stands ready to counter any successful social protests that threaten the established order. As Robert Allen notes, 'under Title II of the 1950 Internal Security (McCarran) Act six detention camps' were established by 1954. Title II gives the President the power to declare an 'internal security emergency' in the event of invasion, war or domestic 'insurrection'. Under the McCarran Act's provisions, the US Attorney General 'is authorized to apprehend and detain "in such places of detention . . . all persons as to whom there is reasonable ground to believe that such person probably will engage in . . . acts of espionage and sabotage"'. Most of the McCarran concentration camps had 'either fallen into disuse' or become part of the US Bureau of Prisons. But most military planners admit 'that detention of dissenters, on at least a limited basis, could conceivably take place . . .'[172] Urban riots supported by Black leaders might provoke martial law. Part of the state's strategy therefore involves the separation of mass leaders in both social movements and the electoral apparatus from their constituencies. On 25 August 1967, FBI Director J. Edgar Hoover ordered Bureau agents to 'expose, disrupt, misdirect and otherwise neutralize Black national groups.' Hoover's original memo included several specific goals: 'Prevent the *coalition* of militant Black nationalist groups; prevent the rise of a Black "Messiah"; [and] discredit the leadership . . .' All means legal or otherwise were permitted: telephone wire-tapping, sending anonymous or fictitious materials to members or groups, the use of paid informants or agents to disrupt an organization or election campaign, leaking damaging information on a leader to the media, creating phoney organizations solely for disruptive purposes, and contacting the employers and neighbours of activists.[173] The FBI, and especially Hoover, had a special loathing for King. In April 1964 Hoover authorized FBI agents to 'neutralize or completely discredit the effectiveness of Martin Luther King Jr as a Negro Leader.' Hoover edited tapes which supposedly documented King's extramarital relations, and sent them to his wife 'in hopes it might ruin King's marriage and thereby diminish his prestige'. The FBI sent an anonymous letter to King, urging him to commit suicide 'before your filthy fraudulent self is bared to the Nation'. The FBI and local police were strangely absent when King was assassinated on 4 April 1968. But when 'the news reached Atlanta, a supervisor in the FBI field office there reportedly danced and shouted, "They got the sonofabitch! I hope he dies!" When the G-man's wish came true an hour later, an atmosphere of general hilarity enveloped the FBI premises.'[174]

Given the repressive nature of the US state, and the institutional racism within both capitalist parties, Black reformers — especially those who are nationalistic — have repeatedly attempted to develop an alternative electoral vehicle that would represent Blacks' interests. As early as 1860, the *Anglo-African* newspaper cautioned the tiny northern Black electorate that 'the two great political parties separate at an angle of two roads, [but] they meet eventually at the same goals. The Democratic Party would make the white man the master and the Black man the slave; the Republican Party . . . though with larger professions for humanity, is by far [our] more dangerous enemy . . . their opposition to slavery means opposition to the Black man — nothing else.'[175] Subsequently Afro-Americans developed a series of short-lived Third Party efforts: the Coloured Independent Party of Pennsylvania in 1883; the Negro Protective Party in Ohio in 1897; the all-Black South Carolina Progressive Democratic Party in 1944; the Mississippi Freedom Democratic Party, which evolved from the southern desegregation campaigns of the 1960s; the Lowndes county Freedom Organization's 'Black Panther Party' of 1965, in Alabama; the Freedom Now Party, based in Michigan and New York in the mid 1960s; and the United Citizens' Party of South Carolina in 1970. All of these formations, like their capitalist counterparts, defined politics in electoral terms, and largely accepted the structural constraints, the rules and official procedures, of the bourgeois democratic process. Not surprisingly, all of them either disappeared, or were absorbed into one of the two major parties.[176]

However, in the early 1970s, for perhaps the first time in Afro-American political history, a significant percentage of Black elected officials and activists advocated the development of some type of independent Black party. Mayor Gibson called for 'a Black political organization along the lines of the Black political party of the one party African state'; Baraka urged the development of a 'National African Party' which must 'represent in totality the Black man's needs' as well as run candidates for public office; and Mervyn M. Dymally, later to be elected California's Lieutenant Governor, advocated the creation of 'not a third party but a third force' which could serve as a vehicle 'within the major party structures'.[177] After a series of major discussions intiated by Hatcher, Baraka and Congressman Diggs, the call for a national Black political convention was issued in late 1971.

The Gary convention of 10-11 March 1972 was the high point of Black nationalist agitation in the post-World War II period, and, in many respects, paralleled the Cleveland, Ohio convention of 1854, called by Delany and other Afro-American nationalists. Integrationist reformers, including Jesse Jackson and Coretta Scott King, stood united with Baraka and other Black nationalists. A 'Black Agenda' denouncing the American system built on 'the twin foundations of white racism and white capitalism' was approved; the assembly of over three thousand delegates created the National Black Political Assembly, which would function as a pre-party formation. Nevertheless, within months many of the Black elected officials who had taken an active part in the historic gathering had defected from the Black party-building process. Jackson, William Clay and Walter Fauntroy endorsed liberal Democrat George McGovern for his party's 1972 presidential nomination; the CBC issued a more moderate 'Black Bill of Rights' to take the place of the radical Black Agenda. Within five years, the Assembly had all but collapsed, retaining the support of only a few hundred progressive Black nationalists and community organizers.[178] The repeated failures to create an independent Black political party have not closed the door to the historical probability that Afro-Americans will finally break from the Democratic Party. Perhaps a majority of CBC members would privately agree with Congressman Dellums's 1982 statement: 'we've arrived at a point where this [two-party] system does not serve us well . . . I am in the Democratic Party because the majority of our people are in it.'[179]

The periodic demand to create a Black political party by both nationalists and liberal reformists is indirectly a consequence of the failure of the American working class as a whole to develop a mass labour or social democratic party over the past century. Both capitalist parties have defended institutional racism, and only through the tremendous efforts of Black social movements has US bourgeois democracy extended some modest measure of civil rights to Black people. Thus the search for an independent political vehicle continues, pushed by the demand for full racial equality, but within a political economy and state apparatus that structurally cannot grant it. The dilemma is, once again, both practical and theoretical. Bourgeois democracy retains its legitimacy among Black working people precisely because we have been denied it. As the editors of the Marxist journal *Line of March* observe, 'the possibilities of achieving the goals of the Black liberation movement through the mechanisms of bourgeois democracy have not been fully tested, let alone exhausted. Consequently, the tendency to pursue this course will rise again and again. And it will continue to re-emerge until the Black masses, through their own experience, become convinced that such a course is fruitless and turn to other political forms through which to defend and advance their interests.'[180] Theoretically, the majority of the Afro-American social fraction has not come to think of 'politics' in terms that transcend bourgeois democratic phenomena. When Black progressives in the past have launched a 'party', it has usually lacked extensive connections with ongoing economic, social and political struggles for power at the community level. Without these extensive links with organic social institutions and struggles, the call for a party becomes purely metaphysical. Furthermore, since almost all the attempts to build such parties have been based on the radicalized Black petty bourgeoisie, vacillation and co-optation of leading figures in the formations have been inevitable. Such efforts have not been guided by a social theory calling for the ultimate construction of a socialist political economy, and as a rule have been slow to commit themselves to coordinated electoral and non-electoral political activities with other oppressed sectors in US society.

It appears quite unlikely that the efforts of reformers to represent the demands of Black workers and the poor via the Democratic Party is a viable strategy over the coming years. The faint possibility does exist that the reformist trend, led in part by Blacks, can push the conservative wing of the party into the Republican Party, creating a historic realignment wherein the Democrats would become qualitatively a social democratic or labour party. A more

probable scenario, given the multiclass composition of the Democratic Party, is the emergence of an anticorporate trend or coherent
bloc within the party, which at some future point will become
organizationally capable of splitting from the Democrats. In either
case, the first decisive step in such a transition is mass Afro-
American involvement in progressive electoral politics. As James
Jennings observes, 'a serious challenge to the distribution of wealth
and influence cannot take place until Blacks increase qualitatively
their level of local electoral activism — within a progressive framework. Economic or social development schemes will not be successful until Black communities are controlled politically and pro-
gressively by the people who live in them.'[181] At no point in US
history have Black people ever obtained anything that approxi-
mates proportional representation in the capitalist state apparatus:
the state has been, and remains, a racist state. The historic failures
of both major capitalist political parties to deliver equality to Black
America, and the many contradictions and compromises evident in
the theory and practice of Black politicians, also indicate that new
forms of electoral political protest and new leadership must emerge
in order for Afro-Americans to make the transition from reform to
socialism. The next stages of this transition, as indicated by both the
Washington and the Jackson campaigns, are political revolts against
the Democratic Party within the party, and open rebellions that
force the petty-bourgeois Black leadership either to commit 'class
suicide' or openly to defend the capitalist *status quo*. Militant,
uncompromising leaders from oppressed social classes emerge only
when the masses themselves, conscious of their capacity for altering
their relationships with dominant structures, seek to create new
history. Ideologically, too, this requires that such women and men
see themselves both as the products of past struggles, and as the
bearers of that radical tradition. As Black poet Kalamu ya Salaam
asks:

Where are our real
    leaders now
Where, the pride bearers
    hope inspirers
The spokespeople
    perceptive articulators
The guides
    keen compasses

> The thinkers
> reality analysers
> Where are today's
> Malcolms?
> In which of us
> does his spirit rise?[182]

The Malcolms and Martins are created only when Black people make demands that are seemingly impossible. Yet the impossible, through struggle, becomes the probable, and the probable becomes reality.

4

Black Power in Chicago
Race and Electoral Politics in Urban America

I stand here like you sit here — as a result of 400 years of travail and struggle in this country. And that travail and struggle has come up with a product called "us". We've been through the crucible. We've been pushed around, shoved around, beat, murdered, emasculated, literally destroyed. Our families have been systematically disrupted. There's been an unfair distribution of all the goodies. No system works for us. We influence no institutions in this country except our own. We have no power. We have no land. But through all that struggle we've stayed together . . . We've become more courageous . . . We've been giving white candidates our votes for years and years, unstintingly, hoping that they would include us in the process, deep-seatedly knowing that they probably would not. And so now it's come to the point when we say, "Well, it's our turn. It's our turn." And we don't have to make excuses for it.

Harold Washington, 14 November 1982

I

The election of Harold Washington as mayor of the third largest city in the US, Chicago, has been described as 'the most astonishing municipal campaign in American history'.[1] Despite being outspent during the electoral campaign by more than ten to one by the Democratic incumbent mayor Jane Byrne, the liberal Black Congressman won the Democratic primary race. In victory, Washington defeated not only Byrne but also the son of Chicago's dictatorial political boss, former mayor Richard Daley. Less than two months later, Washington was able to build an unprecedented coalition of Blacks, Latinos and liberal whites to defeat Republican candidate Bernard Epton, thus becoming the first Black mayor in the city's history. Political observers familiar with Chicago's racial history attempted to explain what had occurred to upset the most powerful political machine in America. Radical journalist Nina Berman noted that tens of thousands of Blacks who had never voted

191

in their lives joined thousands more who had supported the Democratic political machine for half a century, to create a social force that 'resembled a people's movement'. Jesse Jackson viewed the Washington campaign as 'a political riot', an unprecedented act of 'disciplined rage'.[2] Chicago political writer Studs Terkel described the Washington victory as an American 'Soweto', evoking parallels between the racism of the Democratic machine and the apartheid regime.[3] Black political scientists Abdul Alkalimat and Don Gills characterized the election as 'a historic event of great significance . . . Black adults demonstrated that under specific conditions they will defy all expectations and mobilize at unprecedented levels. Indeed, this campaign will be discussed as a permanent event in Black political history, and the history of Chicago.'[4]

The Washington campaign differed qualitatively from most previous Afro-American electoral campaigns for several reasons. Firstly, it represented the culmination of a series of Black social reform movements for socio-economic and political equality which had finally assumed a bourgeois democratic electoral form. Washington's victory was the most recent and most politically advanced expression of a very deep protest tradition which is part of Black Chicago's social history. This protest tradition challenged not only the exploitation of Black workers, but the social manifestations of the racial division of labour — poor housing, inadequate educational facilities, the lack of decent public health-care institutions, and so forth. Secondly, the focus of the mobilization was against the most entrenched and corrupt municipal political organization in twentieth-century America, the Cook County Democratic machine. This movement was 'disciplined' and coordinated across class lines: the ballot had become a weapon for the Afro-American masses to attack institutional racism and political patronage. As such, it was an unambiguous social uprising against the hegemony of the Democratic Party *within* the Democratic Party. As the editors of *Line of March* observe, 'Washington's bid for office became a political lightning-rod precisely because it was *perceived by everyone* as a frontal challenge to the entrenched system of white supremacy in Chicago and to the corrupt Democratic Party machine whose political power sustains and enforces it. The burning issue of white privilege and white power overshadowed all others, arousing intense passions on each side and even rendering party loyalties meaningless after decades of tightly controlled Democratic Party dominance.'[5] Thirdly, the struggle against the Democratic machine highlighted in unambiguous terms the central theme of Black political culture, the historic division within the petty bourgeoisie between the accommodationists and the reformers. The former practised clientage politics as a subsidiary of the Democratic machine, while the latter attempted to advocate programmes that represented the material and political interests of the Black working class. Only when the reformist tendency acquired a mass constituency, drawing upon the resources of Black activists, revolutionary nationalists, and trade unionists to their left, could such a campaign triumph over both the Democratic machine and its Black apologists. Finally, the Washington effort of 1983 illustrated not only the racial divisions within the American working class, but the inherent instability of social class forces that the Democratic Party comprises. The success of Harold Washington, as well as the March on Washington movement that year, were decisive in creating the political conditions necessary for the Jackson campaign to occur.

II

The contemporary struggle for Black power in Chicago can be understood only by reviewing the turbulent history of race and class in this city. Ironically, the city was founded by a Black trader, Jean Baptiste Pointe Du Sable, during the administration of George Washington. Despite this historical footnote, the numbers of Blacks living in the growing town remained relatively small throughout most of the nineteenth century. Sociologists St Clair Drake and Horace Cayton note that there were less than one thousand free Blacks in Chicago in 1860.[6] Thirty years later, the total Afro-American population was 14,271 out of 1.1 million residents, only 1.3 per cent of the city. A variety of external economic, political and social factors — including the rise of racist violence and Jim Crow in the South, and the decline of privately held, Black-owned land after 1910 — increased the trickle of Black emigrants into a roaring tide of humanity. As Charles S. Johnson noted in 1925, Chicago was known throughout the Black South 'for its colossal abattoirs . . . remembered for the fairyland wonders of the World's Fair; home of the fearless, taunting "race paper", and above all things, of the mills clamouring for men.'[7] By 1920, over a hundred thousand Afro-Americans lived and worked in the sprawling city. In the next decade, their numbers increased by 114 per cent, to 233,903 in a city of 3.4 million. Well before the Great Depression, however, Black Chicago was defined by clear and ruthlessly enforced neighbourhood boundaries which formed a pattern of virtual apartheid. In 1900, the majority of working-class Blacks lived on the South Side, between the commercial districts of downtown, and Thirty-ninth Street. By 1910, over 30 per cent of all Blacks 'lived in predominantly Negro sections of the city and over 60 per cent in areas that were more than 20 per cent Negro.' Historian Allan Spear observes that Blacks 'were so limited in their choice of housing, they were forced to pay higher rents in those buildings that were open to them.'[8]

Real estate agents usually received 10 to 15 per cent more in rent fees from Blacks than from whites in so-called 'marginal neighbourhoods'. Perhaps three quarters of all Black families living in predominantly Black neighbourhoods were forced to accept houses that were 'usually dilapidated with boarded-up porches and rickety wooden walks'. Whites living on the periphery of Black neighbourhoods began to band together to preserve the colour line in their communities and public schools. In 1903, 350 liberal white professionals in the Hyde Park area even announced a public crusade against Blacks, which included demands that local 'real estate agents must refuse to sell property in white blocks to Negroes, and landlords must hire only white janitors.' The Hyde Park group 'appointed a committee to purchase property owned by Negroes in white blocks' and gave 'bonuses to Negro renters who would surrender their leases'.[9] Despite the existence of the 1885 Illinois civil rights law which guaranteed 'that all persons shall be entitled to the full and equal enjoyment of the accommodations, advantages, facilities and privileges of inns, restaurants, eating-houses, barber shops, theatres and public conveyances', white supremacy was soon extended into these areas. Black workers were frequently refused service or harassed in public establishments; white taverns often refused to serve Blacks; theatres set aside 'Jim Crow' seats in balconies. As Spear comments, 'Most proprietors would accommodate a Negro if they thought refusal would create a major controversy; Booker T. Washington, for instance, stayed regularly at the plush Palmer House when he visited Chicago.'[10]

Residential apartheid and Jim-Crowed public accommodations mirrored the racist dual labour market of the city. By 1900 'almost 65 per cent of the Negro men and over 80 per cent of the Negro women worked as domestic and personal servants, while only 8.3 per cent of the men and 11.9 per cent of the women were engaged in manufacturing (and most of the women so employed worked in their own homes as dressmakers and seamstresses).'[11] Using the figures for the male work-force in 1910, of the city's 20,210 teamsters, 566 (2.8 per cent) were Blacks; of 14,726 engineers, firemen, motormen and switchmen on railroads, 20 were Blacks (0.1 per cent); of 11,813 deliverymen, 266 were Blacks (2.3 per cent); of 29,820 salesmen, 52 were Blacks (0.2 per cent). Conversely, 30.9 per cent of all male waiters were Blacks, as were 68.3 per cent of all male porters. Of all female 'launderesses', 29.7 per cent were Black women, whereas only 21 out of 11,632 saleswomen were Black. Yet by the end of the nineteenth century, a tiny but relatively affluent Black elite had begun to surface within the South Side and elsewhere. In 1910, the Black community had 44 lawyers, 109 physicians, 76 clergymen, 64 public school teachers (of whom 53 were women), 42 nurses and 218 retail dealers. This elite group was supplemented by a number of Blacks who were independently employed, including barbers (319), hairdressers (316), boarding-house keepers (267), and other entrepreneurs and artisans of various types. Despite their numerical and social fragility, this first generation Negro petty bourgeoisie exerted considerable cultural and ideological weight within the larger Black working-class community. As Drake and Cayton note, the Black elite consciously viewed itself as an emerging petty bourgeoisie, culturally 'refined' and socially if not fundamentally economically more 'advanced' than the thousands of newly arrived Black share-croppers from Mississippi or Arkansas. 'Because of their education and breeding', this elite 'looked down upon . . . the less decorous behaviour of their racial brothers.'[12]

The political and ideological disposition of the bulk of Chicago's Black petty bourgeoisie was unapologetically accommodationist. In politics, this conservative, parvenu stratum was led by men such as Lloyd Wheeler, a manager of a growing tailoring firm and a key organizer of the Chicago branch of the National Negro Business League; S. Laing Williams, a prosperous attorney, founder of a Black literary society, the Prudence Crandall Club, and later a 'ghostwriter' for Washington; and Sandy W. Trice, a clothing store owner who in 1908 purchased a radical Black newspaper, the *Conservator*, fired its anti-Washington editor, J. Max Barber, and published articles praising the conciliatory public line of Washington. Even more influential were George Cleveland, Cyrus Field Adams and Jesse Binga. A doctor, Hall was president of Chicago's Negro Business League branch in 1912, and a powerful ally of Washington. On many occasions, he chastised Blacks for their peculiar inability to advance sufficiently under capitalism. 'The race is not progressing as rapidly in all those things which must

necessarily be acquired,' Hall noted, 'before we can become substantial and highly respected individuals and citizens.' Adams was
managing editor of the *Western Appeal* newspaper, secretary of the
Afro-American Council, and with Washington's influence became
Assistant Registrar of the Treasury in January 1901. Binga was
undoubtedly the most controversial and colourful accommodationist. A member of the National Negro Business League, Binga
made part of his wealth by marrying the sister of John 'Mushmouth'
Johnson, the city's first Black 'gambling lord'. In 1898 he started a
booming real-estate firm, and in 1908 founded Binga Bank. By the
1920s, however, Binga had become the client of 'utilities magnate'
Samuel Insull. Insull's business dealings and his refusal to aid
Binga's many ventures led to the bank's collapse during the Great
Depression.[13]

The reformist elites, conversely, attacked all forms of segregation, and sought to expand Afro-Americans' civil rights and
economic opportunities within the existing bourgeois democratic
system. Black dentist Charles E. Bentley and bookkeeper James B.
Madden were ideological defenders and friends of Du Bois. Both
men attended the famous 1905 Niagara Conference in Ontario
establishing the Niagara Movement. Another Du Boisite was
Ferdinand L. Barrett, Illinois's assistant state attorney for ten
years, and subsequently a municipal court judge in Chicago. Over
Washington's protests, Barret became a major Black leader in the
1904 presidential campaign of Theodore Roosevelt. Edward H.
Morris was yet another Du Bois supporter, the co-founder of the
Illinois Equal Rights League in 1903 and a prominent corporate
attorney. John G. Jones, known to friends and foes alike as 'Indig-
nation Jones', led public protests to create a Black YMCA in 1889,
and prided himself as Booker T. Washington's most 'vitriolic critic'.
But certainly the city's most outstanding reform leader, Black or
white, was Ida B. Wells-Barnett. Born in 1862 in Holly Springs,
Mississippi, Wells first attracted national attention with her fiery
editorials and columns in her Memphis newspaper, *Free Speech and
Headlight.* Her 1893 manifesto denouncing southern lynchings,
United States Atrocities, gained her an international audience. Wells
was an active leader of the Afro-American Council, a noted
feminist and a proponent of women's suffrage. Five years before Du
Bois challenged Washington in his *Souls of Black Folk,* she stood
virtually alone as a national defender of Blacks' civil rights and as
the major critic of the Tuskegee political machine. After Wells
married Barnett, her political work continued. In Chicago, she

developed ties with social worker Jane Addams in the effort to improve the housing and public welfare conditions of the poor. She was the only Chicago Afro-American courageous enough 'to sign the call for the conference that led to the establishment of the NAACP'.[14]

Despite the political differences within the small Black petty bourgeoisie, both tendencies usually submerged their antagonisms in order to build cultural and social institutions benefitting the entire Afro-American community. In 1891 the integrated Provident Hospital was established, led by Dr Daniel Hale Williams, the first surgeon to perform successful heart suture. Accommodationist Lloyd Wheeler was one of Provident's founders, and radical James B. Madden was on the Board of Trustees. The hospital quickly became a symbol of pride for Negroes, and in 1916-1918 Blacks helped to raise $15,000 to expand the facility. Chicago's NAACP branch office was the first founded outside New York, and the city hosted the NAACP's third annual convention in 1912. Black women established a YWCA in 1915, which provided a library, job training courses, an employment reference service, a youth summer camp and exercise facilities for Chicago's Blacks. Black theatres and public entertainment facilities began to thrive with the growing urban Black population. The Chicago chapter of the National Association of Coloured Women was especially active in assisting low-income Black families. The chapter 'maintained kindergartens, day nurseries, sewing and cooking classes, mothers' meetings, penny savings banks [and] helped friendless and homeless girls.'[15] The most influential Black cultural institutions were, of course, the churches. Olivet Baptist Church, with 9,000 members in 1920, was the largest Black church in the city. Olivet retained an efficient staff of sixteen workers who ran 'a labour bureau, kindergarten, nursery, and welfare department, in addition to the usual club and athletic activities'.[16] By 1920, Blacks owned twenty Holiness or Pentecostal churches, thirty-four Methodist and eighty-six Baptist churches. A number of prominent clergy sided with the radical reformers — notably Reverdy Ransom, and also AME pastor Archibald J. Carey, who as a member of the city's motion-picture censorship board, successfully fought against the local release of the viciously racist film *Birth of a Nation* in 1915.

The general situation of Black labour during these decades was complicated by the ambiguous attitude of organized labour to the new emigrants from the South. White trade-union officials and rank-and-file workers were often bitterly racist. When members of the Knights of Labour announced in 1894 that they favoured using federal funds to expel all Afro-Americans to 'the Congo Basin, Liberia, or some other parts of Africa', Blacks were furious. The Chicago Coloured Women's Club responded sharply, 'Negroes have been residents of this country for two hundred and fifty years, and are as much American citizens as anybody. If this country is too small for the Knights of Labour and the Negro, then let the Knights leave.'[17] The hostility between Black and white workers was so great that thousands of Blacks often joined the ranks of strike-breakers, especially in labour confrontations in the stockyards and in the coal companies. As Black Chicago pastor R.R. Wright noted in 1905, 'Negroes [are not opposed] to unions . . . Yet it still remains that in times of industrial peace the more desirable places are closed against Negroes, either because the employers will not hire them or because the men will not work with them.' Wright urged white labour leaders 'to realize in fact, what they have asserted in theory, that the cause of labour cannot be limited by colour . . .'[18] The Chicago Federation of Labour, finally admitting that the unions had deliberately rejected Blacks' applications for membership, made some attempts to redress long-standing griev-ances. In an open statement to Chicago's Black proletariat, the Federation declared: 'The trades-union movement knows no race or colour. Its aims are the bettering of the condition of the wage-earner, whatever his colour or creed . . . Come into our trade unions, give us your assistance and in return, receive our support, so that race hatred may be forever buried, and the workers of the country united in a solid phalanx to demand what we are justly entitled to — a fair share of the fruits of our industry.' Most Black workers joined the unions after these anti-racist appeals. In fact, some 'became so zealous for the cause of unionism, that they even tried the persuasion of violence upon other members of their race, when words were not found strong enough to stop' Black strike-breakers.[19] Within several years there were several Black local union officers, and six Black delegates to the Chicago Federation of Labour. Some white workers even developed friendships with their Black 'comrades'. Radical Railway Carmen's Union organizer William Z. Foster — later to become the chairman of the American Communist Party — was a strong proponent of biracial co-operation within Chicago stockyard's labour-force.

These steps forward towards interracial labour unity, and indeed the steady progress of the entire Black community, were halted with the outbreak of the bloody Chicago race riot of July-August 1919.

Armed vigilante gangs of whites terrorized the Black community, and Blacks fought back in kind. Black students and army veterans armed themselves and protected the Black YMCA, discharging their guns at the car-loads of whites. Black workers without rifles hurled bricks and rocks from their tenement houses and fire-escapes. William M. Tuttle Jr, the historian of the Chicago riot of 1919, oberves that both the police and white ethnic workers were active participants in the widespread atrocities:

> Instances of brutality and actual police collusion with white lawlessness were not rare; indeed it was often the Black victim of the assault rather than the mob itself who was arrested, and policemen frequently vanished into the shadows of alleys and side streets rather than confront the lawless bands of whites who boldly paraded the main arteries . . . [white mobs hunted] for Blacks in the downtown district. Wherever they were spotted — in railroad stations, restaurants, hotels — Black men and boys were dragged into the streets and beaten insensible or shot. Often the motive was not only inflamed racial hatred but also robbery and vandalism. Black men lay dead and wounded in gutters, their pockets turned inside out, while at street-corners stood the white gangsters, boldly dividing up their profits of watches, cash, and rings . . . Italian residents on the West Side . . . set upon a Black youth who happened to ride by on his bicycle. His body [was] riddled with bullets and stab wounds, [and] the mob, in addition, saturated the corpse with gasoline and ignited it.[20]

White union leaders urged white members to abstain from violence, but racism was more powerful than appeals for proletarian unity. Stockyard workers circulated 'petitions demanding that the companies draw the colour line in employment'. When Black workers returned to the yards, 'nearly 10,000 white unionists walked out.' Handbills 'in three languages' circulated by white workers called for a whites-only general strike. In fourteen days 38 persons, including 25 Afro-Americans, were killed; 178 whites and 342 Blacks were seriously injured; one thousand families were left homeless.[21] Despite later instances of Black-white labour unity, particularly during the South Chicago steelworkers' strike of 1937, the distrust and fear generated by the 1919 race riot remained a barrier to future efforts to bring workers together across the colour line. Some white workers might be willing 'in a time of crisis . . . to struggle side by side with Negroes [and] follow them as leaders'; however, 'such behaviour was not . . . accepted as entirely normal by many workers.'[22]

III

All of these factors — the existence of white working-class racism and vigilante violence, residential segregation, Jim-Crowed public accommodations, the dual labour market — had a direct impact upon Black electoral behaviour in Chicago. Like most Afro-Americans prior to the New Deal, Chicago's Black community was overwhelmingly Republican. In his 1933 study, Harold F. Gosnell observed that in presidential elections the Republicans normally 'can count on anywhere from 70 to 95 per cent of the votes cast in the sections inhabited largely by Negroes.' One Black labourer from Alabama explained to Gosnell that 'he could never vote for a Democrat as long as he kept his memory. The Democrats he knew in Alabama were the "imps of Satan".'[23] Nevertheless, Chicago's Black community exhibited some degree of political independence as early as 1888, with the formation of the Cook County Coloured Democratic Club. Black Democrats were still an isolated minority in 1905 when they split into two factions, the Cook County Democratic League and the Tom Jefferson Club. On into the twentieth century, the Republicans still controlled the Black vote. At the state level, Illinois Republican governor Charles S. Deneed, who served from 1905 to 1913, 'used every bit of patronage at his disposal to lure Black voters into the Republican fold', observes Hanes Walton. 'Following Deneed on the local level in 1915 was mayoralty winner William Hale Thompson, who likewise used patronage as freely as possible to elect himself mayor of the city three times from 1915 to 1923 and from 1927 to 1931.'[24] Several political scientists suggest that as the number of Black rural southerners increased dramatically in Chicago between 1910 and 1920, the political behaviour of Black voters split along class lines, the poor and working classes voting Republican and much of the older elite becoming increasingly Democratic. In 1916 about one fifth of Chicago's Blacks voted Democratic. Julius F. Taylor, a militant editor of the *Broad Ax* newspaper, championed a type of William Jennings Bryan populism and urged Blacks to leave the Republican Party. In 1918 the *Broad Ax* endorsed Democratic Senator James Hamilton for re-election, and roughly 45 per cent of Black voters cast the Democratic ticket.[25] A very general pattern of voting was therefore set by the early 1920s: accommodationist elites, tied by conservative ideology and patronage, usually voted for Republicans; reformist elites, inclined towards independence, supported moderate to liberal Democrats, and made a clear distinction between the southern

Democrats, who maintained a rigid segregation code, and their northern counterparts; and the Black working class and displaced agrarians for historical and cultural reasons tended to vote Republican, but under certain circumstances, could favour Democrats in local races.

In the period of political transition between 1920 and 1940, most Blacks gradually shifted their electoral allegiance from the Republican to the Democratic Party.[26] In Chicago, this period coincided with the emergence from the Black elite of the first core of public officials. Indeed, by 1920, Spear states:

> Negroes had more political power in Chicago than anywhere else in the country. They had more appointive and elective offices and exercised greater influence on the dominant political organization than their counterparts in New York, Philadelphia, or Baltimore . . . White political leaders could no longer ignore Negro sensitivities. Frank Lowden, the Republican candidate for Governor of Illinois in 1916, threatened to move his headquarters from a downtown hotel when the management discriminated against Negroes. In 1919, the legislature strengthened the state's civil rights legislation by forbidding landlords, schools and places of public accommodation to advertise a discriminatory policy. When Illinois adopted a new constitution in 1920, it included a strong and explicit civil rights clause.[27]

The Black Chicago politicians of this period had to bridge the cleavages of class within the Black community, and play a delicate balancing-act between the two major parties. The most effective representative of this group was Oscar DePriest. An Alabama emigrant, DePriest arrived in Chicago in 1889. Starting as a house-painter, DePriest gradually made his wealth by the systemic exploitation and manipulation of the newly arrived impoverished Black peasantry. Purchasing whites-only apartment buildings, and thereby prompting their tenants' departure, he then doubled the rent of the Black tenants who took their places. When the migration began in earnest, DePriest's scheme netted thousands of dollars. 'Negroes weren't aware of being overcharged', the entrepreneur reasoned, and if 'he hadn't gotten it, someone else would have.'[28] His entrepreneurial skills elevated him to the leadership of Chicago's National Negro Business League. DePriest then established a powerful Republican base in the city's second ward, and by 1915 he had become an alderman. He first allied himself with Chicago's first Black ward committee-man, E.H. Wright; but DePriest occasionally fought against conservative Republican boss

William Hale Thompson. DePriest formed his own group in 1918, the 'People's Movement', which made 'Black Pride' appeals not unlike those of Garvey, aimed at working-class constituents.[29] Perhaps to gain the support of many reform-minded Black elites, DePriest illustrated his opposition to the Republicans by endorsing a moderate Democrat for mayor, Judge William E. Deven, in 1923. With DePriest's support, and with the vigorous endorsement of Taylor's *Broad Ax*, Deven received 53 per cent of the Black vote and won the election. Despite his frequent flirtations with the Democratic Party, after the mid 1920s he slavishly supported Mayor Thompson's machine, and his loyalty was rewarded in 1928 when he won a Congressional seat at the age of fifty-seven, the first Black Republican to serve in the House since 1901.

For Blacks across the nation, DePriest's 3,800 plurality victory, and his subsequent re-election to Congress both in 1930 and in 1932, was nothing short of a second Jubilee. In his December 1928 editorial in the NAACP journal *Crisis*, Du Bois declared that the former associate of the Washington camp represented 'a vicious political machine, but he cannot be nearly as bad as the white men who run the machine.'[30] Despite his machine-background, Du Bois refused to 'repudiate' DePriest once he was in office, and he explained to readers in a February 1929 essay that Black voters had to use a variety of independent strategies to obtain power.[31] John Hope Franklin explains DePriest's unique contribution to Black political history:

> [DePriest] represented not only his own district, but all the Negroes of the United States. During his three terms in office he was in great demand as a speaker and was pointed to by Negroes everywhere as the realization of their fondest dreams. One Negro newspaper said that his presence in Washington gave the Negro "new hope, new courage, and new inspiration". The white South was alarmed that a Negro had achieved so high a distinction in American political life. When Mrs DePriest attended a tea at the White House for the wives and families of Congressmen, southerners were outraged . . . In Birmingham, where DePriest was scheduled to speak, the Ku Klux Klan burned him in effigy.[32]

DePriest deliberately challenged the 'colour line' in a series of highly publicized acts. He appointed sixteen Blacks to national military academies, sponsored a Non-Partisan Negro Conference in 1931 'to propose Black solutions to the nation's economic problems', and 'carried pistols with him when he mounted the speaker's platform to denounce "race-baiting whites and timid Uncle Toms".[33] To ensure his continued survival, DePriest recruited talented young Black men from the elite to serve in his machine — most prominent among them was a second-generation disciple of the Tuskegee philosophy, William L. Dawson.[34]

The Chicago mayoral races of 1927 and 1931, in combination with the national devastation of the Great Depression, represent the fundamental turning-point in Chicago Black politics. Ironically, the period of Democratic Party hegemony over Black Chicago was initiated by the defeat of Deven by the former incumbent Thompson in 1927. 'Deven knew that he could not break the Black voters' alliance with Thompson, so he tried to build an electoral majority through the persecution of a minority group', Walton observes. Deven 'distributed pictures of Thompson kissing Black children and set calliopes throughout the streets playing "Bye, Bye Blackbird".'[35] Black elites and workers alike united behind Thompson as the lesser of two evils, giving the Republican a resounding 93 per cent Black mandate. However, Thompson would be the last Republican to be elected mayor of Chicago. Bipartisanism was firmly entrenched within the Black community — a legacy of both the Democratic reformist elites and DePriest. In 1928, almost one third of Chicago's Blacks voted for Democratic Presidential candidate Alfred Smith, and in 1932, 21 per cent of all Black voters endorsed Franklin D. Roosevelt. The Democrats won city hall in 1931 with the candidacy of Anton Cermak, despite a Black vote of 84 per cent for his Republican opponent. As Chicago Black historian Charles Branham notes, Cermak 'fired hundreds of Black political job-holders and launched successive raids on South Side gambling in an attempt to persuade Blacks to "play ball" with the Democratic Party.' With Cermak's assassination in 1933, Edward J. Kelly, an Irish South Side Democrat, became mayor, and immediately shifted tactics in dealings with Blacks. Kelly halted the practice of the school system's segregation of Morgan Park High School. He adopted the language of biracial justice and social equality used so successfully by Thompson, and identified himself with the New Deal at the national level. Simultaneously, the white ethnics running the Democratic Party began to recruit accommodationist-oriented Black Republicans from the local Negro elite, in order better to control those more reform-minded Blacks who had long been members of the Democratic Party. Kelly's manoeuvres gradually altered the political contours of the South Side. Roosevelt received 45 per cent of Chicago's Black vote in

1936; the year before Kelly received 72 per cent of Blacks' support in his mayoral race.[36]

The triumph of Kelly's 'moderate' Democratic programmes and the popularity of the New Deal among Black workers nation-wide had the ironic effect of bringing the heirs of Black elite accommodationism and Republicanism into the leadership of Chicago's Black community. This can be illustrated by an assessment of the careers of Chicago's three most influential Black politicians in the period of 1935-1960: Arthur W. Mitchell, Earl Dickerson and William L. Dawson. Mitchell was the perfect Black candidate, as far as the Kelly machine was concerned. A virtual unknown, he had arrived in Chicago only in 1929, and as late as 1930 had been a registered Republican. In 1934, Mitchell ran an effective campaign to unseat DePriest from Congress with the overt aid of the Kelly Democrats. Mitchell used liberal, reformist rhetoric in the local tradition of Julius F. Taylor and Ida B. Wells, charging that DePriest 'had voted against relief and federal jobs programmes for the South Side' and pictured himself 'as a staunch New Dealer'. Mitchell received 53 per cent of the vote, and 'to virtually everyone's surprise', became the first Black Democratic Congressman in US history. Yet this was no triumph for Black progressive reformers. In his undistinguished eight-year career in the House of Representatives, Mitchell proved to be a docile and even inept follower of the worst tendencies of Tuskegee's philosophy of political accommodation. Nationally, Mitchell 'attempted to obstruct the NAACP's crusade for an anti-lynching bill and in contrast to his predecessor, acquiesced to segregation in the nation's capitol.' Mitchell allowed white Democrats to select virtually all of his local appointments in Chicago. 'He survived less on his own merits than as a result of continuing rivalries which prevented the emergence of a powerful Democratic rival.'[37] Mitchell's sole contribution to the struggle for civil rights came in 1937, when he was physically ejected from a Pullman railroad car travelling in the South, and was forced to bring a desegregation suit on the matter to court.[38]

The victory of accommodation over reform among the Negro elites can be more clearly illustrated in the careers of Dickerson and Dawson. Dickerson was an NAACP activist and an articulate proponent of progressive racial reforms. As Branham notes:

> Dickerson set a standard of community consciousness and political courage unsurpassed in Chicago politics . . . He chaired a subcommittee on housing conditions in the black belt that castigated "real estate sharks" and "rent gougers" who charged Blacks 25 per cent more than

whites for equal facilities. He attacked the Department of Public Works for failure to provide adequate garbage collection in his ward. He threatened to block appropriations for Washburn Trade School unless Blacks were admitted, and he led marches to protest delays in the construction of the Ida B. Wells Housing Project . . . Unlike Wright and DePriest, Dickerson did not seek the creation of a political fiefdom within the black belt. He sought nothing less than the breaking down of racial and geographical boundaries, the creation of a coalition of progressive forces across the city to extend the benefits of the New Deal to the homeless, the poor and dispossessed.[39]

After DePriest's defeat in 1934, it appeared that Dickerson would become the next major political leader of the Black community. In a fractious four-way race for city council in 1939, Dickerson defeated DePriest's lieutenant Dawson. Several years before, however, Dawson had begun his move from the Republican Party. In 1935 he crossed party lines to endorse the popular Kelly for mayor. After his failure to be elected to Congress as a Republican candidate in 1938, Dawson left the party and became a Kelly Democrat. With Kelly's material support, Dawson defeated Dickerson in the 1942 Democratic primary for Mitchell's Congressional seat. The next year, to ensure Dickerson's permanent demise, the new Congressman used his new influence to crush Dickerson's effort to secure re-election to city council.

For over a quarter of a century, Dawson ran a subordinate political machine in concert with Kelly and his Machiavellian successor in 1955, Richard J. Daley. Dawson's ideological hero was Booker T. Washington: like the Tuskegee leader, he was absolutely ruthless in rooting out all potential rivals and political liberals who threatened his hegemony over the Black community. Kelly and Daley supplied Dawson's political bloc with the fiscal resources necessary to placate a few of the more serious social ills confronting Blacks, while Dawson gave the Irish Democratic machine a dependable and pliant reservoir of votes every election day. To divide his more progressive critics in Black labour and among the liberal Black elite, Dawson repeatedly 'declared his interest in racial goals and hopes', but 'proceeded to pursue other policies [which] never mentioned Blacks.'[40] Dawson took no role of local leadership in 1946-47 in the Congress of Racial Equality's Chicago campaign to desegregate the work-force at Wonder Bread Bakeries, 'which had a large market in the Negro community but employed Blacks only in menial capacities'.[41] In national politics, Dawson was a non-controversial tool of the Democratic Party's machinery. He was not even on speaking terms with Adam Clayton Powell who was elected to the House in 1944. As political scientist Chuck Stone states, 'Dawson exercised his power carefully, prudently and patiently.' During the Cold War and McCarthyism, Dawson was as hard-line an anticommunist as one could find in the Democratic Party. In the wake of the 1954 Brown decision and the Montgomery County bus boycott of 1955-56, 'Dawson retreated further into silence. He continued to do just three things: win re-election, control Black patronage in Chicago and keep his mouth shut.'[42] The rise of Dawson marks the effective beginning of a Black 'submachine' within the larger city-wide Democratic machine. Black electoral political leverage was tied directly to the number of Black ward committee-men, who were hand-picked by white party leaders.[43]

The legacy of Dawson's corrupt clientage relationship with both Kelly and Daley was devastating to the Black community. Chicago rapidly became, by the 1960s, the most racially segregated city in the nation. The liberal-reform tradition prevalent among broad sections of the Negro petty bourgeoisie was largely divorced from the political culture of the working class. The overwhelming majority of those Black elites who emerged as elected officials were diminutive imitations of Dawson — fawning, cautious in outlook, thoroughly accommodationist in political behaviour. The experience of Martin Luther King Jr in Chicago is particularly instructive here. In late 1965, a group of young turks led by the Reverend Albert A. Raby, president of the Coordinated Council of Community Organizations, invited King and his chief lieutenants, Andrew Young, Walter Fauntroy, Bernard Lee and Jesse Jackson, to help organize a civil rights campaign in the city. Using the successful model of the Christian Leadership Conference-sponsored 'Operation Breadbasket' from Atlanta, King and his associates devised plans to increase the gross income of Chicago's Blacks by $50 million. King met with Superintendent of Police O.W. Wilson, and announced his plans 'to educate people about slum conditions, to organize slum-dwellers into a union to force landlords to meet their obligations, and to mobilize slum tenants into an army of non-violent demonstrators.'[44] A core of reformist community leaders was formed which included John McDermott of the Catholic Interracial Council; Charles Hayes of the Packing House Workers Union; the Reverend Art Brazier, director of the Woodlawn Organization; William Berry of the Chicago Urban League; and Raby. At a massive rally at Soldiers' Field on 10 July

1966, King urged his followers to organize:

> We shall be sadly mistaken if we think freedom is some lavish dish that
> the federal government and the white man will pass out on a silver platter
> while the Negro merely furnishes the appetite. Freedom is never volun-
> tarily granted by the oppressor. It must be demanded by the
> oppressed . . . This day we must decide to fill up the gaols of Chicago, if
> necessary, in order to end slums. This day we must decide that our votes
> will determine who will be the next mayor of Chicago. We must make it
> clear that we will purge Chicago of every politician, whether he be Negro
> or white, who feels that he owns the Negro vote.[45]

But after months of marching, meetings and public confrontations
— which included the stoning of King, Raby and gospel singer
Mahalia Jackson at Marquette Park on 5 August 1966 — the desegregation campaign was forced to come to terms with the Daley
machine. On 5 August, seventy-nine representatives of widely
divergent groups on both sides of the colour line met at Palmer
House and signed the 'Summit Agreement', which effectively
ended the grass roots campaign. A vaguely-worded document, it
included pledges by the Chicago Housing Authority to 'provide a
communally wholesome dispersal of public-housing projects in the
future'; real estate brokers agreed to post summaries of 'the city's
policy on open housing'; the Department of Urban Renewal
declared it would 'vigilantly report cases of discrimination to the
Commission on Human Relations'; and the Chicago Mortgage
Bankers Association agreed to give 'equal service and to lend
mortgage money to all qualified families, without regard to race.'[46]
Daley hailed the Summit Agreement as a 'great day' for Chicago,
and the Democratic machine politicians of both races declared that
King's controversial intervention in the city had brought
Chicagoans a major step forward towards racial equality. The
majority of the South and West Sides' Black poor and working
classes viewed the Summit Agreement as a hypocritical 'sell-out'.
Even SCLC organizers close to King 'admitted that the Movement
failed to achieve its goals. The Black bourgeoisie of Chicago
conceded the insufficiency of the agreement' as well. King's
biographer David Lewis argues that the 'agreement omitted any
mention of a timetable and amounted to little more than a goodwill
pledge from the city, business, and realtors . . . Martin left the local
[Black] leadership with an incomplete and vague agreement.'[47]

King's defeat in Chicago can be attributed to several principal
factors. Firstly, Daley was a skilful follower of the Thompson/Kelly

tradition of benign paternalism towards Blacks. On the same day that King announced plans to demonstrate before city hall, for instance, the city obtained a major grant from the Department of Housing and Urban Development to repair and rebuild thousands of substandard homes. Despite the criticisms from Raby and other liberal reformers, Daley still maintained his political control over the Black wards.[48] Secondly, neither the Cook County Democratic Party nor the white corporate and financial establishment assumed a non-cooperative or blatantly racist posture towards the reforms. Daley simply allowed his bastion of white ethnic constituents — Irish, Germans, Poles, Italians, White Russians, Hungarians, Ukrainians — to represent the racist backlash to King. Thus, when 'open housing' demonstrators ventured into Daley's white ethnic political base in Marquette Park and into the Belmont-Cragin neighbourhood, they were pelted and beaten by thousands of angry whites. As groups of Black and white non-violent demonstrators knelt in prayer, one group of thugs attacked them, while singing the racist ditty:

> I wish I were an Alabama trooper
> That is what I would truly like to be;
> I wish I were an Alabama trooper
> 'Cause then I could kill the niggers legally.

Even the harsh experiences of Birmingham and Selma had left King unprepared for the all-white enclaves of Chicago. 'I have seen many demonstrations in the South,' King observed to reporters, 'but I have never seen anything so hostile as I've seen here . . . '[49]

More decisive to King's failure in 1966 was the lack of political support from broad elements of the Negro elite. Dawson declared that Chicago had no need for a desegregation campaign, and mimicked Albama governor George C. Wallace by denouncing King as an 'outside agitator'. Most of the South Side's Black commitee-men, city councilmen and state representatives played no role in terms of effort. The city's most powerful Black preacher, Dr J.H. Jackson, president of the National Baptist Convention, explicitly denounced King, the SCLC and their reformist allies in Chicago.[50] Jackson and Ernest E. Rather, the leader of the Committee of One Hundred, a Chicago-based interracial coalition, charged that non-violent demonstrations for decent housing, jobs and desegregation were 'a premeditated strategem to trigger civil disruption'. They demanded that King and his associates go back to the South, 'where there was a fertile terrain of flagrant injustice for which his tactics were ideally suited'. Months later, the director of Chicago's NAACP chapter denounced King's 'intemperate campaign' as the reason for the defeat of liberal white Illinois politicians in the November 1966 election. Finally, the desegregation effort was undercut by the noticeable lack of popular support expressed by impoverished ghetto Blacks. The major demonstrations did not attract as many working-class and low-income Blacks as King and other local reformers had expected. After only four weeks in Chicago, some of King's aides wondered aloud whether any popular campaign could mobilize the urban poor. 'I have never seen such hopelessness', Hosea Williams declared in early 1966. 'They don't participate in the governmental process because they're beaten down psychologically. We're used to working with people who want to be freed.'[51] Soon after King's departure from Chicago, Daley was again up for re-election for a fourth term. Unopposed for the third time running, he received 420,200 votes in the Democratic primary, and still won impressive totals in the city's Black South and West Sides. To most political observers, the King campaign was less than ineffectual; the Daley machine controlled the Black community more strongly than ever before.[52]

IV

Throughout Chicago's history there have been only rare moments of working-class harmony across the colour line. Probably the best examples of these occurred during the Great Depression, when overall unemployment in the city had reached 40 per cent by 1931. Black groups initially responded to the economic crisis by pressuring white-owned stores that had exclusively Black clientele to hire Afro-American workers. The Black newspaper the *Chicago Whip* organized 'boycotts against stores in the Black belt that refused to employ Negro clerks'. Du Bois also applauded the campaign as 'the use of mass action by Negroes who take advantage of segregation in order to strengthen their economic foundation'.[53] Such militancy spread to the white working-class districts, and quickly instances of Blacks and whites joining together to fight home evictions began to take place. Rent strikes led to hundreds of arrests and more than a dozen murders. One rent riot in August 1931 'left three people dead and three policeman injured: "News of the riot screamed in the headlines of the evening press. The realization of the extent of unrest in the Negro district threw Chicago into panic." '[54] Spontaneous poor people's riots broke out in Polish,

Irish and Black neighbourhoods, as starving workers mobbed relief stations: 408 such demonstrations occurred in 1931, 566 in 1932.[55] Poor southern Blacks and rural whites from the Midwest flocked to the city by the thousands, many transients sleeping in the streets or in railroad yards, eating from garbage cans to survive. For hungry women and men of both races, the political appeals of the Communists and Socialists, who had organized militant unemployed councils, gained in significance. By mid 1932, the Communist-led councils had 22,000 members in forty-five locals across the city, and the Socialist Party had mobilized another 25,000 poor Black and white Chicagoans. Starvation is the great 'equalizer' in politics, and white workers who had headed lynch mobs in 1919 now found themselves sharing bowls of soup with equally impoverished Blacks. But with the economic recovery during World War II, many of the racist hierarchical patterns in employment of the 1920s reasserted themselves.

After the war, the racial demography of the city continued to change, as thousands of Black farmers and 'debt peons' continued to flee into the great Black Mecca of the South Side.[56] By 1940, Chicago's Black population had reached 277,731, 8.2 per cent of the city's residents. Twenty years later, 22.9 per cent of the city's population was Black. And by 1970, Black Chicago numbered 1,102,620 persons, a figure larger than the Afro-American populations of Los Angeles and Washington DC combined. Before the 1960s, the South Side had surpassed Harlem in size; Chicago's Black metropolis was the second largest concentration of Afro-American workers in the Western hemisphere.[57] Despite its rapid numerical growth, the patterns of labour discrimination shackled to earlier generations of Black workers remained virtually the same in these later decades. First, in terms of occupational discrimination, pitifully few Afro-Americans were hired in professional, technical or managerial positions. The majority of Blacks in the labour force were employed as labourers, service workers, private household workers and operatives. A sector-by-sector analysis of various occupational groups illustrates that Blacks generally received lower wages across the board. For example, the median annual income of white service workers in 1959 was $4,417; Black service workers received $3,437, about 77.8 per cent of whites' incomes. For white sales workers, the median annual income that year was $6,465; for Blacks, $3,506, about 54.2 per cent of whites' salaries.[58]

Secondly, Black Chicagoans generally experienced rates of unemployment higher than the national average. During the early

1960s, a period of relatively high joblessness, white unemployment rates in Chicago were about 4 per cent, while Blacks experienced jobless rates of between 10 and 15 per cent. In the mid 1960s, white unemployment rates fell to 2 per cent, while Black jobless rates levelled off at roughly 6 to 7 per cent. As the overall economic conditions became much worse in the 1970s, the plight of Black workers became more desperate. Statistics from the Chicago metropolitan area in 1975 illustrate that less than 70 per cent of the city's Black men and 50 per cent of its Black women found employment during the twelve month period.[59] By the early 1980s, roughly 22 per cent of the city's Black adults and half of all Black youth were without jobs. 300,000 adults and at least 350,000 children were public aid recipients.[60] Chicago Urban League researchers Harold M. Baron and Bennett Hymer characterized the crisis of Chicago's Black working class in these terms:

> The labour market is divided into two racial components — a sector for the deployment of white labour and a sector for the deployment of Negro labour. Each sector has its own separate institutions and mechanisms for the recruitment, training, and allocation of jobs and workers. Firms are cognizant of this division and have different perceptions of the two labour forces when they shop for labour . . . The Negro labour force has served as a pool of surplus labour used to fill shortages of white labour that occur during war years or periods of rapid economic growth. A large segment of the Negro labour force has been frozen into positions that are regraded as traditionally Negro jobs. These jobs are usually marginal and low-paying; they require little skill or formal training; they often involve physical hazards; they frequently offer only seasonal or cyclical employment; and they are frequently in stagnant or declining industries.[61]

With the decline in Chicago's manufacturing firms after the 1960s, increasing numbers of white and Black employees found work in service-related areas. A major source of employment for the city's Black work-force became the state, federal and municipal governments. By the early 1980s, about one fifth of the city's middle-income Blacks were employed in the public sector, compared with a city-wide figure of 11.2 per cent. In Calument Heights, a South Side middle-income neighbourhood with a 93 per cent Black population in 1980, 14.7 per cent of the adults in the labour-force were employed by the city government; in all, 34 per cent of the neighbourhood's residents worked in the public sector. Other neighbourhoods with large Black populations that also had high numbers of government employees included: Chatham, 99 per cent Black, with 33 per cent in the public sector; Avalon Park, 97 per cent Black and 31 per cent in the public sector; Washington Heights, 98 per cent Black and 32 per cent in the public sector; Oakland, 99 per cent Black and 34 per cent in the public sector; and Grand Boulevard, 100 per cent Black and 30 per cent public-sector workers.[62] By 1982, 10,144 of the city's 37,720 employees were Blacks, representing 26.9 per cent of the total work-force. However, the pattern of a dual labour-market and occupational discrimination described by Baron and Hymer in the private sector was perpetuated within municipal employment. University of Chicago political sociologist Rodney C. Coates noted that the 1982 median annual income of Chicago's public workers was $24,600. The average overall salary for Blacks, at $21,000, was about $5,000 less than that for whites. In the Streets and Highways Department, Blacks averaged $17,260 annually, compared with the average white salary of $22,770. Coates observed that 'Blacks employed by the police department, on the average, make $6,290 less than their white co-workers.' Whites employed in the Utilities and Transportation Department earned $28,450, compared with only $20,210 earned by Blacks.[63] An even more graphic way of examining the racial discrimination in municipal government is to use the figure of $20,000 as an index to determine racial stratification in employment. Only 28.1 per cent of all Black sanitation and sewage employees earned $20,000 or more annually in 1981, while 68.8 per cent of their white co-workers were paid at that level. The worst municipal departments in terms of Blacks' income levels compared with whites' were the Streets and Highways and the Fire Protection departments. In the former, 11.5 per cent of Black workers as compared with 85.4 per cent of the whites received $20,000 or more annually; in the latter, the figure was 9.2 per cent for Blacks and 89.1 per cent for whites.[64]

What is particularly striking about Chicago, therefore, is the surprising affluence of its Black entrepreneurial stratum. The city's metropolitan area had only 10,296 Black-owned firms in 1977, fewer than Los Angeles, New York City, or Washington DC. In proportion to the size of the Black population in the city, Chicago also had a smaller number of Black-owned businesses than Houston, Philadelphia, or Detroit. Yet despite the fact that only 19.4 per cent of Chicago's Black firms had any paid employees, the amount of gross receipts for all its businesses — $800 million — was only slightly less than that of Philadelphia's, Detroit's and Houston's Black-owned businesses *combined*. In a comparison using only one criterion, the amount of annual gross receipts for each firm, Chicago is far and away ahead of all other major cities in the United States, Compared with New York City and Los Angeles, where Black firms' annual gross receipts average $35,200 and $37,600 respectively, Chicago's Black enterprises average $77,800 per year. The Bureau of the Census's *1977 Survey of Minority-Owned Business Enterprises* provides some important comparative data on the Black entrepreneurial strata of the country's three major cities. The median annual gross receipts for firms without paid employees is significantly higher in Black Chicago ($14,658) than in Los Angeles ($10,869), in New York City ($10,736), or than the national average ($11,757). For Black-owned firms with paid employees, the median annual gross receipts for Chicago ($339,799) is again significantly above the national figure ($38,963) and the Los Angeles ($196,059) and New York City ($222,382) averages. Chicago's Black-owned firms tend to employ more workers than comparable firms in other cities. In two specific areas, manufacturing and retailing, Chicago's Black entrepreneurs outdistance their counterparts by wide margins. Chicago's 64 Black-owned manufacturing firms with paid employees had 1,704 workers in 1977, and recorded gross receipts totalling $119,1 million. The city's 825 Black retailers with paid employees made gross receipts totalling $332.9 million.[65]

Probably the most important factor in the relative affluence of Chicago's Black entrepreneurial elite is the rigidly enforced policy of residential segregation. According to the 1980 Census, over five sixths of the metropolitan area's Black population lives in seventeen of the city's fifty wards. In the city's suburbs, Blacks make up only 5.6 per cent of the population.[66] This very high concentration of Black consumers in an urban environment in which over 90 per cent of the local residents are Black provides a logical market for Black retailers, insurance companies, contractors, and entrepreneurs of various types. The absence of intense business competition from whites in many all-Black neighbourhoods has allowed many Black firms literally to co-opt a major share of the Black consumer dollar. Thus, the rigid racial segregation perpetuated by the city's political machine has had the effect, in part, of creating a more favourable climate for Black petty capital accumulation, and consequently, for the development of a small but relatively secure Black entre-preneurial elite. As elsewhere, especially in the South during the era of Jim Crow, segregation served as a barrier to white corporate exploitation of the Black consumer market, and gave birth to the economic foundations of a politically conservative, class-conscious Black small business stratum which favoured accommodation with the economic and political *status quo* that in turn dominated the larger society.

The net socio-economic and political effect upon the Black working class and the poor was a numbing sense of hopelessness and civic apathy. Novelist Richard Wright described the cynical manipulation of Chicago's Black electorate under the Thompson machine:

> Election time was nearing and a Negro Republican precinct captain asked me to help him round up votes. I had no interest in the candidates, but I needed the money. I went from door to door with the precinct captain and discovered that the whole business was one long process of bribery, that people voted for three dollars, for the right to continue their illicit trade in sex or alcohol. On election day I went into the polling-booth and drew the curtain behind me and unfolded my ballots. As I stood there the sordid implications of politics flashed through my mind. "Big Bill" Thompson headed the local Republican machine and I knew he was using the Negro vote to control the city hall; in turn, he was engaged in vast political deals of which the Negro voters, political innocents, had no notion. With my pencil I wrote in determined scrawl across the face of the ballots: *I Protest This Fraud.* I knew that my gesture was futile. But I wanted somebody to know that out of the vast sea of ignorance in the Black Belt there was at least one person who knew the game for what it was.[67]

As the Democratic machine consolidated its power, Black electoral participation rapidly declined. In the 1920s and 1930s, according to Gosnell, Black Chicagoans had higher electoral participation rates than whites. In 1930, between 68 and 77 per cent of all adults in the heavily Black Second Ward, for example, were registered to vote. But within a generation, as Alkalimat and Gills note, the Afro-American 'middle class lost interest in local voting because they had not derived sufficient material gain from it. Further, the machine did not work for a large voter turn-out, so the masses of Blacks were not encouraged to vote.'[68] In the 1955 election, Black wards voted for the machine candidate by a majority of four to one, but with very low voter-participation levels. In the Democratic primary election of 1978, the percentage of registered voters who cast ballots in Black wards ranged from 39.6 per cent down to 24.1 per cent. Voter turn-outs became so embarrassingly low that even Black machine politicians began to address the issue. Twenty-first ward alderman

Bennett Steward, later Congressman, once complained, 'Until Blacks start going to the polls and voting, we can forget about any kind of power in Chicago's political structure. What kind of demands can I make with 39,000 registered voters in my ward and only 10,000 coming out to vote?'[69] However, the Democratic machine still commanded the allegiance of some Black voters simply by the number of patronage jobs it controlled — roughly 45,000 in 1982. The vast majority of these jobs were allotted to white wards; but even the prospect of token employment was usually sufficient to maintain some level of political discipline.[70]

In the final analysis, the real power of the Democratic machine over Black workers was embodied in the repressive actions of Chicago's police force. For generations, the police force had been the bulwark of white supremacy, the coercive apparatus necessary to guarantee the protection of white-owned property, and the relations of production that capital required. For example, prostitution had been legal until 1912; after that date the police were given the task of ensuring that the vice 'continued to be centred in the Black belt'. Black hookers were kept 'away from commercial and white residential areas', and police officers stood in line to receive their share of the trade's revenue. Gamblers like 'Mushmouth' Johnson were expected to turn in a sizeable chunk of their profits to the local police. As the size of the Black South Side increased, about fifty Afro-Americans were hired by the department and posted to Black neighbourhoods but 'few could aspire to become sergeants, lieutenants, or detectives.' White police brutality quickly became notorious, as hundreds of Black men and women were harassed and arrested without criminal evidence. Officers regularly raided the few integrated night-clubs; the police chief in 1908 ordered that 'coloured saloon-keepers must keep white men out of their saloons and the white saloon-keepers are to prevent coloured men from entering their places of business.' As illustrated previously, white officers tolerated and even encouraged vigilante violence against Blacks. Beginning in March 1919 a series of bombings rocked the Black community. Binga's real-estate firm was the target of one bombing; in May 1919 'two explosions rocked a building occupied by Negroes on Grand Boulevard, and a gang of white youths attacked and beat a Negro who entered a "white" saloon'; and on 21 June 'gangs of young hoodlums murdered two Negro men for no more apparent reason than their desire to "get a nigger". Although there were witnesses to the crimes, the police made no arrests.'[71] The Chicago Commission on Race Relations noted that between 1

July 1917 and 1 March 1921, fifty-eight bombs were exploded in the Black community, causing two deaths, numerous injuries, and 'the damage to property amounted to $100,000'. During the period, 'the police and the state's attorney's office succeeded in apprehending but two persons suspected of participation in these acts of lawlessness.'[72] In the Depression, police attacked both Black relief marchers and organized rent strikers. When Black and white striking steelworkers held a peaceful march on Memorial Day in 1937, 'the police shot them down, killing ten and wounding ninety.'[73] Even in the post-World War II period, despite a gradual increase in the number of Black officers, the police continued to be viewed by most Black Chicagoans as a kind of alien, occupying army.

In the 1970s and early 1980s, the number of reported instances of police brutality against Black victims increased sharply, as the size of the Afro-American population city-wide grew. Public criticism of the force, and a modest increase in Black and Hispanic officers, did not lead to more liberal race relations between national minorities and the white police establishment. On the contrary, the explicitly racist prerogative, which any police force has as a coercive apparatus within a multiracial capitalist society, seemed to assert itself even more crudely. For example, throughout 1981 and 1982, a series of blatant police attacks escalated across the Black community. Perhaps the worst instances of police brutality occurred in the aftermath of the 9 February 1982 shooting of two white patrolmen by two Blacks. For several weeks, the police made hundreds of illegal house-to-house searches within the Black community, physically and verbally abusing residents and randomly destroying Blacks' personal property. A number of these unconstitutional attacks by the police have been documented by the publication, *Racially Motivated Random Violence*.[74] On the night of 12 February 1982, two Black men, John Marsh, a small lounge-owner, and Madison L. Brown, a city inspector, were both 'verbally and physically abused as well as arrested by eight white Chicago police officers for reasons unknown to anyone in the lounge':

> Two officers approached Marsh and Brown. They asked who the owner was and, after Marsh replied that he was, the officers said he was going to gaol. The officers allegedly put a revolver to Marsh's throat and dragged him down the stairs. Later Marsh and Brown were handcuffed, dragged outside at gunpoint to the paddy wagon and taken to the eleventh district police station. As a result of the police brutality, Marsh

received injuries to the arms and hands, head, face and leg and was treated at Mt Sinai Hospital. Brown suffered a neck injury, bruises to the left knee, and a broken right thumb.

The next day, Marshall Covington, a 57-year-old Black manager of a drugs and liquor store was accosted by police without cause. 'The officers refused to check his identification, though it was offered, but instead handcuffed him and forced him into the police car.' Police brutally struck the handcuffed Covington in the back with a nightstick. 'Covington was not informed of any charges against him', yet bond for his release was set at $1,000. In yet another brutal incident, on 12 April 1982 white Chicago police raided the home of a Black woman, Mrs Georgia Sims:

> The officers burst past her 19-year-old daughter, who answered the door, and conducted a destructive search of the house, first telling Mrs Sims they were looking for her 21-year-old son Rufus, then saying they were looking for her 24-year-old son Rodney. [Police] threatened to blow Mrs Sims's brains out, and pointed a gun at her daughter. When the officers found a rifle, they arrested Mrs Sims and took her to the precinct. When Rufus came to inquire about his mother's arrest, he was grabbed, thrown on the floor, then locked up. When two other children went to inquire about their mother and brother, they reportedly learned that Rufus had been beaten unconscious and was taken to St Anne's Hospital with a fractured skull. As the brother and sister left the station and approached their parked car, two officers reportedly came up from behind, handcuffed the brother, and jabbed him in the ribs. They grabbed the sister by the hair, picked her up by the breasts and buttocks, and using abusive language against the two, brought them back to the precinct. They were charged with assault, and the sister was reportedly assaulted further. She states her purse fell, and when she later tried to post bond, $118 was missing.

Police brutality incidents increased dramatically in subsequent months. On 23 May 1982, half a dozen plain-clothes police raided one Black family's apartment, supposedly on a drug raid. Without producing any identification or a search warrant, they proceeded to ransack the apartment. One Black man with his arm in a cast was restrained as a police officer 'tried to break the cast with a crowbar'. One occupant, 20-year-old Louis Brown was severely beaten and suffered a ruptured pancreas. Brown was held in jail and denied medical attention for five hours. By July, the City-wide Coalition to End Police Abuse and Misconduct, a coalition of over forty neighbourhood associations, demanded action. Coalition spokesperson

Wallace Davis charged that the Police Department's Office of Professional Standards tolerated illegal and brutal conduct by police officers. But Coalition members themselves were victimized by police brutality — and the incidents continued unabated. Seven Black civil rights activists were beaten and arrested by police at a Chicago Housing Authority meeting on 10 August. Days later, a 24-year-old Black man, Vernard Williams, was shot in the head by an off-duty policeman in a Chicago grocery store during a fight. Williams died within minutes, and the officer stated that his gun went off accidentally.

Even the racist violence against Black citizens in Chicago paled by comparison with the reported racist incidents that occurred in suburban, all-white neighbourhoods. Cicero was a prime example of an American version of apartheid. In 1982, only seventy-four Blacks lived in the city which had a population of 61,200. Not a single municipal worker in the town, out of a total work-force of 400, was Black. Blacks were not even allowed to attend Cicero's public schools. In February 1982 when a Black businessman rented an apartment within the city limits, his automobile was fire-bombed and damaged on three occasions. Complaining to local police, he was promptly arrested for disorderly conduct. On 6 August 1982, three young Black men driving through Cicero at about 8.00 p.m. were stopped by white police officers, guns drawn. One victim, 33-year-old George Goodman, stated later: 'We were told to get out and lay face down on the street. They had guns behind each of our heads. They were laughing all the time and calling us racial names, and then the kicking started. Two Cicero squad cars came, and all hell broke loose.' After a thorough beating, the men were taken to the police station, and cited for speeding, for 'failing to stop for an emergency vehicle', 'evading police', and for transporting open liquor. Before they were dismissed, one white officer asked, 'Now, how did you get those bruises?' When one of the Black men replied that he had fallen down the stairs, the officer responded, 'Good boy . . . Now you may go.'

Two sharply distinct working-class cultures coexisted in Chicago, and police brutality was simply the most decisive manifestation of race/class coercion to ensure the racial division of labour. The white ethnic working class was economically far more secure than non-whites. Capital had largely co-opted the upper strata of white labour, and the majority of less affluent whites could always gauge their position in the social hierarchy to be above that of most Blacks. Whites frequently owned their own homes (39 per cent in

1960, as against 16 per cent for non-whites); their neighbourhoods were less vulnerable to street crime; police were perceived as guardians of civic order and social stability.[75] Thus their political behaviour, in most instances, reinforced the power and corruption of the machine. There were, of course, ethnic rivalries which erupted from time to time. Polish Americans, the largest white ethnic bloc in the city, were upset that no Pole had ever been elected mayor, and that the Irish, who made up only 10 per cent of the population held one third of the City Council positions.[76] But these were family feuds, not class struggles. White ethnics had respectable voter turn-out rates of about 50 per cent during the 1960s and 1970s. The machine continued to produce tangible benefits, and the racist pogroms of the police against Blacks and Latinos evoked little interest. On the other side of the colour line was the increasingly marginal Afro-American working class. The victims of street crime and police violence, manipulated by Black accommodationist politicians within the Daley 'submachine', Black workers had little in common with whites. Despite their overall population share of 34.4 per cent in 1970, Blacks held only 28 per cent of the City Council positions and 15 per cent of the Democratic Ward Committee slots. The lack of meaningful representation in the bourgeois democratic apparatus and the racial division within the city's working class produced the conditions which would culminate in a new social movement for race and class power in the 1980s.

V

Despite the endless series of political abuses, racist violence and the clientage practices of Black 'submachine' politicians, the tradition of Black resistance and social reform was never destroyed completely. In 1963, A A. (Sammy) Rayner, a Black reformer, ran a credible campaign for the City Council seat in the Sixth Ward, losing by a small margin. After being defeated by Dawson in a Congressional race in 1964, Rayner again challenged a machine-controlled opponent in the Sixth Ward race in 1967, and this time won by a wide margin. Carmichael and Hamilton analysed Rayner's victory, commenting that although Rayner had 'rejected the term Black Power', his 'statements, attitudes and programmes' embodied a new militancy. 'The very least that Sammy Rayner can give the Black community is a new political dignity. His victory will begin to establish the habit of saying "No" to the downtown bosses.'[77] When the Chicago police, at the instigation of Democratic State's Attorney Edward V. Hanrahan, viciously executed Chicago Black Panther leaders Mark Clark and Fred Hampton in 1969, and illegally arrested other Black activists, the Afro-American community was outraged. In an unprecedented act of defiance, Black voters by the thousands crossed party lines and elected Republican Bernard Carey over Hanrahan in the 1972 general election. Nine of the then fourteen Black-majority wards went to Carey. By the early 1970s, dozens of prominent Black elected officials and community leaders who had long been aligned with Daley had broken with the machine — most prominent among them were South Side Congressman Ralph Metcalfe and his protégé State Senator Harold Washington. After 1975, the Afro-American electorate consistently voted against machine-supported candidates within Democratic primary races. After Daley's death in 1976, Washington ran a largely symbolic campaign for mayor, winning five out of nine wards in the heavily Black (89 per cent) First Congressional District, and received 77,345 votes city-wide.[78] Two years later, three new Black independents defeated machine candidates and were elected to the city council — Niles Sherman (21st ward), Danny Davis (29th ward) and Robert Shaw (9th ward). The Black vote was most decisive in the Democratic mayoral primary of 1979, when a little-known underdog, Jane Byrne, defeated incumbent mayor Michael A. Bilandic with a narrow (51-49) majority. Running against the Democratic machine, Byrne carried all except two predominantly Black wards. Black voters supported Byrne by a 63 per cent mandate, which allowed her to win the election over a well-financed opponent. As political scientist Michael B. Preston noted, the election of Byrne proved that Black Chicago's voters had become 'increasingly more unloyal, unpredictable, uncontrollable, and undeliverable'.[79]

However, within weeks of Byrne's election, she made peace with Daley's real successor as boss of the Cook County Democratic machine, Edward R. ('Fast Eddie') Vrdolyak, and joined forces with the Regular Democrats. Throughout her term in office, the mayor initiated a series of public policies that alienated many Blacks. Her economic policies catered to the interests of the city's financial and corporate interests: municipal debt increased by 130 per cent in three and a half years; and taxpayers were confronted with a bill totalling $205 million to subsidize white real-estate developers in the North Loop.[80] In Byrne's first two years in office, the city employment of Blacks and Latinos increased by only 83 jobs and 53 jobs respectively. In the appointment of the city's police superintendent, Byrne skipped over Samuel Nolan, a well-qualified Black assistant chief, and named a conservative, law-and-order attorney, Richard J. Brezczek, to the post. In 1979 the mayor refused to appoint Black educator Manfred Byrd as the superintendent of schools, naming instead a white woman, Angeline Caruso. In 1981 she replaced two Black school board members, Leon Davis and Michael Scott, with two whites, one of whom (Betty Bonow) had 'a history of opposition to racial integration of the public schools'.[81] Byrne's policies with regard to minority and low-income women represented a continuation of the Daley-Bilandic Administrations. During Byrne's tenure, Chicago ranked third in infant mortality among the nation's fifty-six largest cities; 40 per cent of battered women and their children were turned away from publicly funded shelters; the mayor appointed no women to head any departments controlling city jobs or funds except Human Services, which was subjected to severe budget cuts; and 'well-baby clinics' were closed and many public health nurses dismissed. Half of the city's physicians seeing adult patients under the city's Department of Health were fired. In 1982, Byrne slashed $2.8 million from the Department of Housing's Home Acquisition Programme, despite widespread working-class and poor people's interest in obtaining funds for decent housing.[82] In short, Byrne's administration was, in the words of one Black alderman, utterly 'ruthless' in its 'lack of sensitivity on numerous occasions to the residents of this city'.[83]

Black opposition to the new mayor and the Democratic machine became apparent when Byrne supporter Bennett M. Stewart was selected to fill the First District House seat of the late Ralph Metcalfe. Harold Washington ran successfully in the 1980 Democratic primary against Stewart, and subsequently became one of the most progressive representatives in Congress. Newspaper publisher and Washington ally Gus Savage defeated machine-supported Black candidate Reginald Brown to win the Second Congressional District race. In the city council, Sherman, Davis, and Marion Humes (8th ward) joined with white independent Democrats (such as Martin Oberman, 43rd ward) in criticizing Byrne's programmes. A few of Byrne's hand-picked Black officials now began to distance themselves from the administration. Allen Streeter, the Black Democrat appointed by the mayor to fill the 17th ward's city council seat, broke with Byrne over Bonow's controversial school board appointment. When Streeter ran for re-election in June 1981, he was vigorously opposed by the machine. Byrne employed literally every method to unseat Streeter: candidates were paid to file against him, including Streeter's next-door neighbour; seventeenth ward Democratic Committee-man William Parker promised 'new colour television sets to precinct captains who [carried] their precincts' for machine candidate Jewel Frierson. With the assistance of Washington, Davis and a wide range of political groups — from Black nationalists to the Communist Party — Streeter survived a nine-candidate race and won the June 29th run-off election over Frierson, with 56 per cent of the vote.[84] Later that summer, the Reverend Jesse Jackson initiated a grass-roots Black boycott of the Byrne-sponsored 'Chicago Fest', a city-sponsored public carnival. Washington, Savage, Davis and other progressive Black politicians endorsed the boycott, and within weeks, some liberal whites also joined the effort — Alderman Lawrence Bloom (5th ward), Alderman Ivan M. Rittenberg (40th ward) and Oberman. Many Black performers, including Stevie Wonder, cancelled appearances to express political solidarity with the progressives. Even a number of Black entrepreneurs painfully withdrew — including Leon Finney, owner of the Leon's Bar-B-Que chain, who claimed to have lost $300,000 through his decision to respect the boycott. Fewer than 5 per cent of the persons attending Chicago Fest were Black. For Jackson, the widespread popularity of the boycott confirmed that Blacks were 'not bound by Chicago's Plantation politics . . . It is better to boycott with dignity than to sing and dance in shame.'[85]

A democratic social movement had begun to take new organizational forms in Black Chicago. Just as SNCC, the CORE and the SCLC had been created by the failures of the NAACP and Urban League to adopt extralegal tactics in the struggle against Jim Crow a generation before, Black Chicagoans mobilized new formations for social protest that went well beyond Jesse Jackson's PUSH, the Chicago Urban League, and the city's NAACP chapter. Foremost among them was the Chicago Black United Communities (CBUC), a Black nationalist-oriented, progressive formation with strong roots in the working class. CBUC was led by Lu Palmer, a militant Black journalist and community leader who was probably the city's most vocal and uncompromising critic of both Byrne and the Democratic machine. Another South Side group, Citizens for Self-Determination, was directed by electoral political activist Mercedes Maulette. Other protest formations included the 'African Community of Chicago'; the 'Concerned Young Adults', based on the South Side and engaged in voter-registration efforts; the Chicago chapter of the National Black United Front; the 'Independent

Grass-roots Youth Organization', which was controlled by a local Black street gang; the 'People's Movement for Voter Registration and Education'; and POWER 'People Organized for Welfare and Economic Reform', formed in 'response to the Reagan austerity programme', and based 'among the growing number of skilled and unskilled workers being added to the ranks of the poor white, Black, and Latino unemployed, and the expanding number of welfare-dependent family heads in the Chicago area'.[86] POWER and other groups, such as CBUC, PUSH and Citizens for Self-Determination, initiated a massive voter-registration effort, which targeted the unemployed and welfare recipients, and which by November 1982 had added 180,000 new Black voters to the rolls.[87] Community activists now approached Washington, who was not yet convinced that a Black candidate could win the Democratic mayoral primary. Byrne had aligned herself with the most conservative and pro-corporate tendencies of the Democratic machine, but it was not possible for a Black challenger to unseat her unless a second white candidate emerged. This problem was resolved on 4 November by the announcement of State's Attorney Richard M. Daley as a candidate for the mayoral race. Ideologically, Daley was a liberal Democrat, like Washington; but in the context of Chicago's corrupt system, Daley was also a supporter of the patronage machine and 'business as usual'. If the newly registered Afro-American and low-income voters could be mobilized to vote, and if Daley and Byrne split the white electorate, Washington had a better than even chance of winning. On 10 November, Washington declared his candidacy. And as Abdul Alkalimat and Doug Gills perceptively noted, Chicago's 'electorate had three choices: Byrne presented the present, Daley the past, and Washington was identified with their aspirations for the future.'[88]

But the political and social contradictions of nearly a century of systemic exploitation do not disappear overnight. Washington's campaign was forced to confront several thorny difficulties. The social movement's candidate had several notable strengths. Washington was by far the most 'qualified' of the three candidates, having been a state legislator for sixteen years and a member of Congress. He was also clearly the most intelligent, commanding the ability 'to engage in straight, no-nonsense dialogue with the "masses" and the "elites", qualities deeply appreciated within Afro-American culture'.[89] Yet his political development had begun under the aegis of the machine; his father, after all, had been a precinct captain, and as a youngster he had laboured for Dawson. Half hidden were other problems. Washington's extensive involvement in community struggles had contributed towards a disorderly personal and professional life. He had frequently failed to pay his utilities bills; his right to practise law had been suspended by the Illinois Bar; he had not paid income taxes for several years at a time. After Washington led a 1971 walk-out of liberals from the Illinois State Legislature during the appearance of then Vice-President Spiro T. Agnew, Internal Revenue agents promptly investigated his record. Although Washington had owed barely $500 in back taxes, he had been ordered to serve forty days in gaol on this misdemeanour conviction. Few Black voters were alienated by this record; given Washington's start in public life under the machine of Daley and Dawson, it was about as good as one could expect.

Far more serious than Washington's background was the social class and racial split among the candidate's supporters. Washington's most enthusiastic and hardest-working cadre came from various Black nationalist or predominantly Black organizations. Even one week before Washington announced his candidacy, a 'Task Force for Black Political Empowerment' had been created by about fifty groups, including the Black United Front, the African Community of Chicago, CBUC and PUSH. Some forces in this Task Force, such as the 'People's College', were Marxist in orientation; some were grass-roots, community-based (such as Maulette's Citizens for Self-Determination); and still others represented nationalist-oriented professionals and elected officials (such as Danny Davis and Al Streeter). The core of Task Force's leadership was controlled by Black professionals, but a sizeable minority (37 per cent) had trade-union or grass-roots, community backgrounds. Nevertheless, despite its ideological eclecticism, it functioned as a 'parallel organization' which attempted to promote working-class involvement in the effort as well as providing the 'direct, immediate "muscle" for the campaign on the streets'.[90] By contrast, the formal Washington campaign organization had a rather different character. The campaign's steering committee was directed by Bill Berry, a veteran of the 1966 King desegregation struggle, who was now functioning as special assistant to the president of a Black-owned corporation, Johnson Products. Alkalimat and Gills's analysis of the steering committee indicates that 71 per cent of the members were Afro-Americans. Most were white-collar professionals or businessmen (67 per cent), and less than one fifth had any background in trade-union or community organizational activities. Any administrative body with this social class composition can be expected to replicate itself at other levels. Thus in the Washington campaign headquarters, Blacks made up only a little over half (56 per cent) the total number of workers by 1 December. Most of the campaign headquarters' staff were white collar professionals (56 per cent) or politicians (19 per cent). To a degree, two different factions of the petty bourgeoisie were competing to control the campaign. The Task Force was more consistently Black national-istic, and inclined towards economic radicalism or at least reform; the official committee was aligned more closely with the liberal bourgeoisie and was favourable towards racial integration. The latter faction was more influential at first. A controversial decision was made, to locate the principal campaign headquarters in down-town Chicago, and to replace acting campaign manager Renault Robinson with Al Raby. Robinson had been a favourite of CBUC and other nationalist-oriented organizations, and Raby was widely distrusted as representing 'the interests of the Black establish-ment'.[91] Since his involvement in the King desegregation campaign, Raby had been the director of the Peace Corps in Ghana, and had later served as director of intergovernmental relations for the ACTION programme under the Carter Administration. Raby's selection was an implicit rejection of a Black nationalist-oriented campaign, and a signal to the city's white liberal petty bourgeoisie and reformers that they would be welcomed in the mobilization.

But Washington's chief problem was the widespread opinion that an Afro-American could not possibly be elected as mayor of Chicago, and that Black accommodationist politicians tied to the machine would splinter Washington's base. Immediately after his candidacy was announced, the media went to work, defining the Black Congressman as a 'symbolic' candidate. Chicago's 'conven-tional political wisdom', stated *Tribune* reporter Monroe Anderson, was that Washington was a 'spoiler', and might throw the election to either Daley or Byrne.[92] Even Renault Robinson admitted, 'Black people are conservative. They won't waste their vote on a candidate who can't win.'[93] Throughout the West and South Sides, the Regular Democrats went to work, calling in political debts, and forcing Black accommodationist politicians to join Byrne's campaign. Sewer Commissioner Edward A. Quigley, a white Democratic committee-man who directed the all-Black 27th ward, pressured five 'obedient' Black committee-men on the West Side to endorse the mayor by mid November.[94] By the end of the month, several South Side committee-men from overwhelmingly Black wards had joined Byrne's campaign, including one of the most militant reform leaders, 9th ward alderman Robert Shaw. Shaw persuaded his precinct captains to back Byrne, and, later, pledged to the machine that he would carry his ward against the Black progressive. Byrne obtained the endorsement of Washington's moderate Black colleague in the House of Representatives, Cardiss Collins of the Seventh Congressional District. The mayor's strongest support came from her most obsequious Black followers. 'We're going to re-elect Jane Byrne mayor of Chicago', vowed alderman William Carothers (28th ward) to a partisan audience at a West Side Baptist church on 13 November.[95] Illinois State Representative Larry Bullock and Assistant House Majority Leader Taylor Pouncey formed a coalition of thirteen Black Chicago assemblymen, who represented over 90 per cent of the Black voters in the city, to campaign for Byrne. In a curious press statement, the Afro-American legislators praised the mayor's 'minority hiring practices', and attacked Washington's Black supporters for not 'understand [ing] the difference between idealism and realism'. Bullock declared that Byrne had 'definitely made mistakes in the Black community, [but] has shown courage in admitting those mistakes and correcting them . . . This city needs continuity in government.'[96] Other Black elected officials recognized the Black community's deep antipathy for Byrne, so they decided to support Daley instead of Washington. The most influential Blacks for Daley were school board member Michael Scott; the director of the Lawndale People's Planning and Action Conference, and Cook County Commissioner John H. Stroger Jr. Stroger predicted that Washington would receive barely half of the Black vote, and characterized his campaign as 'a revolution of expectation rather than one of action'. Stroger added for the record, 'I have not sold out my people.'[97]

The Black Church was also divided. Al Sampson and John Porter, leaders of the Black Methodist Ministers Alliance, were members of the Task Force for Black Political Empowerment. PUSH and Black church organizations held fundraisers and rallies for Washington. Yet the machine was not without its resources to subvert the Black clergy. Byrne's not so subtle strategy mirrored the techniques of Thompson, Kelly and Daley. On 21 November, the incumbent spoke before the South Side church of the Reverend Norman L. Russell, declaring that she had not 'written off the Black community . . . and I love all of you.' Russell warmly praised Byrne as 'a great person with a great big heart'.[98] Former King nemesis J.H. Jackson surfaced as a Byrne supporter, praising 'the

ability, the genius, and the talent' of the mayor. Reverend Jackson
warned darkly that a Black mayor would unleash uncontrollable
forces. 'In these times when there are so many forces seeking to
wreck and ruin our cities', it was important to preserve 'the strength
and the leadership that we already have'.[99] Black ministers who
endorsed Daley were even more explicit. 'If Harold Washington is
elected, the city would go down the tube', warned the Reverend
O.D. White of Love Baptist Church. E.J. Jones, pastor of the First
Unity Baptist Church and a candidate for alderman in the 4th ward,
expressed the opinion that Blacks had 'moved this "Harold Washington for Mayor" too rapidly. I guess we got too excited with the
extra few thousand voter registration.' Jones declared that
hundreds of Blacks would have to be elevated to the boards of large
corporations 'to prevent them from leaving Chicago if a Black were
elected'.[100] About 150 Black ministers, led by the Reverend T.A.
Clark Sr, endorsed Daley in January 1983.[101] Other Afro-American
clergy stepped up their efforts for the Black Congressman. Over 250
ministers representing 14 denominations circulated a strong statement, linking Washington with both 'the tradition of Dr Martin
Luther King Jr [and] the tradition of [Black] liberation and self-
determination'. Washington had not only merited 'our full support,
our prayers, and our combined resources; he also has our promise
that if he fails to live up to his platform on integrity, we will be the
first to condemn him and to work for his removal.'[102]

The strongest support for Washington was generated by the
Black working class. Several Black trade-union bureaucrats came
out early for Byrne, including James Kemp of the Service
Employees' International Union. Transit Union president John
Weatherspoon supported Daley, but nearly all of his union's rank-
and-file activists were 'lined up behind Washington'. The Black
candidate received the enthusiastic support of Black, Latino and
white progressive unionists, including Charles Barton, Secretary-
Treasurer, Local 500-P, Food and Commercial Workers' Union;
Willie Williamson, Co-Chair, Chicago Committee for Trade-Union
Action and Democracy; Charles Hayes, Food and Commercial
Workers' International Vice-President; Rudy Lozano, organizer,
Ladies' Garment Workers' Union; Johnnie Mae Jackson, president
of the Chicago branch of the Coalition of Labour Union Women;
and Haxen Griffin, President, Local 372, Service Employees'
Union.[103] The Charles A. Hayes Labour and Community Edu-
cation Centre became the central training facility for campaign
workers. Also decisive in mobilizing Black workers were the contri-

228

butions of Jorga Palmer's CBUC unit 'Women's Auxiliary for Harold Washington' and Lu Palmer's '1000 Black Men'. These two subgroups of CBUC 'provided much of the unofficial tactical and logistical support for the formal campaign organization', Alkalimat and Gills observe. 'If Renault Robinson and Al Raby were *the* campaign managers, Jorga Palmer was *the* unofficial campaign monitor and publicist for the Black community.' As in every social movement that assumes a dynamic electoral form, political organizations that existed prior to the mobilization were strengthened. PUSH, CBUC and other formations with strong working-class constituencies all experienced 'increased membership, revenue and publicity'.[104] Thus the capacity of Black workers to manifest their own objective interests in political struggles was reinforced by the Washington crusade.

Most of the Black petty bourgeoisie, and especially the small entrepreneurs, were now firmly behind Washington. One of the nation's wealthiest Black businessmen, John Johnson, owner of the Chicago-based *Ebony* magazine, did endorse Daley and donate $10,000 to his campaign.[105] But the majority of Black executives and less affluent merchants recognized the benefits to their social stratum that would accrue if Washington were elected. In the candidate's campaign platform, 'Working Paper on Jobs for Chicagoans', Washington appealed to workers by calling for 'genuine collective-bargaining agreements' for 'all city workers', new programmes that targeted unemployed youth, the creation of a scholarship loan programme financed by tax-exempt bonds 'to prepare the employed in skills for available jobs', and by his promise that his administration would 'support efforts toward employee ownership', closing factories, seeking 'to retrain displaced workers'. This modest social democratic agenda was balanced by programmes that would appeal to the Black entrepreneur: the establishment of 'a well-monitored programme of set-aside contracts for small businesses' to do business with the city; city contracts that would 'have bid-incentives for firms who hire Chicago residents'; the 'direct infusion' of venture capital into small businesses through Small Business Administration mechanisms; and special 'set-aside' contracts on major urban-development projects allocated specifically to Black and Latino businessmen.[106] Washington's economic agenda was neither 'Socialism-in-one-City', nor a Tuskegee-type 'Black Capitalism', but an attempt to split accommodationist-inclined entrepreneurs from the Democratic machine, while keeping his base among workers, socialists, Black nationalists,

Communists and left-liberals in the historic current of Chicago social reform. This popular-front stategy succeeded in attracting a number of corporate executives to serve as 'coaches' to the candidate, including George O'Hare, public relations executive for Sears, Roebuck and Company; David Potter, former editor of the *Chicago Defender* and an executive with Illinois Bell; Black banker Alvin Boutte; and Black businessmen Cirilo McSeen and Edward Gardner.[107]

In the final weeks of the campaign, it was clear that the machine was in deep trouble. In a series of televised debates, Washington came across to the electorate 'as a compelling speaker with a firm grasp of issues and forthright proposals'.[108] When Daley and Byrne repeatedly dodged questions on taxes, Washington openly called for an increased, progressive state income tax which would benefit the city. Chiding his opponents, Washington declared, 'You can run, but you can't hide.' In the context of Afro-American political culture, the statement sparked instant recognition: this was the famous line of Joe Louis, delivered during his boxing match against Max Schmelling, almost fifty years before. 'To Chicago Blacks, Harold Washington became a political Joe Louis, delivering a knock-out punch to the divided, old, creaky machine that had long dominated without delivering.' As Byrne's position dropped steadily in public-opinion polls each day, more poor and working-class Blacks drew greater confidence. When Byrne visited ghetto tenements, 'crowds of young Blacks spontaneously formed and followed her, chanting "We Want Harold" '. Reporter David Moberg observed, 'blue Washington buttons were worn everywhere as badges of pride. Whites and Blacks who supported Washington worked together — or simply greeted each other on the street — with a friendliness and cooperation rare in this city.'[109] The machine fought back viciously. The weekend before the election, Byrne workers distributed photos of Jesse Jackson, claiming that 'if Washington is elected, the real mayor will be the president of Operation PUSH . . . Washington is being used to launch Jesse Jackson's bid for president of the United States.'[110] Party chairman Vrdolyak warned white Democrats on Chicago's North-West Side that 'a vote for Daley is a vote for Washington . . . It's a racial thing. Don't kid yourself. I'm calling on you to save your city, to save your precinct. We're fighting to keep the city the way it is.'[111] The machine even hired a Black street-gang to use their own 'special' means to ensure a Black turn-out for Byrne. The notorious gang, the El Rukns, 'cut a deal which netted as much as $70,000 for "polling" assistance'.[112]

These desperate manoeuvres fell short. On primary day, 22 February 1983, the Democratic machine experienced its most humiliating defeat. Washington led the field with 419,266 votes (36.3 per cent), followed closely by Mayor Byrne's 386,456 votes (33.4 per cent) and State's Attorney Daley's 343,506 votes (29.9 per cent). As expected, Byrne won by substantial majorities in Chicago's North-West and North Sides; Daley carried his father's Polish, Irish and German working-class stronghold on the South-West Side. What astonished independent observers, and dismayed the machine, was the unprecedented response among Black voters. Overall, the turn-out of Afro-American registered voters was 64.2 per cent, compared with 34.5 per cent in the 1979 Democratic primary. In the eleven Black wards with over 90 per cent Black residency, Washington won 77.7 per cent of all ballots cast. In Allen Streeter's ward, Washington carried 84 per cent of the vote. Robert Shaw's vigorous efforts for Byrne were soundly defeated as 76 per cent of the 9th ward's Democrats went to Washington. 'I knew as soon as I saw that turn-out that we had some problems', Shaw explained to reporters. 'They just came out of the woodwork and there was nothing we could do.'[113] Black petty-bourgeois neighbourhoods gave Washington some of his largest majorities, but even poorer communities, still tightly dominated by Black precinct and ward lieutenants, still voted three to one for Washington. The Washington victory also affected the Black aldermanic races. While Byrne loyalists William Carothers (28th ward) and Shaw were held to 39 per cent or less of their precincts' votes, outspoken Danny Davis (29th ward) carried his district by a four to one margin. Daley apologist E.J. Jones managed to win only two per cent of the vote in the 4th ward.[114]

Washington had won the Democratic primary by over 30,000 votes, but he was not yet mayor. As Alkalimat and Gills observed, '84 per cent of Washington's support came from Black voters, 10 per cent from whites, and 6 per cent from Latinos.' Less than one quarter of the Latino electorate had voted, and nearly half of them had supported Byrne. Washington won only 24 per cent of the Latino vote. In the seven wards of the city that were totally white ethnic, 'Washington won only 0.94 per cent of the Democratic votes cast — 2,131 of 227,327 votes.'[115] Washington had done better among white and Latino youth, winning nearly half of the vote of those under thirty-six, and did marginally well among traditionally liberal whites on the 'Lake Front'. The majority of liberal whites —

feminists in the National Organization for Women, middle-class lesbians and gays — tended to vote in accordance with their race rather than with political or class interests.[116] Washington's victory 'would not have been possible if the two white candidates had not split the white vote, which was even more monolithic as a bloc than the Black vote.'[117]

VI

Washington's supporters had predicted that the Democratic machine would 'find some way to steal the mayor's office' if their candidate emerged with the nomination. Only days before the primary election, one Black journalist suggested that either the Republican Party's little-known nominee, Bernard Epton, would 'become the great white hope', or a white Democrat would attempt to run as a third-party candidate, 'even though the filing date is past'.[118] Simultaneously, Irish aldermen of the South-West Side secretly discussed the possibility of running Byrne or another white independent in the general election in the event of the machine's defeat. When the press learned of this, Byrne's campaign manager quickly denounced the idea. 'I rejected it out of hand', stated William Griffin. 'I thought it was blatantly racist.'[119] In the wake of the primary results, Byrne seemed to reconcile herself to defeat. 'The results are very clear', the mayor stated before a packed press conference. '[Washington] is the choice of the people . . . and I will support him.'[120] Several weeks later, however, the erratic mayor announced to a stunned public that she would become a write-in candidate in the general election. Neither Republican candidate Bernard Epton nor Washington 'represents the best interest of Chicago', Byrne declared. Sensitive to charges that the write-in campaign was inspired by racism, the mayor insisted that she was 'not running for Blacks or for whites, the Democratic Party or the Republican Party or any political organization'. The response from national Democratic leaders, who feared a Black backlash in 1984 if Washington was not elected, was swift and uncompromisingly critical. Senator Ted Kennedy, a friend of Byrne's, declared that he was backing Washington 'strongly and without reserve'. Former Vice-President Walter Mondale, who had backed Daley in the primary, and House of Representatives Speaker Thomas O'Neill also voiced strong support for Washington. Charles T. Manatt, the chair of the Democratic National Committee, claimed that the Black Congressman had 'been betrayed by Jane Byrne', and termed the mayor's decision 'mischievous and hopeless'. Massive national pressure was undoubtedly exerted against machine leaders, and they promptly buckled under the collective strain. Vrdolyak did nothing to pull Democratic aldermen and committee-men behind Washington, but was forced to state his formal opposition to 'any write-in campaign' by Byrne. After a frantic yet futile effort to obtain supporters, Byrne finally announced that she would not be a write-in candidate. As one reporter put it, Byrne was 'destined to go out as she came in, a wild loner, but with a tacky heritage of racism and mismanagement'.[121]

Theoretically, the general election should have been only a formality. No Republican had been elected mayor since 1927, and the Republican Party in the city was practically non-existent. In 1979, Byrne had defeated Republican challenger Wallace Johnson by a majority of four to one. Washington had received over 400,000 votes more than Epton in the latter's 1983 primary. Moreover, the Republican challenger was hardly a household name. A Jewish liberal trained as a corporate attorney, Epton had served in the State Legislature for fourteen years, but had no former city-wide campaign experience. He had known Washington for two decades, and the two men had even co-sponsored liberal legislation together. Epton had made his personal fortune as a financial investor and in his political role as the insurance corporations' chief operative in state affairs. Little in the multimillionaire's background indicated that he could run an unabashedly racist campaign, drawing upon the latent yet malignant appeal of white supremacy to check the energy of the Black masses. But as Alkalimat and Gills observe, 'Epton's ambitions to rule made him more than willing' to become the 'pawn' of the Democratic machine. 'For in their attempts to preserve their privilege, the "old guard" had to call upon primitive, barbaric tactics of race hate-mongering, which feeds upon ignorance and fear and arouses the most backward sentiments and passions among the white electorate.'[122] Both Epton and the Democratic machine comprehended that the only strategy that could defeat Washington was the creation of a multiclass, white united front, dominated by reactionary sectors of corporate capital, the labour aristocracy, and white ethnic Democratic Party leaders. The obscure Republican openly projected himself as the solitary 'white hope', and minimized any discussion of specific programmatic differences between himself and Washington. In his first series of media advertisements,

Epton's campaign slogan cut to the core of the issue: 'Vote Bernard Epton Before It's Too Late.' When questioned by the media about his polemics, Epton's supporters turned the issue of racism on its head: 'Is it racist for whites to unite, but not racist for Blacks?' This racist rhetoric had a chauvinistic impact upon many white ethnics, who began to distribute hate-literature. Within weeks, one widely circulated flyer predicted that the city's Police Department emblem would be changed to 'Chicongo Po-lease' under Washington. 'Honkies for Bernie' buttons appeared in ethnic neighbourhoods. Other flyers distributed by Epton campaign workers predicted that 'white women will be raped' and 'property values will decline if "Mr Baboon" gets in power'. As the racist propaganda increased, Democratic stalwarts began to defect openly to Epton. Among the first were Vito Marzullo, the elderly boss of the City Council, and Chicago Park District Superintendent Edmund Kelly. They were soon followed by aldermen Anthony Laurino (34th Ward), Richard Clewis (45th Ward), Aloysius Majerczyk (12th Ward) and Ivan Rittenberg (40th Ward). A few white Democrats, such as alderman Richard Mell (33rd Ward), opted for 'neutrality', which meant that they would do nothing to promote Washington's campaign among their constituents. More hypocritical was the behaviour of Vrdolyak and other Democratic Party bosses, who formally endorsed Washington but 'in every other way worked directly to support Epton's candidacy'.[123] Sensing a potential victory, the national Republican Party quietly poured substantial resources into Epton's campaign. Republican National Committee leader Senator Paul Laxalt aided Epton's fund-raising efforts. Illinois governor James Thompson, a Republican, allowed his own campaign manager, James Fletcher, to coordinate Epton's campaign.

Police chief Brzeczek's brazen support for Byrne now escalated into an all-out war between the city's two thousand Black and eleven thousand white patrolmen. Squad cars were spotted bearing 'Upton for Mayor' stickers. The Afro-American Patrolman's League president Howard Saffold noted, 'It's simple-minded to say that the rift in the department is anything but racial. Police officers never cared who the mayor was before. The only reason they care now is because one of the candidates is Black.' White officers openly distributed pro-Epton literature while on the job, and others aggressively volunteered for Epton on off-duty hours. One week before the general election, Brzeczek announced his resignation as police superintendent. The 43-year-old attorney had declared earlier that 'the city would not be safe under Washington . . .'. His departure from the $85,000-a-year job was timed to assist Epton's campaign. Republican strategists noted that Washington's chief antagonist had been Brzeczek, not Epton, and that the Black Democrat would be forced 'to address the whole issue of the [police] department, and a new superintendent'. Washington's supporters assessed Brzeczek's surprising departure more candidly. 'This is an underhanded attempt to help Epton', Danny Davis argued. 'Brzeczek is hoping to stir up whites even more by saying, "Washington is about to win, therefore I'm going".' As another Washington supporter stated, 'the police issue has become a code-word for race. Some whites worry about what will happen to the police department under a Black mayor. Epton has used this issue to rally white support, and Brzeczek just moved it to the front burner.'[124]

Well above the field of electoral struggle, Chicago's corporate executives and financial leaders viewed the Washington-Epton campaign with some alarm. It was certainly true that Washington was no socialist, and that his economic programme, if implemented, might actually accelerate the development of petty capitalism in the Black community, thus strengthening the conservative position of the Afro-American elite. Washington had recruited several corporate executives to participate in his campaign, and Chicago's most prominent banks, First National and Continental, provided senior administrators for the Democratic candidate. What disturbed the corporate leadership was, first, the mass social class base of Washington's effort, in which a small number of white workers rejected racist appeals to support their own objective interests. After weeks of indecision, most white labour leaders endorsed Washington after the Democratic primary election. Chicago Federation of Labour executive board president William Lee urged the group's three hundred thousand members to support Washington in the general election. CFL affiliates that donated personnel and financial support to Washington included the American Federation of State, County and Municipal Employees, United Auto Workers, the Chicago Federation of Teachers, the Amalgamated Transit Workers, the United Food and Commercial Workers and the Amalgamated Clothing and Textile Workers. Washington pledged to union members that he would 'immediately end' the Byrne-sponsored practice of requiring city employees to work in election campaigns, and supported the extension of 'Civil Service protection to all city workers', as well as recognition of 'the unions of their choice'.[125] Such rhetoric was typical of liberal

Democrats, but Washington seemed sincerely dedicated to a pro-labour agenda. Thomas J. Klutznick, a millionaire real-estate director, expressed his fears to *Business Week:* 'The concern about Washington is that he might be too extreme to pull together the traditional coalition of government, business, and labour.' One former Byrne supporter, Thomas F. Roeser, a vice-president of Quaker Oats Company, complained, 'Washington views the city more as a repository for taxes than as a place where business should be shored up.' Business executives and bankers explained that Washington had little understanding of the 'complexities' of the capitalist market-place, that he was 'naive' about Chicago's 'marginal credit rating and eroding job base'. Instead of talking about police brutality, 'putting more Blacks in city jobs, and revitalizing the schools', corporate critics noted, the Black candidate ought to be 'concentrating on wooing businessmen'. Consequently the majority of capitalists quietly aligned themselves behind the 'white hope', and voiced few complaints when Epton's working class ethnics transgressed the boundaries of racial etiquette. The chairman of Combined International, W. Clement Stone, led a group of corporate donors into the Epton campaign. Stone and other capitalists understood quite well that beneath the façade of race was the fundamental class struggle, which had now assumed a dynamic electoral form. [126]

Washington was able to raise $3 million for the general election campaign, three quarters of which was generated locally. Most of the members of the Congressional Black Caucus had not taken Washington's mayoral race seriously, at least until his successful performance in the televised debates during the Democratic primary. The democratic socialists within the CBC, notably Dellums and Conyers, pushed their colleagues to support Washington. During both the primary and the general election campaigns, Conyers sent his top political organizers to Chicago to assist Washington's staff. CBC members held fundraisers, and donated other resources. Belatedly, fearful that a Washington defeat would create a Black 'backlash' against the Democrats' 1984 presidential candidate, national party leaders journeyed briefly to Chicago to stump for Washington. Epton even turned this into a major issue, by denouncing Democrats such as Senators Ted Kennedy, John Glenn and Alan Cranston as 'carpet-baggers'. Again, in US racist folk-culture, the term 'carpet-baggers' was a white supremacist epithet used by southern whites to denounce northern politicians who came into their region during Reconstruction. Epton continued to feed the most reactionary traits of the mob: he repeatedly described Washington as not 'quite too bright', illiterate, a liar, a tax evader, and even a 'child molester'. These racist characterizations prompted white ethnics into vigilante action. When Washington and former Vice-President Mondale attempted to attend a church service in a white neighbourhood on Palm Sunday, two hundred angry whites booed and threatened them. Screaming racist epithets, the mob was restrained by the police, but not a single demonstrator was arrested. Chicago *Sun Times* columnist Mike Royko noted with disgust, 'Many of [the demonstrators] had palm fronds in their hands — which symbolized their religious devotion — and that was a heck of a good break for Washington. If the religious observance called for them to be carrying broomsticks or baseball bats, instead of delicate palms, he might of had his skull creased.'[127] The media generally promoted the development of the electoral white united front by deliberately avoiding reporting any positive support Washington received from whites. When, on 27 March, Black and white trade-union leaders held a rally of over thirteen thousand Black and white workers for Washington, the media provided scant coverage. One local television station 'editorially criticized the Democratic Party candidate for not campaigning among white people'.[128] Yet some of Washington's most vigorous and vocal supporters were white working-class leaders: Libby Saries, head of the 8000-member Amalgamated Clothing and Textile Workers' Union; Jim Balanoff, former director of United Steelworkers District 31; and Neil Burke of the United Electrical Workers Local 1154, which represented three thousand workers in five area plants.[129]

Washington continued to try to keep the campaign from descending into the gutter. His staff released ten thousand copies of an ambitious political programme, 'The Washington Papers: A Commitment to Chicago, A Commitment to You', which in a comprehensive manner addressed issues on energy, women's rights, education, public safety, housing, jobs and other topics. Cultural workers and intellectuals organized 'Artists for Harold Washington'; Black, white and Latino elderly mobilized the 'Seniors for Harold Washington'.[130] Washington's supporters also continued to register low-income, Black and Latino voters. Between 23 February and 5 April, 31,533 new voters were added to the rolls. The greatest increase in voters occurred in the South Side's 21st Ward, which added 1,256 new voters. This ward alone, which was 98.4 per cent Black, meant at least another 800 votes for Washington. Other major increases occurred in Wards 9, 16, 17 and 34, all on the heavily-Black South Side. The smallest numbers of additional voters were registered in all-white or predominately Latino wards. Washington and his supporters continued to build a firm electoral base within the Black community, in short, and hoped also to reach just enough white workers, Latinos, liberals and socialists who could transcend the Jim Crow barrier which had historically divided the city. [131] White Democratic leaders, however, began to sense that Washington could not win. Vrdolyak publicly stated that his 'projections' showed that Epton would win by a narrow margin. Another white 'supporter' of Washington, 14th Ward Committee-man Edward M. Burke, now bluntly questioned 'Washington's fitness to serve as mayor'. [132]

Almost 1.3 million people voted on 12 April, 82 per cent of the electorate. In Chicago's closest mayoral race in over half a century, Washington obtained 668,176 votes (50.1 per cent) to Epton's 619,926 votes (46.4 per cent). Epton's strategy of building a white united front was largely successful. The Republican won 27 out of 50 wards, and received 86 per cent of his votes from predominantly white wards. About 95 per cent of Epton's total support had come from white voters. This represented a 'stunning reversal of traditional white voting patterns', notes political scientist Edward Thompson. 'Between 1979 and 1983 there was a rough shift of minus 60 percentage points in white support for the Democratic Party candidate. The magnitude of this shift among the strong white Democratic partisans of Chicago leaves the inescapable conclusion that race influenced white voters.' [133] Washington's victory was the product of three basic elements. First, the Afro-American electorate gave Washington over 514,000 votes, 77 per cent of his total. The Black voter turn-out reached 73 per cent, higher than the white turn-out rate of 67.2 per cent. In the brief span of four years, Afro-American voting power had nearly doubled. Less than 2 per cent of all Blacks had voted for Epton — a figure that is probably generous. Washington's nearly unanimous endorsement by Blacks was fuelled by nationalists, who viewed the campaign as a race-conscious effort for self-determination, and by integrationists who recognized the necessity to uproot institutional racism and political inequality. Secondly, a minority of white liberals, trade unionists and progressives refused to be intimidated by the racist barrage, and voted according to their political and social class interests. About one quarter of the votes in the liberal Lake Front wards went to Washington. Epton also did surprisingly poorly among Jewish voters. According to various estimates, Washington pulled about 34 to 38 per cent of Chicago's Jewish electorate — a low figure, given the liberal political behaviour of this group, but about twice the percentage of all other whites who supported Washington in this election. Washington's meagre 12 per cent share in Irish, Italian and Polish working-class and middle-income wards, however, indicates the political weight of racism with US political culture.[134] But the most crucial element was the Latino electorate. In the six wards with 20 per cent or more Latino voters, Washington won only 12,798 votes during the Democratic primary. In the general election, the Latino turn-out of registered voters was still below 25 per cent, but Washington's vote in the six Latino wards now totalled 43,082. Cuban-Americans voted 52 per cent for Washington; Mexican-Americans, 68 per cent; and the largest Spanish-speaking nationality, Puerto Ricans, voted 79 per cent for Washington. As Alkalimat and Gills note, 'Washington made a major effort to attract the Latino vote. Latinos were put into positions of visibility and responsibility within the campaign.' A Spanish-language 'blue button' was produced and widely circulated, and the campaign 'underwrote a newspaper project *El Independiente*', which was distributed in Latino neighbourhoods. It was this major shift in the Latino vote, more than anything else, that enabled Washington to win.[135]

VII

'Washington's victory was a product of a movement, not [an electoral] campaign', observed journalist Nina Berman. 'While his organization was constantly bogged down by inefficiency, bureaucracy and general inexperience, the movement he galvanized showed remarkable unity in terms of ideology and sense of purpose.' Twenty thousand Chicagoans — Black, white, Asian and Latino — cheered their new mayor at an election night celebration held at 1.30 a.m. All felt that 'a milestone had been reached in the struggle against racial barriers'.[136] There were 236 primary candidates who had run for the fifty City Council Seats. Seven of the sixteen incumbent Black aldermen had backed Washington during the Democratic primary, and had been easily re-elected. Six of the nine Blacks who had not originally supported him had been defeated. In all, twenty-one City Council Seats were now controlled by Washington and the reform Democrats, a liberal bloc which included five whites. Most of these aldermen had blue-collar, working-class backgrounds, and almost all had direct links with social reform and grass-roots groups in their wards. Although the Democratic machine had maintained its hold over the City Council, Washington's bloc was large enough to sustain a mayoral veto. Given the new political situation, the city's corporate and financial leaders promptly indicated that they would be willing to come to terms with the mayor elect. They had not taken Epton's racist hysteria campaign too seriously, and despite their problems with the mass character of Washington's movement, they recognized that the Black liberal would not be hostile to them in most respects. Their cold assessment was correct. Washington created two groups that would set into motion the basic policies of the new administration, a 'Transition Oversight Committee', which examined the functions of existing city departments and staff, and a 'Financial Advisory Coordinating Task Force' (FACT Force), which reviewed fiscal policies. The former committee's social composition was similar to that of Washington's formal campaign staff. A small majority of the members were Black or Latino (52 per cent), and almost all were white-collar professionals, businessmen or politicians. Only three of the Transition Oversight Committee's fifty-five members had ties with organized labour or community groups. The FACT Force was even more elitist: 70 per cent of the members were white, all were corporate executives, lawyers or professionals, and none had links with the social protest movement that had put Washington into office.[137]

Relations between Washington and the machine were quite a different story. Although the mayor elect made several overtures to his old opponents, he was in no mood to compromise — nor could he have, even if he had so desired, because the thousands of militants his campaign had created now expected and demanded fundamental change. In his speeches before his inauguration, Washington reaffirmed his commitment to reforming the city government by removing public jobs from the control of the machine, and declared that 'affirmative action' measures would be used to increase the number of women, Blacks and Hispanic workers in government, especially at policy-making levels. The new administration's first priority would be to create 'affordable housing for low- and moderate-income residents'. The machine would have to learn to exist with Black, Latino and progressive white leaders. 'The machine is mortally wounded,' Washington reflected, 'and like a dying animal will drag itself into the woods and die.'[138] This was certainly wishful thinking. Washington and the Black community had won the electoral battle, but the machine now prepared for war. The white ethnic party bosses were blatant racists, to be sure, but 'race' was never the decisive issue that directed their behaviour. What was really at stake was patronage. The mayor's office in Chicago had controlled thousands of jobs which were distributed to loyal Democratic ward committee-men, aldermen, and neighbourhood lieutenants. Occasionally, members of the machine were sent to gaol for their more obvious crimes. Black pro-machine alderman Tyrone Kenner, for instance, was convicted in 1983 for selling electricians' licences and positions in the sheriff's department. Public patronage breeds nepotism and rampant corruption. Vrdolyak, to cite another example, in 1980 owed the federal government $172,000 in back taxes, but, unlike Washington, did not serve a single day in gaol. The son of one Vrdolyak lieutenant was deputy commissioner of streets and sanitation. Vrdolyak's niece, working in the City Comptroller's office, was 'in charge of a secret revolving fund from which Byrne used $12 million for festivals and parties' in 1982. Machine politicians were frequently partners in businesses that received city contracts. Over 40 per cent of all city contracts, in fact, had been awarded on a 'no-bid' basis. Byrne and other mayors had used the power to award contracts as a means of extorting campaign funds. Washington had already promised to set legal restrictions on campaign contributions from such corporations.[139]

The machine was determined to hold its graft by any means necessary. In a secret session of the twenty-nine machine aldermen, Vrdolyak outlined a strategy for a 'machine coup' of sorts. Under the plan, whites would retain almost all committee chairmanships; Edward Burke, Vrdolyak's closest ally, was given the Finance Committee, which controlled all appropriations bills. The police and Council Sergeant of Arms would be placed under the Council's control. The machine would control all police, fire department and zoning matters, and the number of Black Council committee chairmen would be cut from eight to three. At the first Council session on 2 May, the machine unveiled its measures. Washington promptly adjourned the session, and his twenty-one supporters walked out. With Washington and his allies gone, the 'Vrdolyak 29' ratified their proposals in an illegal rump session. Washington quickly denounced the action as 'an illegal, non-binding and illegitimate meeting'. Subsequent sessions were simply shouting matches. 'Goon squads' of machine supporters then invaded City Hall, and both factions went to court to block each other.[140] Throughout the remainder of 1983 and all of 1984, Washington's initiatives were repeatedly blocked by the Vrdolyak 29. After over a year of his being in office, the Council had approved only four of his major administrative appointees. Working around his opponents, the mayor was able to carry out some of his campaign pledges, including the establishment of a city Commission on Women's Affairs, the creation of a new Department of Revenue for the 'fair collection of taxes', and the successful lobbying for a new state law for collective bargaining for public employees. Washington's only major victory occurred on 1 October 1984, when he forced the Vrdolyak bloc to accept an interdepartmental board to review no-bid contracts over $50,000. Vrdolyak compromised only when Washington vetoed a public-works projects appropriation package which totalled $1 billion, and threatened to shut down a massive airport project employing thousands of workers.[141]

Racism was the key to the machine's entire counter-attack against Washington. First, the budding political alliance between the Latino and Afro-American communities had to be destroyed. Less than two months after Washington's election, his chief organizer and adviser, 31-year-old Rudy Lozano, was assassinated in his home. Despite the arrest and conviction of a gang member for the murder, the Chicago Police Department and the Cook County State's Attorney's office failed to follow numerous leads to determine who planned and financed Lozano's assassination.[142] Another opportunity for disruption presented itself in the 1984 controversy over Ruth Love, a conservative Black educator who was appointed public-school superintendent during Byrne's administration. Latinos had genuine grievances against Love, noting that thirty of the city's thirty-four schools cited for overcrowding were in Hispanic neighbourhoods. Latinos also experienced a 70 per cent drop-out rate in the city's high schools. Unfortunately, one of the initial supporters of the 'Dump Love' movement was Carlos Perez, a political conservative who had led the 'Latinos for Epton' group. Complicating matters further was Love's cordial relationship with the Vrdolyak bloc. Under increased criticism, Love claimed that the mayor was 'conspiring to get rid of her'. Although Washington judiciously took a neutral position, and Love was finally dismissed from her post by the Board of Education, Vrdolyak had successfully manipulated the issue to divide Latinos and Blacks, albeit temporarily.[143]

Racist rhetoric and vigilante violence were also part of the strategy. Thus Vrdolyak, at a major trade show sponsored by nine hundred corporate exhibitors in downtown Chicago, charged that the mayor planned 'to "Blacken" the city by forcing white families to leave town, in order to guarantee a majority in the next election'.[144] Such polemics produced predictable results. In early 1984, when a Black family moved into Vrdolyak's 10th Ward, it was immediately subjected to attack. 'After verbal intimidation, property damage to the house, vandalism of their cars and finally, the burning down of their garage', all in the space of only two weeks, the family fled.[145] According to the Chicago Police Department, there were at least 127 'verified' racial incidents in the city in 1984. This rather modest total does not include hundreds of unreported acts of random violence, or the 31 recorded acts of firebombings, cross-burnings and racist attacks against Blacks in the suburbs. Many atrocities can be cited, but two incidents stand out. On the night of Reagan's re-election, a substantial gang of inebriated whites surrounded a Black family's home, located near Cicero on the city's West Side, and stoned it with bricks, rocks and other weapons for a full six hours. Local police tended to classify instances of racist terrorism as juvenile delinquency. When one Black suburban family complained to police when their property had been defaced with Ku Klux Klan symbols, their automobile vandalized, and they had received written threats, the officer in charge of the investigation replied: 'It's not nice . . . but we can't take every piece of chalk away from every kid.'[146] These monotonous attacks took their toll on many Black residents. A young *Chicago Tribune* editorial writer, Leanita McClain, described the vicious media stories on 'the Blacks' as 'an evilness [which] still possesses this town and it continues to weigh down my heart . . . "The Blacks". It is the article that offends. The words are held out like a foul-smelling sock transported two-fingered at the end of an outstretched arm to the hamper while the nose is pinched shut.' McClain related that the mayoral campaign and its aftermath had robbed her 'of most of my innate Black hope for true integration . . . Chicago taught me to hate whites . . .'. Racist aldermen denounced McClain by name, and demanded that she apologize to the city's whites. Increasingly the target of public abuse, the 32-year-old McClain committed suicide on 29 May 1984.[147]

Had Washington fought the 'Vrdolyak 29' only in the smoke-filled corridors of City Hall, in the machine's traditional conspiratorial style, he surely would have been defeated. But instead, the mayor consistently took his case for reform to the people, and reinforced their involvement and mobilization. He cut his own annual salary from $60,000 to $48,000 and froze city hirings and wages. Washington fired 541 employees that Byrne 'had added to the pay-rolls in a last-minute hiring binge'.[148] Three hundred City Hall administrators were 'laid off in order to transfer $13 million in federal community funds from administrative salaries to neighbourhood improvement projects, which would create more than enough jobs to offset the three hundred laid-off employees.' The unity between Latinos and Afro-Americans which characterized the general election was reinforced when the mayor's office funded $60,000 to hold a Puerto Rican festival in Humboldt Park which attracted over a hundred thousand people. Jose Jimenez, chief coordinator of the festival, 'rallied the crowd' by demanding self-determination for Puerto Rico. As Berman noted, 'This was the first time in recent memory that a city-sponsored cultural festival turned into a political event emphasizing community and leftist concerns.'[149] When Alderman Edward Burke initiated a legal suit in May 1984 to remove the mayor from office, leaders of sixty-eight religious and civic groups quickly united to back Washington, including Mgr John Egan, Catholic Archdiocese; Jane Ramsey, executive director of the Jewish Council on Urban Affairs; and James Compton of the Chicago Urban League.[150] Community groups continued to mount voter-registration efforts to expand their electoral base. Some of Washington's progressive allies were appointed or elected to new positions. Renault Robinson was named by Washington to head the Chicago Housing Authority, and he swiftly replaced 'white craftsmen, appointed through their [machine] connections to maintenance jobs at contruction pay, with trainees selected from among impoverished residents of the housing projects, at regular union maintenance wages.' In August 1983, trade-union leader Charles Hayes was elected to Congress to fill Washington's seat, becoming the highest-ranking trade unionist in Congress.[151]

Yet what had the Black community and other oppressed groups actually won? Coleman Young, who was an old hand in such matters, looked beyond the euphoria. Days after Washington's victory, Young predicted that the new mayor would have no easy time 'coming to grips with an ingrained, overwhelmingly white bureaucracy'. Despite Black authority, the Chicago Police Department — 'known across the country as a law unto itself' — would still terrorize national minorities. The real problem was the paradox of Black electoral power. Washington, and every other Black mayor in the US, was 'caught in a local trap', Young noted. They are all 'limited to a local electoral mandate based on local Black majorities whose voices are too feeble to be heard in Washington. Everyone recognizes that there is no Black majority in the United States as a whole. So you are left with nothing but wheeling and dealing.'[152] Young's early tutelage on the left evidently did not go for naught. No Black mayors, whether liberal reformers like Washington or accommodationists like Thomas Bradley, exercise either state power or semi-autonomous authority, as in the case of petty-bourgeois elites in neo-colonial regimes. The structural constraints of bourgeois democracy give them an electoral mandate, but not the actual mechanism of state power. They have managerial responsibilities, some degree of political patronage to reward some of their constituents, and little else. On assuming office they are instantly confronted with the legacy of the mismanagement and blatant graft of their predecessors, and face public rejection at the polls if they are unable to untangle the mess others have created. When Washington became mayor, the city's school system faced a projected $200 million deficit, and his aides 'estimated that the city's general fund could run as much as $150 million short' in 1983. Few Washington supporters had had experience in running the city's massive bureaucracy, so the new mayor was forced to reappoint a number of Byrne administrators. 'Washington could not afford to get rid of many of them, even if he had a free hand', observed David Maberg. 'He needs their knowledge of how the city works, even though as his transition team carries on its massive research into the city's past practices, it is reportedly discovering mind-boggling examples of waste, padding and outright corruption.'[153]

Most Afro-American mayors lack the type of powerful, social protest mobilization that brought Washington into office. Hence they are far more likely to play a role that is more accommodating to capital. In Atlanta, Andrew Young immediately pushed to 'convert his city into an international trade centre, brokering deals between Atlanta businesses and companies in Africa'. He openly courted the banks and corporations, telling them bluntly: 'I can win without you. I can't govern without you.' The head of the National Conference of Black Mayors, Tuskegee, Alabama Mayor Johnny Ford, counselled his peers to become 'pro-business'. In the true spirit of Booker T. Washington, Ford proclaimed that the corporate-Black 'coalition' was a marriage 'of necessity. We're about trying to get jobs. Dollars are the cutting edge.'[154] Few Black mayors, though, were more accommodating to corporate interests than New

Orleans's Ernest Morial. After his election in 1978, Morial created 'a comprehensive New Orleans Economic Development Strategy to end the city's dependence on low-wage service jobs', which were largely Black. A 7,000-acre tract of city land was turned into a large industrial district. To attract a $9 million computer plant, 'the city issued $7.8 million in tax-exempt industrial revenue bonds, purchased mainly by a local bank, and agreed to exempt' the firm from 'a broad array of taxes'. As an immediate pay-off to the local Black entrepreneurial stratum, $79 million in city contracts was given to Black businesses from 1978 to 1982. For the Black petty bourgeoisie, administrative plums were offered. In four years, Black municipal employment was increased by 11 per cent, and Blacks were appointed to head five of City Hall's twelve departments. But what of the Black working class and the poor? Regressive sales taxes, which of all forms of taxation are the most discriminatory in effects, were hiked in 1980 and 1982. Black public education continued to deteriorate: over half of all New Orleans school children do not graduate from high school. Police brutality towards Black radicals, workers and the poor actually increased under Morial. By 1979 'New Orleans police killed more civilians per police officer than in any other city.' Political scientist Monte Pilawsky observes, 'As Morial builds a more effective political machine of his own, the question of what material benefits a Black mayor can deliver for poor Blacks will remain. For the danger of an ambitious politician forsaking his constituents' real interests is no less real for a Black elected official than for a white.'[155]

Washington and other Black mayors confront one other major problem — the necessity of maintaining a high degree of Black voter-participation and mobilization, without which they cannot remain in office. The historical example of Cleveland's Black mayor Carl Stokes provides a fitting parallel. After failing upon his first try, Stokes was elected mayor of Cleveland in 1967, carrying 95 per cent of the Black wards and 19 per cent of the white wards in the general election — almost exactly Washington's percentages in 1983. But Stokes pursued a cautious programme as mayor from 1967 to 1971, and frequently capitulated to the demands of his mostly white police force and local corporations. The city's Black vote splintered after 1971, when white Republican Ralph Perk was elected mayor. The percentage of Black registered voters who cast ballots declined from 81.7 per cent in 1967 to 30.8 per cent in 1978. 'Despite his talent, his energy, and his abiding commitment to the welfare of his people', Mayor Stokes could 'make little headway' against institutional racism and class exploitation. Cleveland's first Black mayor was also, to date, its last. Does Cleveland's history await Chicago?[156]

The 1983 election of Harold Washington certainly represented far more than the decisive defeat of a corrupt, racist political organization. Viewed in the wider context of Black Chicago's social history, it was the victory of the militant-reform tradition over those more cautious and defensive Black elites who advocate accommodation with the *status quo*. It was the belated triumph and vindication of the contributions of Charles E. Bentley, John G. Jones, Ida B. Wells, Earl Dickerson, and hundreds of other articulate Black labour leaders, politicians and clergy who had led the fight against the Thompson, Kelly and Daley machines. But moreover, it was not the reformist elites, but the Black masses, who were the determining factor throughout. The Black welfare mothers, tenants' organizers, postal workers, labourers, unemployed men and women, and many more, finally believed in their own capacity to organize, and rejected four generations of plantation politics. What liberal Black petty-bourgeois elites had failed to achieve in six decades, the Black working class and the poor accomplished in six months. Whether the election of Washington represents a fundamental shift in the balance of racial and class struggle in Chicago, or whether it becomes simply a minor detour in the rule of the machine, depends upon the ability of Black working people to transcend the past, and to continue to make their own history. This means, in short, the overturning of the implicitly capitalist assumptions perpetuated by reform-minded Black intellectuals, labour and religious leaders, and an ongoing campaign to educate and mobilize the poor and the labouring classes. It demands a political war against the corporate interests that temporarily support the Washington bloc, and a pressuring of the reformist petty bourgeoisie either to commit class suicide or to side openly with capital. Whether this strategy can be implemented through the Democratic party is extremely problematical. 'The big question', Alkalimat and Gills ask, 'is how long can the cathartic ritual of voting Black satisfy the hunger of Black people for freedom, since the material benefits of Black elected officials are so limited?'[157]

5

Rainbow Rebellion

Jesse Jackson's Presidential Campaign and the Democratic Party

This candidacy is not for Blacks only. This is a national campaign growing out of the Black experience and seen through the eyes of the Black perspective — which is the experience and perspective of the rejected. Because of this experience, I can empathize with the plight of Appalachia because I have known poverty. I know the pain of anti-Semitism because I have felt the humiliation of discrimination. I know firsthand the shame of bread lines and the horror of hopelessness and despair because my life has been dedicated to empowering the world's rejected to become respected. Thus, our perspective encompasses and includes more of the American people and their interest than do most other experiences.

Jesse Jackson, 3 November 1983.

I

The 1984 presidential campaign of Jesse Jackson represented a new stage of development in Afro-Americans' struggle for equality in the context of US bourgeois democracy. Even white American political analysts unsympathetic with the Jackson campaign recognized this, and groped for words to define Jackson's achievement. After Jackson had received 26 per cent of the New York Democratic primary vote, Theodore White suggested that the Black candidate had emerged 'as a major historical figure . . . a trailblazer of the dimensions of [Martin Luther King]. There is no doubt that henceforth there will always be a Black candidate as an independent force in national Democratic politics, and American politics will never be the same.'[1] The essence of the Jackson campaign was a democratic, antiracist social movement, initiated and led by Afro-Americans, which had assumed an electoral mode. Its direct historical antecedents — the Montgomery bus boycott of 1955-56, the formation of the SNCC and the sit-in movement of 1960, the Birmingham desegregation campaign of 1963 — were revived in a new protest form within bourgeois democratic politics. The roots of this electoral political mobilization were developed in the ambiguous sphere of national Democratic Party politics, with the collapse of legal Jim Crow and the numerical increase of Black elected officials in the 1960s and 1970s. The unprecedented Black revolt against the Democratic Party in the primaries increased the effective political power and the capacity for future resistance among Afro-Americans; but simultaneously, the assertion of Black voting power led to a sharp increase in ethnic confrontations and shattered the 'melting pot' myth, as was manifested in the bitter and escalating conflict between the American Black and the Jewish communities. The campaign illustrated the capacity of a strong social movement to reshape the ideological and political orientation of its leaders, even charismatic but flawed spokespersons such as Jackson. And it also decisively placed on the American political agenda the possibility of a transitional progressive strategy that would create a viable, mass alternative to the two-party, bourgeois democratic system.

One index that reflects the institutional racism of US bourgeois democracy is the fact that until three decades ago, Afro-Americans played no substantial or meaningful role in US presidential politics. In 1952, about 60 per cent of all Afro-Americans had never voted for president, and more than three quarters of all southern Blacks had never participated in a presidential election. The consequences of various segregation laws, such as whites-only Democratic primaries, poll-taxes and literary tests, as previously discussed, effectively disfranchised the bulk of the Afro-American electorate.[2] Nevertheless, there is a long history of efforts made by Afro-Americans to influence presidential elections. Back in 1872, Douglass was nominated as vice-presidential candidate for Victoria Woodhull's National Radical Reformer's Party, which was dedicated to 'obtain[ing] the human rights of all mankind'. By this stage of his career Douglass was a loyal supporter of the Republican Party, and he promptly declined the nomination.[3]

In the twentieth century, Black involvement in presidential politics has taken two basic forms. First, Black activists have tried to circumvent the two-party system by running as third-party candidates, either in all-Black political formations, or as members of socialist or liberal parties. In 1960, for example, the Reverend Clennon King and Reginald Carter announced their candidacies for president and vice-president on the newly formed Afro-American Party, which quickly died for lack of Black support.[4] In 1964, Black activist Clifton DeBerry ran for president on the Socialist Workers'

Party ticket. But confronted with the possibility of right-wing demagogue Barry Goldwater winning as the Republican Party candidate, virtually all of the American left, including the Communist Party, the Students for a Democratic Society and the Social Democrats, united behind Texas Democrat Lyndon Johnson. The Black vote for Johnson in most states exceeded 99 per cent.[5] In 1968 several Black national candidates emerged. Charlene Mitchell became the first Afro-American woman to run for president, as the nominee of the Communist Party. The Socialist Workers' Party selected Newark, New Jersey organizer Paul Boutelle as its vice-presidential candidate. Eldridge Cleaver, Minister of Information of the Black Panther Party, was the candidate of the Peace and Freedom Party. Based primarily among the radical, white petty bourgeoisie and student movement in California, the Peace and Freedom Party projected an antiracist agenda. Cleaver was able to get on the ballot in over nineteen states, and won nearly 200,000 votes. More quixotic was the campaign of cultural critic Dick Gregory, who had lost the Peace and Freedom Party's nomination to Cleaver. In his campaign, Gregory distributed 'money-size bills bearing his picture and a dove instead of George Washington and an eagle'. Although these 'handbills were seized when several found their way into automatic money-changers', Gregory's combination of wit and panache garnered almost 150,000 votes.[6] The vast majority of the Black social fraction had little or nothing to do with these left and protest mobilizations against the two-party system. Even in 1972, at the height of Black nationalist dominance of Afro-American political culture, only 35 per cent of Black voters supported the idea of an all-Black third party; and this figure had declined by the end of the decade.[7] In that year, Julian Bond spoke for most Black activists in rejecting the viability of an independent electoral strategy. 'It is not going to be possible for 11 per cent of the population, disorganized and scattered, to form a third party', Bond observed. At best, Blacks could 'hold ourselves aloof' from a Democratic presidential nominee in order 'to extract important promises . . . Or to run our own candidate, a Black candidate, for President in states where such a candidacy could affect the outcome.'[8]

The second approach has been a concerted attempt to maximize Black electoral participation in voting for individual white presidential candidates, thus forming the decisive margin of victory whenever the white electorate is evenly divided between the parties. In the past quarter of a century, this has occurred only twice. In the presidential election of 1960, Republican Vice-President Richard Nixon was heavily favoured over John F. Kennedy. As Piven and Cloward observe, 'Kennedy made a vigorous appeal to the Black vote in the industrial states by campaigning on strong pledges to deal with civil rights and poverty . . . ' And, although Black scepticism towards the Democratic Party persisted, 'the Massachusetts Democrat received between 69 and 77 per cent of the national Black vote'.[9] In seven states, including Pennsylvania, Texas, Michigan and Illinois, the Afro-American vote was larger than Kennedy's overall margin of victory. Sixteen years later, an obscure one-term Georgia Democratic governor, Jimmy Carter, became the first president elected from the Deep South since 1848. In more than thirteen states, including Texas, Pennsylvania, Ohio, New York and Mississippi, the Black electorate again provided the margin of victory. 90 to 93 per cent of all Black voters had supported Carter, giving some political observers the erroneous impression that Blacks were now 'full partners in the nation's policy-making franchise'.[10]

Effective block voting for white capitalist candidates certainly changed the results of these presidential elections, but it did not represent any meaningful increase in Black political power. During Kennedy's first two years in office, he 'issued a mild executive order banning discrimination in federally-financed housing', but did nothing directly to assist the civil rights social movement.[11] Carter proved to be an even greater disappointment. The Carter Administration halted the creation of new programmes in human-services areas; increased defence spending to all-time highs; and vowed to 'cut inflation and to stimulate the business sector' at the cost of higher unemployment. By late summer 1977, Black Congressman Parren Mitchell, Benjamin Hooks, Urban League director Vernon Jordan and Jesse Jackson, all of whom had campaigned aggressively for Carter, charged the administration with 'callous neglect'. Richard Hatcher even admitted, 'Now it's difficult for any Black leader who pushed the election of Jimmy Carter to face the people he campaigned with.'[12] Five years before, Congresswoman Shirley Chisholm had attempted to implement Bond's strategy by running as a presidential candidate inside the Democratic Party primaries. Most of her CBC colleagues and other Black elected officials, however, ignored or belittled her campaign as irrelevant and Utopian. William Clay, Jesse Jackson and Walter Fauntroy joined George McGovern's campaign; Black Cleveland politician Arnold Pinkney and Mississippi leader Charles Evers endorsed Cold War liberal Hubert Humphrey.[13]

The dilemma confronting Blacks and the left was quite simple. As Michael Parenti argues, 'the two major parties cooperate in various strategems to maintain their monopoly over electoral politics and discourage the growth of radically-oriented third parties.' The Democrats, with an electoral base largely comprising workers and national minorities, but dominated by a fraction of the capitalist class, may advance social programmes more advantageous to the oppressed than the Republicans. But neither party 'has much appetite for the risks of social changes; each helps to make the world safe for the other.'[14] However, in order for the centre of American political culture to be moved toward the left, activists would have to intervene within the Democratic Party, and create the institutional presence necessary for translating their visionary agendas into actually existing public policies. The absence of even a social democratic party in the US forced most radicals to view work within the Democratic Party as a question of tactics, and not in accordance with the classical Trotskyist concept as a matter of principle. The Communist Party's 1936 presidential campaign — like its 1984 campaign — was largely a Popular Front-inspired effort to defeat the Republican rightist candidate and to elect the more liberal Democrat. Blacks and the US left have attempted, with varying degrees of success, to use the Democratic Party as a vehicle for progressive politics. In 1964, the Freedom Democratic Party, led by Fannie Lou Hamer and Lawrence Guyot, challenged the white racist machine in Mississippi.[15] In 1965, a group of white socialists in New York City created the Committee for Independent Political Action, which attempted to advance an anti-Vietnam war agenda within the Democatic Party primary elections. Radical trade unionist Stanley Aronowitz viewed the strategy as a means for 'an independent political movement' to attack the Democratic Party, as well as to 'evolve into a third party'. Revolutionaries who entered the Democratic Party could 'put reform Democrats who are radicals programmatically on the spot', while educating a mass audience.[16] Throughout the 1970s, progressives used the local Democratic Party apparatus to achieve some basic reforms. But at the national level, options still seemed few. Julian Bond sensed that Blacks would have to develop a presidential strategy that would unite them with white progressives in a 'political coalition' to address not simply civil-rights issues, but women's rights, consumerism, American foreign affairs and problems in the environment. A left-liberal Democratic candidate from such a coalition could have a decisive impact upon presidential politics.[17]

The reactionary administration of Ronald Reagan forced Afro-Americans, Latinos and the broad liberal-left to confront the in-adequacies of their approaches to presidential politics. One reason for this was Reagan's sterile, authoritarian rhetoric, which fed national chauvinism and the cultural currents of white supremacy. Even Fauntroy, who does not frequently indulge in polemics, was not exaggerating when he claimed in 1983 that Reaganism had fostered a 'scapegoat mentality' which was manifested in 'anti-Black feelings, directed at Blacks at all levels of life'.[18] Reaganism gave every tiny sect on the extreme right an ideological and political boost, a certain credibility among working-class and poor whites which it would not otherwise have had. And from the gutters of public life, the Ku Klux Klan once again resurfaced to flourish under the benevolent aegis of Reaganism. The KKK initiated white voter-registration drives in Alabama and Georgia; ran openly for federal and state offices throughout the South; and revived its tradition of bombings, shot-gun murders and cross-burnings. The Klan recognized that it represented the activist, vigilante wing of Reagan's conservative social forces. It praised Reagan's new re-actionary Civil Rights Commission as 'the first positive move to free America of communism, affirmative action, rampant give-away programmes [and] forced bussing'. In early 1984, Bill Wilkinson, leader of the Invisible Empire faction of the KKK, endorsed Reagan for re-election, declaring 'anytime you see all the Blacks and minorities in this country opposing, strongly, one man, you know he has got to be doing something good for the white race.'[19] Most of the American left could not be blind to the very real possibility that Reaganism could represent a first decisive step taken by capital towards some sort of unique version of fascism. As Paul M. Sweezy and Harry Magdoff wrote in January 1984, 'What we have is in every respect the most reactionary, right-wing government in the country's history, and in many ways it is doing things that in other countries and at other times are done by fascist governments.' Even though bourgeois democracy had 'deep roots' in the US, the state 'may be able to accommodate a move to the right resulting in a situation which is the functional equivalent of fascism.' The dilemma for the US left, however, was that it 'had no mass base and hence no significant influence on public opinion'. At best, the left could only try to mobilize all democratic forces to defeat the incumbent, and in so doing, 'get a foothold in public opinion and work to expand it into a meaningful base of political operations'.[20]

Throughout much of 1983, the left and the Afro-American community debated various electoral political options for attacking Reaganism. Inspired by the recent successes of the Green parties in Western Europe, the California Peace and Freedom Party initiated a dialogue with the Citizens' Party, Communist Party, Socialist Party, Workers' World Party and several smaller Leninist formations to create a united left campaign which could 'pose an alternative to the Democrats and Republicans'. From the initial June 1983 discussions in Oakland, California, strategic differences divided the left. The Communist Party, which had been heavily involved in the Washington campaign and was then active in the March on Washington mobilization, argued that working with Democratic liberals was a 'tactical question — not a matter of absolute principle'. It doubted the 'viability of a socialist [presidential] campaign without a conscious working class'. The Citizens' Party, although internally divided, and the small Socialist party were already inclined towards running their own symbolic national campaigns, and both viewed any intervention in the Democratic Party primaries with great repugnance.[21] Most Black independent leftists recognized that a united left national campaign, even with an Afro-American presidential candidate, would attract virtually no support from the Black working class; and in principle, they endorsed a Black challenge in the 1984 Democratic primaries. But they also emphasized that the central aim of such an effort would be to advance a comprehensive liberal-left agenda on domestic and international affairs. The individual presidential candidate, as Boston radical Mel King asserted, had to be secondary to 'the articulation of the issues'.[22]

The Black petty bourgeoisie was deeply divided, as usual, with the vast majority of leaders strongly opposed to any kind of Black challenge in the Democratic primaries. Urban League leader John Jacob denigrated the notion as 'a retreat to symbolism' which would 'fragment the Black community' and 'shatter Black expectations'.[23] The NAACP was firmly opposed as well. Joseph Madison, the Association's director of voter education, predicted that the 'maximum number of delegate votes that a Black candidate could depend on would [be] 250. Anyone with any deal of sense knows that the chance of a Black being elected . . . is extremely remote.'[24] Benjamin Hooks curtly dismissed a Black candidacy, exhibiting his confusion between a tactical, educational mobilization and a traditional capitalist campaign to win a party's nomination. 'Afro-Americans are too sophisticated to need a Black presidential candidate to stimulate their going to the polls . . . I don't think we're that dumb.' Hooks maintained that 'a Black person [hasn't] a ghost of a chance of winning in 1984', but added somewhat coquettishly that he was 'gearing up my mechanism to think about running in 1988'.[25] SCLC president Joseph E. Lowery offered qualified support for the move. 'The combined efforts of high unemployment, federal policies that constitute a vicious assault on rights so dearly won, and embarrassing capitulation by Democratic opposition, have created a crisis of frightening dimensions for Afro-Americans', Lowery warned in May 1983. A Black presidential candidate was a 'radical [yet] viable option', which could, under the appropriate set of conditions, advance 'systemic changes' and attack 'structural un-employment'.[26] Ironically, one of the more conservative civil-rights leaders, M. Carl Holman, president of the National Urban Coal-ition, strongly endorsed a Black presidential campaign. 'No white candidate [could express] the ache and anger of Black communities ravaged by joblessness', Holman commented. Many Black poli-ticians still had 'serious reservations', but most 'professional, religious and working-class Black people are saying that the country should start getting used to the idea that a Black may be as genuine a Presidential candidate as anyone else, without having to enlist in some splinter party . . . No amount of ridicule [or] fear [can] eliminate the possibility of such a candidacy as early as 1984.'[27]

A similar division existed among Black elected officials and labour-union leaders. Most Black mayors shared Hooks's misgivings. The most influential Black mayor in the country, Coleman Young, repeatedly declared that 'the major task of Black America today is to get rid of Ronald Reagan. We cannot afford to support a Black candidate who cannot win.' Andrew Young argued that 'Blacks ought to be in any campaign where the candidate is likely to be elected president.' Harold Washington agreed. 'We do not have the luxury to unite behind a Black candidate who can't win and re-elect Ronald Reagan.'[28] Some Black mayors began to make secret agreements to work for the campaign of former Vice-President Walter Mondale. Birmingham mayor Richard Arrington became an 'adviser' to the presidential campaign of South Carolina Senator Ernest Hollings in early 1983, only to switch to Mondale as Hollings declined in public-opinion polls.[29] Most members of the Congressional Black Caucus were decidedly cool in their response to the prospect of a Black candidate. Influential Congressman Charles Rangel of Harlem agreed to serve as national vice-chairman of Mondale's campaign. Congressman Walter Fauntroy feared that a Black candidate might increase right-wing white re-

gistrations and subsequently defeat a number of Black Congressional candidates. Only three Black Representatives, John Conyers
of Detroit, Gus Savage of Chicago and Ronald Dellums of
Oakland-Berkeley, actively pushed the strategy throughout 1983.
For Conyers, the Black candidacy was a response 'to the multiple
failures of federal policy under both Democratic and Republican
administrations, the steady progression in Black and minority
politics, and the need to build a new coalition. It is the logical
application of the experience gleaned in twenty years of struggle.'[30]
Most Black petty-bourgeois leaders remained unconvinced.
Clarence Mitchell, the president of the 357-member National Black
Caucus of State Elected Officials, told the press in September 1983
that a Black candidacy could 'be divisive and hurt local efforts to
gain more influence'. Coretta Scott King boosted Mondale's credentials as a civil-rights proponent with her endorsement.[31] In a
perverse argument, neo-conservative Black journalist Tony Brown
belittled a Black candidacy within the Democatic Party, and urged
Black Republicans 'to seize the moment and run a Black candidate'
in Republican primaries against Reagan.[32] Black labour spokesman
Bayard Rustin predicted that any Black presidential race was
simply 'doomed', because it would take votes away from white
'liberals' like Mondale, and it would 'heighten racial tensions'.[33]

In a series of meetings in Atlanta, Washington DC and Chicago,
Black leaders — including Andrew Young, Coretta Scott King,
Kenneth Gibson, Lowery, Fauntroy, Conyers and Jesse Jackson —
privately debated the Black presidential option. At the Chicago
meeting of 20 June 1983, about two thirds of this group gave
nominal 'approval to the concept', but did not endorse any
particular candidate.[34] Part of the problem among Black middle-
class leaders was an inaccurate assessment of the meaning of the
Chicago election. Many Black leaders, especially Andrew Young
and Congressman Alan Wheat of Kansas City, were fearful that 'if
Washington had lost, there would have been an emotional reaction
to run a Black presidential candidate as a matter of spite.'[35] White
political analysts such as Tom Wicker, for instance, also warned
that a Washington defeat would prompt 'Blacks everywhere' to
charge 'the loss to racism' and would 'lead to a Black presidential
candidacy' in order to 'shake up' the party.[36] When Washington
won, most Black leaders and white liberals concluded that the
pressure was now off. At the NAACP's July 1983 national convention, leaders were privately predicting confidently that the
Black candidacy movement would die out before October. Other

Black leaders, both radicals and moderates, vehemently disagreed. Holman asserted that a Washington victory would 'encourage Black candidates to come forward for local, state and national office'.[37] Conyers argued that the 'important lesson' of Washington's mayoral race was that 'an office-seeker who has something to say about historical class concerns against inequity and injustice will catch on with voters even without having a multimillion-dollar war chest.'[38] Mel King also stated that 'Chicago gives a model of what happens when there's some political organizing going on that confronts the *status quo* and gets people to register to vote — they can make a difference in the electoral process.'[39] And for Jesse Jackson, 'Washington's coalition victory' gave the 'Black presidential candidacy a major boost . . . It demonstrated that while some will join us if we assert ourselves; without such aggressiveness no one else will lead our fight for equitable representation, and some will actively oppose our interests despite past service and loyalty to the party.'[40]

Once again, the real social momentum for power among Black workers and the poor reduced the catatonic composure of the bulk of the Afro-American petty bourgeoisie to irrelevance. Black nationalists who had long criticized electoral politics now rapidly gravitated towards the Black presidential campaign. Maulana Karenga, the leading Black nationalist figure, declared that 'running a Black candidate can produce a spirit of mobilization and organization formations which can be used after the campaign in other projects.' With the 'political timidity of the Democratic Party in the face of the Right', Afro-Americans had to assume 'their traditional role of raising the radical and progressive banner around which others also can rally'.[41] Leading Black clergy generally favoured a Black presidential race. In June 1983, Bishop H. H. Brookins, a presiding bishop of the AME church, denounced John Jacob and others for their capitulation to Mondale. 'When Mr Jacob says we should not field a Black candidate, to me, it is like saying the various organizations that have opposed a Black presidential bid are afraid of losing the traditional support from the white liberal groups that have given them money through the years . . . the Black Church is standing behind the idea of a Black presidential candidate in the Democratic primaries.'[42] However, the most active proponent of the strategy was Jesse Jackson. In hundreds of towns and urban centres, the 42-year-old civil-rights leader reiterated his message:

Blacks have their backs against the wall and are increasingly distressed by the erosion of past gains and the rapidly deteriorating conditions within Black and poor communities. As Black leaders have attempted to remedy these problems through the Democratic Party — to which Black voters have been the most loyal and disciplined group — too often they have been ignored or treated with disrespect . . . A Black candidacy could use an 18-million eligible Black-voter base to put together a "coalition of the rejected", including appealing to six million Hispanics, women, more than 500,000 Native Americans, twenty to forty million poor whites, and an appeal to the moral decency and enlightened economic self-interest of millions of rejected white moderates, liberals and others . . . A Black candidacy would alter the essentially negative and defensive option of the "lesser of two . . . evils", to the positive and offensive alternative of a "live" option. An increase in voter-registration and political participation would have a profound impact upon the *status quo* of the Democratic Party . . . Never again should Blacks live and operate below their political privilege and rights.[43]

Jackson's extensive promotion of the strategy had the effect of focusing the national media on Jackson as the most likely Black Democratic challenger. In one May 1983 national public-opinion poll, Jackson ranked third of all national contenders for the nomination. Jackson was the first choice of 42 per cent of all Black Democratic voters, but of only 3 per cent of white Democrats. Only slightly more than half of all white respondents had even heard of Jackson — but 78 per cent of all Black voters gave him 'a favourable rating' as a leader.[44]

It is appropriate, at this point, to introduce a detailed analysis of Jesse Louis Jackson, because had he not existed, it is extremely doubtful whether any Afro-American leader would have stepped forward to run for the 1984 Democratic presidential nomination. Born in Greenville, South Carolina, on 8 October 1941, Jackson spent his youth in a state that has been termed the 'hotbed of defiant segregationists'. When he was barely thirteen years old, the chief political issue being debated in South Carolina's 1954 gubernatorial election was the candidates' positions on racial integration. The eventual winner of the contest, George Bell Timmerman Jr, had campaigned less against his actual opponent than against 'the viciously subversive NAACP' which sought to 'amalgamate the races in South Carolina into one race'. Four years later, young Jackson was attending the all-Black Sterling High School in Greenville, where he starred in baseball, football and basketball. That fall, Timmerman was replaced by another militantly racist demagogue,

Democratic Lieutenant Governor Ernest Hollings, who also vowed to 'protect and defend the southern way of life'.[45] Jackson's early hatred for the inhumanity of Jim Crow marked the beginning of his political development: 'I am a reaction to and a product of a voice I heard on Spring Street one day in Greenville when I asked the question, "Daddy, why must we go to the back of the bus?"' Jackson later forgave, but could never forget, the role of Democrats like Hollings in preserving the brutal system of racial inequality, this 'southern way of life'. In a single word, Jim Crow was 'humiliation' for Jackson:

> Humiliation: go to the back of the bus even though you pay the same fare. Humiliation: no public parks or libraries you can use even though you pay taxes. Humiliation: upstairs in movies. Back doors in hotels and cafés . . . Humiliation: all-white police with no police warrants who were so absolute in their power until they were called "the law". Humiliation: a dual school system. Black teachers and white teachers working the same hours, only the Black teachers taught more students and taught double shifts and received less pay . . . We used books exactly three years after white students used them. We used desks exactly four years after whites used them. There were no Black schoolboard members . . . We were rewarded for docility and punished for expressing personhood. Men called boys. Women called girls. We called white children "Master" and "Missy".[46]

Like thousands of other southern Black students, Jackson sought to escape racial segregation by gaining admission to the University of Illinois, where he obtained an athletic scholarship. After his university football coach informed him that 'ability notwithstanding, Blacks were linemen and not quarter-backs' on the team, Jackson transferred to the all-Black North Carolina Agricultural and Technical College. Back in the South as the sit-in movement began, Jackson emerged as a major figure in Greensboro's protests. Even before his involvement with the CORE, the young sociology major was elected president of the North Carolina Intercollegiate Council on Human Rights.[47] Participating in the desegregation campaigns of the early 1960s, Jackson came to terms with the shame and alienation with which segregation had marked his personality. He and other Afro-Americans no longer 'suffered' oppression as isolated individuals; within a collective movement, he found 'meaning in the suffering', a sense of purpose, and even a sense of destiny.[48]

From the beginning of his involvement with the SCLC, Jesse

Jackson was different from any of Martin's lieutenants. Ralph Abernathy was unchallenged as King's *'alter ego'*, yet seemed inefficacious when left on his own. Andy Young was now the steady master of conciliation, yet lacked the *élan* of a James Bevel. James Lawson, Fred Shuttlesworth, Wyatt Tee Walker, Walter Fauntroy and other local leaders were invaluable to King's cause, yet these men never quite acquired the charismatic quality of national leaders. Jackson, the youngest and least experienced disciple of Martin, seemed to combine many of the strengths of all his seniors. Arm in arm with Bevel and Raby, Jackson fearlessly led the demonstration of two thousand Black and white Chicagoans into the Belmont-Cragin neighbourhood on 7 August 1966, where they were assaulted by three thousand vicious white ethnics. Yet like Young, Jackson quickly acquired the ability to conduct negotiations. His first significant victory occurred in 1966, when, as head of the SCLC's Operation Breadbasket, he obtained agreements from four large Chicago grocery corporations to 'carry products of Black corporations and to deposit in Black banks the income from their stores located in the ghetto'.[49] Within a year, Jackson's programme had obtained 2,200 jobs for Black Chicagoans in white-owned firms. His success was so striking that King authorized a conference of 150 ministers from 42 cities, held at Chicago Theological Seminary on 20 July 1967, to expand Operation Breadbasket on a national level. The basic strategy proposed and adopted connected Black economic needs with traditional civil-rights protests. Ministers would study data on Black employment in specific firms operating with Afro-American communities, and would subsequently present proposals that would call for 'hiring and upgrading' Blacks 'in proportion to their population in the city'. If negotiations were fruitless, SCLC affiliates would resort to boycotts, picketing, and other forms of non-violent disruption. In Martin's view, the Operation Breadbasket strategy had two singular strengths. First, it moved the SCLC 'into the economic area with greater thrust', attacking 'the system where it hurts — in the pocketbook'. And secondly, this mode of 'effective action for social change' would be built around Black 'clergymen, who are the natural leaders in the Negro community'.[50] King's ambitious plans for the programme were cut short by his assassination less than a year later; predictably, Young, Abernathy and Jackson were at Martin's side when he died. But in 1971, chafing under Abernathy's leadership, Jackson broke with the SCLC to build his own organization along the lines of the Breadbasket approach. In December of that year Jackson initiated Operation PUSH. Four months later, PUSH-East was started in New York City.[51]

Since the founding of PUSH, Jackson has acquired a rather mixed reputation within civil-rights circles, but a strong and popular constituency among millions of working-class and low-income Afro-Americans. Perhaps the best approach in pursuing the hyperbolic enigma of Jesse Jackson is to outline, in brief, the basic theoretical and programmatic views he has expressed consistently since 1970. Our point of departure is his obvious role as a Black Baptist preacher. Ordained in 1968, Jackson became a master orator in the great tradition of the Black Church. A man who described himself as 'just a country preacher' — who was born and raised in a city — Jackson had a relationship with his congregation that was both intimate and reciprocal. Like other Black ministers, 'he talks to them, and they talk back to him.' As Charles V. Hamilton noted in 1972, Jackson 'frequently intersperses his sermon-speeches with "Y'all know what I'm talking 'bout?" The congregation responds with a variety of expressions: "Go 'head on." "Well, all right!" "Yes, yes." "Help him, Lord." "Preach the word." "Come on".'[52] This setting of the Afro-American Church, the foundation for almost every Black social movement, inevitably influenced Jackson's perceptions of the dynamics of social change. 'A Godless people is a hopeless people', Jackson reflected in 1972. 'It is religion that breaks open the councils of despair and creates pillars out of lions' thighs and brings forth music from the growls they make.' Like King, Jackson suggests that the Afro-Americans' faith has a redemptive quality which has permitted us to help 'save' the larger society. 'The Black protest saved America from going absolutely crazy on the whole world', Jackson observed. 'It may be that we were sent here by God to save the human race. Maybe the creative leadership and the soul and the sense of decency' required to transform society, 'the prophetic message for peace and justice has come from this community.' Black religion offered not simply a path towards one's communion with God, but a way of being which was inherently emancipatory.[53]

A second feature of Jackson's thought, the emphasis on Black self-esteem and 'self-help', is a common theme running throughout Afro-American political culture. Repeatedly, Jackson has argued that 'our problem has been for too long a time that we have had no ambition . . . No one is going to give us anything.' Black Americans 'must stand up and fight for ourselves.'[54] Such attitudes are not original, but speak to a rigid socio-economic condition in which

Blacks perceive few social class allies in the battle for racial equality. Thus the struggle must begin internally, as the men and women of a people consciously attempt to change themselves. Long before Jackson popularized the slogan 'I am Somebody', Alexander Crummell urged Afro-Americans to work collectively for 'industrial effort . . . and for mental and moral improvement'. In 1978, Jackson argued, 'A generation lacking the moral and physical stamina necessary to fight a protracted civilizational crisis is dangerous to themselves, their neighbours and future generations. We need a sober, sane, disciplined army to catch up.' With slightly different rhetoric, the doyen of accommodationists had argued the same position in 1902: 'No race of people ever got upon its feet without severe and constant struggle, often in the face of the greatest disappointment.' For Washington, self-help and racial pride were the essential ideological components in building a stable Black petty bourgeoisie and rural landholding class. 'The opportunity to earn a dollar in a factory just now is worth infinitely more than the opportunity to spend a dollar in an opera house', Washington counselled. 'No race that has anything to contribute to the markets of the world is long in any degree ostracized.' Listen to Jackson echo Washington, in the age of multinational capitalism: 'Changes in the mind precede changes in matter . . . The victim has the responsibility to resist the pressure . . . to avoid being tricked and further deceived. The emphasis and the impetus must come from the victim . . . There has never been a case where a victimizer or a slave-master took a group of slaves and tied them and whipped them and beat them until they became doctors and lawyers and scientists and financiers.'[55] The goal of expanding the Black petty bourgeoisie is the same; the desire to 'catch up', to withdraw from earthly pleasures, to make sacrifices for the long ordeal of capital accumulation and self-preservation.

Jackson also shares other traits of Booker T. Washington. For example, Jackson has long been preoccupied with educational issues. In 1972 he complained that Afro-American youth 'are being shot in the head with misinformation'.[56] The 'only protection against genocide', Jackson insisted, was for Blacks to 'develop academic and character excellence. Because we are fighting against the odds trying to survive, we cannot afford to hang around in the Martian meadows of mediocrity.' In 1975 PUSH formed Project EXCEL, a 'self-help programme' designed to reinforce Black students and to promote parent-teacher cooperation. With large grants from the federal government and technical assistance from a core of Black intellectuals, Project EXCEL was adopted by several major metropolitan school districts by the late 1970s.[57] Also in the tradition of both Washington and Du Bois, Jackson has expressed a deep interest in African affairs, and in US foreign policies in under-developed nations. 'We've got African roots and we must not deny them', Jackson observed.[58] PUSH first became involved in the African continent by conducting a national food campaign, ship-ping crates of supplies to six countries suffering from droughts. With the appointment of former King aide Jack O'Dell as PUSH's international affairs director, Jackson began to address inter-national affairs as well as issues directly relevant to Black America. 'For so long, foreign affairs was considered none of the slaves' business', Jackson argued in February 1979. 'That's why we must fight to be people in the world, not just Black people, but people in the world who are Black. I resent anybody referring to me as a "Black" leader.'[59]

But the closest point of affinity between Washington and Jackson is one of economic policy. Jackson's former association with the CORE, and his extensive labours for Operation Breadbasket under King's guidance, have had a decisive impact upon his thought. Like Washington, Jackson perceives the struggle for racial equality as a function of the market-place. As Jackson explained in 1974, 'when we organized Operation PUSH, our stated objective was to help effect and direct a transformation of the Human Rights Movement from emphasis on Civil Rights to one on Civil Economics'. Like Operation Breadbasket, PUSH 'developed the double-edged tech-niques of organized mass consumer boycotts and negotiations directed at affecting the policy of major corporations'.[60] PUSH's principal activity in this regard has been the signing of 'corporate covenants', in which firms commit themselves to certain construc-tive actions. In June 1982 PUSH pressured the Seven Up Corpor-ation to sign a $61 million agreement to invest capital in Black enterprises. The Seven Up covenant called for $10 million for the creation of Black-owned Seven Up beverage wholesalerships, $5 million to be invested in Black-owned life insurance companies, and another $4.35 million for advertisements in Black-owned radio stations and newspapers. The April 1983 covenant with the Burger King Corporation, worth an estimated $450 million, pledged the company to hire more Black employees and managers, to upgrade existing restaurant facilities in Black neighbourhoods, and to place funds in Black-owned banks. PUSH's covenants, despite their wide publicity, actually did little to reduce Black urban unemployment, and some of the companies that signed the covenants either repudiated them within a year, or failed to carry out the agreed measures. PUSH's response to the loss of thousands of Afro-American workers' jobs in the auto industry was the purchase of one hundred shares of stock in Chrysler, American Motors, Ford and General Motors. Jackson explained that this curious investment would 'assure us the right and the platform to voice our concerns' inside the auto corporations. The purpose of these manoeuvres was to promote capitalist development within the Black community — which was precisely the objective of Washington. 'Blacks need trade, not aid', Jackson argued. 'The way to achieve equality is to allow minorities the opportunity to share in the trade with the whole community — to allow them to partake of the benefits.' In short, the PUSH strategy is a sophisticated attempt to reinforce the capitalist spirit among those whom the system has most brutally exploited.[61]

This is not to suggest that Jackson is another Thomas Sowell, an ideologue of *laissez-faire* capitalism and nineteenth-century liberalism. His contact with Martin occurred precisely at a moment when the civil-rights leader began to advance a social democratic economic agenda. This experience, together with the pivotal role of O'Dell inside PUSH, has permitted Jackson to argue for left social democratic goals and for Black Capitalism *simultaneously*. For evidence of the former, examine PUSH's 1976 platform. The first goals of PUSH are to achieve 'the right of every able-bodied person to get a job at useful work and adequate wages', and the public access 'of every person to the best medical services possible . . . regardless of income'.[62] Like Dellums, Cockrell and other Black leftists in electoral politics, Jackson agrees that the Black movement must fight for 'national recognition and acceptance of the right of every person to a job'. He has demanded that the public and private sectors adopt a quota 'in which Black and Spanish-speaking workers are employed at all levels of decision-making in proportion to their size in the local population'.[63] Yet Jackson has more often advanced the political economy of Tuskegee. Before an audience of three thousand Black nationalists and Pan-Africanists in Atlanta in September 1970, Jackson argued that all Afro-Americans, even the unemployed, were 'part of the [capitalist] system'. And for those who 'believe in some creative form of democratic socialism [who] don't believe in the system', Jackson asserted that 'morally you are not of the system but economically you're in it'. Afro-Americans have 'always been judged based on profit and loss, asset and liability. And once you get your economic definitions, if in forty markets you say we don't want Dixie crystal sugar, you can run Nixon into Castro.'[64] At a conference of the New Orleans Business League in July 1982, Jackson essentially submerged civil-rights agitation in the quest for Black Capitalism. 'We must move from Civil Rights to Silver Rights and from aid to trade', PUSH's leader declared. 'We want our share of opportunities for risks and rewards! There's something tricky and vicious about the way we're locked out of the private sector', Jackson reflected. 'The market-place is the arena for our development.' Black churches had to become 'financial institutions as well as soul-saving institutions'. In his enthusiastic advocacy of capitalist development, Jackson was not alone. By the early 1980s, other civil-rights leaders in elective office were saying as much. Andrew Young, for instance, suggested that the decisive integration battle of the decade would be 'the desegregation of the money markets'. In 1982, Morial also called for the development of 'a strong line of communications' between finance capital and Black entrepreneurs.[65] The basic difference, however, between Morial and Jackson is that politicians like Morial make no public or private overtures to the left, in any way. Jackson embodies both capitalist and anti-corporate tendencies, as repre-sented in PUSH's inherently contradictory slogan: 'Full Employ-ment in an Expanding Economy.'

Given Jackson's history and ideological development, what of his political practice? Unlike Walter White, Roy Wilkins and the earlier generation of civil-rights leaders, Jackson aggressively promoted himself and his organization at the expense of other formations. Even under King, Jackson displayed unusual ambition, joining the inner circle of loyal SCLC aides despite his youth and relative inexperience. Left unchecked, this ambition grew to rather large proportions in the 1970s. During the decade he spoke before more than five hundred groups, including the United Negro College Fund, the National Conference of Mayors and the National League of Cities. Jackson became a columnist with the *Los Angeles Times* syndicate, and subsequently negotiated a contract with the Universal syndicate, which distributed his articles to over seventy-five newspapers. Building his reputation as an educator, he accepted an appointment as visiting professor at the University of Southern California, and in 1977 became the recipient of the Golden Key Award of the American Association of School Admini-strators. By 1980, he had been awarded more than twenty-five honorary doctorates from universities and theological schools.[66]

According to one public-opinion poll in October 1983, Jackson was named 'the most important Black leader in America' by 51 per cent of Afro-Americans questioned, overwhelming Andrew Young (at 8 per cent), Benjamin Hooks (2 per cent) and other national figures.[67] The irony of such acclaim was that the extent of Jackson's popularity tended to be inversely proportional to the geographical distance from Chicago. Jackson's frequent trips throughout the rural South, California and New York City established a strong constituency for him, if not necessarily for PUSH. But in May 1982, when the CBUC organized a community-wide poll to determine the strongest potential Black mayoral candidate, Jackson emerged as only the fifth choice.[68] During the 1982-83 mayoral race, Harold Washington astutely kept PUSH's leader 'at arm's length', according to journalist Monroe Anderson. 'When Washington announced his candidacy in November, Jackson was in the audience, not on the platform. And later, when Washington named his inner circle of political advisers, Jackson's name was conspicuously absent.'[69] PUSH's aggressive tactics had also alienated the petty-bourgeois Black leadership. For example, in June 1982 William Perry, the NAACP president in Miami, Florida, proposed that chapter members and supporters hold a 'Black Monday' — a single day when only Black-owned businesses were patronized. Such tactics were anathema to the integrationist-minded NAACP elite and NAACP South-Eastern Regional Director Earl Shinhoster promptly suspended Perry by mail-gram, 'immediately and indefinitely'. Hooks gave Perry 'five days to explain what happened and why his suspension should not be made permanent'. Meanwhile, Jackson quietly intervened in the dispute. The result was Perry's decision to resign as president and to announce the creation of an Operation PUSH chapter in Miami under his leadership.[70]

In electoral politics, Jackson's major political opponents had always been Democrats: southern Democrats during the desegregation campaigns, and the Democratic machine of Daley in Chicago. Thus, more than any other major civil-rights leader, Jackson constantly flirted with the Republican Party. In 1970, he argued that Afro-Americans had to shed any allegiance they held to the Democratic Party. 'Democrats, let somebody come through as our saviour in the form of a Republican. Let him come. Now I didn't say that's good, I said it's real.'[71] Jackson's subsequent political moves continued to perplex his friends and enemies alike. At the Democratic National Convention of 1980, Jackson and his close political ally Richard Hatcher lobbied against economic platform planks that called for increased federal spending for jobs, and supported Carter's renomination over that of the more liberal candidate, Senator Ted Kennedy. During the general election Jackson suddenly made overtures to the Reagan campaign, telling the press that 'the Black community has the responsibility and obligation to listen to what both parties and all candidates have to say'.[72] There were other disturbing qualities about Jackson's politics. Like most Afro-American males, Jackson frequently made sexist statements which revealed a failure to comprehend the particularity of women's oppression. At times, he praised the potential of 'the wombs of our mothers' for producing 'mayors and kings'![73] Despite his degree in sociology, he tended to adopt the social pathological views of Daniel Patrick Moynihan on the crisis of the Black family. In 1979, for example, he argued that Black men were 'the object of castration. We were made to be boys downtown and couldn't even be men at home.' Black women, however, 'at their highest and most mature state', understood that they had to give 'Black men a sense of self-esteem'. Jackson also denounced male-female 'relationships based upon a false sense of equality', noting that the 'mature Black woman' had to 'preserve her family' before building 'her career.'[74] In short, Jackson may best be understood as an ideological and political weather-vane, an inconsistent and changeable indicator of the mind and moods of Black America. His weaknesses were all too obvious — his braggadocio, sexism, organizational sloppiness and self-promotion. His lack of a comprehensive social theory permitted him to promote various schemes that were often theoretically at odds. But obscured were his singular strengths — his intimate connections with the King legacy, his position as a major figure in the Black Church, his willingness to take political risks, and chiefly, his uncanny ability to sense the shifts of Black working-class and rural poor opinion, far better than his petty-bourgeois counterparts in the NAACP and the CBC. As Black opinion moved, so moved Jesse. He was always determined to be at the head of the masses, no matter where they happened to be going.

Thus when Jackson's name first surfaced in early January 1983 as that of a potential presidential candidate, most Black leftists, radical Black nationalists, community organizers and elected officials did not relish the idea at all — but for widely differing reasons.[75] Black newspaper publisher Carlton Goodlett, a socialist, suggested that Jackson's 'efforts to influence the final selection of the Democratic nominee are foolish. America needs a social democratic party which offers hope and promise for using government to change the evils that dominate the present military-industrial political complex.'[76] But despite Jackson's severe limitations, by the summer of 1983 it became apparent to Black progressives that the only Black 'presidential hopeful' we had was the 'country preacher', and that it was going to be either him or no one in 1984. Gradually at first, and then in growing numbers, Black activists, radical intellectuals and organizers began to boost his still tentative candidacy. Randall Robinson, head of the influential lobbying group Transafrica, and US Civil Rights Commissioner Mary Berry became firm supporters of Jackson. Even before the March on Washington took place, many of the mobilization's key organizers, including director Donna Brazile, pledged to work in Jackson's campaign. The Communist Party all but officially endorsed Jackson's challenge. Party leader Charlene Mitchell declared that the 'pressure of some Black leaders against such a candidacy can be directly tied to the ideological divisions that exist within the Afro-American community and the allegiances of most of their spokespersons to the Democratic Party and the monopoly interests it represents.' A Black candidate would 'deepen the unity of Black people and the working class, expanding the all-people's front against Reagan'.[77]

It was now relatively easy for the Black petty bourgeoisie's chief representatives to condemn the Black presidential candidacy strategy, since Jackson had made so many personal enemies within their ranks over the years. *Washington Post* journalists William Raspberry and Milton Coleman attacked Jackson's 'love of the limelight' and his contradictory policy positions. Warith Deen Muhammad, leader of the American Muslim Mission, which formerly had been the Nation of Islam under Elijah Muhammad, 'sharply' condemned Jackson, calling him an 'unsuitable choice' and 'a Black leader who has been created by the media'. Fauntroy now bluntly dismissed Jackson as a man who was 'not a politician', a leader who had 'alienated politicians in many key districts in the Black community'. Congressman Mickey Leland, the chairman of the Black Caucus of the Democratic National Committee, hinted that Jackson might run simply 'to embellish his ego. There is fear that Jesse doesn't feel accountable to anybody but himself.'[78] Veteran bureaucrat and civil-rights authority Carl Rowan blasted Jackson repeatedly. 'There is no reason to believe that Congress, the white power structure, will pay more heed to the advice of Jackson the presidential candidate than they have to Jackson the civil-rights leader. As a political candidate, he would be of minimal, even negative consequences.'[79] John Lewis and Julian Bond argued that Jackson 'might divert Blacks from the effort to remove Reagan from the White House'. Other Black elected officials bluntly described him as 'an egocentric power seeker'.[80] With Kennedy's decision not to contest the 1984 nomination, Mondale stood to lose the most through a potential Jackson candidacy. In July, Mondale and his campaign staff politely attempted to discourage Jackson's entry. Mondale's senior adviser John R. Reilly asked Charles T. Manatt, the Democratic Party's national chairman, 'to give Mr Jackson a substantial party appointment if he left the race', but Manatt refused.[81] The Republican Party responded to the Jackson threat without 'velvet gloves'. Only weeks after Jackson had attacked the Reagan Administration's policies on Central America and South Africa at Operation PUSH's 24-30 July convention in Atlanta, federal auditors claimed that the organization had 'misused' over $1.7 million in government contracts. The Reagan Administration officials 'found fault' with the documentation of expenses, salaries and accounting procedures, but denied that the audits had anything to do with Jackson's potential campaign.[82]

It was ironic that Jackson himself, who had done so much to mobilize thousands of activists to support a Black presidential campaign, was personally undecided as to whether he should become a candidate as late as September 1983. No exploratory 'draft-Jackson committees' existed, and virtually no funds had been solicited by direct mail. In fact, during the first two months after Jackson's announcement, the campaign collected only $183,085. Deadlines for collecting signatures and filing campaign papers to get on state-primary ballots were also rapidly approaching.[83] Privately, Jackson shared the doubts of Coleman Young, Fauntroy and other Black officials about the viability of the campaign. But his political antennae also told him that it was too late to stop the mobilization. Throughout the early autumn, thousands of college students, workers, professionals and Black businessmen were flooding Jackson's public appearances, demanding that he announce his candidacy. Now Jackson was on the spot: if he refused to run, after spending nearly a year on the stump as a would-be candidate, his critics would have a 'field day', and his reputation as a civil-rights leader would be shattered. He would never obtain the mantle of Martin Luther King Jr. That perhaps more than any other single factor convinced Jackson to take the great risk. Preston Love, manager of Andrew Young's successful mayoral campaign, was recruited to serve briefly as national campaign director. Weeks later Arnold Pinkney, who had served as Humphrey's deputy campaign director in 1972, assumed the job. Fundraisers and key staff personnel were also recruited.[84] On 3 November, Jackson announced his candidacy before almost three thousand supporters at the Washington DC Convention Centre Hall. He criticized Reagan for being 'pro-rich, pro-aristocratic, pro-agribusiness, pro-military, and pro-big business'; and he condemned Mondale and other Democratic leaders for remaining 'too silent and too passive in the face of the Reagan Administration's reduction of funds' for civil-rights enforcement; in the face of increased unemployment and the Administration's support for 'repressive foreign governments'. Mondale's 'acceptance' of the endorsement of Vrdolyak and other racist opponents of Harold Washington in late October, he claimed, had been a decisive reason for his own candidacy.[85] Democratic Party leaders were largely unimpressed. Mondale had a 'lock' on the nomination. Conservative Democrat John Glenn was declining rapidly in public-opinion polls, and Mondale was the preference of 40 per cent of all Democratic voters in late October. Jackson, at 10 per cent, remained a distant third, followed by five obscure white candidates. Jackson was now the first choice of only 39 per cent of all Black Democratic voters, while Mondale had a solid 30 per cent of Blacks' support. Mondale also had the endorsement of most national Afro-American political leaders, including the backing of the Coalition of Black Trade Unionists, and the unofficial endorsement of both the NAACP and the National Urban League. Several political observers believed that Jackson 'would need an almost monolithic Black vote' to win as many as 200 delegates to the Democratic national convention. Others thought that Jackson would 'be hard pressed to get more than 75 delegates'. Given his late start and 'narrow political base', it was highly unlikely that Jackson would even be in the running by March 1984.[86]

II

Had Jackson run a 'traditional' electoral campaign and attempted to project himself as a 'serious' candidate, devoid of direct contact with any social movement, he would quickly have disappeared into the crowd. But several political factors converged at this precise time, permitting the electoral campaign to assume the shape of a democratic, anti-corporate social movement. The first, as previously discussed, was the timely absence of the bulk of the national Black petty-bourgeois leadership from the internal campaign apparatus. The media interpreted this as a crucial weakness: in reality, it was the second most important element in the campaign. The vacuum was filled, in part, by Black nationalists, Black, Latino and white Marxists and white liberals, who were all usually forced to operate on the periphery of liberal and Black electoral campaigns. Thus in Jackson's national campaign headquarters in Washington DC one could find environmentalist Barry Commoner, who four years before had helped to start the Citizens' Party. Commoner had been the party's 1980 presidential candidate, and had received a quarter of a million votes. Also in the national office was anti-nuclear power activist Anna Gyorgy, a democratic socialist. Directly advising Jackson were Howard University political scientist Ronald Walters, a progressive Black nationalist who had been involved in the National Black Political Assembly throughout the 1970s; Carliotta Scott, a top congressional aide to Dellums; and Jack O'Dell. Jackson's south-east regional campaign director was Cleveland Sellers, who had been the SNCC's programme secretary two decades before.

In many states and cities, the tardy behaviour of Black elected officials and NAACP leaders also permitted Black radicals, nationalists, peace activists and other left forces to seize key roles in local campaign mobilizations. In Brooklyn and dozens of other major cities, the large Black nationalist bloc was mobilized by the National Black United Front, led by the Reverend Herbert Daughtry and activist Jitu Weusi; in Harlem, local organizers and activists included Kevin Mercadel, Harlem coordinator of the Communist Party, and Jim Haughton, veteran Black workers' organizer and leader of Harlem Fight-Back; in Louisville, Kentucky, the key white radical activist for Jackson was Anne Braden, head of the Southern Organizing Committee for Economic and Social Justice; in Mississippi, the state coordinator was desegregation leader Hollis Watkins; in North Carolina, one key supporter was Jennifer Henderson, director of the North Carolina Hunger Coalition; in Nashville, Tennessee, the city's co-chair was a Black Marxist-Leninist, Frank Cuthbertson; in Portland, Oregon, one central white activist was Beverly Stein, a radical attorney and a national leader of the Democratic Socialists of America. And in California, for example, an eclectic bloc of left political forces with histories of bitter factional fighting with one another — the Communist Party, the Workers' World Party, the Democratic Workers' Party, the November 29th Committee for Palestine, the *Line of March* grouping, and so on — threw their collective resources and cadre behind Jackson. This is not to suggest that the inner core of the campaign was dominated by the left. The principal advisers and supporters — national campaign director Arnold Pinkney, Richard Hatcher, Kenneth Gibson, New York businessman Eugene Jackson, former Manhattan Borough President Percy Sutton and Tuskegee mayor Johnny Ford — had histories of being ideologically to the right of many of Mondale's Black supporters, such as Julian Bond and Coleman Young. They frequently tried to keep the mobilization within 'safe' boundaries of bourgeois democratic discourse and practice, and often succeeded. But as in the Henry Wallace presidential campaign of 1948, many of the actual cadre and local leaders of the movement were to the left of the candidate himself. And as the 1984 campaign progressed, their participation and deep involvement had an impact on the programmatic content of the electoral mobilization, and on Jackson's speeches. Ideologically, the campaign soon assumed a left social democratic tone, and in later instances even became forthrightly anti-imperialist and anti-corporate in content. The 'egocentric' proponent of Black Capitalism, in short, became one of the most left-wing national spokespersons in a national presidential campaign since Eugene V. Debs.[87]

A second — but most crucial — factor was the unprecedented participation of the Black Church. As a Black minister, Jackson astutely comprehended that the Afro-American Church was the corner-stone of all community-based activism in the non-violent assault against Jim Crow laws. To be a 'good Christian' for Blacks twenty-five years ago meant to break 'unjust laws', to organize sit-ins, to register Blacks to vote. Legal segregation in American society had been destroyed, but institutional racism, unemployment and poverty remained. Now the task was to revive this moral and ideological protest tradition within the context of contemporary bourgeois electoral politics. Listening to Jackson's candidacy announcement, the Reverend Benjamin F. Chavis, Deputy Director of the Commission for Racial Justice of the United Church of Christ, recognized immediately the conscious concepts of 'liberation theology' in the speech. 'His address was more of a sermon, in the tradition of great Black Baptist preachers, than a speech by an aspiring politician', Chavis observed. 'Throughout his speech, many in the audience shouted "Amen . . ." Jackson's theology is a theology of liberation, informed by the Black Church religious experience and in dialogue with the religious and political experiences of the world community, particularly the Third World.'[88] Throughout the campaign, Jackson would repeatedly attack the

Reagan Administration for inverting 'the basic notions of our Judaeo-Christian ethic, encouraging us to spend millions to beat our ploughshares into swords, while leaving the disadvantaged begging for bread'. Jackson deliberately linked the issues of peace and social justice, calling not simply for the removal of Reagan from office, but for a moral and social transformation of the society as a whole. 'My concern is to lift the boats stuck on the bottom; to fight to provide education that is not based on one's ability to pay; to fight to provide health care for all Americans on the basis of need not wealth; to provide a strong and adequate national defence, but end the massive waste, fraud, [and] abuse . . . to campaign on behalf of a national and fair immigration policy; to move beyond our current racial, sexual and class battleground to economic and political common grounds . . .'[89]

Thus Jackson successfully revived the basic moral and political principles of King, in his own way. The campaign throughout retained both the character of a Black religious revival and the special idealism that had motivated the desegregation efforts of the 1960s. Over 90 per cent of the Black clergy in the US endorsed Jackson within two months of his candidacy being announced. The National Baptist Convention, USA, with a membership of 6.5 million Blacks, was the first major organization to pour resources into the campaign. Convention president T.J. Jemison characterized his churches' support for Jackson as 'moral, spiritual and financial'. Other Black denominations, including the National Baptist Convention of America, with 2 million members, and the Pentecostal Church of God in Christ, with an additional 3.7 million followers, also endorsed Jackson. Black church leaders were active in all aspects of the campaign: transporting Black voters to the polls, distributing literature, organizing political motorcades, and raising the vast majority of Jackson's early funds.[90] Pinkney characterized the vital support of Black church leaders as something that was as significant as 'the endorsement of the AFL-CIO' for any other candidate. 'It brings masses of people, financial resources and a fantastic credibility to the candidacy.' For the Black clergy, 'Jesse's running has made people understand the importance of government', stated Bishop Brookins. 'The impact of it will be revolutionary.' Well before the end of the campaign, a synthesis of Black religious beliefs and progressive politics embodied in the 'Rainbow Coalition' of Jackson became nearly hegemonic among the Afro-American social fraction. Just as King's SCLC had once been described as the 'home mission department of the Black Church', so the Rainbow Coalition had become the central 'political activity of the Black Church'.[91]

This powerful combination of religious appeals and a progressive political agenda rapidly captured the mood of most of the national Black electorate. In city after city, hundreds of thousands of Blacks participated actively in the electoral process for the first time in their lives. The initial caucus voting in Virginia on 25 March 1984 was typical of the response Jackson evoked from Blacks. In Norfolk, a city that is 35 per cent Black, a huge Black turn-out gave Jackson all 163 delegates from the city. In Virginia Beach, a town with only 10 per cent Black voters, Black participation gave Jackson a plurality victory of 62 delegates, as against Mondale's 50 delegates and Hart's 30 delegates. One reporter from the *New York Times* noted that 'at some sites party leaders ran out of registration forms. At others, participants had to stand in line for a couple of hours before they could get in. Throughout the Tidewater area, Jackson supporters filled the streets, using bull-horns to exhort people to vote and distributing flyers and maps.' State-wide, Jackson won 31 per cent of Virginia's vote in the early delegate-selection process.[92] Six days later, five thousand people came to a rally at 'African Square' in Harlem to hear the candidate. Members of the Black United Front, the Alliance of Women Against Oppression, the Communist Party and various new formations (such as 'Jews for Jackson', 'Latinos for Jackson', 'Trade Unionists for Jackson', 'Asian-Americans for Jackson', and so forth) were out in force. Daughtry, Commoner and Ramon Jimenez, co-founder of Latinos for Jackson, exhorted the crowd with speeches; cultural workers including Amiri Baraka, the National Black Theatre and others kept up the spirit. Finally Jackson arrived at the head of a march of twenty thousand. Electrifying the crowd, Jackson declared, 'We are going to be the conscience of this campaign!' On 3 April, a massive number of Black New Yorkers went to the polls. Despite the lack of any political advertising on behalf of Jackson — candidate Gary Hart spent over $600,000 on advertisements in New York — Jackson received 87 to 89 per cent of the Afro-American vote state-wide, and 34 per cent of all ballots in New York City. In five Congressional districts with substantial numbers of Latino and Afro-American voters (Districts 6, 11, 12, 16 and 18) in Brooklyn, Queens, Manhattan and the Bronx, Jackson received 183,739 votes (63.5 per cent) to Mondale's 81,206 votes (28.1 per cent) and Hart's 24,477 votes (8.5 per cent). In Harlem, despite Congressman Rangel's vigorous and expensive campaigning for Mondale,

Jackson thrashed the former Vice-President by a majority of over eight to one. State-wide, Jackson received 92 per cent of the vote of Blacks aged between 18 and 29; 36 per cent of the vote of all families earning $12,500 or less annual income; and two thirds of the support of all first-time voters.[93]

A third element contributing to the success of the campaign was its multinational character. Within the framework of 'Rainbow Theology', to employ Chavis's term, religious activists involved in the mobilization believed that 'racism and sexism are sins that defy' the notion that 'all human beings [are created] in the image of God. The call for African, Hispanic, Asian and Native Americans to join with progressive Anglo-Americans, women and the poor to work together politically and spiritually is to affirm through social action the oneness of humanity created by God in God's image.'[94] The actual model of a successful 'Rainbow Coalition' had recently developed in Boston, around the 1983 mayoral campaign of Black socialist Mel King. King lost in the run-off election to a South Boston populist, Ray Flynn. But King's 'Rainbow Coalition' achieved several major victories: it increased Black registration significantly (about 95 per cent of all Blacks voted for King); over 20 per cent of white voters and 66 per cent of Latinos supported King; and thousands of gays and lesbians, feminists, progressive clergy, labour leaders and Blacks were brought together for a common cause in that racially divided city.[95] The general political approaches taken during the King 'Rainbow' mobilization were once again used at a national level, but with a candidate who was ideologically to the right of King.

Most Jackson campaign literature reflected this ethnic pluralism. In flyers to Hispanic voters printed in English and Spanish, Jackson called for bilingual education programmes, the application of the 1965 Voting Rights Act to combat the 'gerrymandering' and the lack of 'voting rights' of Hispanics, and opposed US 'aid to rebels trying covertly to overthrow the Government of Nicaragua'.[96] Such positions were anathema to Cuban-American emigrants, but found widespread praise among Mexican-Americans and Puerto Ricans. In New York State's primary, Jackson won 34 per cent of the Puerto Rican vote despite the nearly unanimous endorsement of Mondale by Puerto Rican officials.[97] In San José, California, at the 12-13 May Mexican American Political Association (MAPA) Endorsing Convention, members substantially embraced Jackson's progressive policy agenda, which included opposition to the repressive Simpson-Mazzoli immigration bill, then being debated in Congress.

Despite predictions that Mondale would be a 'shoo-in for the MAPA endorsement', nearly five hundred 'Mapistas' voted for Jackson. Mondale received the Chicano group's endorsement by the slender margin of four votes.[98] Three weeks later, Jackson received almost one fifth of California's Latino vote. In Arizona, a state with a Black population of only 3 per cent, Jackson received 14 per cent of the Democratic caucus vote on 14 April. Significant support here came from Chicago state representative Jesus Higuera and from several Native American Indian leaders in the state.[99] Jackson was the only candidate to attend the annual conference of the National Congress of American Indians, and he used the opportunity to declare: 'On a moral level, how America treats American Indians is the "litmus test" for this country's character.' Many Indian leaders were convinced.[100] As Indian journalist Buck Martin observed, 'Jackson was either extremely well briefed, or else there is a natural affinity between his and Indian thinking . . . Jackson is demonstrating people of colour do not have to be satisfied with the existing political leadership. He is a national minority leader who has captured the imagination of people of colour, other than Blacks.'[101] Among Asian and Pacific American voters, Jackson again received a strong response. Under the coordination of Cindy Ng, Bill Chong and Lyle Wing, 'Asians for Jackson' committees sprang up in Honolulu, Los Angeles, San Francisco, Seattle, New York and other cities. Such groups raised over $15,000 towards the national campaign. Jackson received 21 per cent of the Asian-American vote in California, and 25 per cent in New Jersey.[102]

Among white voters, Jackson found support among liberal-left peace activists, and, less predictably, among thousands of unemployed and low-income blue-collar workers. The Rainbow Coalition's peace platform was qualitatively to the left of any Democrat's in recent memory: a 20 to 25 per cent cut in the Pentagon budget, with the billions of dollars in funds reallocated to domestic social programmes; a bilateral nuclear freeze; the removal of the Pershing II and cruise missile from Western Europe, and US-Soviet negotiations to reduce both sides' nuclear arsenals; unconditional opposition to US military intervention in Central America, the Caribbean, the Middle East and southern Africa; and the cancellation of all strategic defence initiatives including the ballistic missile defence system and anti-satellite weapons. Jackson repeatedly called for normalized diplomatic relations with Cuba, an end to all military aid to the El Salvador regime, and the destruction of the US military complex in Honduras. Reverend William Sloan-

Coffin, a prominent peace leader, termed Jackson 'a genuine peace candidate. Be it the need to reduce the military budget, or to end American interventions in Central America, or to reverse the nuclear arms race — on every peace issue, Jackson stands head and shoulders above the other candidates.'[103] Other key peace leaders who endorsed the campaign and who travelled with the candidate included Richard Deats, Executive Secretary of the Fellowship of Reconciliation; Dave Dellinger, Mobilization for Survival leader; Rev. Robert Moore, Executive Director, Coalition for Nuclear Disarmament; Sister Marjorie Tuite, Director of Citizen Action, Church Women United; and Rev. William Howard, former President, National Council of Churches. On virtually every major public issue — from economic policy to the environment, women's rights to foreign affairs — Jackson represented the left wing of Democratic Party opinion. Only George McGovern, former liberal Senator and 1972 presidential nominee, stood almost as far to the left as the Black candidate; but with McGovern's withdrawal from the race in early March, only Jackson ideologically represented peace, liberal and left constituencies.

In economically depressed areas, thousands of white workers found other aspects of the Rainbow Coalition programme attractive. In Homestead, Pennsylvania, for example, Local 1397 of the United Steelworkers bucked their national leadership by endorsing Jackson. The 7000-member local had lost half of its jobs due to recent plant closures, and Jackson's calls for legislation to restrict capital flight across state lines won the approval of white steelworkers. Mike Stout, a member of the local's executive committee, explained to the press that Jackson was 'the only one talking about the issues. He is the only one talking about creating jobs for steelworkers who have lost them and of taking money from the military budget and applying it to jobs here at home.'[104] In several rural states, Jackson campaigned effectively among small farmers by riding around on a farm tractor. With less symbolism but more to the point, he called for extensive federal assistance to family farmers to reduce their estimated $227 billion debt. In Columbia, Missouri, hundreds of white small farmers rallied on behalf of the candidate. Many of them had paper bags 'over their heads for fear of reprisal from the Farmers Home Administration', which controlled their farms' mortgages. After giving Jackson a cheering standing ovation, Roger Allison, leader of the Missouri American Agriculture Movement, announced for his organization that 'farmers, like Blacks, are on the bottom — locked out. Together we will form a Rainbow Coalition, and we shall overcome.'[105] Subsequently, the Ohio-based Farm Labour Organization contributed its own organizers to campaign for the Black candidate.

In New York State, almost one third of all union members voted for Jackson, as well as 36 per cent of all women working outside their homes. Some white bus drivers in predominantly Afro-American locals in Boston and Philadelphia also challenged their leadership by backing Jackson. White labour support such as this, combined with a fraction of white liberal support, produced small totals for Jackson in states with Black electorates of 5 per cent or less: 11 per cent in Wisconsin; 12 per cent in Connecticut; 8 per cent in Rhode Island; 9 per cent in Nebraska and Oregon. In Vermont, the Rainbow Coalition earned nearly 15 per cent of the state's April caucus vote; less than one thousand Blacks live in the entire state. In states with large numbers of minorities, Jackson did generally worse: his share of the white vote in Illinois and in Pennsylvania was only 4 per cent, 3 per cent in Georgia, 2 per cent in Florida and barely 1 per cent in Alabama. But as the campaign progressed, more white voters began to look beyond race and to identify with Jackson's progressive agenda. In California, only half of the 8,000 participants in Jackson's Democratic caucuses were Black; 28 per cent were white, 14 per cent Latino, 7 per cent Asian and 1 per cent American Indian.[106] In the state's 5 June primary election, Jackson won over 10 per cent of all whites' votes. By late April, according to a *New York Times* poll, 21 per cent of all white voters and 31 per cent of all Democrats had an 'overall favourable opinion' of Jackson. 63 per cent of whites thought that 'he has eased the path for future Black candidates' and another 28 per cent felt he 'had earned a say' in the Democatic platform on US foreign policy'.[107]

The most interesting question concerning Jackson's support among whites was his — at best — lukewarm standing among the traditional liberal petty bourgeoisie and the white left. On feminist-related issues, for instance, Jackson was clearly the most progressive candidate. Despite his personal opposition to abortion, Jackson called for government-funded abortions, massive social spending on women's service programmes, and expanded affirmative action for women in the labour force. Despite Mondale's long-standing opposition to gender quotas that would advance women workers, the National Organization of Women endorsed the Minnesota Democrat. The 200,000-member liberal feminist formation declared that Mondale, not Jackson, 'understood women's issues' and could more likely 'unite the Democratic coalition'. For different reasons, many white socialist-feminists abstained from the Rainbow Coalition. One radical feminist publication, *Off Our Backs,* argued that Jackson was clearly 'committed to the Black community . . . but he is really committed to being a candidate for feminists?' White radical feminists had to be as 'sceptical about Jackson's campaign as of any other political campaign'.[108] White gays and lesbians also tended to vote according to their race rather than class interests. Prominent gay socialist Harry Britt, a San Francisco Council member, urged constituents to vote for Hart. Lesbian and gay Democratic clubs in New York endorsed Mondale, despite Jackson's support for expanding the 1964 Civil Rights Act 'to prohibit discrimination based on sexual orientation', and his advocacy of an executive order 'banning discrimination based on sexual orientation by government agencies, federal contractors and the military'. Neither Hart nor Mondale, both being fearful of offending homophobic interests, endorsed Jackson's position. Gil Gerald, executive director of the National Coalition of Black Gays, joined the Jackson staff but was perplexed by the candidate's failure to win significant numbers of white lesbian and gay votes. Most white homosexual activists were 'placing bets with the likely winners — Mondale or Hart — as a vehicle to get to the convention', Gerald suggested.[109] Jackson attributed the problem of winning liberal white support to 'whites' lack of regard for the intelligence and hard work of Black people. It remains a moral challenge, however, to white leadership to make judgements based on character and not based on race.'[110]

The success of Jackson was also all the more remarkable given the political obstacles it had to confront at virtually every level. Extremists picketed several Rainbow Coalition offices throughout the country. In Jersey City, New Jersey, five Jackson workers distributing literature were 'arrested, verbally abused, harassed and threatened' by police officers. Arresting policemen threatened one Black campaign worker, warning that he would 'break the lock of the cage and beat his head in'.[111] Democratic Party officials tried at first to ignore Jackson's presence in the race. After the New Hampshire primaries, when most of the would-be presidential aspirants dropped from the race, members of the House of Representatives' Democratic Study Group drafted a joint fund-raising letter with Mondale's and Hart's signatures to aid House candidates, After mailing over sixty thousand letters, somebody finally noticed that Jackson was *still* in the race, and hadn't been invited to sign![112] And despite his repeated overtures to white voters, not a single white member of Congress, governor or white-owned newspaper ever endorsed Jackson. Collectively, as Jackson stated, they were 'the first to urge me to fall in behind a white candidate'.[113]

Under genuinely democratic circumstances, Mondale should have been denied the Democratic Party's nomination in 1984. As other white candidates dropped out of the contest, Gary Hart also emerged as an effective 'neo-liberal' challenger to the rather lack-lustre choice of the party machine. Hart won the Democratic primaries in New England, Florida, Ohio, Indiana and all of the western states. He consistently captured the support of white young people, white families with annual incomes above $35,000, and the 'independent' Democrats who had voted either for Reagan or for independent presidential candidate John Anderson in the 1980 election.[114] The final combined national vote of Jackson (19 per cent) and Hart (36 per cent) was significantly larger than that of Mondale (38.5 per cent). Mondale did win about 18 per cent of the total Afro-American vote, and usually a majority of the votes of other national minorities. But the former Vice-President had three decisive advantages over his opponents, which were, in the final analysis, absolutely critical. The first, of course, was money. By late May, Mondale had collected $18 million in campaign contributions, compared with $9 million raised by Hart and a paltry $1.7 million by Jackson. Mondale received another $800,000 from 132 AFL-CIO-dominated political-action committees. In New Hampshire alone, a state that Mondale lost to Hart, his campaign exceeded legal expenditure ceilings by almost $100,000.[115] These spending ratios neatly compare with the percentage of delegate votes each can-didate ultimately obtained at the San Francisco convention: Mondale, 2191 votes (56.8 per cent); Hart, 1200.5 votes (31.1 per cent); Jackson, 465.5 votes (12.1 per cent).[116] Secondly, the Demo-cratic National Committee and Manatt did everything possible to assist Mondale and to undermine Jackson's leverage within the party. To be awarded delegates at the national convention, presi-dential candidates had to earn at least 20 per cent or more of the popular primary vote in a congressional district. Given that the bulk of the Black and Hispanic electorate is concentrated in a relatively small number of urban Congressional districts, a minority candidate like Jackson could emerge with substantial victories in metropolitan areas, but receive only a handful of delegates, because of a failure to receive 20 per cent of the vote in overwhelmingly white districts. Complicating matters further, Democratic leaders also named 586 'superdelegates' not selected by the public. By mid May, Mondale had received the public endorsement of 107 Senators and Representatives, plus the backing of 78 mayors and local officials from this group.[117] Jackson repeatedly attacked the 'lack of democracy' within the Democratic Party's rules, but failed to obtain any redress.[118]

Thus the Jackson campaign was pressured throughout the spring to prove the 'viability' of a Black presidential challenge, while burdened beneath undemocratic rules. In Mississippi, Jackson defeated both Mondale and Hart, winning almost half of the votes in the 17 March caucuses. But because of the state's regressive caucus rules, Jackson and Mondale each received roughly the same number of delegates. After other delegates had been selected by white party leaders, Mondale had twice as many delegates as Jackson. In Pennsylvania Jackson earned 17 per cent of the state-wide vote, but at the convention, Mondale (who had received 45 per cent of the state's vote) had 177 delegate votes to Jackson's 18. In Arkansas, Mondale narrowly defeated Jackson in state-wide caucuses, 6411 votes to 6011, while Hart ran a poor third. But Mondale eventually won 26 delegate votes, Hart received 9, and Jackson only 7. In the Ohio Democratic primary, Jackson received 251,332 votes, about 16 per cent of the total, but out of 154 state-wide delegates received only 8. In several instances, state Democratic Party committees refused to provide financial resources to enable the elected Jackson delegates to travel to the San Francisco convention. Before the last primaries, Jackson frequently spoke about the negative impact of the party's rules on his movement. Millions of Blacks, Hispanics and progressive whites who had voted for him had been effectively disfranchised. Warning that he would use 'all procedures available' to win their full representation, Jackson declared that 'Party unity is one thing, but we need justice.'[119]

But one of Mondale's decisive advantages over both Hart and Jackson was his support from substantial elements of the Black petty-bourgeois leadership, which produced several critical state-wide victories won with Black votes. In Alabama's Democratic primary, the state's most influential Black official, Richard Arrington, organized dozens of phone banks and put hundreds of city workers into the street to distribute Mondale campaign literature. The mayor and Joe Reed, chairman of the all-Black Democratic Conference, urged Alabama Blacks to 'be realistic' and not to 'throw their votes away'.[120] On primary day, Jackson won 60 per cent of the state's Black vote, and Blacks voted for Jackson over Mondale by a majority of more than three to one outside Birmingham. But in Birmingham, where Black turn-out was twice as high as in the rest of the state, Afro-Americans voted two to one for Mondale. Since virtually no Blacks voted for Hart, Mondale won the state by a narrow margin.[121] In Georgia, Coretta Scott King, Bond and other petty-bourgeois leaders championed Mondale's 'civil-rights credentials', and the Minnesota Democrat won almost one third of the Black vote. In Philadelphia, Black mayor Wilson Goode used slightly different tactics to aid Mondale. Jackson captured 75 per cent of the Black vote in Pennsylvania, and most Black officials who were allied with Goode endorsed Jackson, according to one Black union leader, because they feared being 'seen as out of control of their constituents. But they made damn sure that [Jackson] got no delegates.' Thousands of sample ballots were distributed to Blacks with Jackson's name at the top of the voting slate, but with the names of Mondale delegates at the bottom. Many Blacks voted for Jackson but simultaneously voted for Mondale's delegates to the convention.[122]

Not without some cause, many Afro-Americans began to view Black Mondale supporters as little better than 'traitors' to the Black movement. One journalist, Gerald A. Anderson, bitterly denounced Goode, Young, Los Angeles mayor Tom Bradley, Coretta Scott King, Bond and others as betrayers of 'the masses of Black people', who had sold 'the Black vote for personal gain'.[123] Most Afro-American petty-bourgeois leaders lacked the integrity of a Rangel or Bond, who had to justify their allegiance to Mondale before increasingly hostile Black constitutencies. Black leaders in Congress who had recently touted Mondale attempted desperately to join the Rainbow Coalition. In early June, fifteen of the twenty-one Black Caucus members met with Jackson for three hours, and pledged their unswerving fidelity. Congressman Julian C. Dixon declared that the group was 'united behind Rev. Jackson', a Black leader who 'has spoken out not only for minorities, but has raised very serious issues that we think many Americans are concerned about'.[124] John Lewis suggested that Jackson was now unquestionably 'the undisputed Black leader . . . He's creating the climate for some Black man or Black woman to come along and be elected President of this country.' With the vast majority of NAACP members supporting Jackson, Hooks had little choice except to applaud his effort. With the fervour of a late convert, Hooks exclaimed, 'Jackson has proved to the white community what many Blacks knew all along: that Blacks are intelligent enough to deal with Presidential issues . . .'[125] Nevertheless, for the bulk of white

America, it seemed, the Jackson campaign was almost non-existent. In one April 1984 poll, 18 per cent of all whites said 'they would not vote for a Black man for President, even if he were qualified and was a party nominee'. As political theorist Clarence Lusane observed:

> With the exception of a relatively small proportion of progressives, whites of every social class have rejected the Jackson candidacy. To put it bluntly, working-class whites have not responded in massive numbers to the Rainbow-call . . . Throughout US history, with some notable exceptions, the racist defence of their privileged status relative to minorities has inhibited the development of even a rudimentary class consciousness in the white sector of the US working class. In politics this has often enough been reflected in white workers and Black workers taking divergent or even diametrically opposite positions on the key questions of the day. This dynamic is once again being played out in the Jesse Jackson campaign and obscuring it will not make it go away. If anything, the forthrightness with which Jackson has spoken to the key issues facing the major social reform movements only serves to throw the problem into sharper relief. [126]

III

The greatest mistake in the Jackson mobilization was made by the candidate himself. Black reporter Milton Coleman heard Jackson use an anti-Semitic slur: he referred to Jews as 'Hymies' and to New York City as 'Hymie-town'. For much of February and early March, the campaign was bogged down with charges that Jackson was an anti-Semite. Jackson finally admitted his remarks were wrong and apologized, but his initial denials undercut his 'moral standing' among many constituents. Progressive Jews found it impossible to work within the Rainbow Coalition, and hundreds of liberal and left activists, Jewish and non-Jewish, were lost permanently from the mobilization. Moreover, within the context of 'Rainbow Theology', any statement reflecting anti-Semitic views was clearly intolerable.

Jackson's difficulties with American Jewish leaders were nothing new. In 1979, Andrew Young, then US Ambassador to the United Nations, was fired for his unauthorized discussion with PLO observer Zehdi Labib Terzi. In the immediate outburst of controversy after Young's dismissal, Jackson met with PLO leader Yasser Arafat. Jack O'Dell is a member of the Board of Directors of the Palestine Human Rights Campaign, and has been a proponent of the Palestinian struggle for 'self-determination'.[127] Jackson's cordial relations with Syrian President Hafez Assad paved the way for the dramatic release of Lt Robert Goodman, a captured US Navy pilot, in December 1983.[128] Domestically, almost alone among major civil-rights leaders, Jackson and Operation PUSH cultivated close relations with international Arab groups. The League of Arab States donated $200,000 to Operation PUSH, and Libya donated $10,000 — both of which were legal contributions. Thus, well before his presidential candidacy, Jewish leaders had grave misgivings about Jackson. In 1983, the Anti-Defamation League (ADL) of B'nai B'rith circulated a nineteen-page critique of Jackson which was leaked to the media, a document weaving together quotations, taken out of context, from statements made by Jackson since 1973. The national leaders of the American Jewish Committee met with Jackson in the fall, and let it be known that they were 'disturbed by his views on Israel and the Middle East generally'. In November 1983, a 'Jews Against Jackson' group was formed by the ultraconservative Jewish Defence League. Militant right-wing Zionists threw pickets around Jackson-for-President campaign offices and at his home, chanting 'Ruin, Jesse, Ruin'. Even after Jackson's public apology, when the candidate spoke before a Jewish audience, pickets chanted 'Jackson is a racist pig' and 'Jew hater!' Jackson was constantly subjected to death-threats.[129]

Most Black supporters of Jackson, including those who had criticized their candidate's language, recognized that he was being judged unfairly. Immediately following Jackson's apology, a group of prominent Jackson supporters in New York issued a statement chastising their candidate. 'The language admitted by Jesse Jackson is impermissible when said by anyone on or off the record. It is not in the best interest of the Black and Jewish communities, that have a commonality of ethnic victimization, to permit these unacceptable remarks to divide our long-standing and vital relationships.' Jackson campaign aides caucused with leaders of the progressive New Jewish Agenda in an attempt to restore political harmony. After Jackson's apology, a number of Jewish leaders urged a reconciliation between Blacks and Jews. Rabbi Alexander Schindler, president of the Union of American Hebrew Congregations (Reform), declared 'I hope this matter is now behind us . . . we welcome Mr Jackson's call to renew the dialogue among Blacks and Jews. We have indeed much more in common than in conflict.'[130]

Yet criticism of Jackson increased. Howard I. Friedman, president of the American Jewish Committee, insisted on 27 February that Jackson's *mea culpa* was insufficient. 'While we welcome this particular acknowledgement,' Friedman suggested, 'we call upon him now to re-examine other statements he has made in the past about Jews, about Israel, about the Holocaust, about so-called Jewish power.'[131] One ADL leader, Leonard Zakim, explained that neither the American Jewish Committee nor the ADL was genuinely interested in a dialogue with the Rainbow Coalition. 'What you've got is the Jewish agencies condemning Jews Against Jackson' and Meir Kahane's Jewish Defence League 'and then playing the same kind of politics behind closed doors', stated Zakim. 'It's stupid and sad.'[132]

Blacks were perturbed by two factors. First, Jackson's positions on the Middle East were hardly those of the PLO. Repeatedly, Jackson referred to Israel as being 'the centre of democracy in the Middle East'. He advocated 'Israel's right to exist with security and with internationally recognized boundaries'. He did not oppose the 1977 Camp David accords, nor did he ever call for the creation of a 'democratic, secular Palestine', which is the PLO's official position. Jackson criticized American military aid to Israel, and like nearly all Black Americans, opposed the strengthening military and economic relationship that existed between the South African regime and Israel. In the context of international politics, Jackson's Middle East policies were roughly similar to those of Pope John Paul II. As one reporter put it: 'Jackson is attacked because he has breached a wall of silence; he has dared to speak out on a peace issue which had been taboo in American politics.'[133] In another radical departure from US bourgeois politics, Jackson actively courted the one million Arab-American constituency. In November 1983, for example, Jackson spoke before a national organization of Arab-Americans and invited them to join the Rainbow Coalition. Subsequently in Houston, Detroit, Boston and other cities, thousands of Arab-Americans contributed to Jackson's effort. 'Other politicians have been intimidated by the Jewish lobby', stated Essa Sackiah, an Arab-American leader in Houston. 'It's time to come out of the closet and be a voice, and Reverend Jackson has given us that opportunity.'[134]

The second factor was the historically complex relationship between progressive Black political organizations and the Jewish community. For over two decades many Black activists had been increasingly critical of Jewish involvement in Black political affairs.

Older Black progressives recalled that Jewish contributions had largely financed the desegregation campaigns of the CORE in the early 1960s. But with the CORE's espousal of 'Black Power', incoming funds stopped almost instantly.[135] When the SNCC published a brief essay on Palestine in its July 1967 newsletter, the executive director of the American Jewish Congress attacked the article as 'shocking and vicious anti-Semitism'. Almost every Jewish leader denounced the SNCC, and moderate civil-rights officials, including Urban League leader Whitney Young, Rustin and Randolph, also attacked the group.[136] Black nationalists such as Malcolm X had long attacked the 'Zionist control' over the NAACP and other civil-rights agencies. In 1959, Malcolm X argued that 'Jews sap the very life-blood of the so-called Negroes to maintain the state of Israel, its armies and its continued aggression against our brothers in the East . . . We make no distinction between Jews and non-Jews so long as they are all white.'[137] As Blacks began to emerge within electoral politics and the trade unions, they often conflicted with Jewish leaders who, in previous generations, had acquired positions of authority. Many Jewish groups actively opposed racial quotas in affirmative-action programmes, while Blacks demanded quotas as an effective means of redressing discrimination. Black intellectual Harold Cruse spoke for many Afro-American nationalists in 1967: 'One cannot deny the horror of the European Jewish holocaust, but for all practical purposes . . . Jews have not suffered in the United States. They have, in fact, done exceptionally well on every level of endeavour . . . The average Negro is not going to buy the propaganda that Negroes and Jews are "brother sufferers" in the same boat.'[138] Speaking in Atlanta in April 1970, Stokely Carmichael was even more blunt: 'Whenever Jewish senators take the floor, they wage propaganda for Israel. They [say] Africa has no right to have any guns, but Israel has the right to have all the guns she wants . . . Israel [occupies] land in Palestine that doesn't belong to [it].'[139]

In the 1970s and 1980s, Jewish support for Black progressive candidates was mixed. Only half of all Philadelphia Jews supported Wilson Goode in his successful race for mayor in 1983.[140] The case of New York City is most instructive. In 1973, Jewish districts voted overwhelmingly for Jewish moderate Abraham Beame over Puerto Rican liberal Herman Badillo. In the 1982 Democratic gubernatorial primary, Jews voted heavily for New York mayor Ed Koch, a 'neo-conservative' and aggressive opponent of Black and Hispanic interests, while Blacks substantially backed an Italian-

American liberal Mario Cuomo, who won. Increasingly some Afro-Americans, Latinos and Asian-Americans charged that Jews maintained a disproportionate share of political power in New York City. In 1984, non-whites made up over 48 per cent of the city's population, compared with about 24.5 per cent Jews. Yet of the three city-wide officials, two were Jewish, and of the five borough presidents, four were Jewish. As Arnold Linhardt of New York's American Jewish Congress noted, Jews have become 'more receptive to candidates and political platforms' that favour 'issues such as neighbourhood preservation — an issue that non-whites often view with distrust and perceive as meaning segregation — rather than the old liberal concerns such as social welfare'. The decline of the local white population and the rise of Black political activism 'has made the Jewish community even more apprehensive and concerned with protecting its political "power".' Consequently, many New York Blacks concluded that Jewish criticism of Jackson was actually an attempt to maintain local white ethnic hegemony over the national minority electorate. On New York State's primary day, only 5 per cent of Jewish voters backed Jackson.[141]

By mid March 1984, the national Black press was dominated by harsh reactions against American Jewish leaders, and the criticism was fuelled less by the 'Hymie controversy' than by those older, half-hidden grievances. John Kilimanjaro, editor/publisher of the *Carolina Peacemaker* stated that the 'Stop Jesse Movement had finally seized on an issue' in order to 'derail the Jackson Presidential Limited in its stride for the Democratic nomination . . . Far too many Jews are firmly ensconced in reactionary camps and are guilty of passing themselves off as liberals when it suits their purpose. It is these wolves in sheep's clothing who come down hard on Blacks whenever they dare raise their hand in independent fashion.'[142] Black economist Curtis Perkins denounced Jackson's critics as those who had also obtained the firing of Andrew Young from the UN. Young was 'a victim of Zionist power in the US, who are against any overtures to the PLO and to most Arabs'. Now Jackson shared Young's fate. 'We will defy those who try to bully us, dangle their money to tempt us or not allow our views to be heard', Perkins warned.[143] Another controversial statement was issued by Carlton Goodlett, the nation's most influential Afro-American publisher: 'Blacks resent the fact that Jews have taken the Big Brother attitude in most civil-rights struggles . . . When Blacks are only presenting our own point of view on what's best for Black folks, far too many of our Jewish friends think of us as anti-Semitic. The hell raised over the small aspersion upon Jews made by Jackson was a smoke-screen behind which the anti-Jackson movement among Jews was projected and gained momentum.'[144] The Jewish response was often in a similar vein. Leonard Fein, editor of the Jewish monthly *Moment*, retorted, 'Jackson's actions, his evasions and his statements have done grave damage to this nation . . . Blacks deserve better leadership than Jesse Jackson offers . . .'[145]

Black-Jewish relations then deteriorated to a nadir with the emergence of the 'Farrakhan controversy'. The leader of the Nation of Islam religious group, which had approximately five to ten thousand members, Farrakhan maintained a substantial political following which well exceeded his own organization. Farrakhan was a featured speaker at the 1983 March on Washington, and was one of the earliest supporters of Jackson's candidacy. For the Muslim leader, the campaign illustrated that 'the power and presence of Allah [God] is being felt in the activity of the children of slaves, who, in quest of their own freedom, must make a thrust for the freedom of all others'.[146] Fluent in Arabic and a charismatic speaker, Farrakhan was an undeniable asset at first, reaching both the growing community of American Muslims and a large sector of the militant Black nationalist movement which had previously opposed electoral participation.[147] When Jackson came under attack for the 'Hymie' slur, Farrakhan responded with his own verbal jibes. In a radio broadcast on 11 March, he attacked Milton Coleman as a 'betrayer' to his race for reprinting remarks which had been made 'off the record'. Coleman was warned: 'One day soon we will punish you with death.' Farrakhan referred to Adolph Hitler as 'wickedly great', and declared that if Jackson's candidacy was not taken seriously by the Democratic National Convention he would 'lead an army' to Washington DC to 'negotiate for a separate state or territory of our own'.[148] Jackson immediately disavowed Farrakhan's statements, and defended Coleman as a 'tough' and 'professional reporter'. But he did not repudiate Farrakhan's endorsement of his candidacy, declaring, 'I am not going to negotiate away my integrity trying to impress somebody'.[149] Virtually every white American leader was outraged by Jackson's refusal to condemn a 'racial demagogue'. Hundreds of newspaper editorials denounced Jackson again, linking Farrakhan's Black Muslim beliefs with those of the Baptist minister. Two Reagan appointees to the US Civil Rights Commission described Farrakhan as 'a man who preaches hate', and demanded that Jackson 'disavow' his support unconditionally.[150] The US Justice Department promptly investigated Farrakhan's broadcast transcript for 'evidence to prosecute' him for 'threatening the life' of Coleman.[151] In an opportunistic attempt to link Mondale and Hart to the Farrakhan controversy, Vice-President George Bush attacked all three Democratic candidates for failing to 'denounce the intrusion of anti-Semitism into the American political process'.[152] Quietly Jackson asked Farrakhan not to work publicly for the campaign. But only in June, when Farrakhan was quoted as calling Judaism a 'gutter religion' and the establishment of the Israeli state as an 'outlaw act', did Jackson forcefully condemn his statements as 'reprehensible and morally indefensible'.[153] Several weeks later, however, Jackson charged that Mondale had refused to consider him as a possible running mate because 'Jewish leaders' had tried to 'make me a pariah and isolate our support'. Once more, Jewish leaders attacked Jackson. Henry Siegman, the executive director of the American Jewish Congress, warned Democratic Party officials that continued support for Jackson was 'a partnership that can only lead to disaster'.[154]

If we assume a long historical view, the most interesting dimension of the Afro-American/Jewish controversy was that few of its major participants seemed to exhibit theoretical or political clarity about the genuine roots of the disagreement. The first problem was the repetitive and incorrect equation of 'anti-Semitism' with 'racism'. For many years, Marxists and non-Marxists alike have tended to draw direct parallels between white supremacy which targets non-whites and anti-Semitism targeting Jews. Du Bois was no exception. Throughout his career he equated the campaign to uproot anti-Semitism with the political struggles of 'disadvantaged groups' that experienced racial and national oppression, such as Afro-Americans and the Irish.[155] One of the few social scientists who attempted to explain the critical distinctions between racism and anti-Semitism was Oliver Cromwell Cox. 'The dominant group is intolerant of those whom it can define as antisocial, while it holds race prejudice against those whom it can define as subsocial', Cox noted. Thus the white, Christian majority could persecute Jews, an 'antisocial' group, while perpetuating racism against Afro-Americans, a group deemed 'subsocial'. 'In other words, the dominant group or ruling class does not like the Jew at all, but it likes the Negro in his place', observed Cox. 'The condition of its liking the Jew is that he cease being a Jew and voluntarily become like the generality of society, while the condition of its liking the Negro is that he cease trying to become like the generality of society and remain contentedly a Negro.' In a racist capitalist social form-ation, racists are frequently anti-Semitic, and the brutal methods used to oppress Blacks — destroying their houses of worship, the denial of academic opportunities, restrictions on certain vocations, the bombing of homes, and so on — have been used against Blacks and Jews alike. But as Cox emphasized, similar or even identical cases of violence do not stem from the same social dynamics. 'Intolerance demands recantation and conversion'; it presumes that the outsider may, at some point, be integrated into the cultural mainstream. 'A Jewish pogrom is not exactly similar to a Negro lynching', Cox added. 'In a pogrom the fundamental motive is the extermination of the Jew; in a lynching, however, the motive is that of giving the Negro a lesson in good behaviour.'[156]

A common heritage of victimization and struggles against adver-sity has brought Afro-Americans and American Jews together his-torically. For over a century, Black leaders with widely differing views have pointed to the socio-economic mobility of the national Jewish community as an example worthy of imitation. Booker T. Washington urged Blacks to pattern themselves after 'the Jews, who through unity and faith in themselves were becoming more and more influential'.[157] Du Bois applauded the creation and expansion of the United Hebrew Trades in the late nineteenth century as a type of racial 'self-segregation' which would help to destroy anti-Semitism inside organized labour.[158] Despite these and other simi-larities, the social class position of the majority of American Jews in the past thirty years has been radically different from that of the bulk of Americans of African descent. Lenni Brenner argues:

> . . . the typical class relationship between a Black person and a Jewish person is one in which the Jew is in the superior social position. Few Jewish students have the experience of being taught by more than one Black teacher, if that. Few Jews patronize Black-owned stores. Fewer still have utilized the services of a Black attorney or a Black physician. The number of Jews with Black landlords must be miniscule, and has there ever been a Black person who had a Jewish maid? In contrast, sociologist Seymour Martin Lipset estimates that a majority of white families residing outside the South with full-time servants are Jewish, and 40 to 60 per cent of middle-class Jewish families have their Black cleaning lady.[159]

The American Jewish community has a deep ideological and political history of combating racism. Nevertheless, there are Jews who are racist, and there are Afro-Americans who are anti-Semitic.

One key difference between the two social groups is that Afro-Americans usually lack the institutional or organizational capacity to inflict systemic anti-Semitic actions upon most Jews, who tend to occupy a more privileged socio-economic status. Racists who happen to be Jews may have greater access to coercive apparatuses that disrupt Afro-Americans' lives. It is important to emphasize that access does not mean utility. White supremacy has a miniscule audience among Jews, and contrary to some media assertions in recent years, anti-Semitism has never found a mass audience among Afro-Americans. But it is difficult not to observe that the socio-economic conditions of Afro-Americans, which as we have seen, have steadily deteriorated since the early 1970s, can be brushed aside as immaterial in any contemporary analysis of Black-Jewish relations.

A third point involves the politics of Zionism. Historically, most Afro-American political leaders, both accommodationists and reformers, have tended to accept the view that Zionism was the principal — and indeed at times the only — significant expression of Jewish politics. Black leaders since the 1950s who have criticized the state of Israel — including Malcolm X, Farrakhan and Carmichael — may have not known that some of their ideological mentors were firm proponents of Zionism. Pan-Africanists and Black nationalists especially viewed Jewish Zionism through the prism of Africa. Thus in December 1918, when Du Bois prepared to organize the first Pan-African Congress session in Paris, he stated that 'the African movement means to us what the Zionist movement must mean to the Jews, the centralization of race effort and the recognition of a racial fount'.[160] For four decades, Du Bois was one of the most prominent non-Jewish American defenders of Zionism. In 1948, Du Bois drafted a moving appeal defending the creation of the state of Israel, observing that 'the plight of the Jews throughout the world has been even harder and more desperate than anything the Negroes have passed through in modern times'.[161] Garvey disagreed with Du Bois about many things, but Zionism was not among them. The UNIA leader frequently drew parallels between his 'Back to Africa' programme and that of Jewish Zionists for Palestine. Garvey accepted financial contributions from a Jewish Zionist, Louis Michael, who had declared that 'no justice or peace' could exist 'until the Jew and the Negro both control side by side Palestine and Africa'. Garvey told supporters that he was fully 'in sympathy with the Zionist movement', and on at least one occasion stated that Jewish Zionists had in part 'inspired' his own activity.[162] Part of the reason for the 180-degree shift in Afro-American nationalists' recent attitudes towards Zionism may be traced to the state of Israel's extensive economic relationship with apartheid South Africa, and to the role of Israel's overseas arms sales, which supplied some of Portugal's weapons during its genocidal wars against Mozambique, Angola and Guinea-Bissau.[163] But in terms of domestic US politics, there is still a pronounced tendency among Black leaders, whether favourable towards or critical of Israeli policies in the Middle East, to equate the entire American Jewish community with the politics of Zionism. How accurate is this characterization? According to Fred Massarik and Alvin Chenkin, 60.2 per cent of all American Jews in 1973 were 'unaffiliated with any Jewish organization, religious or Zionist'. Fewer than one out of six Jewish Americans have ever visited Israel, and a 'majority of Jews in the United States have yet to give a single penny' towards Israel's support.[164]

American Jewish electoral behaviour has indeed moved further to the right in recent years, but supporters of Reaganism within the Jewish community are a distinct minority. In 1944 about 90 per cent of all Jewish voters supported Roosevelt, a proportion significantly larger than that of Afro-American voters, or any other group for that matter. It was only during the 1960s that Black Americans surpassed Jews as the most consistently liberal bloc in presidential elections. Despite the appeals of the Israeli ambassador to the US, Yitzhak Rabin, urging American Jews to vote for Richard Nixon in 1972, only 35 per cent of the Jewish vote went to the Republican incumbent. In 1980 Reagan received almost 40 per cent of the Jewish vote, and in neo-conservative Jewish circles there was a strong belief that this percentage would reach a majority by 1984.[165] This did not occur. Despite the intense polemics about the Jewish/Afro-American debate, public-opinion polls carried out in late May 1984 indicate that both groups remain clearly on the liberal spectrum within US bourgeois democracy. Both favour the ratification of the Equal Rights Amendment (Blacks 74 to 21 per cent, Jews 79 to 20 per cent); both back affirmative action 'without rigid quotas' (Blacks 73 to 19 per cent, Jews 70 to 20 per cent); and both support a 'freeze' on the production and deployment of nuclear weapons by majorities of over nine to one. Jews gave Reagan a 61 to 38 negative assessment to Afro-Americans' 80 to 18 rating. Both termed Jesse Jackson 'an attractive, forceful personality and a real leader' (Blacks 80 to 19 per cent, Jews 55 to 36 per cent).[166] It is quite possible, as Hyman Bookbinder notes, that as many as 50 per cent of all Jews were prepared to support Reagan immediately after the Farrakhan incident in mid 1984. But given the strong weight of political liberalism within the community, and Reagan's manipulation of primitive evangelicalism to obtain conservative Christian support, Jewish voters voted against Reagan overwhelmingly, by a national majority of about 68 to 32 per cent. The electoral repudiation of Reaganism by most Jews forced Jewish neo-conservatives to scramble, subsequently to claim that pollsters had undercounted heavily Conservative, Hasidic and Orthodox neighbourhoods across the country. But even these frustrated neo-conservatives could not deny that Jews almost alone among the middle to upper-income white voters, had maintained their ideological commitment against the US right, which translated into a sharp rebuke to the Reagan administration.[167]

Jackson's verbal blunder was costly to the Rainbow rebellion, but perhaps something constructive came out of the dissension, something that may prove beneficial to long-term progressive politics. A left-liberal, multiracial, multiclass coalition can function within bourgeois democratic politics only if all parties recognize and respect areas of historical and social differences among themselves. Afro-Americans who are socialized to react sharply against racism must recognize that the democratic struggles against forms of intolerance, and specifically against anti-Semitism, must be supported vigorously and without qualification. Conversely, progressive Jews certainly recognize that a political programme that criticizes the policies of Israel does not have to connote any element of anti-Semitism. The real tragedy of the recent debate was that the anti-Semites and racists who *do* actively exercise power within the US state and in the capitalist ruling class were able to escape much public criticism from a unified progressive movement.

IV

None of the supporters of the Rainbow Coalition anticipated that Jackson had any possibility of receiving the Democratic Party's presidential nomination. 'Even the vice-presidential nomination, a traditional consolation prize for unsuccessful presidential candidates, seemed extremely unlikely', noted political scientists Thomas E. Cavanagh and Lorn S. Foster. Thus the 'criteria for evaluating the campaign's success' had to be different from those for other mundane efforts.[168] Perhaps the most remarkable accomplishment was the capacity of a social protest movement to transform its own 'leader'. Most progressives retained private doubts about Jackson during the early stages of the campaign. We had seen his hasty retreat from the National Black Political Assembly a decade before; his lack of organizational follow-through after his moving into a Black community for a series of highly publicized rallies; his opportunistic manipulation of the press. But we should have known that the social class pressure from below, from the inner-city streets and factories and churches, would dictate the flow of the social movement. And as that uneven process swept aside the wavering Black petty bourgeoisie, the elected officials who had desperately tried to protect their interests within the party hierarchy, we saw Jackson grow rapidly in his social vision. Bustamante and King, Mondlane and Nkrumah had not been, at the outset of their careers, the 'leaders' they became: they learned to listen to the people, and in the process they began to transform themselves. So too with Jackson. The Rainbow Coalition candidate struggled with his own contradictions, and tried to explain his growing aspirations for the social movement he now represented. As he stood before the Acorn housing projects in Oakland, California, on 5 June, a small group of supporters formed a prayer circle. Jackson was physically exhausted, but seemed at peace with himself. 'There comes a point when leaders can't take you any further', he stated softly. 'I've brought you as far as I could bring you. You must shoulder the burden and the responsibility and go across the chilly Jordan. Each one has to swim for his or herself.'[169] With these words, some felt a shudder of recognition: Martin Luther King's last major address had expressed the identical sense of completion, the achievement of a new level of Black hope and struggle.[170] In the cold eye of the national media, other criteria were used to measure the full dimensions of this internal revolt against the Democratic Party. Jackson had won over three and a half million popular votes; he had defeated Mondale and Hart in sixty Congressional districts; he had carried popular majorities or pluralities in the District of Columbia, Virginia, South Carolina, Louisana and Mississippi. To be sure, some Blacks had voted for Jackson primarily because he was an Afro-American. But the Rainbow Coalition found its popular base because of its advanced political programme, not simply because of the national-minority identity of its spokesperson. Jackson came to be the voice of the progressive mass post-World War II constituencies, as Barry Commoner observed: 'for civil rights; against nuclear-weapons testing; for women's and gay rights; against the war in Vietnam; for the environment; against nuclear power and for solar energy; against nuclear war. Each of these movements expresses a moral critique of a major national policy. Taken together they represent millions of voters, yet they have never been linked together into a political force.'[171]

The Jackson effort had its biggest impact in the South. The region had fewer than 3,000 Black elected officials out of a total of 79,000 (3.8 per cent), despite a 21 per cent Black region-wide population in 1984. Southern Blacks had only one Congressional representative, and but seven mayors of cities with populations of 50,000 and above. With the Jackson mobilization, thousands of non-registered Blacks were motivated to participate in the electoral process. Between January 1983 and April 1984, over 183,000 new Black voters were enrolled in just five southern states — Georgia, South and North Carolina, Alabama and Louisiana. The significance of this mobilization was not lost upon many traditional political bosses. In 1980, for example, there were 85,000 unregistered Black voters in Arkansas, a state Reagan carried in the general election by 5,123 votes. In Tennessee, Reagan's 1980 victory margin of 4,710 votes was dwarfed by the 158,000 previously non-registered Black voters; in South Carolina, Reagan's margin of 11,456 votes disintegrated with any significant registration of the state's 292,000 non-registered Blacks.[172] In Louisiana, white leaders attempted to undermine both the Jackson campaign and Black registration efforts by cancelling the state's 1984 Democratic primary. Conservative Democratic governor Edwin W. Edwards urged voters to 'boycott' the election, and the State Legislature refused to approve a budget request for $150,000 to pay for printing the ballots. The federal courts required that the election be held, and the worst fears of local racists came true: Jackson received 42 per cent of the state-wide vote, trouncing both Mondale and Hart, and in the process brought tens of thousands of new Black voters to the polls. In Tennessee, Jackson was the winner in Memphis, Nashville, Chattanooga and Knoxville, the state's four largest cities.[173] In Kentucky, the massive Black turn-out for Democratic caucuses stunned party regulars. State-wide, 24 per cent of the caucus participants were Jackson supporters. Jackson carried Louisville, the largest metropolitan area (with a 15 per cent Black voting population) with 51 per cent of the caucus vote. Lexington, with a 13 per cent Afro-American population, produced a 53 per cent majority for the Rainbow Coalition.[174] In Georgia, the Jackson state chair, State Representative Tyrone Brooks, observed: 'We had no paid staff and not one radio or TV ad; we didn't get a cent from the Washington office until March. But we had five hundred volunteers in and out of the Atlanta office everyday. And we raised $300,000 for the national campaign.'[175]

One central political demand that Jackson called for throughout the campaign was the abolition of 'run-off primaries' — which force the two top vote recipients in a Democratic primary to hold a second election if no one obtains 50 per cent of the vote. In theory, the second primary system ensured that the strongest possible candidate would emerge from the Democratic Party into the general election. But in practice, given the extreme reluctance whites exhibit in voting for Black candidates, it usually eliminated Blacks before they reached general elections. Not coincidentally, the only states that still maintain run-off primaries are in the South. Many southern politicians of both races, including Bond, insisted that 'the second primary has helped progressive causes as often as it has hurt'. Georgia Lieutenant Governor Zell Miller, a white liberal Democrat, stated that 'without the run-off primary, you would polarize the state along racial lines'.[176] Most observers suggested that the abolition of the run-off primaries would increase Afro-American Congressional representation significantly, but that several million white southern Democrats would shift their political allegiance to the Republican Party, thus ensuring conservative hegemony at the national level. At the San Francisco convention, however the Jackson minority platform plank in opposition to run-off primaries was overwhelmingly defeated by the delegates.

Another important contribution of the Rainbow campaign was its impact upon various foreign-policy debates. In a racist social formation, Blacks are not expected to possess the capacity to comprehend, much less articulate, sensitive positions on international affairs. As discussed in the chapter on the Washington march, perhaps the most serious charge levied against the 1983 organizers was that of their commitment to address foreign-affairs questions, linking domestic social transformation with the battle for world peace and nuclear-arms reductions. In the tradition of Robeson and Du Bois, Malcolm X and Martin Luther King Jr, Jackson refused to parochialize the broader meaning of the Black freedom movement. As the campaign progressed, Jackson moved further to the left. 'For example, at the November 12 [1983] March on Washington in support of Central America, Jackson was ambiguous about the presence of US troops in Lebanon and called for Europe and Japan to build up their military forces to take the place of cuts in the US military budget', Marxist journalist John Trinkl noted. Within five months, progressive campaign staff and researchers sharply influenced Jackson's international positions. During the New York primary, Jackson's condemnation of the bipartisan foreign policies of the US were as radical as that of any socialist. On Central America, Jackson declared, 'our government [is] on the wrong side of history, taking the side of dictators against the people. We must re-examine our foreign policy of history around the world, we must seek to wage peace, to take the side of oppressed people . . . '[177] Speaking before the North American Regional Conference for Action Against Apartheid in New York, Jackson called for federal legislation prohibiting new US corporate investment in South Africa, and for 'a timetable for the removal of the more than 350 American corporations doing business there'. Denouncing US foreign policy as a tool of corporate capitalism, Jackson thundered: 'Choosing dollars over dignity not only in South Africa, but in El Salvador, Chile, the Philippines and elsewhere around the world is leading us as a nation down the road to moral suicide.'[178] In late July, Jackson met with the leaders of the Sandinista government in Nicaragua, and travelled to Cuba, where he obtained the release of forty-eight American and Cuban prisoners. Even before Jackson returned to the US, Secretary of State George Shultz denounced the release as a Cuban 'propaganda ploy', and the Supreme Court reinstated the Reagan Administration's strict travel curbs on visiting Cuba. The *New York Times* viciously attacked Jackson's 'burgeoning traffic in prisoners from dictatorships' as a 'collaboration with the enemies of democracy'.[179] Perhaps the *Times,* the voice of bourgeois democracy, was most distressed by the conclusion of Jackson's speech at the University of Havana: *'Viva el Presidente Fidel Castro! Viva Martin Luther King! Viva Ché Guevara! Viva Patrice Lumumba! Dios les bendiga!'*[180]

At the Democratic convention during the week of 16 July, the Rainbow Coalition continued to mobilize. As most of the Mondale and Hart delegates sat in the Moscone Convention Centre on the night of 16 July, Jackson, Dellums and thousands of dissidents held their own rally outside in the centre's parking lot. In the streets, several hundred thousand Jackson supporters, workers, gay and lesbian activists, peace proponents and other radical reformers continued to demonstrate throughout the week.[181] The Rainbow forces inside the convention placed before the delegates several minority platform positions, including 'no first use' of nuclear weapons, support for affirmative action programmes without the use of strict quotas, and a demand for 'substantial reductions' in Pentagon spending. Mondale was opposed to all of these positions, but was unable to impose discipline on his Afro-American delegates. The Black Caucus of the Democratic National Committee, chaired by Mondale supporter Mickey Leland, voted to support all of Jackson's progressive minority planks to the Democratic platform. Well over 80 per cent of the 968 Black delegates voted with Jackson's positions. But despite the defection of several hundred Latino and liberal white delegates to the Rainbow Coalition, Mondale and Hart delegates voted according to the demands of the prospective nominee. The plank for majority reductions in the military budget was defeated by more than two to one. A compromise plank was approved on affirmative action, but many Jackson delegates stated angrily that 'the approved version was weakened to the point of becoming meaningless'. The Jackson minority plank to put the party 'on record as unconditionally opposed to any first use of nuclear weapons' also lost, but obtained the support of 1,406 delegates, or 39 per cent of all those voting on the issue. [182] The plank calling for the elimination of the South's run-off primaries was crushed by three to one. During the floor debate, Black delegates were stunned to see Andrew Young waltz to the platform to support the dual elections. Throughout his ten-minute speech, Afro-American delegates 'booed and heckled' him from the convention floor. The general view of most Blacks was that Mondale had 'despicably used Andy' to leave 'the Black community high and dry'. Coretta Scott King subsequently chastised Black delegates who had 'wronged' Young — and she too was promptly booed. Only Jackson's timely intervention kept some degree of order. Embracing Young, he reprimanded the hecklers, stating that their conduct 'was rude and unnecessary'. [183] But Jackson also recognized the frustration of his followers. One Jackson delegate, Pennsylvania State Representative Dave Richardson, explained: 'We have to have something to take back to our people to save face.' [184]

Fresh from the defeat of the Rainbow Coalition's platform planks, Jackson could have vented his anger before a national audience. But his major televised address was a masterful performance. 'The network cameras made the whole nation a cathedral for an experience previously common only on Sundays, in the Black churches of America', wrote one reporter. Filling the 'moral and political vacuum at the centre of Black America' once occupied by King, Jackson came 'as a man who would not be denied, creating an opportunity no Black man had had before'.[185] Apologizing to American Jews, he stated: 'If in my low moments, in word, deed or attitude, through some error of temper, taste or tone, I have caused anyone discomfort, created pain or revived some-one's fears, that was not my truest self.' Jews and Blacks were 'bound by shared blood and shared sacrifices'.[186] Jackson then offered a *moral* critique of the Reagan Administration, noting that it 'must be held accountable for increasing infant mortality among the poor'. He evoked hilarious cheers when he stated: 'I would rather have Roosevelt in a wheelchair than Reagan on a horse!' He placated Mondale delegates by announcing that he would be 'proud to support the nominee of this convention', but he refused to repudiate any of the progressive positions he had advocated in the previous six months. And in a break with his own previous history, he reminded his supporters: 'I am not a perfect servant. I am a public servant. As I develop and serve, be patient. God is not finished with me yet.' Jackson's speech, which was rumoured to have been drafted in part with the assistance of Senator Kennedy's speech-writers, received nearly total acclaim. Some white Mondale delegates even admitted that 'if Jesse Jackson were a white man, he would win the presidency hands down'. The Black press praised Jackson's speech as 'the rhetorical highlight of the convention'.[187] Moderate Black elected officials such as Congresswoman Cardiss Collins termed the Reverend's speech a 'watershed for democratic politics'.[188] John Jacob expressed the hope that Mondale, now safely nominated, would 'understand that Jesse Jackson is critical to getting out the Black vote'. But Black Marxists, Black nationalists and more progressive reformers shared a radically different view of the entire proceedings. Joseph Lowery complained that 'even after all that Jesse did to show what Black voters can do, it's the same old thing . . . .'. Amiri Baraka demanded, 'Why are we going home with nothing?' Herbert Daughtry was 'disappointed and disgusted' with the entire process. Taking Jackson aside, he urged the minister to hand Mondale an ultimatum: 'You respond to our demands, or you get your backside whipped by Reagan.'[189]

Daughtry and other progressive Blacks' hopes were quickly dashed. Despite the massive Jackson social movement which had nearly denied Mondale the nomination, the cautious Cold War liberal had learned nothing new. Mondale's staff had prepared a 250-page study in the weeks immediately preceding the Democratic convention, assessing his chances in the general election. The study concluded that 'the only way Mondale can win is by pitching his appeal to the white working class and minorities, not the middle class'. With the registration of an additional six million new Latino, Black, poor and blue-collar voters, he could defeat Reagan. To secure a large minority turn-out, a Black politician had to be selected as his vice-presidential running mate. Mondale's staffers suggested Los Angeles mayor Tom Bradley. Mondale's response was to select a three-term, Italian-American Congresswoman, Geraldine Ferraro. Despite her working-class origins, Ferraro had little in common with most white, Black or Latina women. Ferraro's husband was a millionaire real-estate operator in New York City. Politically liberal on some economic issues, she had also voted against bussing for school desegregation, and supported the Pershing II missile programme and the Trident nuclear submarine, which took billions of dollars from human-service programmes needed by working women. Of all white female Democratic leaders, she was the one whom 'the men in the back room find most acceptable'.[190] Chosen several days before the convention began, Ferraro was the first woman selected by a major capitalist party as a national candidate. Jackson quickly praised Ferraro's selection as 'long' overdue and well-deserved. But Jackson had been the first Democratic candidate in history to promise during the campaign that he would select a woman running mate if nominated. Campaign aides noted that Mondale 'never took seriously' a list of minority women vice-presidential possibilities that Jackson had given him two weeks before the convention. Many Afro-American women and Latinas argued that there were many other minority women leaders far more qualified than Ferraro.[191] The alienation of the Rainbow forces from Mondale further increased when the party nominee froze many Jackson supporters out of campaign roles, and appointed Rangel as his national-campaign co-chair. By late July, Jackson was forced to announce that he would campaign for the Democratic ticket only when Mondale and Ferraro sent a 'message to inspire the masses'. That message was not forthcoming.[192]

Technically, Reagan should have had a difficult time seeking re-election. During the conservative Republican's first term in office real interest rates, factoring for inflation, had increased from 0.2 per cent to 4.7 per cent. Real home-mortgage rates were also up from 2 per cent to 6.4 per cent after inflation. Real farm incomes had fallen by over 50 per cent between 1981 and 1984. The only beneficiaries of Reaganomics were the large corporations and the households in the top fifth income bracket, which had gained 8.7 per cent after taxes and inflation in four years under Reagan.

Moreover, the Jackson campaign had mobilized hundreds of thousands of new voters, who were largely prepared to vote for anyone in the general election in order to defeat the incumbent. Unfortunately, Mondale's campaign was both poorly conceived and badly executed. The two themes that could have unified the warring factions of the national Democratic Party were the issues of 'fairness' and 'peace'. Reagan's budget reductions had hurled millions into poverty, and the vast majority of workers and low-income Americans had not been touched by the economic recovery of 1983-84. The modern peace movement and the demand for a freeze on nuclear weapons had the support of a majority of Americans. Instead, Mondale focused his critique on the un-inspiring issue of budget deficits, and on the necessity to increase the taxes of all families with annual incomes over $25,000. Instead of demanding a major reduction in the Pentagon budget, Mondale called for annual military increases of 3 to 4 per cent over the rate of inflation. Instead of calling for massive social democratic-type pro-grammes to reduce unemployment and to improve national edu-cational, housing and health-delivery systems, the former Vice-President insisted upon another $29 billion reduction in social and civilian expenditures to reduce the federal deficit. On major foreign-policy matters, Mondale applauded the illegal invasion of Grenada, never criticized US intervention in Central America, and was practically mute on Reagan's 'constructive engagement' policies which support apartheid. In short, Mondale offered the electorate not a choice, not even an echo, but a whimper. It was 'Reaganism with a human face', and it bewildered and angered Afro-Americans, Puerto Ricans, Chicanos and other strong sup-porters of Jackson. Mondale and Ferraro pitched their entire campaign towards the affluent white middle class, and to a lesser extent, to blue-collar ethnics. In brief, they all but ignored the advice of liberal analysts like James Ridgeway: 'Mondale's pre-sidential campaign depends on the Rainbow. Without it, he has no chance in the big cities, not a prayer in the South, in Texas or California.'[193]

Under these circumstances, the major concern of the Republican national campaign managers was to insulate their candidate from public scrutiny. The president of the United States became a 'phantom candidate': no news conferences were held for a period of six months during 1984; all public appearances were carefully staged, complete with brass bands and American flags. Only once did the mask slip, during Reagan's first televised debate with

Mondale, when the veteran actor seemed incoherent and quite at a loss without his script. If Reagan was nearly devoid of details concerning his own administration's policies and personnel, at least his managers maintained a surer grasp of political priorities. Reagan's aides deliberately attempted to construct an electoral bloc that was in most respects the social class opposite of the Rainbow Coalition: non-Black, non-Latino, non-poor, non-unemployed. In the South, this strategy was expanded to include overt appeals to working-class and poor whites: in essence, a white united front. Ideologically, millions of white workers supported the Republican because of his rhetoric of white supremacy, national chauvinism and anti-Communism. Evangelical Christians, led by right-wing minister Jerry Falwell's 'Moral Majority', spearheaded a massive voter-registration drive to recruit low-to-moderate-income conservatives. The Republicans spent more than $10 million on voter registration; as a result, first-time voters went for Reagan by a majority of 60 to 39 per cent. The Democrats devoted less than one quarter of this amount to voter registration, fearful that the addition of more Black, Latino and poor white voters into the party would strengthen the Rainbow Coalition's constituency after the election. As a result, the November election's results were entirely predictable. Reagan-Bush received 59 per cent of the popular vote, which amounted to 30 per cent of all eligible voters. Within this bloc, the Republicans received their strongest support from political conservatives (81 per cent), white 'born again' Christians (80 per cent), all southern whites (72 per cent), and voters with personal annual incomes above $50,000 (68 per cent). Mondale-Ferraro managed to carry only one state and the District of Columbia. Their primary electoral base consisted of Afro-Americans (90 per cent), Jews (68 per cent), Latinos (65 per cent), and unemployed workers (68 per cent) — which was essentially the core of the Rainbow's constituency. Mondale's blatant appeals to the white upper middle class contributed to lower totals among key groups from which he needed more substantial support. The Democratic ticket obtained only 53 per cent of the votes from members of union households, 53 per cent from workers earning less than $12,500 annually, and 52 per cent from women with less than a high-school education.[194]

The presidential election results of 1984 raise several disturbing questions for national minorities, liberals and the left. We should take small comfort from the fact that only 52.9 per cent of all voters went to the polls, because of those whites who did exercise their franchise, 66 per cent supported Reagan. To judge by any criteria, when 73 per cent of all white Protestants, regardless of social class, vote for one candidate, something fundamental has taken place within bourgeois democratic political culture. When 64 per cent of all white women voters, regardless of social class, support an incumbent president who is vehemently opposed to the Equal Rights Amendment, to comparable worth or equal pay for jobs regardless of sex, and to abortion rights, something has happened that requires a thoughtful critique. Since the New Deal, when the majority of the electorate became identified with the liberal capitalist policies of the Democratic Party, American political scientists have awaited the next ideological realignment. Since Eisenhower's re-election in 1956, however, the Republicans have not held a majority in the House of Representatives, and only in the 1980s have they obtained a narrow majority in the Senate. Democrats consistently control most state legislatures, and have won about 60 per cent of all gubernatorial elections over the past two decades. The Reagan 'mandate' of 1984 produced a net gain of only fifteen House seats and the Republicans actually lost two seats. So the wait for the great political realignment still continues in most quarters. This orthodox perspective, which is shared by many liberals and conservatives, is badly flawed, because 'realignment' is defined incorrectly in purely partisan terms. In the last nine elections since 1952, Democratic presidential candidates have received an average of 42.2 per cent of whites' votes, compared with 84.1 per cent of the Afro-American vote. In the past three elections, the racial stratification of the electorate has become more polarized, with whites' support for Democrats declining to 38.9 per cent, and Black support at about 90 per cent. In fact, since 1952 a majority of white Americans have voted for a Democratic presidential candidate only once — for Lyndon Johnson in 1964.[195] Consequently, many white middle-class Democrats running in local, state and Congressional races have tailored their message to appeal to a more affluent, better-educated, white professional social class. These Democratic leaders recognize that neither the AFL-CIO, which represented the old industrial working-class base inside the New Deal coalition, nor the National Organization of Women, which tries to articulate the interests of white liberal, petty-bourgeois women, has the political capacity to deliver any reliable percentage of votes in national elections. They understand, like the Reaganites, that vulgar appeals to national chauvinism and racial solidarity can induce millions of blue-collar and semi-skilled white workers to vote against their own material interests. They also comprehend that it is much easier for them to shift their ideological orientation than to leave one party for another. In US bourgeois democratic politics, incumbency is far more important than party affiliation. In the November 1984 elections, of the 410 House incumbents who sought re-election, only twelve were defeated; in the Senate, only three incumbents failed to win re-election out of twenty-nine.[196] Thus the realignment has largely taken place: the ideological 'centre' of bipartisan politics has clearly moved to the right during the past decade, and whether there is a Democrat or a Republican in the White House matters relatively little within the general framework of public policies. This political realignment is, broadly understood, a response to the structural crisis of American capitalism which intensified after 1973, and to which no permanent solutions exist within the established order.

Throughout the remainder of the 1980s, the national Democratic Party will probably continue this drift to the right, towards greater fiscal conservatism, in an effort to recruit Reagan's constituency. Where will this leave the Rainbow Democrats? Jackson hinted at the next stages of the Rainbow Coalition's development at the Democratic National Convention: 'Our campaign was not the end but the beginning of a new movement that can change the direction of this country. There are three schools of thought: conservatives, who want things to stay as they are; liberals, who want to reform what is; and progressives, who want to change things. We represent the progressive school of thought.' Rainbow theoreticians have attempted to project an 'inside-outside' strategy *vis-à-vis* the regular Democrats. 'We are not talking about a third party, but a second party', O'Dell explains. Activists will continue to reform the existing party apparatus and programmes, which would 'make the Democratic Party a real alternative to the Republican Party. If the Democratic Party does not understand that,' O'Dell predicts, 'it will go out of existence, and the Rainbow Coalition will become the second party.' The essence of this new formation would be 'a grass-roots, human-rights organization' that takes part in electoral political activities, notes Cleveland Sellers. 'The main base will be Black, but we will reach out to more Hispanics, Native Americans, and other groups nationally, and in the South more progressive whites, especially workers who are losing their jobs as plants move overseas.'[197] Frank Watkins, a top Jackson aide, revealed plans in mid 1984 to create a permanent Rainbow Coalition, with its national headquarters at the Operation PUSH centre in Chicago. The centre 'would be equipped with television studios, a direct-mail organization and offices for voter registration and fund-raising'.[198]

The difficulties involved in carrying out this ambitious strategy, in the face of political reaction, should not be minimized. The lack of operating capital means that the Rainbow Coalition's 'message' is largely controlled by the capitalist media. During the 1984 primaries, the Jackson campaign spent less than $10,000 on all its political advertising throughout February, and no money was spent on television advertisements until the 5 June California primary. Jackson was 'successful at generating visibility and coverage', but he had absolutely 'no control over the content of this coverage', comment Cavanagh and Foster. Consistently the press emphasized Jackson's role as the 'Black' candidate, and said little about the progressive and comprehensive public policies of the Rainbow programme. During the 'hymie' controversy, 'the media seemed almost relieved to be able to criticize a Black candidate in the name of defending liberal values'.[199] If the Jackson campaign develops into a viable 'second party', running its own candidates on a left social democratic programme, the media's negative coverage will certainly increase, making it difficult to reach new constituencies, especially white workers.

Another problem yet to be resolved is what I would term the 'Messiah complex' within Afro-American politics. Repeatedly within Afro-American political culture a 'Black Messiah' or 'Black Moses' has arisen, challenging the system of institutional racism, motivating thousands of Blacks to march, and inspiring a new vision of social relations. The political discourse is almost always connected with the Old Testament saga of Moses. For Afro-Americans during the Civil War, Jewish biblical history was merged with their intense commitment to achieving freedom. Slaves' songs spoke of the 'rough, rocky road' that Moses travelled. As historian Eugene D. Genovese notes, 'the image of Moses, the this-worldly leader of his people out of bondage' was central to the politics of 'deliverance'.[200] After World War I, Marcus Garvey was seen by his contemporaries as a 'Black Moses' who had precipitated 'a new era of militant Black leadership'.[201] Martin, Malcolm X, and now Jesse Jackson are seen within this Black redemptive tradition, the synthesis of spiritual salvation and temporal transformation. The weaknesses of this perspective are obvious, at least in the case of Jackson. The intense socio-economic crisis of the 1980s in Black America created the social foundations for a Black revolt against the Democratic Party; but given the lack of a socialist alternative, the revolt occurred within the Democratic Party. Jackson, long the representative of the Black entrepreneurial elite, became the conduit of the Black social revolt. History forced greatness upon Jackson. This new 'Black Moses' accepted it, and rose to the occasion, despite several detours. But until the Rainbow Coalition forms a strong but decentralized structure that is independent of PUSH and the Democratic Party, the possibility of accommodation is ever present. As writer Bill Fletcher observes, 'Regardless of how progressive Rev. Jackson may now be, no leader can be held accountable to and by the base, and no movement can realize its potential if it does not set clear goals and have a workable, realistic structure. A big danger to Rainbow politics is Jackson's freedom to make deals and set direction relatively free of discussion and exchange with the base.'[202]

Does the Jackson electoral campaign represent the first phase of the transition to a socialist movement? The specific goals of the Rainbow are to deepen and to enrich American democracy to include all the members of society who are exploited. But as Cox reminds us, 'accomplished democracy — democracy with its substance residing in the people — will be finally attained only when the democratic form has been fully impregnated with power to control the State and its economic resources. When the economic power of the State has been completely won from the bourgeois plutocracy by the great mass of people, the bourgeoisie will have, of course, been liquidated and capitalism will have come to an end.'[23] Through their practical struggles to build a viable 'second party' that may at some point break from the Democratic Party, the masses may come to recognize the unity between full democracy and social class equality: the necessity not to administer the state, but to transform capitalist society from the bottom up. This process will require political forms that will ultimately transcend the Rainbow Coalition, but the precise character of these future structures will be determined by the masses themselves, and by their expanding capacity to change their consciousness and political culture through struggle. 'All development takes place as a result of self-movement', affirms James, 'not organization or direction by external forces.'[204] The next stage in the struggle to uproot racism, gender oppression, and social class inequality, requires that Afro-Americans and other oppressed sectors begin to think of politics in a new way, and perceive that the power to transform capitalist society is already in their hands.

Notes

1 Historical Prologue: Towards a General Theory of Black Politics

1. Nicos Poulantzas, *Political Power and Social Classes*, London 1978, p. 104.

2. Ralph Miliband, *Marxism and Politics*, New York 1977, p. 6.

3. Quoted in Horace B. Davis, *Toward a Marxist Theory of Nationalism*, New York 1978, p. 4.

4. Edward L. Paynter, 'Value Premises in Race Research: The Evolution of Environmentalism', in Peter Orleans and William Russell Ellis Jr., eds., *Race, Change and Urban Society*, Beverly Hills, California 1971, p. 23.

5. Decisive in this regard were the early works of W.E.B. Du Bois, *The Negro*, New York 1915; Franz Boas, *The Mind of Primitive Man*, New York 1911; Melville J. Herskovits, 'On the relation between Negro-white mixture and standing in intelligence tests', *Pedagogical Seminary*, vol. 33, 1926, pp. 30-42; Herskovitz, *The American Negro*, New York 1930; Herskovits, *The Anthropometry of the American Negro*, New York 1930; O. Klineberg, *Race Differences*, New York 1935; E. Franklin Frazier, *The Negro Family in the United States*, Chicago 1939; and Charles S. Johnson, *The Negro in American Civilization*, New York 1930.

6. Henry Pratt Fairchild, ed., *Dictionary of Sociology*, Totowa, New Jersey 1966, p. 25.

7. Anthony Smith, *The Body*, New York 1968, p. 14.

8. Victor Perlo, *Economics of Racism USA: Roots of Black Inequality*, New York 1975, p. 4.

9. Ira Katznelson, 'Power in the Reformulation of Race Research', in Orleans and Ellis, eds., *Race, Change and Urban Society*, p. 64.

10. Oliver Cromwell Cox, *Caste, Class and Race: A Study in Social Dynamics*, New York 1970, pp. 317-322.

11. See Louis Dumont, 'Caste, racism and "stratification", reflections of a social anthropologist', *Contributions to Indian Sociology*, vol. 5, October-November 1961, pp. 21-43; Oliver C. Cox, 'Race and Caste: a distinction', *American Journal of Sociology*, vol. 50, March 1945, pp. 360-368; Gerald D. Berreman, 'Caste in India and the United States', *American Journal of Sociology*, vol. 66, September 1960, pp. 120-127; John Dollard, *Caste and Class in a Southern Town* New York 1957; Lloyd I. Rudolph and Suzanne H. Rudolph, *The Modernity of Tradition*, Chicago 1967; and Sidney Verba, Bashiruddin Ahmed and Anil Bhatt, *Caste, Race, and Politics: A Comparative Study of India and the United States*, Beverly Hills, California 1971.

12. Martin Orans, 'Caste and Race Conflict in Cross-Cultural Perspective', in Orleans and Ellis, eds., *Race, Change, and Urban Society*, pp. 116-123.

13. Bernard Makhosezwe Magubane, *The Political Economy of Race and Class in South Africa*, New York 1979, p. 4.

14. See M. I. Finley, *Ancient Slavery and Modern Ideology*, New York 1983. On race and slavery in antiquity, see also F.M. Snowden, *Blacks in Antiquity*, Cambridge, Massachusetts 1970; M.I. Finley, *The World of Odysseus*, New York 1959; M.I. Finley, ed., *Slavery in Classical Antiquity*, Cambridge 1960; and A.M. Duff, *Freedmen in the Early Roman Empire*, Cambridge 1958.

15. David Brion Davis, *The Problem of Slavery in Western Culture*, Ithaca 1966, pp. 66, 70, 94-96, 107.

16. Cox, *Caste, Class and Race*, p. 321.

17. Davis, *The Problem of Slavery in Western Culture*, p. 51.

18. 'Introduction', in Barry N. Schwartz and Robert Disch, eds., *White Racism: Its History, Pathology and Practice*, New York 1970, pp. 6-10.

19. *Ibid.*, p. 13.

20. Davis, *The Problem of Slavery in Western Culture*, pp. 96-97.

21. 'Introduction', in Schwartz and Disch, eds., *White Racism*, p. 17.

22. Magubane, *The Political Economy of Race and Class in South Africa*, p. 3.

23. Perlo, *Economics of Racism USA*, p. 5.

24. Magubane, *The Political Economy of Race and Class in South Africa*, p. 5.

25. Manning Marable, *Blackwater: Historical Studies in Race, Class Consciousness and Revolution*, Dayton, Ohio 1981, pp. 73-75.

26. Magubane, *The Political Economy of Race and Class in South Africa*, pp. 224-225.

27. Melville J. Herskovits, *The Myth of the Negro Past*, Boston 1958, p. 2.

28. Frantz Fanon, *Black Skin, White Masks*, New York 1967, pp. 110-116.

29. Social fractions within a nation may be a numerical minority, e.g., Afro-Americans in the United States, or it may be an absolute majority in one state, e.g., South Africa's African majority. Social fractions comprise more than one class, but function within the general context of class struggle. In other words, members of social fractions may speak a 'different language' from members of corresponding social classes, but the general patterns of class conflict prefigure the terms of the debate, and set the range of historical possibilities in the pursuit of power.

30. Poulantzas, *Political Power and Social Classes*, p. 113.

31. See *Ibid.*, p. 113; and Miliband, *Marxism and Politics*, p. 8.

32. Quoted in Miliband, *Marxism and Politics*, p. 8.

33. Poulantzas, *Political Power and Social Classes*, p. 118.

34. Karl Marx and Friedrich Engels, *The Communist Manifesto*, Baltimore 1967, p. 93.

35. W.E.B. Du Bois, 'A Forum of Fact and Opinion', *Pittsburgh Courier*, April 17 1937.

36. Fanon, *Black Skin, White Masks*, p. 140.

37. Jean-Paul Sartre, 'Sartre Today', translated in *Telos*, no. 9, 1971, pp. 110-116.

38. Edward Roux, *Time Longer Than Rope: A History of the Black Man's Struggle for Freedom in South Africa*, Madison 1965, p. 129.

39. E.P. Thompson, *The Poverty of Theory and Other Essays*, New York 1978, p. 171.

40. An interesting discussion of Toussaint in the light of Hegel's *Phenomenology of Mind* is found in David Brion Davis, *The Problem of Slavery in the Age of Revolution, 1770-1823*, Ithaca, New York 1975, pp. 557-564.

41. See Sterling Stuckey, 'Remembering Denmark Vesey', *Negro Digest*, vol. 15, February 1966, pp. 28-41; William W. Freehling, *Prelude to Civil War: The Nullification Controversy in South Carolina, 1816-1836*, New York 1968, pp. 43-65; Robert S. Starobin, *Denmark Vesey: The Slave Conspiracy of 1822*, Englewood

Cliffs, New Jersey 1970 and John Oliver Killens, ed., *The Trial Records of Denmark Vesey*, Boston 1970.

42. Studies of Black slave rebelliousness in Jamaica include: Orlando Patterson, *The Sociology of Slavery*, London 1967; B.W. Higman, *Slave Population and Economy in Jamaica, 1807-1834*, Cambridge 1976; Mavis C. Campbell, *The Dynamics of Change in a Slave Society*, Rutherford, New Jersey 1976; and Michael Craton, *Searching for the Invisible Man: Slaves and Plantation Life in Jamaica*, Cambridge, Massachusetts 1978.

43. C.L.R. James, *The Future in the Present: Selected Writings*, Westport, Connecticut 1980, pp. 265-268; and James, *Spheres of Existence*, Westport, Connecticut 1980, p. 182.

44. Gilberto Freyre, *The Masters and the Slaves: A Study in the Development of Brazilian Civilization*, New York 1971, pp. xivi, 330, 351, 353.

45. As David Brion Davis observes, 'under the Hammurabi Code, a man who killed someone else's slave was merely required to pay compensation to the owner . . . A master might kill his slave with impunity, however, in Homeric Greece, ancient India, the Roman Republic, Saxon England, Kievan Russia, and, under certain circumstances, in China of the Former Han period. The Pali canon, Tipitaka, provided no redress for a bondswoman who, forced to sleep with her master, had her nose and ears cut off by his jealous wife . . . Rome was notorious for ghastly atrocities; Vedius Pollio, for example, was said to have fed the meat of slaves to his pet fish.' Davis, *The Problem of Slavery in Western Culture*, pp. 60-61.

46. Vincent Harding, *The Other American Revolution*, Los Angeles 1980, p. 39. Lenin makes the crucial observation: 'An oppressed class that does not strive to learn to use arms, to acquire arms, only deserves to be treated like slaves. We cannot forget . . . that we are living in a class society, that there is no way out of this society, and there can be none, except by means of the class struggle. In every class society, whether it is based on slavery, serfdom, or as at present, on wage labour, the oppressing class is armed . . . any army which does not train to use all the weapons, all the means and methods of warfare that an enemy possesses . . . [behaves] in an unwise or even criminal manner.' V.I. Lenin, ' "Left-wing" Communism: An Infantile Disorder', published in Lenin, *On the Dictatorship of the Proletariat*, Moscow 1976, p. 303.

47. Immanuel Wallerstein, 'Capitalism and the World Working Class: Some Premisses and Some Issues for Research and Analysis', in Wallerstein, ed., *Labor in the World Social Structure*, Beverly Hills, California 1983, p. 19.

48. Cox, *Caste, Class and Race*, pp. 344-345.

49. Nikolai Bukharin, *Historical Materialism: A System of Sociology*, Ann Arbor 1969, p. 301.

50. Frances Fox Piven and Richard Cloward, *Poor People's Movements*, New York 1979, pp. 4-5.

51. Clayborne Carson, *In Struggle: SNCC and the Black Awakening of the 1960s*, Cambridge, Massachusetts 1981, p. 9.

52. Angela Y. Davis, *Women, Race and Class*, New York 1981, pp. 127-148. Also see Gerda Lerner, ed., *Black Women in White America: A Documentary History*, New York 1972; and Alfreda M. Duster, ed., *Crusade for Justice: The Autobiography of Ida B. Wells*, Chicago 1970.

53. Walter Rodney, *A History of the Guyanese Working People, 1881-1905*, Baltimore 1981, pp. 190-192.

54. William H. Harris, *The Harder We Run: Black Workers since the Civil War*, New York 1982, p. 78.

Other sources on the Brotherhood of Sleeping-Car Porters includes: William H. Harris, *Keeping the Faith: A. Philip Randolph, Milton P. Webster, and the Brotherhood of Sleeping-Car Porters, 1925-37*, Urbana 1977; Brailsford R. Brazeal, *The Brotherhood of Sleeping-Car Porters: Its Origins and Development*, New York 1946; and Bernard Mergen, 'The Pullman Porter: From George to Brotherhood', *South Atlantic Quarterly*, vol. 73, Spring 1974, pp. 224-235.

55. Florestan Fernandes, *The Negro in Brazilian Society*, New York 1969, pp. 177, 183, 187.

56. Brian Bunting, *The Rise of the South African Reich*, Baltimore 1969, pp. 158-164.

57. Carson, *In Struggle*, pp. 9, 11. On the 'sit-in' movement, also see Ruth Searles and J. Allen Williams Jr., 'Negro College Students' Participation in Sit-ins', *Social Forces*, vol. 40, March 1962, pp. 215–220; and Charles U. Smith, 'The Sit-Ins and the New Negro Student', *Journal of Intergroup Relations*, vol. 2, Summer 1961, pp. 223–229.

58. Fernandes, *The Negro in Brazilian Society*, pp. 200-201. Other recent studies on racial oppression in Brazil include: Abdias do Nascimento, *Mixture or Massacre: Essays in the Genocide of a Black People*, Buffalo, New York 1979; Anani Dzidzienyo, *The Position of Blacks in Brazilian Society*, London 1971; Thomas E. Skidmore, *Black into White*, New York 1974; and Elisa Larkin Nascimento, *Pan-Africanism and South America: Emergence of a Black Rebellion*, Buffalo, New York 1980.

59. Albert Luthuli, *Let My People Go*, New York 1962, pp. 116-117.

60. Carson, *In Struggle*, pp. 11, 13.

61. Harding, *The Other American Revolution*, pp. 157-159.

62. Carson, *In Struggle*, p. 64.

63. *Ibid.*, p. 12.

64. August Meier and Elliott Rudwick, CORE: *A Study in the Civil Rights Movement, 1942-1968*, New York 1973, pp. 102, 111, 112.

65. Fernandes, *The Negro in Brazilian Society*, pp. 196, 211-212. The *Frente Negra* was outlawed by the government in 1937. Subsequently it became the *União Negra Brasileira*.

66. Rodney, *A History of the Guyanese Working People, 1881-1905*, pp. 201, 105.

67. *Ibid.*, pp. 193, 207.

68. Magubane, *The Political Economy of Race and Class in South Africa*, p. 306.

69. Cherri D. Waters, 'Black Women and Social Change: Proceedings of Trans-Africa Forum Seminar', *TransAfrica Forum*, vol. 2, Summer 1983, p. 35.

70. Amilcar Cabral, *Unity and Struggle: Speeches and Writings*, New York 1979, pp. 134-137. 'The revolutionary petty bourgeoisie must be capable of committing *suicide* as a class, to be restored to life in the condition of a revolutionary worker completely identified with the deepest aspirations of the people to which he belongs.' (p. 136).

71. Rodney, *A History of the Guyanese Working People, 1881-1905*, pp. 203-204.

72. Davis, *Women, Race and Class*, pp. 129, 131-132, 135.

73. Carson, *In Struggle*, pp. 21, 25, 42, 69-70.

74. Bureau of the Census, *The Social and Economic Status of the Black Population in the United States: An Historical View, 1790-1978*, Washington DC 1980, pp. 90, 93.

75. Harris, *The Harder We Run*, pp. 79, 81, 83; and Manning Marable, 'A. Philip Randolph and the Foundations of Black American Socialism', in James Green, ed., *Workers' Struggles, Past and Present*, Philadelphia 1983, p. 222.

76. Carson, *In Struggle*, pp. 32, 67, 105, 134, 202-204, 229, 239, 251.

310

77. Allan G.B. Fisher and Humphrey J. Fisher, *Slavery and Muslim Society in Africa: The Institution in Saharan and Sudanic Africa and the Trans-Saharan Trade*, Garden City, New York 1971, pp. 107-108.

78. Walter Rodney, *How Europe Underdeveloped Africa*, London 1972, pp. 90-91.

79. *Ibid.*, p. 91; and Basil Davidson, *A History of West Africa*, Garden City, New York 1966, p. 297.

80. Chinweizu, *The West and the Rest of Us: White Predators, Black Slavers and the Africa Elite*, New York 1975, p. 50.

81. Robin Hallett, *Africa Since 1875, A Modern History*, Ann Arbor 1974, p. 281.

82. N.E. Davis, *A History of Southern Africa*, Essex, England 1978, pp. 65-66.

83. Davis, *The Problem of Slavery in Western Culture*, p. 161.

84. See Claude Levy, 'Slavery and the Emancipation Movement in Barbados, 1650-1833', *Journal of Negro History*, vol. 55, January 1970, pp. 1-14.

85. John Hope Franklin, *From Slavery to Freedom: A History of Negro Americans*, third edition, New York 1969, p. 68.

86. 'Confession', in Herbert Aptheker, *Nat Turner's Slave Rebellion*, New York 1968, p. 138.

87. The fiery symbol of Nat Turner lives on among radical Blacks. Writer John Oliver Killens noted in 1968: 'Nat Turner, in the tradition of most Black Americans, was a man of tragedy, a giant . . . Every Black American, then and now, is a potential Nat Turner.' For political scientist Charles V. Hamilton, 'Nat Turner is our hero, unequivocally understood. He is a man who had profound respect and love for his fellow Blacks and who respected Black womanhood and held utter contempt for those white slave-masters who violated the purity and beauty of our Black women. Nat Turner *was a success* because he perpetuated the idea of freedom — freedom at all cost.' See John Henrik Clarke, ed., *William Styron's Nat Turner: Ten Black Writers Respond*, Boston 1968, pp. 34-37, 78; and John B. Duff and Peter M. Mitchell, eds., *The Nat Turner Rebellion: The Historical Event and the Modern Controversy*, New York 1971. Other historical studies of the Nat Turner revolt include: Frank R. Johnson, *The Nat Turner Slave Insurrection*, Murfreesboro, North Carolina 1966; Eric Foner, *Nat Turner*, Englewood Cliffs, New Jersey 1971; Henry I. Trangle, *The Southampton Slave Revolt of 1831*, Amherst 1971; and Stephen B. Oates, *The Fires of Jubilee: Nat Turner's Fierce Rebellion*, New York 1975.

88. Vincent Harding, *There is a River: The Black Struggle for Freedom in America*, New York 1981, pp. 104-192. There are about one dozen biographies of Douglass, including Benjamin Quarles, *Frederick Douglass*, Englewood Cliffs, New Jersey 1968; Nathan I. Huggins, *Slave and Citizen: The Life of Frederick Douglass*, Boston 1980; Philip S. Foner, *The Life and Writings of Frederick Douglass*, New York 1950; and Dickson J. Preston, *Young Frederick Douglass: The Maryland Years*, Baltimore 1980. Studies by or about Delany include: his famous 1851 manifesto, *The Condition, Elevation, Emigration, and Destiny of the Colored People of the United States*, New York 1968; Delany, *Blake: Or, The Huts of America*, Boston 1970; Cyril E. Griffith, *The African Dream: Martin R. Delany and the Emergence of Pan-African Thought*, University Park 1975; and Victor Velman, *Martin R. Delany: The Beginnings of Black Nationalism*, Boston 1971. General works on Black abolitionism in the US include: Jane H. Pease and William H. Pease, *They Who Would Be Free: Blacks' Search for Freedom, 1830-1861*, New York 1974; Benjamin Quarles, *Black Abolitionists*, New York 1969; and Sterling Stuckey, ed. *The Theological Origins of Black Nationalism*, Boston 1972. Important recent essays on major Black abolitionists include: Richard Blackett, 'Martin R. Delany and Robert Campbell: Black

Americans in Search of an African Colony', *Journal of Negro History*, vol. 62, January 1977, pp. 1–25; Robert L. Harris Jr, 'H. Ford Douglas: Afro-American Antislavery Emigrationist', *Journal of Negro History*, vol. 62 July 1977, pp. 217–234; Les Wallace, 'Charles Lenox Remond; Abolitionist', *Negro History Bulletin*, vol. 40; May-June 1977, pp. 696-701; and Robert P. Smith, 'William Cooper Nell: Crusading Black Abolitionist', *Journal of Negro History*, vol. 55, July 1970, pp. 182-199.

89. E. Bradford Burns, *A History of Brazil*, New York 1970, p. 189. Also see Robert Conrad, *The Destruction of Brazilian Slavery, 1850–1888*, Berkeley 1972; Joaquim Nabuco, *Abolitionism: The Brazilian Antislavery Struggle*, Urbana 1977; Robert B. Toplin, *Freedom and Prejudice: The Legacy of Slavery in the United States and Brazil*, Westport, Connecticut 1981; and James Kennedy, 'Luiz Gama: Pioneer of Abolition in Brazil', *Journal of Negro History*, vol. 59, July 1974, pp. 255–267.

90. Gabriel Debien, 'Maroonage in the French Caribbean', in Richard Price, ed., *Maroon Societies: Rebel Slave Communities in the Americas*, Baltimore 1979, p. 108.

91. Herbert Aptheker, 'Maroons Within the Present Limits of the United States', in *Ibid.*, p. 159.

92. August Meier, *Negro Thought in America, 1880-1915: Racial Ideologies in the Age of Booker T. Washington*, Ann Arbor, Michigan 1963, pp. 147-148.

93. Arthur A. Anderson, 'Prophetic Liberator of the Coloured Race', in John H. Bracey Jr, August Meier and Elliott Rudwick, eds., *Black Nationalism in America*, Indianapolis 1970, pp. 177-187.

94. C. Eric Lincoln, *The Black Muslims in America*, Boston 1961, p. 95. On the development of all-Black communities in the United States after 1865, see John G. Van Deusen, 'The Exodus of 1879', *Journal of Negro History*, vol. 21, April 1936, pp. 111-129; Mozell Hill, 'The All-Negro Communities of Oklahoma: The Natural History of a Social Movement', *Journal of Negro History*, vol. 31, July 1946, pp. 254-268; William Bittle and Gilbert Geis, 'Racial Self-fulfilment and the Rise of an All-Negro Community in Oklahoma', *Phylon*, vol. 17, Third Quarter 1957, pp. 247-260; August Meier, 'Booker T. Washington and the Town of Mound Bayou', *Phylon*, vol. 15, Fourth Quarter 1954, pp. 396-401; and Joseph Taylor, 'The Rise and Decline of a Utopian Community, Boley, Oklahoma', *Negro History Bulletin*, vol. 3, April 1940, pp. 105-106.

95. On the Republic of New Africa, see Imari A. Obadele, 'The Struggle is for Land', *Black Scholar*, vol. 3, February 1972, pp. 24-36; Obadele, 'The Struggle of the Republic of New Africa', *Black Scholar*, vol. 5, June 1974, pp. 32-41; Obadele, 'National Black Elections Held by Republic of New Africa', *Black Scholar*, vol. 6, October 1975, pp. 27-30; Obadele, 'People's Revolt Against Poverty', *Black Scholar*, vol. 9, May-June 1978, pp. 35-39; and Chokwe Lumumba, 'Short History of the US War on the RNA', *Black Scholar*, vol. 12, January-February 1981, pp. 72-81.

96. Herbert Aptheker, ed., *A Documentary History of the Negro People in the United States: From the Reconstruction Years to the Founding of the NAACP in 1910*, Secaucus, New Jersey 1972, vol. 2, pp. 805–806.

97. Burns, *A History of Brazil*, pp. 364–365, 371.

98. Hallett, *Africa Since 1875*, p. 529.

99. August Meier and Elliott Rudwick, *From Plantation to Ghetto*, New York 1976, p. 297. General biographies and political critiques of Martin Luther King Jr, include: Lerone Bennett, *What Manner of Man: A Biography of Martin Luther King Jr*, Chicago 1964; David L. Lewis, *King: A Critical Biuography*, New York 1970; Lionel Lokos, *House Divided: The Life and Legacy of Martin Luther King*, New Rochelle, New York 1968: James Alonzo Bishop, *The Days of Martin Luther King Jr.*, New York 1971; Laurence Dunbar Reddick, *Crusader Without Violence: A*

312

Biography of Martin Luther King Jr, New York 1959; and Lee Augustus McGriggs, *The Odyssey of Martin Luther King Jr*, Washington DC 1978. Essays that examine the role of Black churches in the Civil Rights movement of the 1950s–1960s include: C. A. Green, 'The Negro Church: A Power Institution', *Negro History Bulletin*, vol. 26, October 1962, pp. 20–22; and Gary T. Marx, 'Religion: Opiate or Inspiration of Civil Rights Militancy Among Negroes?', *American Journal of Sociology*, vol. 32, February 1967, pp. 64-72.

100. Philip S. Foner, *Organized Labor and the Black Worker, 1619-1981*, New York 1981, p. 22.

101. *Ibid*, p. 49.

102. There are numerous studies that document the political evolution of the Afro-American working class. Some classic contributions to the field are: Ira De A. Reid, *Negro Membership in American Labor Unions*, New York 1969; Sterling D. Spero and Abram L. Harris, *The Black Worker: The Negro and the Labor Movement*, New York 1931; Charles H. Wesley, *Negro Labor in the United States*, New York 1927; Lorenzo H. Greene and Carter G. Woodson, *The Negro Wage Earner*, Washington DC 1930; and Horace R. Cayton and George S. Mitchell, *Black Workers and the New Unions*, Chapel Hill 1939. Other more recent studies include: Ray Marshall, *The Negro and Organized Labor*, New York 1965; Benjamin Wolkinson, *Blacks, Unions and the EEOC*, Lexington, Kentucky 1973; and William B. Gould, *Black Workers in White Unions: Job Discrimination in the United States*, Ithaca 1977. Articles on the early organizing experiences of Black labour include: Herman D. Bloch, 'Labor and the Negro, 1866-1910', *Journal of Negro History*, vol. 50, July 1965, pp. 163-184; Sumner Eliot Matison, 'The Labor Movement and the Negro during Reconstruction', *Journal of Negro History*, vol. 33, October 1948, pp. 426-468; Sidney Kessler, 'The Organization of Negroes in the Knights of Labor', *Journal of Negro History*, vol. 38, July 1952, pp. 248-276; and Philip S. Foner, 'The IWW and the Black Worker', *Journal of Negro History*, vol. 60, January 1970, pp. 45-64.

103. Allen Isaacman and Barbara Isaacman, *Mozambique: From Colonialism to Revolution, 1900-1982*, Boulder, Colorado 1983, pp. 69-70.

104. Hallett, *Africa Since 1875*, p. 530.

105. George M. Frederickson, *White Supremacy: A Comparative Study in American and South African History*, New York 1981, pp. 221-222.

106. Dan Georgakas and Marvin Surkin, *Detroit: I Do Mind Dying; A Study in Urban Rebellion*, New York 1975, p. 35.

107. *Ibid.*, pp. 36-37.

108. Literature on Black radical union activism in the late 1960s includes: James A. Geschwender, *Class, Race and Worker Insurgency: The League of Revolutionary Black Workers*, Cambridge 1977; John C. Legget, *Class, Race and Labor: Working Class Consciousness in Detroit*, New York 1968; William B. Gould, 'Black Power in the Unions: The Impact Upon Collective Bargaining Relationships', *Yale Law Review*, vol. 79, November 1969, p. 46; Herbert Hill, 'Black Protest and the Struggle for Union Democracy', *Issues in Industrial Society*, vol. 1, January 1969, pp. 19-29; Orley Ashenfelter, 'Racial Discrimination and Trade Unionism', *Journal of Political Economy*, vol. 80, May-June 1972, pp. 435-464; Thomas R. Brooks, 'DRUMbeats in Detroit', *Dissent*, vol. 17, January-February 1970, pp. 16-24; Thomas R. Brooks, 'Black Upsurge in the Unions', *Dissent*, vol. 17, March-April 1970, pp. 124-134; and Ernie Allen, 'Dying From the Inside: the Decline of the League of Revolutionary Black Workers', in Dick Cluster, ed., *They Should Have Served That Cup of Coffee:*

Seven Radicals Remember the Sixties, Boston 1979, pp. 71-109.

109. See W.E.B. Du Bois, 'As the Crow Flies', *Amsterdam News*, July 3 1943 and May 27 1944; and *Behold the Land*, Birmingham, Alabama 1946.

110. Isaacman and Isaacman, *Mozambique: From Colonialism to Revolution, 1900-1982*, p. 78.

111. Rodney, *How Europe Underdeveloped Africa*, p. 299.

112. And yet Fanon was never completely accepted by the Algerian revolutionaries. As Irene L. Gendzier observes, Algerian officials were attempting to 'de-Fanonize Algeria' and to 'de-Algerianize Fanon'. The Black radical was, after all, a foreigner. Some suggested ten years after his death that 'he helped with our cause; [but] he was not one of us'. When Dr Mohammed el Mili, writer and Director of the Algerian Ministry of Information and Culture, was asked to select the most significant 'theoretician of the Algerian Revolution', he replied that Fanon 'would have been the man', *if* he 'had been an Algerian'. See Irene L. Gendzier, *Frantz Fanon: A Critical Study*, New York 1973, pp. 244, 247. Other studies on Fanon include: Robert C. Smith, 'Fanon and the Concept of Colonial Violence', *Black World*, vol. 22, May 1973, pp. 23–33; M. Frank Wright, 'Frantz Fanon: His Work in Historical Perspective', *Black Scholar*, vol. 6, July-August 1975, pp. 19-29; Chester J. Fontenot, *Franz Fanon*, Lincoln 1979; David Caute, *Frantz Fanon*, New York 1970; and Peter Geismar, *Fanon: The Revolutitnary as Prophet*, New York 1971.

113. Gerald W. Mullin, *Flight and Rebellion: Slave Resistance in Eighteenth-Century Virginia*, New York 1972, pp. 110-113.

114. Many studies of the Communist Party published in the US retain an anti-Marxist bias, which must be taken into account in any review of the literature. Besides those of Angela Davis, the political writings of Black Communists Henry Winston, James E. Jackson, Claude M. Lightfoot and Hosea Hudson provide an overview of the Party's approach to issues of race and class. See Henry Winston, *Strategy for a Black Agenda*, New York 1971; Winston, 'Reagan's Election, the Black Vote and the Struggle for Equality', *Political Affairs*, vol. 60, February 1981, pp. 1-6; James E. Jackson, *Revolutionary Tracings in World Politics and Black Liberation*, New York 1974; Jackson, 'CPSU Congress Highlights Peace Now', *Political Affairs*, vol. 60, April 1981, pp. 4-9; Claude M. Lightfoot, *Ghetto Rebellion to Black Liberation*, New York 1968; and Hosea Hudson, *Black Worker in the Deep South, A Personal Record*, New York 1972. See also Nell Irvin Painter, *The Narrative of Hosea Hudson: His Life as a Negro Communist in the South*, Cambridge, Massachuetts 1979. Books to avoid are Wilson Record, *The Negro and the Communist Party*, Chapel Hill 1951, and William Nolan, *Communism Versus the Negro*, Chicago 1951.

115. On John Brown, see W.E.B. Du Bois, *John Brown*, New York 1962; Herbert Aptheker, *John Brown: American Martyr*, New York 1960; and Stuart Knee, 'John Brown and the Abolitionist Ministry', *Negro History Bulletin*, vol. 45, April-June 1982, pp. 36-37.

116. Bridget Brereton, *A History of Modern Trinidad, 1783-1962*, London 1981, pp. 167, 169. Also see W. Knowles, *Trade-Union Development and Industrial Relations in the British West Indies*, Berkeley 1959.

117. Sheila Rowbotham, *Woman's Consciousness, Man's World*, New York 1973, p. 117.

118. Manning Marable, *How Capitalism Underdeveloped Black America: Problems in Race, Political Economy and Society*, Boston 1983, pp. 9-10.

119. Rowbotham, *Woman's Consciousness, Man's World*, p. 35.

120. Bettina Aptheker, *Woman's Legacy: Essays on Race, Sex and Class in American History*, Amherst 1982, p. 87.

121. Angela Y. Davis, *Women, Race and Class*, New York 1981, pp. 6, 7, 17-18, 23.

122. In March, 1978, the median number of years of school completed by American white women in the US civilian labour force was 12.6, compared with 12.4 for Black women. However, for professional and managerial positions, Black women averaged 16.0 years of training as against 15.7 years for white women. About 4 per cent of all white women workers are managers, compared with 1.5 per cent of all Black women workers. One seventh of Black women are private household workers, compared with only 2.1 per cent of white women. Almost a quarter of all Black women are service workers, labourers of operatives. See Phyllis A. Wallace, *Black Women in the Labor Force*, Cambridge, Massachusetts 1980, pp. 112, 123.

123. Joyce A. Ladner, *Tomorrow's Tomorrow: The Black Woman*, Garden City, New York 1971, pp. 276-277.

124. Judith Resnik and Nancy Shaw, 'Prisoners of Their Sex: Health Problems of Incarcerated Women', in Ira P. Robbins, ed., *Prisoners' Rights Sourcebook, Volume II*, New York 1980, pp. 319-413.

125. Lynora Williams, 'Violence Against Women', *Black Scholar*, vol. 12, January-February 1981, pp. 18-24.

126. Davis, *Women, Race and Class* pp. 115-118. Davis notes that Afro-American women were betrayed at every turn, 'spurned and rejected by the leaders of the lily-white women suffrage movement. For suffragists and clubwomen alike, Black women were simply expendable entities when it came time to woo Southern support with a white complexion.' (p. 148). A similarly racist dynamic occurred in South Africa. The racist Hertzog government, looking for a means to 'reduce the importance of non-European vote in the Cape' during the late 1920s, advocated women suffrage. As Pierre L. van den Berghe observes, white supremacy and the white woman's right to vote were part of a single plan: 'The Women Enfranchisement Act of 1930 extended voting rights to white women only, and thereby reduced by half the relative weight of the non-white vote; the Franchise Laws Amendment Act of 1931 waived the property, income, and education qualifications for white voters but not for non-whites; finally, the Native Representation Act of 1936 eliminated Africans from the common electoral roll in the Cape . . . ' See van den Berghe, *South Africa: A Study in Conflict*, Berkeley 1970, p. 126.

127. C. Eric Lincoln, *The Black Muslims in America*, Boston 1961, pp. 51, 55, 82, 128.

128. Malcolm X, *The Autobiography of Malcolm X*, New York 1965, pp. 294-295.

129. Philip S. Foner, ed., *The Black Panthers Speak*, Philadelphia 1970, pp. 25-26, 58–59.

130. Georgakas and Surkin, *Detroit: I Do Mind Dying*, pp. 84, 170-171.

131. See Friedrich Engels, *The Origin of the Family, Private Property and the State*, New York 1972. See also David McLellan, *Friedrich Engels*, New York 1977, pp. 47-54.

132. Barbara Christian, *Black Women Novelists: The Development of a Tradition, 1892-1976*, Westport, Connecticut 1980, p. 219.

133. There is a substantial and growing corpus of historical studies on the role of Afro-American women in the freedom struggle in the US. Sources concerning Black women abolitionists, intellectuals and their organizations during the eighteenth and nineteenth centuries include: Debra Newman, 'Black Women in the Era of the

American Revolution in Pennsylvania', *Journal of Negro History*, vol. 61, July 1976, pp. 276-289; Charles W. Akers, ' "Our Modern Egyptians": Phyllis Wheatly and the Whig Campaign Against Slavery', *Journal of Negro History*, vol. 60, July 1975, pp. 397-410; Gerda Lerner, 'Early Community Work of Black Club Women', *Journal of Negro History*, vol. 59, April 1974, pp. 158-167; Janice Sumler-Lewis, 'The Forten-Purvis Women of Philadelphia and the American Antislavery Crusade', *Journal of Negro History*, vol. 66, Winter 1981-1982, pp. 281-289; John E. Fleming, 'Slavery, Civil War and Reconstruction: Black Women in Microcosm', *Negro History Bulletin*, vol. 38, August-September 1975, pp. 430-433; Dorothy Sterling, *Black Foremothers: Three Lives*, Old Westbury, New York 1979; Gerda Lerner, ed., *Black Women in White America: A Documentary History*, New York 1972; Johnnetta Cole, 'Militant Black Women in Early US History', *Black Scholar*, vol. 9, April 1978, pp. 38-44; Marie Harlow, 'Sojourner Truth: The First Sit-In', *Negro History Bulletin*, vol. 29, Fall 1966, pp. 173-174; E. Jay Ritter, 'Sojourner Truth', *Negro History Bulletin*, vol. 26, May 1963, p. 254; August Strong, 'Negro Women in Freedom's History Battles', *Freedomways*, vol. 7, Fall 1967, pp. 302-315; Arthur H. Fausett, *Sojourner Truth*, New York 1971; Hertha E. Pauli, *Her Name Was Sojourner Truth*, New York 1962; and Bert James Loewenberg and Ruth Bogin, eds., *Black Women in Nineteenth-Century American Life*, University Park 1976.

134. Mary McLeod Bethune, Mary Church Terrell and Ida B. Wells were central figures in the civil-rights struggles during the Jim Crow period. Studies by and about these leaders include: Mary McLeod Bethune, 'Clarifying Our Vision with the Facts', *Journal of Negro History*, vol. 23, January 1938, pp. 12-15; Rackham Holt, *Mary McLeod Bethune: A Biography*, New York 1964; C.O. Pearce, *Mary McLeod Bethune*, New York 1951; B. Joyce Ross, 'Mary McLeod Bethune and the National Youth Administration', *Journal of Negro History*, vol. 60, January 1975, pp. 1-28; Ida B. Wells-Barnett, *On Lynching*, New York 1969; David M. Tucker, 'Ida B. Wells and Memphis Lynching', *Phylon*, vol. 32, Summer 1971, pp. 112-122; Mary Church Terrell, *A Colored Woman in a White World*, Washington DC 1940; and Gladys B. Sheppard, *Mary Church Terrell*, Baltimore 1959.

135. Foner, *Organized Labor and the Black Worker*, pp. 231, 261, 296, 389, 390.

136. Meier and Rudwick, *Core*, pp. 225, 247, 393, 406–407.

137. *Ibid.*, pp. 153, 205, 250.

138. *Ibid.*, pp. 380, 412. McKissick also had a pronounced tendency towards mixing Black nationalism with fascism. Demanding that CORE centralize its political authority, he noted that Marcus Garvey 'was not a democratic leader, in fact, he was a dictator. He had ritual, discipline, and benefits for the membership . . . We need to study his style.' (p. 422). Not surprisingly, McKissick eventually became a leading proponent of Black Capitalism in the early 1970s, and in 1972 'had tactfully moved toward the Nixon Administration and begun to support the Republican Party'. See Marable, *Blackwater*, pp. 98. 101.

139. Gendzier, *Frantz Fanon*, p. 259. The inability to transform the traditional oppression of women during the early post-revolutionary period was only one indicator of the directions of the Algerian revolution. One might argue that the transition to socialism under Boumedienne was registering material benefits to women. But the political composition of the regime and the state bureaucracy are dominated almost exclusively by men. The Algerian constitution mandates Islam as the state religion, and thereby provides the ideological basis for retarding the social and political liberation of women. See B. Etienne, *L'Algérie: Cultures and Revolution*, Paris 1977; I. Clegg, *Workers' Self-Management in Algeria*, London 1971; Hugh Roberts, 'The Algerian Bureaucracy', *Review of African Political Economy*, 24

316

May-August 1982, pp. 39-54; and David C. Gordon, *Women of Algeria*, Cambridge, bridge, Massachusetts 1968.

140. Le Roi Jones, *Home: Social Essays*, New York 1966, p. 216; and Eldridge Cleaver, *Soul on Ice*, New York 1968, pp. 102-110.

141. Linda C. Powell, 'Black Macho and Black Feminism', in Barbara Smith, ed., *Home Girls: A Black Feminist Anthology*, New York 1983, p. 287.

142. Gloria Anzaldúa, 'Speaking in Tongues: A Letter to 3rd World Women Writers', in Cherrie Moraga and Gloria Anzaldúa, eds., *This Bridge Called My Back: Writings by Radical Women of Color*, New York 1983, p. 165. Works by and about Afro-American lesbians include: Audre Lorde, 'Scratching the Surface: Some Notes on Barriers to Women and Loving', *Black Scholar*, vol. 13, Summer 1982, pp. 20-24; Lorraine Bethel and Barbara Smith, eds., *Conditions 5: The Black Women's Issue*, Autumn 1979; Joan Gibbs and Sara Bennett, eds., *Top Ranking: A Collection of Articles on Racism and Classism in the Lesbian Community*, Brooklyn, New York 1980; Audre Lorde, *Uses of the Erotic: The Erotic as Power*, Brooklyn, New York 1978; J. R. Roberts, *The Black Lesbian Bibliography*, Tallahassee, Florida 1981; and Anita Cornwell, *Black Lesbian in White America*, Tallahassee, Florida 1983.

143. Literature about Black feminism includes:Michele Wallace, 'A Black Feminist's Search for Sisterhood', *Village Voice*, 28 July 1975, pp. 6-7; Michele Wallace, *Black Macho and the Myth of the Superwoman*, New York 1979; Bell Hooks, *Ain't I A Woman: Black Women and Feminism*, Boston 1981; Gloria T. Hull, Patricia Bell Scott and Barbara Smith, eds., *All the Women are White, All the Blacks are Men, But Some of Us are Brave: Black Women's Studies*, Old Westbury, New York 1982; Elizabeth F. Hood, 'Black Women, White Women: Separate Paths to Liberation', *Black Scholar*, vol. 14, September-October 1983, pp. 26-37; Pat Crutchfield Exum, *Keeping the Faith: Writings of Contemporary Black American Women*, Greenwich, Connecticut 1974; Linda LaRue, 'The Black Movement and Women's Liberation', *Black Scholar*, vol. 1, May 1970, pp. 36-42; Ann Allen Shockley, 'The New Black Feminists', *Northwest Journal of African and Black American Studies*, vol. 2, Winter 1974, pp. 1-5; Sharon Harley and Rosalyn Terborg-Penn, *The Afro-American Woman*, New York 1978; Gloria I. Joseph and Jill Lewis, *Common Differences*, Garden City, New York 1981; Frances S. Foster, 'Changing Concepts of the Black Woman', *Journal of Black Studies*, vol. 3, June 1973, pp. 433-454; Delindus R. Brown and Wanda F. Anderson, 'A Survey of the Black Woman and the Persuasion Process: The Study of Strategies of Identification and Resistance', *Journal of Black Studies*, vol. 9, December 1978, pp. 233-248; Inez Reid, *Together Black Women*, New York 1972; and E. Frances White, 'Listening to the Voices of Black Feminism', *Radical America*, vol. 18, March-June 1984, pp. 7-25. The most prominent Black feminist who is also a Marxist is Angela Davis. Works about Davis include: Regina Nadelson, *Who is Angela Davis?*, New York 1972; Reginald Major, *Justice in the Round: The Trial of Angela Davis*, New York 1976; Bettina Aptheker, ed., *The Morning Breaks: The Trial of Angela Davis*, New York 1975; J.A. Parker, *Angela Davis: The Making of a Revolutionary*, New York 1973; Blythe Finke, *Angela Davis: Traitor or Martyr of the Freedom of Expression*, Charlottesville, New York 1972; Sid Cassese, 'Angela Davis — Ten Years Later', *Essence*, vol. 12, April 1981, pp. 60-61; and Cecil Williams, 'A Conversation with Angela', *Black Scholar*, vol. 3, March-April 1972, pp. 36-48.

144. John E'Emilio, *Sexual Politics, Sexual Communities: The Making of a Homosexual Minority in the United States, 1940-1970*, Chicago 1983, p. 172.

145. Zoila Ellis and Cynthia Ellis Higinio, 'Women in the Home — Why Not in

the House?', and 'On-the-Job Sexual Harassment', in *Disweek*, 29 June 1984 and 13 July 1984.

146. Errol Lawrence, 'In the abundance of water and the fool is thirsty: sociology and black "pathology"', in Centre for Contemporary Cultural Studies, ed., *The Empire Strikes Back: Race and Racism in 70s Britain* London 1982, pp. 95-142.

147. Hazel V. Carby, 'White women listen! Black feminism and the boundaries of sisterhood', in *Ibid.*, pp. 214, 231-232.

148. See Nelson Peery, *The Negro National Colonial Question*, Chicago 1974, pp. 133-158.

149. Robert L. Allen, *Black Awakening in Capitalist America: An Analytic History*, Garden City, New York 1970, pp. 102-103.

150. See Harry Haywood, *Black Bolshevik: The Autobiography of an Afro-American Communist*, Chicago 1978.

151. Jackson, *Revolutionary Tracings*, pp. 216-245.

152. See George Breitman, ed., *Leon Trotsky on Black Nationalism and Self-Determination*, New York 1967.

153. Trotskyist critiques on the Black movement in the US are represented by: 'The Fight for Black Liberation: The Current Stage and Its Tasks', in Jack Barnes et al., eds., *Prospects for Socialism in America*, New York 1976, pp. 170-204; Tony Thomas, *In Defense of Black Nationalism*, New York 1971; Derrick Morrison, 'The Combined Character of the Coming American Revolution', Tony Thomas, 'Leninism, Stalinism, and Black Liberation', and Maxine Williams, 'Why Women's Liberation is Important to Black Women', all in Tony Thomas, ed., *Black Liberation and Socialism*, New York 1974; and Cathy Sedwick and Reba William, 'Black Women and the Equal Rights Amendment', *Black Scholar*, vol. 7, July-August 1976, pp. 24-29.

154. Cox, *Caste, Class and Race*, p. 402.

155. Davis, *Toward a Marxist Theory of Nationalism*, pp. 8-9.

156. *Ibid.*, p. 7.

157. *Ibid.*, pp. 3-31, 41-42. Davis argues that the Left cannot take a 'position' on nationalism, 'for or against. One does not take a position for or against a hammer, or a can-opener, or any other implement. When used for murder, the hammer is no doubt a weapon; when used for building a house, it is a constructive tool.' (p. 31).

158. Cox, *Caste, Class and Race*, pp. 374, 376.

159. V.I. Lenin, 'Report of the Commission on the National and the Colonial Questions', (delivered at the Second Congress of the Communist International, July 26 1920), in Institute of Marxism–Leninism, ed., *Lenin: Selected Works*, Moscow 1977, pp. 596-597.

160. Davis, *Toward a Marxist Theory of Nationalism*, pp. 239, 241.

161. James, *Spheres of Existence*, p. 177.

162. See Johnnetta Cole, 'Afro-American Solidarity with Cuba', *Black Scholar*, vol. 8, Summer 1977, pp. 73-75.

163. Eugene D. Genovese, *Roll, Jordan, Roll: The World the Slaves Made*, New York 1974, pp. xv, 280.

164. W.E.B. Du Bois, *The Souls of Black Folk: Essays and Sketches*, Greenwich, Connecticut 1961, pp. 16-17.

165. W.E.B. Du Bois, *Dusk of Dawn: An Essay Toward an Autobiography of a Race Concept*, New York 1968, p. 305. Nothing illustrates the difficulties in determining whether Afro-Americans are or are not a nation better than the ambiguity of W.E.B. Du Bois. Du Bois usually affirmed the cultural distinctiveness of Black

America. During the late 1890s, a period of rampant race violence and political disfranchisement, and during the 1930s and 1940s, he advanced the concept of 'Negro nationhood' within the US. In his 1947 'Appeal to the World' to the United Nations, for instance, Du Bois repeatedly noted that Blacks constituted 'one of the considerable nations of the world.' But at other moments, he specifically denied that Blacks were a nation. In 1953, he even declared that Negroes 'do not even form a complete cultural unit'. See W.E.B. Du Bois, *The Conservation of Races,* Washington DC 1897; 'A Negro Nation Within the Nation', *Current History*, vol. 42, June 1935, pp. 265-270; 'As the Crow Flies', *Amsterdam News*, 10 April 1943; *An Appeal to the World: A Statement on the Denial of Human Rights to Minorities in the Case of Citizens of Negro Descent in the United States and an Appeal to the United Nations for Redress*, New York 1947; and 'One Hundred Years in the Struggle for Negro Freedom', *Freedom* [Harlem, New York], January 1953.

166. See Theodore G. Vincent, *Black Power and the Garvey Movement*, Berkeley, California 1971, pp. 74-85; and Robert A. Hill, ed., *The Marcus Garvey and Universal Negro Improvement Association Papers, Volume I*, Berkeley 1983, pp. 1xx — 1xxi.

167. W.E.B. Du Bois, 'Ireland', *Crisis*, vol. 12, August 1916, p. 167; 'England Again', *Crisis*, vol. 19, March 1920, p. 238; 'Opinion', *Crisis*, vol. 21, February 1921, p. 149.

168. Hill, ed., *The Marcus Garvey and Universal Negro Improvement Association Papers*, pp. 1xx-1xxviii, 355, 472, 501-507. British colonial officials despised Garvey, and drew parallels between the UNIA and the Irish republicans. In June, 1923, one official declared that Garvey's *Negro World* attacked Britain 'with a malignity reminiscent of the *Irish World*'. See John Henrik Clarke, ed., *Marcus Garvey and the Vision of Africa*, New York 1974, p. 426.

169. Not coincidentally, this was the same year that the Trinidad Working-men's Association and Henry Sylvester Williams's Pan-African Association were established. See Brereton, *A History of Modern Trinidad, 1783-1962*, pp. 109, 148-149.

170. Rodney, *A History of the Guyanese Working People, 1881-1905*, pp. 156-157.

171. W.E.B. Du Bois, 'The African Roots of the War', *Atlantic Monthly*, vol. 115, May 1915, pp. 707-714.

172. *New York Evening Post*, 22 September 1917.

173. W.E.B. Du Bois, 'India', *Amsterdam News*, 7 October 1931; 'Europe in India', *Amsterdam News*, 14 October 1931; and 'A Forum of Fact and Opinion', *Pittsburgh Courier*, 11 April 1936.

174. W.E.B. Du Bois (unsigned), 'Gandhi and India', *Crisis*, vol. 23, March 1922, pp. 203-207.

175. W.E.B. Du Bois, 'The Freeing of India', *Crisis*, vol. 54, October 1947, pp. 301-304, 316-317; 'The Greatest Man in the World', *Unity*, vol. 134, May-June 1948, pp. 25-26; and 'India', *Freedomways,'* vol. 5, Winter 1965, pp. 115-117.

176. Hanes Walton Jr, *The Political Philosophy of Martin Luther King Jr* Westport, Connecticut 1971, pp. 24-25.

177. Meier, *Negro Thought in America, 1880-1915*, p. 66.

178. Henry M. Turner, 'The Negro Has Not Sense Enough', in John H. Bracey Jr, August Meier and Elliott Rudwick, eds., *Black Nationalism in America*, Indianapolis 1970, pp. 172–174. On Afro-American emigrationism, see George Brown Tindall, 'The Liberian Exodus of 1878', *South Carolina Historical Magazine*, vol. 52, July 1952, pp. 133–145; Edwin S. Redkey, 'Bishop Turner's African Dream', *Journal of American History*, vol. 54, September 1967, pp. 271–290; William Bittle and Gilbert Geis, *The Longest Way Home: Chief Alfred Sam's Back to Africa Movement*,

Detroit 1964; Howard Bell. 'The Negro Emigration Movement, 1849–1854: A Phase of Negro Nationalism', *Phylon*, vol. 20, Summer 1959, pp. 132-142; Howard Bell, 'Negro Nationalism: A Factor in Emigration Projects 1858-1861, *Journal of Negro History*, vol. 47, January 1962, pp. 42-53. On nineteenth-century Black nationalism, see also: Kathleen O'Mara Wahle, 'Alexander Crummell: Black Evangelist and Pan-Negro Nationalist', *Phylon*, vol. 29, Winter 1968, pp. 388-395; August Meier, 'The Emergence of Negro Nationalism', *Midwest Journal*, vol. 4, Winter 1951-1952, pp. 96-104; a d William Toll, *The Resurgence of Race: Black Social Theory from Reconstruction to the Pan-African Conferences*, Philadelphia 1979.

179. The ideological and programmatic connections between Black nationalism in the US and Pan-Africanism are discussed in St Clair Drake, 'Negro Americans and the African Interest', in John P. Davis, ed., *American Negro Reference Book*, Englewood Cliffs, New Jersey 1965, pp. 662-705; George Shepperson, 'Notes on Negro-American Influences on the Emergence of African Nationalism', *Journal of African History*, vol. 1, 1960, pp. 299-312; and Raymond L. Hall, *Black Separatism in the United States*, Hanover, New Hampshire 1978. Recent contributions to the political and historical literature of Pan-Africanism include: Maulana Karenga, 'Which Road: Nationalism, Pan-Africanism, Socialism?', *Black Scholar*, vol. 6, October 1974, pp. 6-14; Amiri Baraka, *Afrikan Revolution*, Newark, New Jersey 1973; Amiri Baraka, ed., *African Congress*, New York 1972; Imanuel Geiss, *The Pan-African Movement*, New York 1974; Robert Chrisman and Nathan Hare, eds., *Pan-Africanism*, Indianapolis 1974; Elegna Mbuyinga, *Pan-Africanism or Neo-Colonialism?* London 1982; P.O. Esedebe, *Pan-Africanism: The Idea and Move-ment, 1776-1963*, Washington DC 1982; Max Stanford, 'The Pan-African Party', *Black Scholar*, vol. 2, February 1971, pp. 26-31; Tony Monteiro, 'The Sixth Pan-African Congress', *Freedomways*, vol. 14, 1974, pp. 295-302; George Bennett, 'Pan-Africanism', *International Journal*, vol. 18, Winter 1962-1963, pp. 91-96; and Colin Legum, *Pan-Africanism: A Short Political Guide*, New York 1962.

180. Bracey, Meier and Rudwick, eds., *Black Nationalism in America*, pp. xlii, 248.

181. Walter Rodney, 'The African Revolution', *Urgent Tasks*, no. 12, Summer 1981, p. 8.

182. John Henry Smyth, 'The African in Africa and the African in America', in Martin Kilson and Adelaide Hill, eds., *Apropros of Africa: Afro-American Leaders and the Romance of Africa*, Garden City, New York 1971, p. 67.

183. The best assessment of Blyden's political thought is provided in Hollis R. Lynch, *Edward Wilmot Blyden: Pan-Negro Patriot*, New York 1967. Also see M.Y. Frenkel, *Edward Blyden and American Nationalism*, Moscow 1972.

184. On Henry Sylvester Williams, see O.C. Mathurin, *Henry Sylvester Williams and the Origins of the Pan-African Movement*, Westport, Connecticut 1975; and James Hooker, Henry Sylvester Williams: Imperial Pan-Africanist, London 1975.

185. W.E.B. Du Bois, 'The American Negro Intelligentsia', *Présence Africaine*, vol. 5, December 1955-January 1956, pp. 34-51. Some of Du Bois's writings on the 1900, 1919, 1921, 1923 and 1945 Pan-African Congresses include: 'The American Negro at Paris', *American Monthly Review of Reviews*, vol. 23, November 1900, pp. 575-577; 'The Future of Africa', *Advocate of Peace*, vol. 81, January 1919, pp. 12-13; 'Manifesto to the World', *Nation*, vol. 113, 12 September 1921, pp. 357-358; 'A Second Journey to Pan-Africa', *New Republic*, vol. 29, 7 December 1921, pp. 39-41; 'The Negro Takes Stock', *New Republic*, vol. 37, 2 January 1924, pp. 143-145; 'The Winds of Time', *Chicago Defender*, 26 May 1945, 3 November 1945, 17 November 1945 and 24 November 1945.

186. The literature on Garvey and Garveyism is monumental. One should begin by reading what Garvey's contemporary critics had to say about him, pro and con. See W.E.B. Du Bois, 'Marcus Garvey', *Crisis*, vol. 21, December 1920, pp. 58-60, and January 1920, pp. 112-115; Du Bois, 'The Black Star Line', *Crises*, vol. 24 September 1922, pp. 210–214; Du Bois, 'The UNIA', *Crisis*, vol. 25, January 1923, pp. 120-122; Du Bois, 'Back to Africa', *Century Magazine*, vol. 105, February 1923, pp. 539-548; E. Franklin Frazier, 'Garvey: A Mass Leader', *Nation*, vol. 123, 18 August 1926, pp. 147-148; and Kelly Miller, 'After Marcus Garvey — What of the Negro?', *Contemporary Review*, vol. 131, April 1927, pp. 492-500. Garvey presents his rebuttal and his own Pan-Africanist Programme in Amy Jacques Garvey, ed., *The Philosophy and Opinions of Marcus Garvey*, New York 1969, and Amy Jacques Garvey, *Garvey and Garveyism*, New York 1970. The two major Garvey scholars are Tony Martin and Robert A. Hill. Martin's studies include: *Race First: The Ideological and Organizational Struggles of Marcus Garvey and the Universal Negro Improvement Association*, Westport, Connecticut 1976; *Literary Garveyism: Garvey, Black Arts and the Harlem Renaissance*, Dover, Massachusetts 1983; and *The Pan-African Connection: From Slavery to Garvey and Beyond*, Dover, Massachusetts: 1984. Hill is the director of the Marcus Garvey and Universal Negro Improvement Association Papers, and is currently editing a ten-volume survey of 30,000 archival documents and manuscripts, which is being published by the University of California Press. Other secondary literature on Garvey includes: Lenford Sylvester Nembhard, *Trials and Triumphs of Marcus Garvey*, Millwood, New York 1978; Adolph Edwards, *Marcus Garvey*, London 1967; Elton C. Fax, *Garvey*, New York 1972; Daniels Davis, *Marcus Garvey*, New York 1972; Ben F. Rogers, 'William E.B. Du Bois, Marcus Garvey, and Pan-Africa', *Journal of Negro History*, vol. 40, April 1955, pp. 154-165; Elliott M. Rudwick, 'Du Bois Versus Garvey: Race Propagandists at War', *Journal of Negro Education*, vol. 28, Fall 1959, pp. 421-429; John Henrik Clarke, 'Marcus Garvey: The Harlem Years', *Black Scholar*, vol. 5, December 1973-January 1974, pp. 17-24; Mark D. Matthews, ' "Our Women and What They Think', Amy Jacques Garvey and the *Negro World'*, *Black Scholar*, vol. 10, May-June 1979, pp. 2-13; and Amy Jacques Garvey, 'Garvey and Pan-Africanism', *Black World*, vol. 21, December 1971, pp. 15-18.

187. Padmore's major theoretical work was *Pan-Africanism or Communism?*, Garden City, New York 1971. Works by and about Padmore include: Padmore, *How Russia Transformed her Colonial Empire*, London 1946; Padmore, *Africa: Britain's Third Empire*, New York 1969; and James R. Hooker, *Black Revolutionary: George Padmore's Path from Communism to Pan-Africanism*, New York 1967.

188. Rodney, 'The African Revolution', p. 9.

189. Studies on modern Afro-American nationalism include: John Henrik Clarke, 'The New Afro-American Nationalism', *Freedomways*, vol. 1, Fall 1961, pp. 285-295; Wilson Record, 'The Negro Intellectual and Negro Nationalism', *Social Forces*, vol. 32, October 1954, pp. 10-18; Irene Tinker, 'Nationalism in a Plural Society: The Case of the American Negro', *Western Political Quarterly*, vol. 19, March 1966, pp. 112-122; Eugene D. Genovese, 'Black Nationalism and American Socialism', in *In Red and Black: Marxian Explorations in Southern and Afro-American History*, New York 1971, pp. 188-199; Harold Cruse, 'Revolutionary Nationalism and the Afro-American', *Studies on the Left*, vol. 2, 1962, pp. 12-25; A. James Gregor, 'Black Nationalism: A Preliminary Analysis of Negro Radicalism', *Science and Society*, vol. 26, Fall 1963, pp. 415-432; Allen, *Black Awakening in Capitalist America;* and Harold Cruse, *The Crisis of the Negro Intellectual*, New York 1967. The major Black nationalist theoretician in the US is Maulana Karenga. Creator of the 'Kwanzaa'

celebration in 1965 which is practised by millions of Afro-Americans, Karenga developed a unique Afrocentric value system *nguzo saba*. Karenga's works include: *Essays on Struggle: Position and Analysis*, San Diego 1978; 'Afro-American Nationalism: Beyond Mystification and Misconception', *Black Books Bulletin*, vol. 6, Spring 1978, pp. 7-12; *Beyond Connections: Liberation in Love and Struggle*, New Orleans 1977; 'Black Art: A Rhythmic Reality of Revolution', *Negro Digest*, vol. 17, January 1968, pp. 5-9; 'The Crisis of Black Middle-Class Leadership: A Critical Analysis', *Black Scholar*, vol. 13, Fall 1982, pp. 16-32; *Kawaida Theory: An Introductory Outline*, Los Angeles 1980; 'Carter and His Black Critics: The Dialogue and Its Lessons', *Black Scholar*, vol. 9, November 1977, pp. 52-54; and 'Jesse Jackson and the Presidential Campaign: The Invitation and Oppositions of History', *Black Scholar*, vol. 15, September-October, 1984, pp. 57-71.

190. Poulantzas, *Political Power and Social Classes*, pp. 97, 107.

191. Hoare and Smith, eds., *Selections From the Prison Notebooks of Antonio Gramsci*, pp. 147-157. At one point, Gramsci suggests that 'a newspaper or a review is a "party" or "fraction of a party" or "a function of a particular party".' (p. 148).

192. Hill, ed., *The Marcus Garvey and Universal Negro Improvement Association Papers, Volume I*, pp. 521-527. Also see Vincent, *Black Power and the Garvey Movement*, pp. 74-85. Briggs became national secretary of the American Negro Labour Congress in October 1925, and was elected to the central executive committee of the us Communist Party in March 1929. Ten years later he was expelled from the Party for his 'Negro nationalist way of thinking'. In 1948 Briggs was permitted to rejoin the Party; he died in October 1966.

193. The NAACP's history and policies are documented in: Charles Flint Kellogg, *NAACP: A History of the National Association for the Advancement of Colored People*, Baltimore 1967; Warren D. St James, *The National Association for the Advancement of Colored People: A Case Study in Pressure Groups*, New York 1958; Daniel W. Wynn, *the NAACP Versus Negro Revolutionary Protest*, New York 1955; Walter White, *A Man Called White*, Garden City, New York 1948; Jack Abramowitz, 'Origins of the NAACP', *Social Education*, vol. 15, January 1951, pp. 21-23; Robert L. Zangrando, 'The NAACP and a Federal Antilynching Bill, 1934-1940', *Journal of Negro History*, vol. 50, April 1965, pp. 106-107; Gilbert Ware, 'Lobbying as a Means of Protest: The NAACP as an Agent of Equality', *Journal of Negro Education*, vol. 33, Spring 1964, pp. 103-110; and John A. Morse II, 'The National Association for the Advancement of Colored People and Its Strategy', *Annals of the American Academy of Political and Social Science*, vol. 357, January 1965, pp. 97-101.

194. W.E.B. Du Bois, *The Autobiography of W.E.B. Du Bois: A Soliloquy on Viewing My Life from the Last Decade of Its First Century*, New York 1968, pp. 328-339.

195. W.E.B. Du Bois to Walter White, 10 October 1946, in Herbert Aptheker, ed., *The Correspondence of W.E.B. Du Bois, Volume III: Selections, 1944-1963*, Amherst 1978, pp. 120-124.

196. Piven and Cloward, *Poor People's Movements*, pp. 27, 29.

197. Poulantzas, *Political Power and Social Classes*, p. 109.

198. Piven and Cloward, *Poor People's Movements*, pp. 22-23.

199. Theda Skocpol, *States and Social Revolutions: A Comparative Analysis of France, Russia, and China*, Cambridge 1979, p. 4.

200. *Ibid.*, p. 47.

201. Rodney, *How Europe Underdeveloped Africa*, p. 125.

2 Marches on Washington, 1941, 1963, 1983: The Social Movement for Racial Equality

1. Frederick Douglass, 'What to the Slave is the Fourth of July?', *Black Scholar*, vol. 7, July-August 1976, pp. 33-37.

2. Roberta Yancy Dent, ed., *Paul Robeson: Tributes and Selected Writings*, New York 1976, pp. 98, 100.

3. Vincent Harding, *The Other American Revolution*, Los Angeles 1980, p. 229.

4. Cox, *Caste, Class and Race*, p. 495.

5. C. Vann Woodward, *The Strange Career of Jim Crow*, third revised edition, New York 1974, pp. 111-112.

6. *Ibid.*, p. 113.

7. C. Vann Woodward, *Origins of the New South, 1877-1913*, Baton Rouge Louisiana 1951, p. 352.

8. Allison Davis, Burleigh B. Gardner and Mary R. Gardner, *Deep South: A Social Anthropological Study of Caste and Class*, Chicago 1941, p. 302.

9. Monroe Berger, *Equality by Statute: The Revolution in Civil Rights*, Garden City, New York 1968, p. 86. Also see Edward F. Waite, 'The Negro in the Supreme Court', *Minnesota Law Review*, vol. 30, March 1946, pp. 219-304; Paul A. Freund, 'Separate-But-Equal: A Study of the Career of a Constitutional Concept, *Race Relations Law Reporter*, vol. 1, February 1956, pp. 283–292; Clement E. Vose, *Caucasians Only: The Supreme Court, the NAACP and the Restrictive Covenant Cases*, Berkeley 1959; and Sarah M. Lemmon, 'Transportation Segregation in the Federal Courts since 1865', *Journal of Negro History*, vol. 38, April 1953, pp. 174-193.

10. Woodward, *Origins of the New South*, p. 355.

11. Woodward, *The Strange Career of Jim Crow*, pp. 117-118.

12. Franklin, *From Slavery to Freedom*, p. 547.

13. Woodward, *Origins of the New South*, p. 354.

14. Cox, *Caste, Class and Race*, pp. 548-551.

15. Bernard B. Fall, ed., *Ho Chi Minh on Revolution: Selected Writings, 1920-66*, New York 1968, pp. 51-55.

16. Cox, *Caste, Class and Race*, p. 487.

17. Foner, *Organized Labor and the Black Worker*, p. 215.

18. Piven and Cloward, *Poor People's Movements*, pp. 196-197. There are a number of critiques of the New Deal's response to — and neglect of — the needs of Afro-Americans. See Raymond Wolters, *Negroes and the Great Depression: The Problem of Economic Recovery*, Westport, Connecticut 1970; Leslie H. Fishel, 'The Negro in the New Deal Era', *Wisconsin Magazine of History*, vol. 48, Winter 1964, pp. 111-126; Wolters, 'Section 7a and the Black Worker', *Labor History*, vol. 10, Summer 1969, pp. 459-474; Robert L. Zangrando, 'The NAACP and a Federal Antilynching Bill', *Journal of Negro History*, vol. 50, April 1965, pp. 106-117; Charles H. Houston and John P. Davis, 'TVA: Lily-White Reconstruction', *Crisis*, vol. 41, October 1934, pp. 290-291, 311; John P. Davis, 'The Plight of the Negro in the Tennessee Valley', *Crisis*, vol. 42, October 1935, pp. 294-295, 314-315; Ralph J. Bunche, 'A Critique of New Deal Planning as It Affects Negroes', *Journal of Negro Education*, vol. 5, January 1936, pp. 59-65; and Bunche, 'The Roosevelt Record', *Crisis*, vol. 47, November 1940, p. 343.

19. Foner, *Organized Labor and the Black Worker*, p. 180.

20. *Ibid.*, pp. 216-217.

21. *Ibid.*, p. 214. Also see A. Philip Randolph, 'Why I Would Not Stand for Re-election as President of the National Negro Congress', *Ameriian Federationist*, vol. 48, July 1940, pp. 24-25.

22. Richard M. Dalflume, 'The "Forgotten Years" of the Negro Revolution', in Bernard Sternsher, ed., *The Negro in Depression and War: Prelude to Revolution, 1930-1945*, Chicago 1969, p. 305.

23. Piven and Cloward, *Poor People's Movements*, pp. 58-67.

24. V.I. Lenin, 'What Is to be Done? Burning Questions of our Movement', in Robert C. Tucker, ed., *The Lenin Anthology*, New York 1975, pp. 23-33.

25. Dalflume, 'The "Forgotten Years" of the Negro Revolution', p. 306.

26. *Ibid.*, p. 306; and Meier and Rudwick, *From Plantation to Ghetto*, p. 272.

27. Dalflume, 'The "Forgotten Years" of the Negro Revolution', p. 305.

28. Foner, *Organized Labor and the Black Worker*, p. 240.

29. *Ibid.*, p. 241.

30. Historian William H. Harris observes that the central 'characteristic of Randolph's personality that he would show again and again throughout his illustrious career' was his belief in 'the big bluff'. In 1928 the Brotherhood called for a strike against the Pullman Company, setting the date for 8 June. In the weeks before the strike, however, Randolph issued a public statement in which 'he assured everyone that a strike vote did not necessarily mean that the porters would actually strike'. He informed Pullman director J. Pierpont Morgan that 'the union intended to ensure that the employees continued their loyalty to the company'. His actions not only confused the Brotherhood, but reassured the Pullman Company that no strike would take place, despite the workers' intense preparations. On the morning of 8 June, Randolph called off the strike. Demoralized, thousands of porters left the union. By 1933 the Brotherhood had only 658 national members, and 'Randolph was almost finished as a labour leader'. See Harris, *The Harder We Run*, pp. 86-88; and Marable, 'A. Philip Randolph and the Foundations of Black American Socialism', pp. 223-225.

31. Herbert Garfinkel, *When Negroes March*, Glencoe, Illinois 1959, p. 60.

32. Foner, *Organized Labor and the Black Worker*, p. 242.

33. See Louis C. Kesselman, *The Social Politics of FEPC: A Study in Reform Pressure Movements*, Chapel Hill 1948.

34. Afro-American leaders continued to express their dissatisfaction with Roosevelt's Administration throughout World War II. See A. Philip Randolph, 'Why Should We March?', *Survey Graphic*, vol. 31, November 1942, pp. 488-489; James A. Bayton, 'The Psychology of Racial Morale', *Journal of Negro Education*, vol. 11, April 1942, pp. 150-153; Horace Mann Bond, 'Should the Negro Care Who Wins the War?', *Annals of the American Academy of Political and Social Science*, vol. 223, September 1942, pp. 81-85; Guion G. Johnson, 'The Impact of the War upon the Negro', *Journal of Negro Education*, vol. 10, July 1941, pp. 596-611; and Lester B. Granger, 'Barriers to Negro War Employment', *Annals of the American Academy of Political and Social Science*, vol. 223, September 1942, pp. 72-81.

35. The best detailed account of the Montgomery County bus boycott written during the civil-rights movement was a five-part series by Norman W. Walton, 'The Walking City, A History of the Montgomery Boycott', *Negro History Bulletin*, vol. 20, October 1956, pp. 17-21; November 1956, pp. 27-33; February 1957, pp. 102-104; April 1957, pp. 147-152, 166; and vol. 21, January 1958, pp. 75-76, 81. Also see Martin Luther King Jr, 'We Are Still Walking', *Liberation*, vol. 5, December 1956, pp. 6-9; and King, *Stride Toward Freedom*, New York 1958.

36. Thomas Gentile, *March on Washington: August 28, 1963*, Washington DC 1983, p. 8.

37. Carson, *In Struggle*, p. 35.

38. Gentile, *March on Washington: August 28, 1963*, p. 24.

39. *Ibid.*, pp. 24-26.

40. Carson, *In Struggle*, p. 90.

41. Piven and Cloward, *Poor People's Movements*, p. 244.

42. Carson, *In Struggle*, p. 91.

43. Gentile, *March on Washington: August 28, 1963*, p. 14.

44. *Ibid.*, p. 12. Rustin's political thought during the civil-rights movement was reflected in a series of his essays, including: 'The Watts "Manifesto" and the McCone Report', *Commentary*, vol. 41, March 1966, pp. 29-35; 'The Meaning of Birmingham', *Liberator*, vol. 8, June 1963, pp. 7-9, 31; 'The Meaning of the March on Washington', *Liberator*, vol. 8, October 1963, pp. 11-13; 'From Protest to Politics: The Future of the Civil Rights Movement', *Commentary*, vol. 39, February 1963, pp. 25-31; ' "Black Power" and Coalition Politics', *Commentary*, vol. 42 September 1966, pp 35–40; and 'The Failure of Black Separatism', *Harper's*, vol. 140, January 1970, pp. 25-34. Rustin's growing affinity for conservatism is reflected in *Down the Line*, Chicago 1971, and *Strategies for Freedom: The Changing Patterns of Black Protest*, New York 1976.

45. Carson, *In Struggle*, p. 29.

46. Gentile, *March on Washington: August 28, 1963*, p. 8.

47. *Ibid.*, pp. 36, 39.

48. *Ibid.*, p. 42.

49. Carson, *In Struggle*, p. 91.

50. Gentile, *March on Washington: August 28, 1963*, p. 49.

51. *Ibid.*, pp. 122-123.

52. *Ibid.*, pp. 42-43.

53. *Ibid.*, pp. 123, 200.

54. Foner, *Organized Labor and the Black Worker*, pp. 349-350.

55. Gentile, *March on Washington, August 28, 1963*, pp. 208-245.

56. *Ibid.*, p. 252.

57. *Ibid.*, pp. 175-183; Carson, *In Struggle*, pp. 93-95. Other sources on the 1963 March on Washington include: Margaret Long, 'March on Washington', *New South*, vol. 17, September 1963, pp. 3–17; 'For Jobs and Freedom: Three Views of the Washington March', *Midwest Quarterly*, vol. 5, Winter 1964, pp. 99–116; and Martin Luther King Jr., *Why We Can't Wait*, New York 1964, pp. 122-125.

58. Foner, *Organized Labor and the Black Worker*, pp. 350-351, 354. Studies of the 1964 Civil Rights Act include: Clifford M. Lytle, 'The History of the Civil Rights Bill of 1964', *Journal of Negro History*, vol. 51, October 1966, pp. 275-296; Alexander M. Bickel, 'The Civil Rights Act of 1964', *Commentary*, vol. 38, August 1964, pp. 33-39; Donald S. Strong, *Negroes, Ballots and Judges: National Voting Rights Legislation in the Federal Courts*, University, Alabama 1968; and Lytle, 'The Controversy over the "Equal Opportunity" Provisions of the Civil Rights Bill', *Congressional Digest*, vol. 43, March 1964, pp. 67-96.

59. Bureau of the Census, *The Social and Economic Status of the Black Population in the United States: An Historical View, 1790-1978*, p. 90.

60. Lynn Webber Cannon, 'Trends in Class Identification among Black Americans from 1952 to 1978', *Social Science Quarterly*, vol. 65, March 1984, pp.

112-126.

61. Diane Ravitch, 'The Ambiguous Legacy of Brown vs Board of Education', *New Perspectives*, vol. 16, Summer 1984, pp. 6-13.

62. W.E.B. Du Bois, 'On Being Ashamed of Oneself: An Essay on Race Pride', *Crisis*, vol. 40, September 1933, pp. 199-200.

63. Marion D. Thorpe, 'The Future of Black Colleges and Universities in the Desegregation and Integration Process', *Journal of Black Studies*, vol. 6, September 1975, p. 105.

64. W.E.B. Du Bois (Herbert Aptheker, ed.), *The Education of Black People: Ten Critiques, 1906-1960*, New York 1973, pp. 150-152.

65. See Carnegie Commision on Higher Education, *From Isolation to Mainstream*, New York 1971.

66. See Manning Marable, 'The Quiet Death of Black Colleges', *Southern Exposure*, vol. 18, March-April 1984, pp. 31-39; and Marable, ' "Color-Blind" Colleges: A Cop-Out', *Guardian*, 10 October 1984.

67. Marian Wright Edelman, 'Black College Opportunities Eroding as America's Wealth Increases', *Carolina Peacemaker*, 23 June 1984.

68. See Manning Marable, 'Black families: What's in "crisis" — and what's not', *Guardian*, 30 May 1984.

69. See Manning Marable, *Race, Reform and Rebellion: The Second Reconstruction in Black America, 1945-1982*, London 1984, pp. 196-198.

70. Marable, 'Black families: What's in "crisis" — and what's not'.

71. Richard McGahey, 'Industrial Policy: Minority Economic Interests and American Political Response', *Review of Black Political Economy*, vol. 13, Summer-Fall 1984, pp. 85-96.

72. Adam Fairclough, 'Martin Luther King Jr, and the War in Vietnam', *Phylon*, vol. 45, July 1984, pp. 19-39.

73. Marion Anderson, 'Bombs or Bread, Black Unemployment and the Pentagon Budget' and Manning Marable, 'Nuclear War and Black America', in *National Scene*, vol. 53, January 1984, pp. 8-12, 30 and pp. 14, 18-19.

74. 'Organizer's Manual for the Twentieth Anniversary Celebration of the 1963 March on Washington', 1983. Copy in possession of author.

75. Bayard Rustin and Norman Hill to Mrs Martin Luther King Jr, the Rev. Joseph Lowery, Chairman and Members of the Black Leadership Forum, memo regarding 'Proposed Anniversary of 1963 March on Washington', 19 October 1982. Copy in possession of author.

76. Carson, *In Struggle*, pp. 93-94.

77. Lovell Beaulieu, 'NAACP plans anniversary march in Washington August 27', *Times-Picayune*, 14 July 1983.

78. According to one source, Lowery 'delivered a radical speech using a spiritual theme, "Down by the Riverside" '. Lowery declared that American citizens must 'face imperialism wherever it raises its ugly head . . . and support the right of self-determination for the people of El Salvador, Nicaragua, Chile, South Africa . . .'. The most urgent task of peace activists was to halt 'the deployment of [US] missiles in Europe'. Atiba Mbiwan, US Media's Betrayal of the American Public', *Ebenezer Grapevine*, Providence RI August 1983. Also see Alice Palmer, 'World Assembly calls for Peace', *Black Press Review*, vol. 2, June/July 1983, pp. 1, 16.

79. Franklin, *From Slavery to Freedom*, p. 449. The National Urban League was

established in 1911 as a bridge between Blacks and the corporate and governmental elites. It achieved numerous reforms in racial hiring policies and improved the urban socio-economic conditions of Afro-Americans, but it never embraced militant social protest. See L. Hollingsworth Wood, 'The Urban League Movement', *Journal of Negro History*, vol. 9, April 1924, pp. 117–126; 'Fifty Years of the Urban League', *Negro History Bulletin*, vol. 24, October 1960, pp. 13–14; and Arvarh E. Strickland, *History of the Chicago Urban League*, Urbana 1966.

80. 'NUL Concludes Four-Day Conference In New Orleans', *Bulletin*, Sarasota, Florida 26 August 1983.

81. 'American Jewish Congress Endorses March on Washington' and 'Israel to mark Martin Luther King "I Have A Dream" Anniversary With Tree-Planting Ceremony in Galilee', *Chronicle* [Charleston, SC], 27 August 1983.

82. 'Zionists smear August 27 March', *Militant*, 26 August 1983; John Trinkl, ' "Jobs, peace, freedom" demand proving popular', *Guardian*, 10 August 1983.

83. 'Organizer's Manual for the Twentieth Anniversary Celebration of the 1963 March on Washington'.

84. *Ibid.*

85. Charley Spektor, 'Widespread support for August 27 March', *Daily World*, 16 June 1983.

86. 'Many activities planned to build for Aug. 27 march', *Daily World*, 30 June 1983.

87. George Johnson, 'Steelworkers say: march Aug. 27; Jobs, peace, freedom rally gains labor support', *Militant*, 8 July 1983.

88. List of buses leaving from New York City to March on Washington, prepared mid August 1983. Copy in possession of author.

89. 'Cities, mobilize for "We Still Have a Dream" march', *Portland Observer*, 10 August 1983.

90. 'Hundreds From Charleston To Take Part In March On Washington This Week-end', *Chronicle*, Charleston, SC 27 August 1983.

91. 'NAACP to Participate in March', *Carolina Peacemaker*, Greensboro, NC 20 August 1983.

92. Charles Barnett and Richard Bolitho, 'Va. Aug. 27 group backs Bell strike', *Militant*, 2 September 1983.

93. Rashaad Ali, 'Unionists in New Orleans back rally', *Militant*, 22 July 1983.

94. Don Mackle, 'Aug. 27 builds in Philadelphia', *Militant*, 22 July 1983.

95. Ann Rilkey Owens, 'St Louis conference held for march', *Militant*, 27 July 1983.

96. Trinkl, ' "Jobs, peace, freedom" demand proving popular'.

97. John Trinkl, 'Fighting the Same Enemy, August 27', *Guardian*, 27 July 1983.

98. 'Organizer's Manual for the Twentieth Anniversary Celebration of the 1963 March on Washington'.

99. One of the more active left groups that promoted the March was the Socialist Workers' Party (SWP). On balance, however, the SWP did not seem to comprehend that the theoretical underpinnings of this time of left-centre mass formation owed far more to Georgi Dimitrov and the Popular Front thesis advanced at the Seventh Congress of the Communist International in 1935 than to Leon Trotsky. SWP writer Malik Miah argued that the march would be a 'direct challenge to the rulers' attacks', an action against the bosses' efforts 'to force working people to pay for the crisis of the capitalist system'. It is doubtful whether the rest of the Left, not to mention the civil-rights reformers and liberals, viewed their actions in this context. See Miah, 'August 27 March', *Militant*, 22 July 1983.

100. Henry Winston, 'Dimitrov and Our Fight for Peace', *Political Affairs*, vol. 61, August 1982, p. 2.

101. Frances M. Beal, 'August 27 March Attempts to Revive Civil Rights Coalition', *Frontline*, 27 June 1983.

102. 'What is the significance of August 27?', *Unity*, San Francisco 12 August-8 September 1983.

103. Jones, *Home: Social Essays*, p. 148.

104. Amiri Baraka, 'The real fight for democracy and self-determination', *Unity*, San Francisco 12 August-8 September 1983. LeRoi Jones (Amiri Baraka) was the most important artist/intellectual/activist to emerge from the Black Power period. There are a number of works that examine his evolution from being an avant-garde poet of the late-1950s beat generation, through Black nationalism in the 1960s, and finally to a variety of Marxism in the mid 1970s: Theodore R. Hudson, *From LeRoi Jones to Amiri Baraka*, Durham 1973; Kathryn Jackson, 'LeRoi Jones and the New Black Writers of the Sixties', *Freedomways*, vol. 9, Third Quarter 1969, pp. 232-247; C. Lynn Munro, 'LeRoi Jones: A Man in Transition', CLA *Jounal*, vol. 17, September 1973, pp. 58-78; Mary D. Dippold, 'LeRoi Jones: Tramp with Connections', Ph.D. dissertation, University of Maryland, College Park, 1971; Clenora F. Hudson, 'The Political Implications in the Works of Imamu Amiri Baraka', MA thesis, Atlanta University, 1971; Kimberly W. Benston, *Baraka: The Renegade and the Mask*, New Haven 1976; Werner Sollors, *Amiri Baraka/LeRoi Jones: The Quest for a Populist Modernism*, New York 1978; and Lloyd Brown, *Amiri Baraka*, Boston 1980.

105. Trinkl, ' "Jobs, peace, freedom" demand proving popular'.

106. Here again, an analysis of the DC 'feeder marches' reveals the multi-national, multi-issue character of the march generally. The smaller marches were organized by unions (AFSCME), religious organizations (the AME Church, Baptists, Lutherans, Unitarians, Presbyterians, Catholics, etc.), Black 'Greeks' (Zeta Phi Beta Sorority and Omega Psi Phi Fraternity), gays, lesbians, Howard University students and Hispanics. See 'Feeder Marches', *Washington Post*, 26 August 1983.

107. John Burgess and Sandra R. Gregg, 'No Major Mishap as 250,000 Celebrate', *Washington Post*, 28 August 1983.

108. *Ibid.* The US Park Police first estimated the crowd at 250,000, but, as a rule, their estimates of the number of participants tend towards the low side.

109. Lincoln, *The Black Muslims in America*, p. 153.

110. 'Excerpts of Speeches', *Washington Post*, 28 August 1983.

111. *Ibid.*

112. *Ibid.*

113. Trinkl, 'Fighting the Same Enemy August 27'.

114. Rev. Herbert Daughtry to Walter Fauntroy, 25 July 1983, copy in possession of author. Duplicate copies of the letter were also sent to NBUF Vice-Chairpersons and Regional Coordinators, as well as to Lowery, Coretta King, Representative Major Owens and several others.

115. 'March to Seek National Agenda for "Jobs, Peace and Freedom",' *Washington Post*, 25 August 1983.

3 Black Politicians and Bourgeois Democracy

1. Alexis de Tocqueville, *Democracy in America*, New York 1981, pp. 46, 457, 467.

2. See Stuart R. Schram, *The Political Thought of Mao Tse-Tung*, New York 1969.

3. Karl Marx and Friedrich Engels, *Selected Works, Volume III*, Moscow 1973, pp. 326-327.

4. Lenin, *On the Dictatorship of the Proletariat*, excerpt from *The State and Revolution*, p. 35.

5. Marx and Engels, *Selected Works, Volume III*, pp. 327-328.

6. Quintin Hoare and Geoffrey Nowell Smith, eds., *Selections from the Prison Notebooks of Antonio Gramsci*, New York 1971, pp. 208, 258.

7. *Ibid.*, pp. 210, 276.

8. Ralph Miliband, *Class Power and State Power: Political Essays* London 1983, p. 41.

9. There are several historical examples of this. The English aristocracy was defeated by the Puritan army at Marston Moor, and King Charles was beheaded in 1649. Yet after a little more than a decade of Cromwell's dictatorship, Charles's son was again on the throne, and the aristocracy back in command.

10. Cox, *Caste, Class and Race*, pp. 155-156.

11. Lenin, *On the Dictatorship of the Proletariat*, p. 114.

12. Barrington Moore Jr, *Social Origins of Dictatorship and Democracy: Lord and Peasant in the Making of the Modern World*, Boston 1967, pp. 414, 429.

13. Erik Olin Wright, *Class, Crisis and the State*, London 1979, p. 21.

14. Cox, *Caste, Class and Race*, p. 163.

15. Skocpol, *States and Social Revolutions*, pp. 192, 201, 234.

16. Cox, *Caste, Class and Race*, p. 230.

17. Nicos Poulantzas, *Classes in Contemporary Capitalism*, London 1978, p. 99.

18. James O'Connor, *The Fiscal Crisis of the State*, New York 1973, p. 6.

19. Hoare and Smith, eds., *Selections from the Prison Notebooks of Antonio Gramsci*, p. 243.

20. *Ibid.*, p. 5.

21. *Ibid.*, p. 335.

22. O'Connor, *The Fiscal Crisis of the State*, p. 224; and Perlo, *Economics of Racism USA*, p. 211.

23. O'Connor, *The Fiscal Crisis of the State*, p. 225.

24. Miliband writes that the state helps capitalist mass parties 'to fulfil their role, and also in competing on terms of advantage with their working-class rivals'. However, 'it is only in periods of acute and prolonged crisis, when these parties show themselves incapable of performing their political task, that their role may be taken over by the state'. *Class Power and State Power*, p. 42.

25. Benjamin R. Barber, *Strong Democracy: Participatory Politics for a New Age*, Berkeley 1984, pp. 140-144.

26. Milton Friedman, *Capitalism and Freedom*, Chicago 1962, p. 5. Friedman's central arguments are more ludcidly stated in the earlier writings of Frederick Hayek. See Hayek, *The Road to Serfdom*, Chicago 1944, and *Law, Legislation and Liberty*, Chicago 1976.

27. Evan Durbin, 'A Socialist View of Democracy', in Irving Howe, ed., *Essential Works of Socialism*, New Haven 1976, pp. 557-563.

28. Friedman, *Capitalism and Freedom*, pp. 6-7.

29. Robert L. Heilbroner, *Between Capitalism and Socialism: Essays in Political*

Economics, New York 1970, p. 145.

30. Davis, *The Problem of Slavery in the Age of Revolution*, p. 24. Jefferson, a classical liberal, was philosophically opposed to slavery. In the 1783 proposal for Virginia's state constitution, 'he provided for the freedom of all children born of slaves after the year 1800'. The 'great father of democracy' nevertheless owned many slaves, and suggested that Black emancipation was 'like abandoning children'. Blacks were 'prone to theft', 'carefree and submissive', 'never thought about the future', 'were promiscuous in their sexual attachments', and had absolutely 'no capacity for delicate or resined love', (pp. 174-176, 179, 194).

31. Franklin, *From Slavery to Freedom*, pp. 142-144.

32. Davis, *The Problem of Slavery in the Age of Revolution*, pp. 111, 139, 143.

33. Lenin, *On the Dictatorship of the Proletariat*, (excerpt from *The Proletarian Revolution and the Renegade Kautsky*), pp. 142-143.

34. Carl N. Degler, *Neither Black Nor White: Slavery and Race Relations in Brazil and the United States*, New York 1971, p. 280.

35. Lerone Bennett Jr, *Black Power USA: The Human Side of Reconstruction 1867-1877*, Baltimore 1967, pp. 322-324.

36. Carson, *In Struggle*, pp. 189-190.

37. In 'Two Tactics of Social Democracy', Lenin notes that 'from the vulgar bourgeois standpoint the terms dictatorship and democracy are mutually exclusive. Failing to understand the theory of class struggle and accustomed to seeing in the political arena the petty squabbling of the various bourgeois circles and coteries, the bourgeois understands by dictatorship the annulment of all liberties and guarantees of democracy, arbitrariness of every kind, and every sort of abuse of power in a dictator's personal interest.' From the point of view of those at the bottom of the social order, however, bourgeois democracy appears to be exactly what it is — a dictatorship of the bourgeoisie. See Lenin, 'Two Tactics of Social Democracy in the Democratic Revolution', in Tucker, ed., *The Lenin Anthology*, p. 142.

38. *Ibid.,* pp. 123-124.

39. Marx's description of Bonapartism reads as follows: '. . . State power does not hover in mid air. Bonaparte represents a class, indeed he represents the most numerous class of French society, the small peasant proprietors. Just as the Bourbons were the dynasty of big landed property and the Orleans the dynasty of money, so the Bonapartes are the dynasy of the peasants, i.e., of the mass of the French people. The chosen hero of the peasantry is not the Bonaparte who submitted to the bourgeois parliament but the Bonaparte who dispersed it . . . [However,] the Bonaparte dynasty represents the conservative, not the revolutionary peasant: the peasant who wants to consolidate the condition of his social existence, the small-holding . . . It represents the peasant's superstition, not his enlightenment; his prejudice, not his judgment; his past, not his future . . .'. Marx, *The Eighteenth Brumaire of Louis Bonaparte,* in David Fernbach, ed., *Karl Marx, Political Writings, Volume II: Surveys from Exile,* New York 1974, pp. 238-240.

40. Palmiro Togaliatti, *Lectures on Fascism,* New York 1976, p. 1.

41. Miliband explains: 'The point is not, of course, to claim for bourgeois-democratic forms of the capitalist state virtues that they do not possess; or to suggest that such regimes are not given to repression and to Bonapartist-type modes of behaviour; or to imply that the dominant classes in *any* of them are immune from Bonapartist temptations and promptings, given the right circumstances and opportunities . . . But to say all this is not the same as obliterating differences between forms of the capitalist state which are of crucial importance, not least to working-class movements.' *Class Power and State Power,* pp. 45-46.

42. Brian Bunting, *The Rise of the South African Reich*, Baltimore 1969, p. 80.

43. *Ibid.*, pp. 30-31. Boer nationalist leader J.B.M. Hertzog praised Bolshevism in 1919. The following year Malan declared that 'the aim of the Bolshevists was that Russians should manage their own affairs without interference from outside. That was the same policy that Nationalists would follow in South Africa.'

44. *Ibid.*, pp. 56, 59-62, 64-65, 111.

45. Magubane, *The Political Economy of Race and Class in South Africa*, pp. 143, 244-245.

46. Miliband, *Class Power and State Power*, pp. 94, 96.

47. *Ibid.*, p. 96.

48. Cox, *Caste, Class and Race*, pp. 231-232.

49. V.I. Lenin, 'Communism and the East: Theses on the National and Colonial Questions', in Tucker, ed., *The Lenin Anthology*, p. 620.

50. V.I. Lenin, ' "Left-Wing" Communism: An Infantile Disorder', in Lenin, *On the Dictatorship of the Proletariat*, p. 270.

51. Cox, *Caste, Class and Race*, p. 150.

52. *Ibid.*, p. 226.

53. Karl Marx, 'Address of the Central Committee to the Communist League, March 1850,' in David Fernbach, ed., *Karl Marx: Political Writings, Volume I: The Revolutions of 1848*, New York 1974, pp. 322-323.

54. Lenin, *On the Dictatorship of the Proletariat*, (excerpt from *The State and Revolution*), p. 113.

55. Jane J. Mansbridge, *Beyond Adversary Democracy*, Chicago and London 1983, pp. 3-5.

56. *Ibid.*, pp. 18-19.

57. Charles S. Johnson, *Backgrounds to the Patterns of Negro Segregation*, New York 1970, pp. 323-324.

58. Tocqueville, *Democracy in America*, pp. 588-593.

59. Joseph Schumpeter, *Capitalism, Socialism and Democracy*, London 1943, p. 162.

60. Robert Cruden, *The Negro in Reconstruction*, Englewood Cliffs, New Jersey 1969, p. 5.

61. *Ibid.*, p. 6; and Abram L. Harris, *The Negro as Capitalist: A Study of Banking and Business Among American Negroes*, New York 1936, pp. 12, 17-18.

62. Benjamin Quarles, *Frederick Douglass*, New York 1969, pp. 255, 279, 320, 335-339.

63. Meier, *Negro Thought in America, 1880-1915*, pp. 36, 213, 248, 297; and Franklin, *From Slavery to Freedom*, p. 320.

64. W.E.B. Du Bois, *Black Reconstruction in America, 1860-1880*, New York 1975, pp. 362-363, 528-529; and John Hope Franklin, *Reconstruction: After the Civil War*, Chicago 1961, p. 88.

65. Du Bois, *Black Reconstruction in America, 1860-1880*, pp. 513, 520-521.

66. *Ibid.*, p. 442; and Franklin, *Reconstruction: After the Civil War*, p. 88.

67. Franklin, *From Slavery to Freedom*, p. 318; and Du Bois, *Black Reconstruction in America, 1860-1880*, p. 402.

68. The best study on Black politics in post-war South Carolina is by Thomas Holt, *Black over White: Negro Political Leadership in South Carolina During Reconstruction*, Urbana 1977. Other general studies on the topic include: Joel Williamson, *After Slavery: The Negro in South Carolina During Reconstruction*, Chapel Hill 1965; Okon Edet Uya, *From Slavery to Public Service: Robert Smalls, 1839-1915*, New York 1971; Peggy Lamson, *The Glorious Failure: Black Congressman Robert Brown*

Elliott and the Reconstruction in South Carolina, New York 1973; Herbert Aptheker, 'South Carolina Negro Conventions, 1865', *Journal of Negro History,* vol. 31, January 1946, pp. 91-97; and Lawrence C. Bryant, *Negro Lawmakers in the South Carolina Legislature,* Orangeburg 1968.

69. Holt, *Black over White,* pp. 65-66.

70. *Ibid.,* pp. 59-60, 165.

71. John W. Blassingame, *Black New Orleans, 1860-1880,* Chicago 1973, pp. 154-161.

72. Meier, *Negro Thought in America, 1880-1915,* pp. 54, 76-77.

73. Holt, *Black over White,* pp. 36-38.

74. *Ibid.,* pp. 132-133; and Franklin, *Reconstruction: After the Civil War,* p. 87.

75. Franklin, *Reconstruction: After the Civil War,* p. 91.

76. Holt, *Black over White,* pp. 107, 132. Randolph was not consistently radical and in fact had voted in favour of conservative qualifications on suffrage. But in his major address before the convention, he urged delegates to back a constitutional provision banning racial discrimination in all public accommodations. 'The day is coming', he warned, 'when we must decide whether the two races shall live together or not.' Evidently, the delegates decided that the time had not yet arrived, for the resolution was defeated. Elected as Chairman of the Republican state central committee in 1868, Randolph was soon assassinated by white terrorists.

77. Cruden, *The Negro in Reconstruction,* p. 59.

78. Du Bois, *Black Reconstruction in America, 1860-1880,* pp. 337-338. The greatest tragedy of Black Reconstruction was the failure of Afro-Americans to obtain Stevens's goal of 'forty acres and a mule'. Other sources on the 'land question' and Black politics include: LaWanda Cox, 'The Promise of Land for the Freedmen', *Mississippi Valley Historical Review,* vol. 45, December 1958, pp. 413-440; Manuel Gottlieb, 'The Land Question in Georgia During Reconstruction', *Science and Society,* vol. 3, Summer 1939, pp. 356-388; Christie Farmham Pope, 'Southern Homesteads for Negroes', *Agricultural History,* vol. 44, April 1970, pp. 201-222; Paul W. Gates, 'Federal Land Policy in the South', *Journal of Southern History,* vol. 6, August 1940, pp. 303-330; Joseph D. Reid Jr, 'Sharecropping in History and Theory', *Agricultural History,* vol. 49, April 1975, pp. 426-440; and Jay R. Mandle, *The Roots of Black Poverty: The Southern Plantation Economy after the Civil War,* Durham 1978, especially chapters 1-4, pp. 3-51.

79. Cruden, *The Negro in Reconstruction,* p. 37.

80. Peter Camejo, *Racism, Revolution, Reaction, 1861-1877: The Rise and Fall of Radical Reconstruction,* New York 1976, pp. 94-95.

81. Franklin, *Reconstruction: After the Civil War,* p. 91.

82. Holt, *Black over White,* pp. 125-128, 131, 156.

83. *Ibid.,* pp. 36, 48, 112, 164-165.

84. *Ibid.,* pp. 168-169.

85. Du Bois, *Black Reconstruction in America, 1860-1880,* pp. 350-351.

86. Holt, *Black over White,* pp. 60, 74-75, 106.

87. Meier, *Negro Thought in America, 1880-1915,* p. 65.

88. Franklin, *Reconstruction: After the Civil War,* p. 90.

89. McKinlay, Bosemon, Sasportas and most of Charleston's coloured elite strongly opposed railroad subsidies, state expenditures for internal improvements, and bond issues to pay for these programmes. These Negroes had a financial stake in real estate, pre-Civil War securities and other ventures which could have been hurt by the taxation or fiscal policies of the new state government.

90. See C. Vann Woodward, *Reunion and Reaction: The Compromise of 1877 and*

332

the End of Reconstruction, New York 1956.

91. Cruden, *The Negro in Reconstruction*, p. 163.

92. Meier, *Negro Thought in America, 1880-1915*, pp. 239-240, 251-255.

93. W.E.B. Du Bois, *The Autobiography of W.E.B. Du Bois*, New York 1968, p. 239.

94. Meier, *Negro Thought in America, 1880-1915*, pp. 114, 159, 174-180.

95. W.E.B. Du Bois to John Hope, 22 January 1910, in Herbert Aptheker, ed., *The Correspondence of W.E.B. Du Bois: Volume I*, Amherst 1973, p. 167.

96. Du Bois, *The Autobiography of W.E.B. Du Bois*, pp. 236–237. Du Bois could examine the strengths of Washington's programme only some time after their historic conflict. Twenty years after Washington's death, Du Bois reflected that his adversary had 'minimized political power and emphasized industrial education'. Nevertheless, 'his earnestness, shrewd common sense and statesman-like finesse in interracial contacts mark his greatness; and Tuskegee Institute stands as his magnificent monument'. Du Bois, 'Washington, Booker Taliaferro', in Edwin R.A. Seligman, *Encyclopedia of the Social Sciences*, New York 1935, vol. 15, pp. 365-366.

87. Meier, *Negro Thought in America, 1880-1915*, p. 171.

98. W.E.B. Du Bois to Booker T. Washington, 24 September 1895, in Aptheker, ed., *The Correspondence of W.E.B. Du Bois: Volume I*, p. 39.

99. Louis R. Harlan, *Booker T. Washington: The Making of a Black Leader, 1856-1901*, New York 1972, pp. 298-302. Several essays that indicate Washington's interest in civil rights, political reform and Pan-Africanism are: Louis R. Harlan, 'Booker T. Washington and the White Man's Burden', *American Historical Review*, Burden', *American Historical Review*, vol. 71, January 1966, pp. 441-467; Harlan, 'The Secret Life of Booker T. Washington', *Journal of Southern History*, vol. 37, 'Toward a Reinterpretation of Booker T. Washington', *Journal of Southern History*, vol. 23, May 1957, pp. 220-227; J. Donald Calista, 'Booker T. Washington: Another Look', *Journal of Negro History*, vol. 49, October 1964, pp. 240-255; Jack Abramowitz, 'The Emergence of Booker T. Washington as a National Negro Leader'. *Social Education*, vol. 32, May 1968, pp. 445-451; and Manning Marabic, 'Booker T. Washington and African Nationalism', *Phylon*, vol. 35, December 1974, pp. 398-406.

100. Meier, *Negro Thought in America, 1880-1915*, pp. 31-33, 70, 184, 213-214, 221, 232, 241, 250-251, 254-255.

101. *Ibid.*, pp. 110, 248-249. The unctuous behaviour of Councill did little good — white racist 'night riders' once set fire to his college and burned several buildings to the ground. See Matthew Holden Jr, *The Politics of the Black 'Nation'*, New York 1973, pp. 46-47.

102. 'Along the Color Line', *Horizon*, vol. 5, November 1909, p. 9.

103. Reverdy C. Ransom, 'The Negro and Socialism (1896-97)', in Philip S. Foner, ed., *Black Socialist Preacher*, San Francisco 1983, pp. 282-289.

104. Verna Chandler Foster and Robert D. Reid, 'The Negro in Politics', in Jessie Parkhurst Guzman, ed., *Negro Year Book: 'A Review of Events Affecting Negro Life, 1941-1946*, Tuskegee Institute, Alabama 1947, pp. 281–287.

105. W.E.B. Du Bois, 'The Right to Work', *Crisis*, vol. 40, April 1933, pp. 93-94.

106. W.E.B. Du Bois, 'A History of the Negro Vote', *Crisis*, vol. 40, June 1933, pp. 128-219.

107. Holden, *The Politics of the Black 'Nation'*, pp. 57-58.

108. Carson, *In Struggle*, pp. 21-22, 57, 232, 306.

109. Emily Rovetch, ed., *Like It Is: Arthur E. Thomas Interviews Leaders on Black America*, New York 1981, pp. 144–145. Sources by and about Julian Bond

include: John Neary, *Julian Bond: Black Rebel*, New York 1971; Herbert Shapiro, 'Julian Bond', *Nation*, vol. 202, 2 February 1966, pp. 145–148; Reese Cleghorn, 'Here Comes Julian Bond', *New York Times Magazine*, 20 October 1968, pp. 38–39; Julian Bond, 'Non-violence: An Interpretation', *Freedomways*, vol. 3, Spring 1963, pp. 159–162; Bond, *A Time to Speak, A Time to Act*, New York, 1972; Bond, *Black Candidates: Southern Campaign Experiences*, Atlanta 1969; Bond, 'Better Voters, Better Politicians', *Southern Exposure*, vol. 7, Spring 1979, pp. 68–70; and Bond, 'Politics Makes a Difference', *Southern Exposure*, vol. 12, February 1984, pp. 12–14.

110. Angela Y. Davis, *Angela Davis: An Autobiography*, New York 1974, pp. 79, 83, 141-43, 180.

111. Carson, *In Struggle*, pp. 162–163, 306. Carmichael was the pivotal figure in the emergence of Black Power in 1966. The evolution of his social thought can be traced in Carmichael, 'What We Want', *New York Review of Books*, vol. 7, 22 September 1966, pp. 5-6, 8; 'Toward Black Liberation', *Massachusetts Review*, vol. 7, Autumn 1966, pp. 639-651; Carmichael and Charles V. Hamilton, *Black Power: The Politics of Liberation in America*, New York 1967; and *Stokely Speaks: Black Power Back to Pan-Africanism*, New York 1971.

112. Perry Anderson, *Considerations on Western Marxism*, London 1979, p. 26.

113. Meier and Rudwick,CORE, p. 5.

114. *Ibid.*, p. 170; and Manning Marable, *Blackwater* pp. 98, 101.

115. Leonard A. Cole, *Blacks in Power: A Comparative Study of Black and White Elected Officials*, Princeton 1976, pp. 74-76.

116. Ernest Patterson, *Black City Politics*, New York 1974, pp. 206-208.

117. Lewis, *King: A Critical Biography*, pp. 137, 278; and William Robert Miller, *Martin Luther King Jr: His Life, Martyrdom and Meaning for the World*, New York 1968, pp. 19, 122. On Andrew Young's career and political thought, see: Lee Clement, ed., *Andrew Young at the United Nations*, Salisbury, North Carolina 1978; Carl Gardner, *Andrew Young, A Biography*, New York 1978, Eddie Stone, *Andrew Young: Biography of a Realist*, Los Angeles 1979; and Joseph Howard Holland, 'Toward the Just Society: The Ideological Heritage of Andrew Young', MA thesis, Cornell University, 1979.

118. Miller, *Martin Luther King Jr*, pp. 47, 185; and Marable, *Blackwater*, pp. 156-157.

119. Rovetch, ed., *Like It Is*, pp. 56-57.

120. Monte Piliawsky, 'The Limits of Power: New Orleans', *Southern Exposure*, vol. 12, February 1984, pp. 71-72.

121. William E. Nelson Jr and Philip J. Meranto, *Electing Black Mayors: Political Action in the Black Community*, Columbus 1977, pp. 197-199.

122. Meier and Rudwick, CORE, pp. 218-219.

123. Rovetch, ed., *Like It Is*, pp. 158-159.

124. Robert Staples, 'Tom Bradley's Defeat: The Impact of Racial Symbols on Political Campaigns', *Black Scholar*, vol. 13, Fall 1982, pp. 40-41.

125. Gerald A. Anderson, 'A Question of Blackness', *Charleston Chronicle*, 14 July 1984.

126. Rovetch, ed., *Like It Is*, pp. 32-33.

127. Rod Bush, ed., *The New Black Vote: Politics and Power in Four American Cities*, San Francisco 1984, pp. 43, 324-326.

128. Foner, *Organized Labor and the Black Worker*, pp. 294-296, 301.

129. Georgakas and Surkin, *Detroit: I Do Mind Dying*, pp. 69, 222-225.

130. *Ibid.*, pp. 24, 88-89; and Rod Bush, 'Detroit: Victory of a Black Radical: An Interview with Ken Cockrel', in Bush, ed., *The New Black Vote*, pp. 183-197.

131. Bureau of the Census, *The Social and Economic Status of the Black Population*, p. 174.

132. Steven V. Roberts, 'Rules of Party Playing Desired Role, Poll Finds', and '*New York Times* Delegate Survey: Who the Delegates Are', *New York Times*, 15 July 1984. The *New York Times*'s survey results are similar to the social profiles of Black politicians compiled by Leonard A. Cole in 1976. 58 per cent were between 30 and 49 years of age; 39 per cent either had college diplomas or had studied in college, and another 52 per cent had post-graduate degrees; 23 per cent were business owners or managers, 7 per cent were clergymen, and another 20 per cent were either accountants or engineers. See Cole, *Blacks in Power*, pp. 40-43.

133. 'Median Family Income in 1960 and 1970 to 1982 by Race', in Williams, ed., *The State of Black America, 1984*, p. 21.

134. See Manning Marable, 'The Crisis of the Black Working Class: An Economic and Historical Analysis', *Science and Society*, vol. 46, Summer 1982, pp. 145-147.

135. Martin, *The Pan-African Connection*, p. 127.

136. Marable, *How Capitalism Underdeveloped Black America*, pp. 172-176.

137. Richard Hatcher, in Baraka, ed., *African Congress*, p. 69.

138. Charles V. Hamilton, 'Black Americans and the Modern Political Struggle', *Black World*, vol. 19, May 1970, p. 78.

139. Karenga, 'The Crisis of Black Middle-Class Leadership', p. 21.

140. James Jennings, 'Blacks and Progressive Politics', in Bush, ed., *The New Black Vote*, p. 203.

141. Shirley Chisholm, 'Coalitions — the Politics of the Future', in Nathan Wright Jr, *What Black Politicians are Saying*, New York 1972, p. 86.

142. Cole, *Blacks in Power*, pp. 83-86.

143. Nelson and Meranto, *Electing Black Mayors*, p. 388.

144. Cole, *Blacks in Power*, p. 104.

145. Nelson and Meranto, *Electing Black Mayors*, p. 18.

146. Jennings, 'Blacks and Progressive Politics', p. 210.

147. See Herrington J. Bryce and Alan E. Warrick, *Black Women in Electoral Politics*, Washington DC 1973.

148. In Jewel L. Prestage's 1977 survey of 32 Afro-American women state legislators, she was told that women's liberation was a 'very low priority'. See Prestage, 'Political Behavior of American Black Women', in Rodgers-Rose, ed., *The Black Woman*, p. 244.

149. James Early, 'Rainbow Politics: From Civil Rights to Civil Equality: An Interview with Jack O'Dell', *Black Scholar*, vol. 15, September-October 1984, pp. 50-56.

150. Rovetch, ed., *Like It Is*, pp. 65, 68.

151. Chuck Stone, *Black Political Power in America*, New York 1970, p. 10.

152. Meier, *Negro Thought in America, 1880-1915*, pp. 109-110.

153. Kenneth Gibson, in Baraka, ed., *African Congress*, pp. 19-20.

154. Whitney Young Jr, in *Ibid.*, p. 40.

155. Lewis, *King*, pp. 88, 162.

156. Harlan, *Booker T. Washington*, pp. 300, 308-309.

157. Rustin, ' "Black Power" and Coalition Politics', pp. 35-40.

158. Marable, *Blackwater*, p. 156.

159. Cole, *Blacks in Power*, pp. 54-55.

160. See Henry Lee Moon, *Balance of Power: The Negro Vote*, New York 1948.

161. Clay quoted in Anna R. Langford, 'How I "Whupped" the Tar out of the Daley Machine', in Wright, ed., *What Black Politicians Are Saying*, p. 30.

162. Rovetch, ed., *Like It is*, p. 68.

163. Hatcher, in Baraka, ed., *African Congress*, p. 72.

164. Carmichael and Hamilton, *Black Power*, pp. 54, 75, 82-83.

165. Marable, *How Capitalism Underdeveloped Black America*, pp. 43-44.

166. Michael Parenti, *Democracy for the Few*, New York 1977, pp. 201-203, 207, 222-223, 232.

167. Wright, *Black Boy*, p. 219.

168. On Powell's charismatic rise and fall, see James Q. Wilson, 'The Flamboyant Mr Powell', *Commentary*, vol. 41, January 1966, pp. 31-35; and Wilson, 'Two Negro Politicians: An Interpretation', *Midwest Journal of Political Science*, vol. 4, November 1960, pp. 346-369.

169. Marguerite Ross Barnett, 'The Congressional Black Caucus: Illusions and Realities of Power', in Preston, Henderson and Puryear, eds., *The New Black Politics*, pp. 44-45.

170. Institute for the Study of Labour and Economic Crisis, ed., *The Iron Fist and the Velvet Glove: An Analysis of the US Police*, San Francisco 1982, p. 116.

171. Michael Newton, *The FBI Plot: How the FBI Fought Against Civil Rights in America*, Los Angeles 1981, p. 176. Also under police scrutiny as 'radical organizations' were the American Civil Liberties Union, the Gay Activists Alliance, the American Friends' Service Committee and the Academy of Political Science.

172. Allen, *Black Awakening in Capitalist America*, pp. 203-205.

173. Institute for the Study of Labour and Economic Crisis, ed., *The Iron Fist and the Velvet Glove*, pp. 110, 112-115.

174. Newton, *The FBI Plot*, pp. 114-122.

175. Walton, *Black Politics*, p. 122.

176. *Ibid.*, pp. 123-131.

177. Baraka, ed., *African Congress*, pp. 20, 115; and Mervyn M. Dymally, 'The Rise of Black Political Leadership in California', in Wright, ed., *What Black Politicians Are Saying*, p. 41.

178. Marable, *Blackwater*, pp. 105-107.

179. Rod Bush, 'Peace, Justice and Politics: An Interview with Congressman Ronald V. Dellums', in Bush, ed., *The New Black Vote*, p. 367.

180. 'The New Motion in Black Politics and the Electoral Arena', *Line of March*, 15, Spring 1984, p. 74.

181. Jennings, 'Blacks and Progressive Politics', in *Ibid.*, p. 212.

182. Kalamu ya Salaam, 'For Malcolm, For Us', *Steppingstones: A Literary Anthology Toward Liberation*, Winter 1983, p. 38.

4 Black Power in Chicago: Race and Electoral Politics in Urban America

1. Studs Terkel, 'The Chicago Machine Is a Junk Heap', *New York Times*, 17 April 1983.

2. Nina Berman, ' "Disciplined rage" shakes up Chicago', *Guardian*, 9 March 1983.

3. Terkel, 'The Chicago Machine Is a Junk Heap'.

4. Abdul Alkalimat and Don Gills, 'Black Political Protest and the Mayoral Victory of Harold Washington: Chicago Politics, 1983', *Radical America*, vols. 17-18, November 1983-February 1984, pp. 111, 125.

5. 'The New Motion in Black Politics and the Electoral Arena', *Line of March*, pp. 25-26.

6. St Clair Drake and Horace R. Cayton, *Black Metropolis: A Study of Negro Life in a Northern City, Volume I*, New York 1962, pp. 32-45.

7. Charles S. Johnson, 'The New Frontage on American Life', in Alain Locke, ed., *The New Negro*, New York 1977, p. 278.

8. Allan H. Spear, *Black Chicago: The Making of a Negro Ghetto, 1890-1920*, Chicago 1967, pp. 12–13. Also see Devereaux Bowly Jr, *The Poorhouse: Subsidized Housing in Chicago, 1895_1976*, Carbondale 1978.

9. *Ibid.*, pp. 17, 22-24.

10. *Ibid.*, pp. 41-42.

11. *Ibid.*, pp. 32-33.

12. Drake and Cayton, *Black Metropolis*, p. 48.

13. Spear, *Black Chicago*, pp. 66-67, 72-75, 80, 227. Also see Inez Cantey, 'Jesse Binga', *Crisis*, vol. 34, December 1927, p. 239; August Meier, 'Booker T. Washington and the Negro Press', *Journal of Negro History*, vol. 38, January 1953, pp. 67-90.

14. *Ibid.*, pp. 57-63.

15. Meier, *Negro Thought in America, 1880-1915*, p. 135.

16. Spear, *Black Chicago*, p. 178.

17. Foner, *Organized Labor and the Black Worker, 1619-1981*, pp. 62-63.

18. R.R. Wright, 'The Negro in the Chicago Labor Movement, 1900-1905', in Herbert Aptheker, ed., *A Documentary History of the Negro People in the United States, Volume II*, pp. 838-842.

19. *Ibid.*, p. 839. General studies of Blacks and organized labour in Chicago include: Alma Herbst, *The Negro in the Slaughtering and Meat Packing Industry in Chicago*, Boston 1932; William M. Tuttle Jr, 'Labor Conflict and Racial Violence: The Black Worker in Chicago, 1894-1919'. *Labor History*, vol. 10, Summer 1969, pp. 408-432; and Catherine E. Lewis, 'Trade-Union Policies in Regard to the Negro Worker in the Slaughter and Meatpacking Industry of Chicago', Master's thesis, University of Chicago, 1945.

20. *William M. Tuttle Jr, Race Riot: Chicago in the Red Summer of 1919*, New York 1974, pp. 43, 46, 49.

21. *Ibid.*, pp. 60.

22. Drake and Cayton, *Black Metropolis*, p. 325. Other secondary sources that examine the 1919 race riot include: Chicago Commission on race Relations, *The Negro in Chicago*, Chicago 1922; Carl Sandburg, *The Chicago Race Riots*, New York 1919; Walter White, 'Chicago and Its Eight Reasons', *Crisis*, vol. 18, October 1919, pp. 293-294; Guido Dobbert, 'A History of the Chicago Race Riot of 1919'. MA

thesis, University of Chicago, 1957; and Arthur I. Waskow, *From Race Riot to Sit-In*, New York 1965.

23. Harold F. Gosnell, 'The Chicago "Black Belt" as a Political Battleground', *American Journal of Sociology*, vol. 39, November 1933, pp. 337-338.

24. Walton, *Black Politics*, pp. 105, 107. It is noteworthy, however, that one Democratic candidate for mayor, Harrison Carter I, received about 50 per cent of the Black vote in 1885. His son, Harrison Carter, II, won 65 per cent of the Black vote in his successful mayoral race in 1897. Charles Branham, 'A History of Black Politics, Part One', *Chicago Journal*, 19 January 1983.

25. Walton, *Black Politics*, p. 107. Spear, *Black Chicago*, pp. 82, 114.

26. Studies on the history of Afro-American politics in Chicago include: Ralph J. Bunche, 'The Thompson-Negro Alliance', *Opportunity*, vol. 7, March 1929, pp. 78-80; John M. Allswang, 'The Chicago Negro Voter and the Democratic Consensus: A Case Study, 1918-1936', *Journal of the Illinois State Historical Society*, vol. 60, Summer 1967, pp. 145-175; Harold Gosnell, *Negro Politicians: The Rise of Negro Politics in Chicago*, Chicago 1935, reprinted, 1969; Harold M. Baron, 'Black Powerlessness in Chicago', *Transaction*, vol. 6, November 1968, pp. 27-33; Dianne Pinderhughes, 'Interpretations of Racial and Ethnic Participation in American Politics: The Case of the Black, Italian and Polish Communities in Chicago, 1910-1940', Ph.D. dissertation, University of Chicago, 1977; and Charles Branham, 'Black Chicago: Accommodationist Politics Before the Great Migration', in Peter Jones and M. Hollis, eds., *The Ethnic Frontier*, Grand Rapids, Michigan 1977, pp. 212-262.

27. Spear, *Black Chicago*, p. 191.

28. Gosnell, *Negro Politicians*, pp. 169-171. Unlike the more conservative accommodationists, DePriest always exhibited an independent streak, a tendency to barter with white Democrats and Republicans alike, which won the grudging respect of some reformers, and the admiration of many fo the Black poor (whom DePriest so effectively and cruelly exploited). In 1904 and 1906 the young businessman was elected as a Republican on the Cook County Board of Commissioners. A brief feud with white Republican Congressmen Martin B. Madden, who represented the South Side, forced DePriest out of office. Off and on, DePriest was part of the Republican Party's machinery for the next two decades. But unlike his more loyal and less imaginative Black counterparts, DePriest continued to break with Republican leaders whenever it served his own interests. In 1912 he campaigned for white Democrat Maclay Hoyne against the Republican nominee in Hoyne's successful bid to become State's Attorney. DePriest won a five-way struggle to become the Republican Party's nominee for 2nd ward alderman in 1915 by building a powerful Black coalition, which included the Hotel Waiters' Association, Black dentists, physicians, women's church groups, barbers, and the major leaders of the Black Baptist and Methodist churches. In the general election, DePriest defeated a white Progressive Party candidate and the white Democrat.

29. As Branham observes, DePriest's tactical struggle with the Thompson Machine 'was clearly self-serving and the People's Movement had no programme save returning the former alderman to political power'. Yet in the devastation of Chicago's 1919 race riot, which left 38 dead and 520 injured, DePriest 'emerged as a genuine hero', saving Black workers from assaults and 'braving hostile white mobs'. Branham, 'A History of Black Politics, Part One'.

30. W.E.B. Du Bois, 'Postcript', *Crisis*, vol. 35, December 1928, p. 428.

31. W.E.B. Du Bois, 'Postcript', *Crisis*, vol. 36, February 1929, p. 57.

32. Franklin, *From Slavery to Freedom*, pp. 525-526.

33. Charles Branham, 'A History of Black Politics, Part Two', *Chicago Journal*, 19

January 1983.

34. Dawson's early history in politics is most revealing. A Fisk University graduate, he received his legal training at Northwestern University. By the mid 1920s, the majority of the First Congressional District's population was Black. Taking this racial constituency into account, the young Dawson ran a militant, almost 'Garveyist', campaign against Madden. With open appeals to Black pride and consciousness, Dawson told community audiences that he was 'better fitted to represent the district' owing to his 'birth, training and experience'. Madden was 'a white man' who did 'not even live in the district. Therefore, for those two reasons, if no others, he can hardly voice the hopes, ideals and sentiment of the majority of the district.' In the Republican primary, however, Dawson received only 29 per cent of the vote. As fate would have it, Madden died only months later, and Mayor Thompson turned to the somewhat more reliable DePriest to run as the district's Republican candidate in the fall of 1928. Dawson's turn to fill the seat did not occur until 1942, after he had purged himself of any dangerous militant Black nationalistic political tendencies and had become a dependable cog in the machine. See Gosnell, *Negro Politicians: The Rise of Negro Politics in Chicago*, p. 79.

35. Walton, *Black Politics*, pp. 108-109. Du Bois's view of the 1927 Chicago election is of some interest. Describing the defeat of the Democratic incumbent as a 'serious mistake', he denounced Thompson as 'a well-known demogague who represents open house to gamblers, bootleggers and prostitutes'. The NAACP leader admitted that the Democratic nominee had made 'overtures' to Negroes, but that his racist campaign propaganda had alienated thousands of Black voters. 'For bullheaded asininity, commend us to the Democratic party.' Du Bois, 'Postscript', *Crisis*, vol. 34, June 1927, p. 131.

36. Branham, 'A History of Black Politics, Part Two'; Gosnell, *Negro Politicians*, p. 54; Bunche, 'The Thompson-Negro Alliance', p. 79.

37. Branham, 'A History of Black Politics, Part Two'.

38. In 1937, Congressman Mitchell was forcibly removed from a Pullman railroad car travelling between Chicago and Hot Springs, Georgia. Mitchell argued that he 'was entitled to railroad accommodations equal to those provided for whites'. In the 1941 Supreme Court decision, Chief Justice Charles Evans Hughes ruled that the action of the railroad officials 'was manifestly a discrimination against [Mitchell] in the course of his interstate journey and admittedly that discrimination was based solely upon the fact that he was a Negro'. The denial of equal accommodations in interstate travel was a violation of the 14th Amendment and in view of the nature of the right and of our constitutional policy, it cannot be maintained that the discrimination as it was alleged was not essentially unjust'. Guzman, ed., *Negro Year Book: A Review of Events Affecting Negro Life, 1941-1946*, p. 298.

39. Branham, 'A History of Black Politics, Part Two'.

40. Walton, *Black Politics*, pp. 63, 207.

41. Meier and Rudwick, CORE, pp. 27-28.

42. Stone, *Black Political Power in America*, pp. 177-179.

43. See Wilson, *Negro Politics: The Search for Leadership*.

44. Lewis, *King: A Critical Biography*, p. 316.

45. *Ibid.*, p. 332.

46. *Ibid.*, pp. 346-347.

47. *Ibid.*, pp. 351-352.

48. 'Daley received an average of 77.4 per cent of the Black vote during his entire political career, and between 1955 and 1963 his primary support had come from Black Belt wards in the inner city.' After the 1966 desegregation campaign, Daley's

mandates began to slip in Black wards, 'and he began to shift his base of support from the inner city to the white outer wards. After 1970 Daley appealed increasingly to white blue-collar Southwest and North Side wards . . .'. Branham, 'A History of Black Politics, Part Two'.

49. Lewis, *King: A Critical Biography*, p. 339.

50. Joseph H. Jackson's hatred of King transcended even the boundaries of death. 'The Chicago City Council voted to change the name of South Park Boulevard to Dr Martin Luther King Jr Drive' after his assassination. Jackson's 'Olivet Baptist Church is on the corner of 31st and South Park Boulevard. Its original address was 3101 South Park Boulevard. When the street-name was changed, Reverend Jackson had the address of the church changed to 401 East 31st Street!' Charles V. Hamilton, *The Black Preacher in America*, New York 1972, p. 27. James Q. Wilson observed that the majority of Black leaders in Chicago were members of 'the Negro upper-class churches — Episcopalian, Presbyterian, Congregational, Lutheran, and Roman Catholic'. The majority of Black workers, conversely, were Baptists or Methodists. Thus Jackson's attack on King could have played a decisive role in the demoralization of many Black poor and working-class Chicagoans. See Wilson, *Negro Politics*, pp. 11-12.

51. Lewis, *King: A Critical Biography*, pp. 313, 336-337.

52. 'Democratic Mayoral Primaries Since Daley Era Began in 1955', *Chicago Sun-Times*, February 23 1983. In the aftermath of the Summit Agreement, and with Daley's subsequent re-election, the city's administration assumed a more vicious and repressive posture towards Blacks. For example, after the April 1968 uprisings following King's assassination, Daley announced his displeasure at the fact that his officers had not given 'shoot-to-kill orders'. Any arsonist or anyone with a 'Molotov cocktail' should be shot on sight. The mayor also told police to 'shoot looters [in order] to detain them' at the scene of the crime. Within months, Chicago spent over $150,000 on 'three helicopters designed to serve as airborne command posts during [future] riots'. Allen, *Black Awakening in Capitalist America*, pp. 196-197.

53. W.E.B. Du Bois, 'Segregation in the North', *Crisis*, vol. 41, April 1934, pp. 115-117.

54. Piven and Cloward, *Poor People's Movements*, p. 55.

55. *Ibid.*, p. 59.

56. Occasionally irate white plantation-owners would pursue their 'runaway Blacks' into the North. One infamous case occurred in Chicago in 1939, when William T. Cunningham, a Georgia planter, took a local police officer and followed the trail of 'four of his indebted labourers to Chicago'. Cunningham 'persuaded the Chicago police to aid in rounding them up'. See Daniel, *The Shadow of Slavery*, p. 175.

57. The greatest concentrations of Black Americans in 1970 were in six major cities. New York had 1,667,000 Black residents; Chicago, 1,103,000; Detroit, 660,000; Philadelphia, 654,000; Los Angeles, 504,000; and Washington DC, 538,000. See Marcus E. Jones, *Black Migration in the United States With Emphasis on Selected Central Cities*, Saratoga, California 1980, pp. 69, 70.

58. In the Chicago metropolitan area in 1960, 55.8 per cent of all Black men and 53.9 per cent of Black women were operatives, private household workers, service workers or labourers. In the same group, figures for white males were 31.5 per cent; for white females, 28.8 per cent. 23.5 per cent of all white male workers were professionals, managers or proprietors, compared with 14.5 per cent of white women; Black men, 4.8 per cent; Black women, 7.9 per cent. See Harold M. Baron and Bennett Hymer, 'The Negro Worker in the Chicago Labor Market', in Julius

340

Jacobson, ed., *The Negro and the American Labor Movement,* Garden City, New York 1968, pp. 252, 255.

59. US Department of Labour, *Work Experience and Earnings in 1975 by State and Area,* Washington DC 1976, pp. 11-12.

60. 'New Poverty Traps 600,000 Chicagoans — Permanently', *Chicago Reporter,* vol. 9, February 1980, pp. 1, 4-5.

61. Baron and Hymer, 'The Negro Worker in the Chicago Labor Market', p. 259.

62. Larry S. Finley, 'Production Jobs in Decline', *Chicago Sun-Times,* 18 July 1982; Alan P. Henry and Dennis Byrne, 'Blacks find jobs refuge in public sector', *Chicago Sun-Times,* 19 December 1982.

63. Chinta Strausberg, 'Charges Blacks Paid Less', *Chicago Defender,* 27 November 1982.

64. 'Occupational Discrimination in Chicago Municipal Government — 1981', *Chicago Defender,* 27 November 1982.

65. Bureau of the Census, *1977 Survey of Minority-Owned Business Enterprises,* Washington DC December 1979, pp. 5, 42, 51, 54.

66. Some of Chicago's most heavily segregated neighbourhoods are on the West Side: West Garfield Park, 98.8 per cent Black; East Garfield Park, 99.0 per cent Black; North Lawndale, 96.5 per cent Black. On the South Side, Woodlawn is 95.7 per cent Black; West Pullman, 90.6 per cent Black; Riverdale, 96.7 per cent Black; Auburn Greeham, 98.4 per cent Black. Conversely, the Ashburn neighbourhood on the Southwest Side — directly west of Auburn Greeham — is 36.6 per cent Irish, 24.3 per cent German, 18.4 per cent Polish and 10 per cent Italian, with fewer than a handful of Black families. See Dennis Byrne, 'Ethnic roots deep in City Suburbs', *Chicago Sun-Times,* 2 January 1983.

67. Richard Wright, *American Hunger,* New York 1977, pp. 41-42.

68. Alkalimat and Gills, 'Black Political Protest and the Mayoral Victory of Harold Washington', p. 113; Gosnell, 'The Chicago "Black Belt" as a Political Battleground', p. 331.

69. 'Chicago Board of Election Commissioners', *Chicago Reporter,* vol. 8, April 1979, p. 8; *Chicago Reporter,* vol. 7, January 1978, pp. 4-5.

70. Andrew H. Malcolm, 'Chicago Politics: The "Machine" Today', *New York Times,* 13 February 1983; Harry Golden Jr, 'Four Wards Hold 20 Per cent of City Jobs', *Chicago Sun-Times,* 21 December 1982. Richard M. Daley's 11th Ward and three other all-white wards on the city's South-west Side contain only 8 per cent of Chicago's population but held 20 per cent of the patronage jobs. Daley's cousin in the 18th Ward, John M. Daley, alone controlled 2,196 jobs in 1982.

71. Spear, *Black Chicago,* pp. 25, 35-36, 44, 212-213.

72. Johnson, *Backgrounds to Patterns of Negro Segregation,* p. 178.

73. Piven and Cloward, *Poor People's Movements,* pp. 143-144; Drake and Cayton, *Black Metropolis,* pp. 322-325.

74. *Racially Motivated Random Violence,* vol. 2, June-July 1982, pp. 1-2, 5; and vol. 2, August-September 1982, pp. 2, 5-7.

75. Karl. E. Taeuber and Alma F. Taeuber, 'The Negro as an Immigrant Group: Recent Trends in Racial and Ethnic Segregation in Chicago', *American Journal of Sociology,* vol. 69, January 1964, p. 377.

76. Alkalimat and Gills, 'Black Power vs Racism', p. 64.

77. Carmichael and Hamilton, *Black Power,* pp. 173-175.

78. Monroe Anderson, 'Black may redo mayor script', *Chicago Tribune,* 8 November 1982.

79. Michael B. Preston, 'Black Politics and Public Policy in Chicago: Self-Interest

Versus Constituent Representation', in Preston, Henderson and Puryear, eds., *The New Black Politics*, pp. 162, 170-171.

80. George Atkins, 'City Debt Increased 130 Per cent Since 1979', *All Chicago City News*, 31 December 1982-14 January 1983.

81. Preston, 'Black Politics and Public Policy in Chicago', pp. 167-168.

82. People's College, ed., *Black Power in Chicago*, pp. 2A-6, 2C-74. [Author's note: Many of the newspaper sources cited here were also reproduced in the monograph *Black Power in Chicago*.]

83. Chinta Strausberg, 'Ward Bosses, Washington in "secret" meet', *Chicago Defender*, 23 November 1983.

84. Marc Zalkin, 'Streeter Faces Byrne Power in South Side Election', *All Chicago City News*, 16 April 1982-30 April 1982; David Axelrod, 'South Side maverick has become hero', *Chicago Tribune*, 27 June 1982; Marc Zalkin, 'Streeter victory sends message downtown', *All Chicago City News*, 11 June 1982-25 June 1982.

85. Roger Simon, 'Jackson Hits Byrne where it hurts', *Chicago Sun-Times*, 30 July 1982; Chinta Strausberg, 'Fest Boycott no longer a Black issue', *Chicago Defender*, 2 August 1982.

86. Rod Bush, 'Black Enfranchisement, Jesse Jackson, and Beyond', p. 25; and Alkalimat and Gills, 'Black Power vs Racism', pp. 86-87, in Bush, ed., *The New Black Vote*.

87. George Atkins, 'POWER: Most successful vote registration drive in Chicago history', *All Chicago City News*, 10 September 1982-24 September 1982; Helen Shiller, 'Voter Registration Drive Exceeds Expectations', *All Chicago City News*, 8 October 1982-22 October 1982; Juanita Bratcher, 'Huge voter turn-out enhances mayoral bid', *Chicago Defender*, 4 November 1982.

88. Alkalimat and Gills, 'Black Power vs Racism', pp. 91, 95-96.

89. *Ibid.*, p. 107.

90. *Ibid.*, pp. 111-113.

91. Chinta Strausberg, 'Washington announces "blue ribbon" team', *Chicago Defender*, 14 December 1982; Lillian Williams, 'Washington Camp Wooing Ex-Byrne Aide', *Chicago Sun-Times*, 18 December 1982; Lillian Williams, 'Three Prominent Coaches Join Washington', *Chicago Sun-Times*, 5 December 1982.

92. Anderson, 'Black may redo mayor script'.

93. Lillian Williams, 'Two Dem. Leaders Back Washington', *Chicago Sun-Times*, 9 November 1982.

94. Basil Talbott Jr and Lillian Williams, 'Byrne to run: Dem. slating likely', *Chicago Sun-Times*, 17 November 1982.

95. 'Black politicians choose up sides in Mayor's race', *Chicago Defender*, 16 November 1982.

96. 'Black Reps Endorse Byrne', *Chicago Observer*, 5 February 1983.

97. Chinta Strausberg, 'Stroger defends support for Daley', *Chicago Defender*, 18 November 1982; David Axelrod and Monroe Anderson, 'Daley best for blacks, aide says', *Chicago Tribune*, 2 December 1982; Chinta Strausberg, 'Daley gains support with Scott backing', *Chicago Defender*, 16 November 1982.

98. William Recktenwald, 'Won't let race become issue, Byrne declares', *Chicago Tribune*, 22 November 1982.

99. 'The Black Role in the Byrne Administration', *Chicago Defender*, 8 January 1982.

100. Chinta Strausberg, 'Clerics: A black can't win', *Chicago Defender*, 13 January 1983.

101. ' "Protest ministers" support of Richie Daley for mayor', *Chicago Defender*,

13 January 1983; Mitchell Locin and Jane Fritsch, 'Black clergy for Washington hit pro-Daley colleagues', *Chicago Tribune*, 13 January 1983.

102. 'The Black Church Supports Harold Washington For Mayor!!!', *Chicago Defender*, 12 February 1983.

103. Willie Williamson, 'Chicago Trade Unionists Say: Washington for Mayor', *Labor Today*, February 1983, p. 1; James Strong, 'City unions in a bind on support', *Chicago Tribune*, 20 February 1983; Brian Kelly and James Warren, 'Mayor's race splits Chicago labor ranks', *Chicago Sun-Times*, 9 February 1983.

104. Alkalimat and Gills, 'Black Power vs Racism', pp. 116-117.

105. 'Ebony Magazine Publisher Supports Daley with $10,000', *Westside Journal*, 13 January-20 January 1983;.

106. 'Congressman Harold Washington's Working Paper on Jobs for Chicagoans', *Black Power in Chicago*, pp. 2C-59-2C-67.

107. Lillian Williams, 'Three Prominent Coaches Join Washington', *Chicago Sun-Times*, 5 December 1982; 'Washington for Mayor Campaign Unveils Steering Committee', *Black Power in Chicago*, pp. 2C-4, 2C-5.

108. David Moberg, 'Blacks, left spark Washington win', *In These Times*, 2-8 March 1983; Jerry Crimmins and Andy Fegelman, 'Viewers rehash debate', *Chicago Tribune*, 19 January 1983; Chinta Strausberg, ' "Man in Street" calls Washington winner in first mayoral debate', *Chicago Defender*, 20 January 1983; Basil Talbott, Jr, 'Washington dominates 2nd meet', *Chicago Sun-Times*, 24 January 1983; Eugene Kennedy, 'Mayor debates bad for Byrne', *Chicago Tribune*, 5 January 1983; Basil Talbott Jr, 'Debates were remarkable', *Chicago Sun-Times*, 3 February 1983. Talbott observed that 'Washington got more out of the debates than the other candidates. Neither Byrne nor Daley really wanted debates'.

109. Moberg, 'Blacks, left spark Washington win'.

110. Vernon Jarrett, 'Evidence of pre-election racism', *Chicago Tribune*, 18 February 1983.

111. Mike Royko, 'Racist Finale: An odorous Byrne ploy', *Chicago Sun-Times*, 22 February 1983.

112. Alkalimat and Gills, 'Black Political Protest and the Mayoral Victory of Harold Washington', p. 121. The El Rukn street-gang distributed Byrne literature across the South Side. Gang members gave away groceries in return for 'the recipients' voter-registration cards, addresses and phone numbers so they could contact them for political purposes. In each food bag were eight-page folders promoting Byrne's re-election and a card with the mayor's photo. When Byrne supporter Ed Vrdolyak was asked about Black gang involvement, he replied curtly, 'We'll take support wherever we can get it . . . ' See David Axelrod and Lynn Emmerman, 'Group tied to El Rukn', *Chicago Tribune*, 4 February 1983; John White and David Axelrod, 'Mayor disavows aid of gangs', *Chicago Tribune*, 5 February 1983.

113. David Axelrod, 'Byrne gives support to Washington', *Chicago Tribune*, 24 February 1983.

114. People's College, ed., *Black Power in Chicago*, p. 3; 'Aldermanic Vote', *Chicago Sun-Times*, 23 February 1983.

115. Alkalimat and Gills, 'Black Political Protest and the Mayoral Victory of Harold Washington', p. 121.

116. For four years, Byrne had earned a poor record on women's rights-related issues. According to one union-sponsored study, Byrne had cut public services for poor women, had contested and eventually lost 'a wage discrimination suit brought against the city by Black women' and had hired 'relatively few women — and then at low pay'. In stark contrast, as a state assemblyman and senator Washington had 'won

numerous awards for his work and pushed legislation on behalf . . . of women'. In Congress, he had received top legislative rankings from the National Women's Political Caucus, and had fought for abortion rights, the ERA, and anti-rape legislation. Nevertheless, the local National Organization for Women (NOW) chapter publicly backed Byrne. Black and white radical feminists bitterly denounced NOW's decision. As Black local activist Nancy Jefferson told one reporter: 'They should add another "W" to their name . . . National Organization for White Women'. See David Moberg, 'Mayor race divides labor, white liberals', *In These Times*, 16-22 February 1983. There was also a solid base of support for Washington among many gay and lesbian progressive leaders, but others found many questionable excuses for not endorsing him — perhaps in order to dodge charges of racism. Washington probably lost some gay support in the primary by not attending an endorsement meeting of the Greater Chicago Gay and Lesbian Democrats, an event which Byrne did attend. Many gays had praised repressive police chief Richard Brzeczek for his positive conduct towards them, and they 'questioned whether any replacement that Washington might select could fill Brzeczek's shoes in terms of gay relations'. Even the coordinator for gays and lesbians under Byrne, Angelo Galicia, admitted to the press that most white gays were 'not really being fair to Washington'. Galicia stated that not a few white gays had denounced the Black candidate with 'racist comments'. Chicago *Gay Life* columnist F. Jay Deacon declared, 'Plenty of gay and lesbian Chicagoans are going to vote *against* the Black congressman, the candidate who happens to possess the strongest record on the rights of gay and lesbian people. They're going to vote against him *because* he is Black, and they're saying so.' See Karlis Streips and Albert Williams, 'Gay voters react to Washington win', *Gay Life*, vol. 8, 3 March 1983; Paul Cotton, 'Gay-Lesbian Dems endorse Washington after debate', and F. Jay Deacon, 'A bold, splendid chance for Chicago', *Gay Life*, vol. 8, 24 March 1983.

117. Moberg, 'Blacks, left spark Washington win'.

118. Leanita McClain, 'Fear of post-election theft', *Chicago Tribune*, 18 February 1983.

119. Willie Cole, 'Save Our City', *Chicago Reporter*, vol. 12, March 1983, p. 2.

120. Andrew H. Malcolm, 'Representative Washington, Chicago Victor, Sets Ambitious City Hall Agenda', *New York Times*, 24 February 1983.

121. Nathanial Sheppard Jr, 'Mayor Byrne Sets Write-in Campaign For Chicago Vote', *New York Times*, 17 March 1983; David Moberg, 'Jane's looking-glass politics,' *In These Times*, 23-29 March 1983. Byrne's decision to run as a write-in candidate was based on the belief that Epton would capture only 18 per cent of the electorate in a general race, and that she could pick up the majority of the 343,000 votes that had been cast for Daley in the primary. Contemptuously dismissing the primary results, she claimed that the general election should be a 'run-off' between the two highest vote recipients. See Nathaniel Sheppard Jr, 'Mayor Byrne Developing Strategy to Make Chicago a Write-In City', *New York Times*, 22 March 1983.

122. Alkalimat and Gills, 'Black Power vs Racism', p. 137.

123. *Ibid.*, pp. 132-133, 135; 'The New Motion in Black Politics and the Electoral Arena', *Line of March*, pp. 35, 50; and *In These Times*, 13-19 April 1983. One flyer distributed by a group called 'Democrats for Epton' asserted that a vote for the Republican candidate 'will stop contamination and the occupation of city hall by a Mr Baboon . . . elected racially with the vote of thousands of baboons . . . '

124. David Axelrod and Philip Wattley, 'Police and mayor's race: Brzeczek quits; move seen as boost for Epton'; Lynn Emmerman, 'Politics of race divides police' and Philip Wattley, 'Brzeczek goal: A businesslike police force', *Chicago Tribune*, 6

344

April 1983; Beth Fallon, 'What Chicago means to us', *Daily News*, 4 April 1983.
During the Democratic primary, Brzeczek appeared in a television commercial for Byrne and enthusiastically supported her re-election bid. Washington turned the issue of police behaviour into a central issue of his campaign. He advocated the elimination of the Office of Police Standards and the creation of a new and independent civilian review board to supervise and discipline the police. For Blacks, this was a powerful incentive to work actively for Washington's campaign. For example, at an 'electrifying' rally of supporters in the University of Illinois field-house, on 6 February, Washington declared, 'One of the first things I do when I walk into that office is . . .'. Even before he could finish, the audience of twelve thousand strongly resounded: 'Fire Brzeczek, fire Brzeczek, fire Brzeczek!'. After Byrne's primary loss, Brzeczek bitterly charged that Washington's aides had falsely reported death-threats in order to receive police protection for the candidate, and that he would not under any circumstances work for the Black man. Washington replied that the 'overworked' police chief had become 'hysterical. I would suggest he should seek his doctor and get some quieting pills. I suggest he may lose his mooring and fly off to the moon.' See Moberg, 'Blacks, left spark Washington Win'; and Robert Davis, 'Washington says Brzeczek is "hysterical" ', *Chicago Tribune*, 26 February 1983.

125. Ted Pearson and Charles Wilson, 'Labor support for Washington builds', *Daily World*, 3 March 1983; Si Gerson, 'Chicago's elections and a labor-Black alliance', *Daily World*, 3 March 1983.

126. Winston Williams, 'Business Leaders Wary on Chicago Contest Role', *New York Times*, 12 April 1983; Andrew H. Malcolm, 'Chicago's Loop Is Coming Back Alive', *New York Times*, 1 February 1983; 'An Outsider Upsets Chicago's Machine', *Business Week*, 7 March 1983.

127. Anne Keegan, 'Issues obscured by election drama', *Chicago Tribune*, 6 April 1983; Andrew H. Malcolm, 'Democrat Assailed for Seeking Campaign Aid Outside Chicago', *New York Times*, 3 April 1983; Maurice Carroll, 'Chicago Candidate Receives $93,000 in New York City', *New York Times*, 31 March 1983; Malik Miah, 'Chicago socialist candidate condemns racist attack on Harold Washington', *Militant*, 8 April 1983; and Alkalimat and Gills, 'Black Power vs Racism', p. 140.

128. Ted Pearson, 'How Big Biz Whips Up Racism', *Daily World*, 31 March 1983. Most of the national media tended to portray the Washington-Epton race as a case where both politicians were 'guilty of racism'. Washington was attacked for not going after white votes; whenever he went into white neighbourhoods, some critics accused him of 'baiting' whites into making racist statements. The *New York Times* criticized Epton, but warned in an editorial that Washington had erred by giving 'the impression that his victory would indeed find Blacks claiming a huge share of the power and perks of City Hall . . . The cause of ethnic power or pride can be driven too far. Mr Washington knows, or should know, that he can become mayor only with a fraction of white votes and could govern only if he enters office with the confidence of a cross-section of voters'. See Editorial, 'Party vs Race in Chicago', *New York Times*, 6 April 1983.

129. Tim Wheeler, 'A Movement that challenges the Chicago machine', *Daily World*, 31 March 1983.

130. Alkalimat and Gills, 'Black Power vs Racism', pp. 142-147.

131. Tim Franklin and Robert Davis, 'Eight Black wards show biggest gains in voters', *Chicago Tribune*, April 6, 1983. Not all elements of the left were supporters of Washington. The Socialist Workers' Party ran their own Black candidate, Edward Warren, in the general election. Warren dismissed Washington as simply the capitalists' candidate. Not surprisingly, Warren's quixotic 'ultraleft' campaign received less

than 4,000 votes, but it objectively aided Epton by undermining the Washington mobilization. See Malik Miah, 'Chicago socialist candidate condemns racist attack on Harold Washington', *Militant*, 8 April 1983; and Miah, 'Should Marxists Back Harold Washington?', *Militant*, 1 April 1983.

132. David Axelrod, 'Vrdolyak tells Washington he could be loser', *Chicago Tribune*, 6 April 1983.

133. Edward Thompson III, 'Race and the Chicago Election', *Journal of Ethnic Studies*, vol. 11, Winter 1984, p. 6.

134. Washington's 17 per cent vote among Chicago's whites was typical for Afro-American mayoral candidates. In their initial races, Richard Hatcher of Gary had obtained 7 per cent of the white vote, Maynard Jackson of Atlanta, 21 per cent, Coleman Young of Detroit, 8 per cent, and Carl Stokes of Cleveland, 19 per cent. See 'The New Motion in Black Politics and the Electoral Arena', *Line of March*, p. 37.

135. Alkalimat and Gills, 'Black Political Protest and the Mayoral Victory of Harold Washington', p. 124; and Nathaniel Sheppard Jr, 'Hispanic Vote Seen as a Key Factor By Both Chicago Mayoral Candidates', *New York Times*, 11 April 1983.

136. Nina Berman, 'A movement starts to transform Chicago', *Guardian*, 27 April 1983.

137. Alkalimat and Gills, 'Black Power vs Racism', pp. 155-156.

138. Nathaniel Sheppard Jr, 'Chicago Mayor Elect Vows Reforms', *New York Times*, 14 April 1983.

139. Nathaniel Sheppard Jr, 'The Spoils of Chicago's Political War: Money and Power Go to the Winners', *New York Times*, 14 May 1983; Sheppard, 'A Gritty Alderman in Chicago', *New York Times*, 13 May 1983; and Curtis Black, 'Mayor wins battle in war with white-run council', *Guardian*, 17 October 1984.

140. Nina Berman, 'Mayor's honeymoon ends fast as hacks start feud', *Guardian*, 18 May 1983; Nathaniel Sheppard Jr, '"Chicago Democrats Fail to Heal Rift', *New York Times*, May 11 1983; and Mike Giocondo, 'Chicago machine attempts coup', *Daily World*, 5 May 1983.

141. Mike Giocondo, 'Chicago mayor hits corruption', *Daily World*, 23 August 1984; and Black, 'Mayor wins battle in war with white-run council'.

142. Nina Berman, 'Lozano Remembered in Chicago', *Guardian*, 27 June 1984.

143. Tim Thomas, 'Chicago School Superintendent Ruth Love fired', *Unity*, 31 August-13 September 1984.

144. Ted Pearson, 'Chicago: Class Struggle in the Electoral Arena', *Political Affairs*, vol. 62, November 1983, p. 31.

145. Nina Berman, 'Whites' War on Washington Brings City to the Brink', *Guardian*, 13 June 1984.

146. Kevin B. Blackistone, 'Racial Violence and Harassment Escalate in Chicago Area', *Chicago Reporter*, vol. 14, January 1985, pp. 1, 5-6.

147. Leanita McClain, 'How Chicago Taught Me To Hate Whites', *Washington Post*, 24 July 1983; Walter Dozier, '. . . And contributes to a Black journalist's suicide', *Guardian*, 13 June 1984.

148. David Moberg, 'Washington tangles with machine pols', *In These Times*, 11-17 May 1983.

149. Nina Berman, 'So Far, Washington is Keeping Most of his Promises', *Guardian*, 13 July 1983.

150. Washington filed a campaign financial form several weeks late, and Burke claimed that Washington had forfeited his office under Illinois state law. The Vrdolyak 29 then appointed Richard Mell, a machine loyalist, as acting mayor.

Washington had to speak on radio stations to dispel fears about this latest 'attempted coup'. Burke's legal ploy was later dismissed in Cook County Circuit Court. See Mike Giocondo, '68 civic groups back Chicago mayor', *Daily World,* 26 May 1984; and Berman, 'Whites' War on Washington Brings City to the Brink'.

151. Pearson, 'Chicago: Class Struggle in the Electoral Arena', pp. 31-32; Mike Giocondo, 'Chicago voter registration fight', *Daily World,* 22 June 1984; and Berman, 'Whites' War on Washington Brings City to the Brink'.

152. Frank Viviano, 'Coleman Young's view: What Chicago did — and did not — do', *Portland Observer,* 20 April 1983.

153. Moberg, 'Washington tangles with Machine pols'.

154. Joel Dreyfuss, 'Black mayors, business join hands', USA *Today,* 12 May 1983; and Tom Dent, 'New Orleans Versus Atlanta', *Southern Exposure,* vol. 7, Spring 1979, pp. 64-68. Dent comments that 'in Atlanta the power interests of Black and white money often coincide . . . This is the real reason why [Atlanta's new motto] is "the city too busy to hate". They are busy making money'. (pp. 64-65).

155. Piliawsky, 'The Limits of Power: New Orleans', pp. 70-76.

156. Nelson and Meranto, *Electing Black Mayors,* pp. 162, 372; and William E. Nelson Jr, 'Cleveland: The Rise and Fall of the New Black Politics', in Preston, Henderson and Puryear, eds., *The New Black Politics,* pp. 201, 205.

157. Alkalimat and Gills, 'Black Political Protest and the Mayoral Victory of Harold Washington', p. 127.

5 Rainbow Rebellion: Jesse Jackson's Presidential Campaign and the Democratic Party

1. Theodore H. White, 'Jackson, Democratic Revolutionary', *New York Times,* 5 April 1984.

2. Gerald B. Finch, 'Physical Change and Partisan Change: The Emergence of a New American Electorate, 1952-1972', in Louis Maisel and Paul M. Sacks, eds., *The Future of Political Parties, Vol. I,* Beverly Hills, California 1975, p. 47.

3. Quarles, *Frederick Douglass,* pp. 263-264.

4. Walton, *Black Politics,* p. 126.

5. Duncan Williams, ed., *The Lesser Evil? The Left Debates the Democratic Party and Social Change,* New York 1977, p. 46.

6. Walton, *Black Politics,* pp. 126-129, 136-139. Also see Hanes Walton Jr, 'Blacks and the 1968 Third Parties', *Negro Educational Review,* vol. 21, April 1970, pp. 19-23.

7. Finch, 'Physical Change and Partisan Change', pp. 54-55.

8. Bond, *A Time to Speak, A Time to Act,* p. 140.

9. Frances Fox Piven and Richard A. Cloward, *Regulating the Poor: The Functions of Public Welfare,* New York 1971, p. 255.

10. Manning Marable, *From the Grassroots: Social and Political Essays Toward Afro-American Liberation,* Boston 1980, p. 28.

11. Walton, *Black Politics,* p. 117.

12. Marable, *From the Grassroots,* p. 30.

13. Marable, *Blackwater,* p. 107.

14. Parenti, *Democracy for the Few,* pp. 200-201.

15. On the early development of the Mississippi Freedom Democratic Party, see

Lawrence Guyot and Michael Thelwell, 'Toward Independent Political Power', *Freedomways*, vol. 6, Spring 1966, pp. 120-132; Jack Minnis, 'The Mississippi Freedom Democratic Party', *Freedomways*, vol. 5, Spring 1965, pp. 264-278; and Leslie B. McLemore, 'The Freedom Democratic Party and the Changing Political Status of the Negro in Mississippi', Master's thesis, Atlanta University, 1965.

16. Williams, ed., *The Lesser Evil?*, pp. 73, 75.

17. Bond, *A Time to Speak, A Time to Act*, p. 162.

18. 'Unemployment, Inflation Has Scapegoat Showing Anti-Black Feelings', *Charleston Chronicle*, 9 July 1983.

19. 'Klan Holds White Voter Registration Drives, Backs Candidates', *Klanwatch Intelligence Report*, July 1984, p. 4; 'Klansman Praises New Civil Rights Commission', and 'Reagan Slow to Disavow KKK Backing', *National Anti-Klan Network Newsletter*, Winter-Spring 1984, p. 8.

20. Paul M. Sweezy and Harry Magdoff, 'The Left and the 1984 Elections', *Monthly Review*, vol. 35, February 1984, pp. 1-3.

21. Tod Ensign and Joyce Stroller, 'Will left parties run in tandem in '84?', *Guardian*, 13 July 1983.

22. Akinshiju C. Ola, 'Will a Black go for the White House in '84?', *Guardian*, 13 July 1983.

23. Celes Tisdale, 'Yes, There Should Be A Black Presidential Candidate in '84,' *Buffalo Challenger*, 25 May 1983.

24. Sheila Rule, 'NAACP to Focus on Black Voter Drive in North', *New York Times*, 14 July 1983.

25. 'Will Ben Hooks Run for President in 1988?', *Sacramento Observer*, 1-7 September 1983.

26. Joseph E. Lowery, 'The 1983 Election Agenda', *Carolina Peacemaker*, 21 May 1983.

27. M. Carl Holman, 'A Black for '84', *New York Times*, 22 April 1983; James H. Cleaver, 'Coalition Backs Black For President', *Charleston Chronicle*, 16 July 1983; and Holman, 'Black presidential candidate in '84?', *Amsterdam News* [New York], 9 April 1983.

28. 'Black Mayors Disagree on Black Presidential Candidate, Agree Reagan Must Go', *Westside Gazette*, 1 September 1983.

29. Ann Woolner, 'Birmingham's mayor likely to back Hollings', *Atlanta Journal* 25 March 1983.

30. John Conyers, Jr, 'Why We Should Work for Jesse Jackson', *The Organizer*, vol. 10, Spring, 1984, pp. 31-32; and Gus Savage, 'An Independent View from Capital Hill', *Pensacola Voice*, 3-9 March 1983.

31. Ronald Smothers, 'Black Caucus Weights Candidacy by Jesse Jackson', *New York Times*, 26 September 1983; and 'Should There Be A Black Presidential Candidate in 1984?', *Buffalo Challenger*, 18 May 1983.

32. Tony Brown, 'Can Black Republicans Pull Off Presidential Race?', *Carolina Peacemaker*, 14 May 1983.

33. Bayard Rustin, 'Black Presidential Candidate Doomed', *Los Angeles Sentinel*, 2 June 1983.

34. 'Support Growing for Jackson Presidential Bid', *Statesman* [Florida], 12 May 1983; and Howell Raines, 'Group of Black Leaders Supports Idea of Bid by Black for Presidency', *New York Times*, 21 June 1983.

35. 'Chicago's Effect', *Charleston Chronicle*, 30 April 1983.

36. Tom Wicker, 'Blacks and Chicago', *New York Times*, 12 April 1983.

37. Holman, 'A Black for '84'.

38. 'Democrats Don't Want a Black Candidate', *Buffalo Challenger*, 27 July 1983.

39. Ola, 'Will a Black go for the White House in '84?'.

40. Allen, 'People's victory jolts Reaganites'.

41. Maulana Karenga, 'Running A Black Presidential Candidate: Pros, Cons and Caveats', *Buffalo Challenger*, 7 September 1983.

42. James H. Cleaver, 'Brookins Rebuts Black President Dissenters', *Charleston Chronicle*, 18 June 1983.

43. Jesse L. Jackson, 'Advantages of a Black Presidential Candidacy', *Westside Gazette*, 28 April 1983.

44. James H. Cleaver, 'Jesse Jackson Could Seek US Presidency', *Charleston Chronicle*, 12 March 1983; Fay S. Joyce, 'Alabama Legislature Hears Jackson', *New York Times*, 25 May 1983; 'Black Presidential Candidacy Endorsed', *Minority News Review* [Chicago], September 1983, p. 15; 'Jesse Jackson Says He May Run For President in 1984', *Florida Star*, 12 March 1983.

45. Earl Black, *Southern Governors and Civil Rights: Racial Segregation as a Campaign Issue in the Second Reconstruction*, Cambridge, Massachusetts 1976, pp. 79-82.

46. Jesse Jackson, 'The New Spirit of '76', in Wright, ed., *What Black Politicians are Saying*, pp. 60-61.

47. Rovetch, ed., *Like It Is*, p. 158.

48. Jackson, 'The New Spirit of '76', pp. 64-65.

49. Lewis, *King: A Critical Biography*, p. 339, 366.

50. Miller, *Martin Luther King Jr*, pp. 268-269.

51. Hamilton, *The Black Preacher in America*, p. 130.

52. *Ibid.*, p. 28.

53. Jackson, 'The New Spirit of '76', p. 56.

54. *Ibid.*, pp. 57, 66.

55. Rovetch, ed., *Like It Is*, pp. 160–161; Meier, *Negro Thought in America, 1880-1915*, pp. 43, 101, 105; and Jesse Jackson, 'Confronting Monopoly and Keeping the Movement Moving', in Ernest Kaiser, ed., *A Freedomways Reader: Afro-America in the Seventies*, New York 1977, p. 356.

56. Jackson, 'The New Spirit of '76', p. 55.

57. Rovetch, ed., *Like It Is*, pp. 159-160.

58. Jackson, 'The New Spirit of '76', p. 55.

59. Rovetch, ed., *Like It Is*, p. 167.

60. Jackson, 'Confronting Monopoly and Keeping the Movement Moving', p. 355.

61. Manning Marable, 'The Paradox of Reform: Black Politics and the Democratic Party', *Southern Exposure*, vol. 12, February 1984, p. 22; and Marable, 'Why Black Americans are not Socialists', in Phyllis Jacobson and Julius Jacobson, eds., *Socialist Perspectives*, Princeton, New Jersey 1983, pp. 84-85.

62. Jesse Jackson, 'Philosophy and Program of PUSH', Chicago 19 November 1976.

63. Jackson, 'Confronting Monopoly and Keeping the Movement Moving', p. 353.

64. Jesse Jackson in Baraka, ed., *African Congress*, pp. 22-34.

65. Marable, 'Why Black Americans are not Socialists', p. 85.

66. Rovetch, ed., *Like It Is*, p. 159; and Henry J. Young, *Major Black Religious Leaders Since 1940*, Nashville 1979, pp. 130-131.

67. Thomas E. Cavanagh and Lorn S. Foster, *Jesse Jackson's Campaign: The Primaries and Caucuses*, Washington DC 1983, p. 2.

68. Alkalimat and Gills, 'Black Power vs Racism', p. 85.

69. Monroe Anderson, 'Jackson didn't steal the show, but he was a big part of it', *Chicago Tribune*, 27 Febraury 1983.

70. Marable, 'Why Black Americans are not Socialists', p. 86. Jackson's desire to build a political base in Miami was no secret. In May 1980, during the Miami Rebellion, Jackson flew into the city to quell racial unrest, only to meet outrage from many local Black community activists. He was rejected as an 'outsider' and one well-publicized Jackson media event in the central ghetto, Liberty City, attracted only twleve people, six of whom were television reporters. See Marable, *Blackwater*, pp. 130, 133.

71. Jackson, in Baraka, ed., *African Congress*, p. 30.

72. Marable, *Blackwater*, pp. 155-156.

73. Jackson, in Baraka, ed., *African Congress*, p. 33.

74. Rovetch, ed., *Like It Is*, p. 165.

75. A personal note: I first learned about the possibility of a Jackson candidacy from my friend Bertram Gross, author of *Friendly Fascism*, on 1 January 1983. Gross was working on a piece of legislation for Conyers, and the Detroit Congressman floated the name of Jackson as a possibility. When Gross informed me, my initial reaction was to laugh so hard that I very nearly fell out of my chair. Given Jackson's chequered history in the Black movement, and his lack of credentials among white leftists, peace, gay and feminists groups, it was hard to imagine at that time a less appropriate choice. The obvious candidates were Dellums, Conyers, US Civil Rights Commissioner Mary Berry, Parren Mitchell and perhaps Julian Bond. For various reasons, none of these individuals emerged in 1983. Jackson's name-recognition alone, at least among millions of Afro-Americans, gave instant credibility to the concept of a Black presidential candidacy. Only after the March on Washington, and after an intense two-hour discussion with Dellums in mid September 1983, was I fully convinced that Jackson could represent a progressive public policy agenda effectively. Of the strategy itself, I never had any doubts: it was the only way to mobilize millions of Americans to fight both Reaganism and the drift towards the right by white national Democratic Party leaders. I also knew that Jackson had always been something of an ideological chameleon. If Black progressives and the left got involved in the campaign across the country, and influenced Jackson's views on major issues, the mobilization could easily become a very anticorporate, anti-imperialist movement.

76. Editorial, 'Jackson Candidacy Raises Questions', *Sun Reporter* [San Francisco], 27 July 1983.

77. Charlene Mitchell, 'Black Presidential Aid: for the whole working class', *Daily World*, 9 June 1983.

78. Tony Brown, 'A Black President on the "Family Plan" ', *Statesman*, 14 April 1983.

79. Brown, 'Can Black Republicans Pull Off Presidential Race?'.

80. Fay S. Joyce, 'Presidential Decision Nears for Jesse Jackson,' *New York Times*, 27 September 1983.

81. Howell Raines, 'Mondale Backers Watching Jackson', *New York Times*, 16 July 1983.

82. Editorial, 'PUSH Takes Nothing for Granted', *Carolina Peacemaker*, 30 July 1983; Maceo Dixon and Stuart Crome, 'Operation PUSH condemns US war against people of Central America', *Militant*, 26 August 1983; and 'Two Jesse Jackson Groups Misused $1.7 Million, US Auditors Say', *New York Times*, 20 August 1983.

83. Cavanagh and Foster, *Jesse Jackson's Campaign*, pp. 12, 27.

84. Ronald Smothers, 'Decisions Face Jackson on Key Contests and Workers in Field', *New York Times*, 25 November 1983; Smothers, 'Ohio Politician Says He'll Run Campaign For the Rev. Jackson', *New York Times*, 16 November 1983; and

John W. Lewis Jr, 'Jesse-Watching', *Carolina Peacemaker*, 3 December 1983.

85. Ronald Smothers, 'Jackson Declares Formal Candidacy', *New York Times*, 4 November 1983.

86. 'Provocative Candidate Posing Challenge for Party' and 'Poll Finds Mondale Widens Lead Over Glenn', *New York Times*, 4 November 1983.

87. 'The Jackson Campaign in the South: A Victory Already Won', *Southern Fight-Back*, vol. 9, July 1984, pp. 1-4, 5; Speeches by Anne Braden, Jim Haughton, Jitu Weusi and Carliotta Scott, in NCIPA *Newsletter*, vol. 1, April 1984, pp. 8-10; Carson, *In Struggle*, p. 151; and Barry Commoner, 'Jackson's Historic Campaign', *New York Times*, 10 July 1984.

88. Benjamin F. Chavis Jr, 'Theology Under the Rainbow', *The Witness*, vol. 67, May 1984, pp. 6-7.

89. *Ibid.*, pp. 6-7.

90. Gerald M. Boyd, 'Black Churches a Mainspring of Jackson's Efforts', *New York Times*, 14 February 1984; 'Progressive Baptists Seek to Register 500,000', *Buffalo Challenger*, 7 September 1983; and 'Gospel Fest to Raise Funds for Jackson', *Buffalo Challenger*, 1 February 1984.

93. Kevin Mercadel, 'Harlem Communists and the 1984 Elections', *Black Liberation Journal*, vol. 7, Summer 1984, pp. 11-13; Frankl Lynn, 'Primary Poll', *New York Times*, 5 April 1984; Akinshiju C. Ola, 'History Was Happening in Harlem', *Guardian*, 11 April 1984.

94. Chavis, 'Theology Under the Rainbow', p. 8. Chavis also notes that 'rainbow theology should not be viewed as an attempt to engage in some vague type of pluralism that lacks theological clarity. Rather it is a justice-seeking theology that is evolving out of conrete political praxis . . . '.

95. James Green, 'The Making of Mel King's Rainbow Coalition: Political Changes in Boston, 1963-1983', *Radical America*, vols. 17-18, November 1983 February 1984, pp. 9–33. Green observes that 'one third of the white voters interviewed' after the Boston mayoral election stated thatey 'would not vote for a Black candidate *under any circumstances*, no matter how appealing the candidate's proposals happened to be'. (p. 13).

96. '*Jesse Jackson Acerca De Los Asuntos Hispanos*', campaign pamphlet, Jackson for President Committee, Washington DC 1984.

97. Hector Rivera, 'Latinos aim to defeat Reaganism', *Daily World*, 9 June 1984.

98. William Gallegos, 'MAPA endorsing convention sets progressive agenda', *Unity*, 25 May–14 June 1984.

99. Kevin J. Kelley, 'To confront or conciliate: That is Jackson's question', *Guardian*, 13 June 1984. Also see Fay S. Joyce, 'Jackson, in California, Presses for Minority Votes', *New York Times*, 17 May 1984; and 'Jackson Woos Asian-Americans', *New York Times*, 18 May 1984.

100. Bob Massey, 'What's in store for Democratic race?', *Unity*, 20 April-10 May 1984.

101. Buck Martin, 'Editorial: An Indian Viewpoint', *National Minority Campus Chronicle*, vol. 2, May 1984, p. 2.

102. 'Asian-Pacific Americans', *The Rainbow Organizer*, vol. 1, July 1984, pp. 4-5.

103. 'Jesse Jackson: Study War No More', pamphlet published by 'Peace Leaders for Jackson', Washington DC 1984. Also see Reese Erlich, 'Why the Peace Movement must support Jesse for president', *Unity*, 20 April-10 May 1984.

104. 'Women, Jesse Jackson and the Rainbow Coalition', pamphlet published by the Alliance Against Women's Oppression, San Francisco May 1984; Howell Raines, 'Democrats Focus on Key Delegates', *New York Times*, 17 May 1984; Peter

Shapiro, 'How Jesse Jackson has opened the doors for workers', *Unity*, 25 May-14 June 1984.

105. Roger Allison and Dee Reilly, 'Missouri FMHA director refuses Blocu order to meet with farmers' and Roger Allison, 'Farm issues radio hosts Jackson', *North America Farmer*, vol. 1, 25 April 1984.

106. 'California Delegates Names for Jackson', *Sacramento Observer*, 15-21 March 1984; and Massey, 'What's in store for Democratic race?

107. Howell Raines, 'Standing of Jackson Increases in Poll', *New York Times*, 29 April 1984.

108. 'Women, Jesse Jackson and the Rainbow Coalition'.

109. Dan Bellm, 'Improved views earn Jackson more support', *Guardian*, 25 April 1984.

110. Gerald M. Boyd, 'Jackson Assesses Low White Vote', *New York Times*, 22 March 1984.

111. 'Five Arrested and Threatened by Jersey Police While Distributing Jesse Jackson Material', *Buffalo Challenger*, 25 April 1984.

112. 'And Jackson Makes Three', *New York Times*, 28 March 1984.

113. Kevin J. Kelley, 'Mondale's nomination might be suicide pact for Democrats', *Guardian*, 20 June 1984.

114. In the New York Democratic primary, for example, Hart received about 45 per cent of the votes of whites aged 18 to 44; one third of the votes of whites whose family incomes exceeded $35,000 annually; and the support of 56 per cent of all Democrats who had voted for John Anderson four years before. See 'Primary Poll', *New York Times*.

115. Kevin J. Kelley, 'The Long and Winding Trail — That Leads Nowhere?', *Guardian*, 6 June 1984.

116. 'Roll-Call Vote on President', *New York Times*, 20 July 1984.

117. Howell Raines, 'Democrats Focus on Key Delegates', *New York Times*, 17 May 1984.

118. Howell Raines, 'Democratic Drive for Unity Starts Renewed Fighting', *New York Times*, 6 May 1984; Wallace Turner, 'Complaints by Jackson Get No Action by Party', *New York Times*, 11 May 1984.

119. 'Carolina Party "Favors" Jackson as Favorite Son', *New York Times*, 12 March 1984; Kevin J. Kelley, 'Jackson Movin' On Up', *Guardian*, 28 March 1984; Amiri Baraka, 'On the Jesse Jackson campaign to date', *Unity*, 9 March 1984.

120. Ronald Smothers, 'Black Leaders Who Back Mondale in Alabama Arguing for Pragmatism', *New York Times*, 12 March 1984.

121. John Corry, ' "Frontline" Views Alabama Primary', *New York Times*, 5 April 1984.

122. Howell Raines, 'Democratic Contenders Turning to Second Half,' *New York Times*, 12 April 1984; Phil Gailey, 'Philadelphia's Vote is Seen as a Factor in Jackson Influence', *New York Times*, 9 April 1984; Bob Sanders, 'Philadelphia Story: Winner loses and loser wins', *Guardian*, 25 April 1984.

123. Anderson, 'A Question of Blackness'.

124. 'Caucus Solidly Behind Rev. Jackson', *Sacramenato Observer*, 14–20 June 1984.

125. Fay S. Joyce, 'Jackson Candidacy Is Giving New Shape to Politics in US', *New York Times*, 13 April 1984.

126. *Ibid.*; and Clarence Lusane, 'Building a Progressive Alliance — Where's the Rainbow?'; pamphlet, 'Jesse Jackson's Challenge', San Francisco 1984, p. 13.

127. In the *Rainbow Organizer*, O'Dell called the support of 'the right of the

Palestinian people to self-determination as the key to peace in the Middle East'. O'Dell, 'From "White" Democratic Primary to the Rainbow Coalition', *Rainbow Organizer*, vol. 1, July 1984, p. 13.

128. A.W. Singham, 'Foreign Policy Held Hostage: The Jackson Rescue Mission', *Freedomways*, vol. 24, First Quarter 1984, pp. 15-22.

129. Fay S. Joyce, 'Jackson Outlines His Views to Jewish Group', *New York Times*, 28 February 1984; Kevin J. Kelley, 'Jackson Tries to explain', *Guardian*, 7 March 1984; and Kelley, 'Rainbow repair work as Jackson reaches out to Jews', *Guardian*, 14 March 1984. Jackson received more death-threats during the campaign than all other candidates combined. Fearful of Black retaliation if Jackson were to be assassinated during the primaries, Reagan's Secretary of the Treasury, Donald T. Regan, authorized Secret Service protection of Jackson more than two and a half months ahead of the other Democratic presidential candidates. Immediately following the San Francisco convention, Secret Service protection of Jackson was pulled, despite Jackson's repeated requests for its continuation. See 'Secret Service Protecting Jackson Months Before Other Candidates', *New York Times*, 12 November 1983; and 'Jackson Request Denied On Secret Service Guards', *New York Times*, 23 July 1984.

130. Kelley, 'Rainbow repair work as Jackson reaches out to Jews', Morris U. Schappes, 'Around the World', *Jewish Currents*, vol. 38, April 1984, p. 46.

131. Schappes, 'Around the World'.

132. Ben Bradlee Jr, 'Jackson-Jewish group meeting off, then on', *Boston Globe*, 25 February 1984.

133. 'The Democrats and Palestine', *Palestine Focus*, no. 7, July 1984, p. 1.

134. See 'Jackson on the Arabs', *New York Times*, 20 March 1984; Fay S. Joyce, 'Jackson Outlines His Views to Jewish Group'; Fay S. Joyce, 'Reporter's Notebook: Days Grow Long in Jackson Camp', *New York Times*, 28 April 1984.

135. Meier and Rudwick, CORE, pp. 336, 411.

136. Carson, *In Struggle*, pp. 267-269.

137. Lincoln, *The Black Muslims in America*, pp. 148-149, 166. Also see Robert G. Weisboro, *Bittersweet Encounter: The Afro-American and the American Jew*, Westport, Connecticut 1970, pp. 18, 93-97, 107, 148, 152, 182.

138. Cruse, *The Crisis of the Negro Intellectual*, pp. 482-483.

139. Carmichael, *Stokely Speaks*, p. 206.

140. Franklin Williams, 'Jewish Political Support', *Amsterdam News*, 4 February 1984.

141. Arnold Lindhardt, 'New York's Jewish Voter: Losing Clout?', *Jewish Currents*, vol. 38, June 1984, pp. 4-6. Jackson's city-wide vote promoted immediate speculation that a Black or Hispanic candidate could capture the mayor's office in the 1985 election. See Sam Roberts, 'Black Strength in City Voting', *New York Times*, 5 April 1984.

142. John Marshall Kilimanjaro, 'Jesse and that Hymie Slur', *Carolina Peacemaker*, 17 March 1984.

143. Curtis Perkins, 'The Maligning of Jesse Jackson', *Buffalo Challenger*, 7 March 1984.

144. Carlton Goodlett, 'In Defense of Jesse', *Buffalo Challenger*, 14 March 1984.

145. Fein also condemned Jews 'who regularly refer to *shvartzes* sanctimoniously to condemn those who use "Hymie" . . . It is time for us to stop pretending that our history of persecution has immunized us against prejudice.' See Morris U. Schappes, 'Around the World', *Jewish Currents*, vol. 38, June 1984, p. 45.

146. Chavis, 'Theology Under the Rainbow', p. 8.

147. In Detroit, Farrakhan introduced Jackson before a crowd of 8,000 Arab-American supporters, speaking in fluent Arabic. See Jim Jacobs and Herb Boyd, 'Facing the Headwind', *Metro Times* [Detroit], 11-17 January 1984.

148. 'Jackson Disagrees With Secession Idea', *New York Times*, 23 April 1984; E.R. Shipp, 'Farrakhan Statements Reflect His Background', *New York Times*, 17 April 1984. Farrakhan's broadcast of 11 March included the following commentary: 'The Jews don't like Farrakhan, so they call me Hitler. Well, that's a good name. Hitler was a great man. He wasn't great for me a Black person, but he was a great German. Now I'm not proud of Hitler's evil against Jewish people, but that's a matter of public record . . . But don't compare me with your wicked killers.' See 'Farrakhan on Race, Politics and the News Media', *New York Times*, 17 April 1984.

149. Fay S. Joyce, 'Jackson, Citing "My Integrity", Upholds His Ties to Farrakhan', *New York Times*, 6 May 1984.

150. Fay S. Joyce, 'Black Muslim Leader's Support', *New York Times*, 2 May 1984.

151. US Calls Evidence Insufficient', *New York Times*, 6 May 1984.

152. David Shribman, 'Bush Faults Democrats as Failing to Deal with Anti-Semitism Issue', *New York Times*, 10 April 1984. Jackson responded that Bush's remarks 'come from an Adminitration that supported regimes in Chile and El Salvador', both gross violators of human rights. Bush's platitudes, as such, were at best 'self-righteous'.

153. Robert Pear, 'Mondale is trying to patch the Jewish-Black Rift', *New York Times*, 18 July 1984. Jackson's extensive repudiation of Farrakhan's statements included the following remarks: 'I am a Judaeo-Christian and the roots of my faith run deep in the Judaeo-Christian tradition . . . Such statements are inflammatory to the context of the Middle East and are damaging to the prospects for peace there . . . I will not permit Minister Farrakhan's words, wittingly or unwittingly, to divide the Democratic Party. Neither Anti-Semitism nor anti-Black statements have any place in our party.' 'Text of Statement By Jackson', *Buffalo Challenger*, 3 July 1984.

155. W.E.B. Du Bois, 'Opinion', *Crisis*, vol. 24, August 1922, pp. 154-155.

156. Cox, *Caste, Class and Race*, pp. 400-401.

157. Meier, *Negro Thought in America, 1880-1915*, pp. 105-106.

158. W.E.B. Du Bois, 'As the Crow Flies', *Amsterdam News*, 25 November 1939.

159. Lenni Brenner, 'The Misguided Search for Black/Jewish Unity', *Freedomways*, vol. 24, Second Quarter 1984, p. 112.

160. W.E.B. Du Bois, 'Letters from Du Bois', *Crisis*, vol. 17, February 1919.

161. W.E.B. Du Bois, 'The Case for the Jews', *Chicago Star*, 8 May 1948; and Du Bois, 'The Winds of Time', *Chicago Defender*, 15 May 1948.

162. Marcus Garvey, speech in Philadelphia, 12 October 1919; Garvey, speech at Liberty Hall, Harlem, 6 March 1920; and Garvey, speech at Madison Square Garden, New York, 3 August 1920, in Hill, ed., *The Marcus Garvey and Universal Negro Improvment Papers, Volume II*, pp. 94, 235, 502.

163. William Minter, *Portuguese Africa and the West*, 1972, p. 136.

164. Brenner, 'The Misguided Search for Black/Jewish Unity', pp. 116-117.

165. *Ibid.*, p. 113.

166. Afro-Americans are not immune to anti-Semitism, unfortunately. Yet Harris's poll also notes this important fact: 'By an overwhelming 77-78 per cent majority, Blacks feel that "The same people who would like to keep down Jews would also like to keep other minorities down".' Lou Harris, 'Comparative Outlook on Politics and Issues between Black and Jewish voters', *National Scene*, vol. 53, July 1984, pp. 26-27.

167. Walter Goodman, ''84 Poll Results Disputed by Jews', *New York Times*, 18 December 1984.

168. Cavanagh and Foster, *Jesse Jackson's Campaign*, pp. 2–3.

169. Gerald M. Boyd, 'Reporter's Notebook: Jackson's Brand of Politics', *New York Times*, 15 June 1984.

170. The night before his assassination, King stated: 'I don't know what will happen now. But it really doesn't matter to me now. Because I've been to the mountain top . . . And I've looked over, and I've seen the promised land. I may not get there with you, but I want you to know tonight that we as a people will get to the promised land.' See Manning Marable, 'Evaluating King's Journey', *Democratic Left*, vol. 11, September-October 1983, p. 15.

171. Commoner, 'Jackson's Historic Campaign'.

172. Conyers, 'Why We Should Work for Jesse Jackson'; and Elsie Davis, 'Campaign 1984: Blacks, Poor Could Decide Election', *Southern Neighbourhoods*, vol. 8, May-June 1984, pp. 1, 7.

173. Phil Gailey, 'Louisiana Voter Apathy Seen as Aiding Jackson', *New York Times*, 5 May 1984.

174. Anne Braden, 'Kentucky', *NCIPA Newsletter*, vol. 1, June-July 1984, pp. 7-8.

175. 'The Jackson Campaign in the South.'

176. Julian Bond, 'Testing the "Litmus Test" ', *Sacramento Observer*, 31 May-6 June 1984, and Phil Gailey, 'Run-off Issue Puts Democrats on Spot', *New York Times*, 3 May 1984.

177. John Trinkl, 'Millions for the People, Not Another Cent for War', *Guardian*, 11 April 1984; Gerald M. Boyd, 'Jackson Describes the Reagan Administration as "Warmongering" ', *New York Times*, 26 April 1984.

178. Norman Richmond, 'Jackson Attacks Reagan's Policies at UN', *Buffalo Challenger*, 11 July 1984. Other participants at the anti-apartheid conference included US Communist leader Angela Davis, Andrew Young, and San Nujoma, leader of the South West Africa People's Organization.

179. Gerald M. Boyd, 'Jackson Flies to Cuba to Pick Up Prisoners and Take Them to the US'; Bernard Gwertman, 'Cuba Move Called Propaganda Ploy' and Linda Greenhouse, 'High Court Restores Curbs on Tourist Travel to Cuba', *New York Times*, 29 July 1984; Editorial, 'Mr Jackson's Prisoner Dealings' and Gerald M. Boyd, 'Jackson Says Attack by Reagan Cloaks Failures in Foreign Policy', *New York Times*, 6 July 1984; and Karen Wald, 'Jackson the Peacemaker', *Guardian*, 11 July 1984.

180. Text of Jackson's speech at the University of Havana, 27 June 1984. Copy provided to author by the Cuban Mission, United Nations, New York. The near-unanimous opinion of Afro-Amricans regarding Jackson's Cuban trip was very positive. One Jackson backer, South Carolina State Representative Robert R. Woods, was particularly miffed at the white media's negative reaction. White American leaders were 'suddenly up in arms' Woods exclaimed, because they had been 'forced to watch from the sidelines as a real leader takes over and shows the world how things are done!' 'Lawmaker Sees Jesse's Cuban Trek as a "Christian Success"; White Media Reaction No Surprise', *Charleston Chronicle*, 7 July 1984.
25 July 1984. Most US newspapers wrote virtually nothing about the series of mass demonstrations held by the liberal-left in San Francisco. On 13 July, Jackson spoke before a Rainbow rally of four thousand in San Francisco's Union Square; the 'National March for Lesbian/Gay Rights' brought 100,000 into the street on 15 July; on 16 July, over 100,000 activists marched to Moscone Centre in a 'Vote Peace in '84' rally; and on 14 July over 4,000 older people rallied to denounce the Reagan

Administration's attacks on Social Security.

182. John Wojcik, 'Black delegates call for Dem party unity', *Daily World*, 17 July 1984; Warren Weaver Jr, 'Jackson Plank on Weapons is Voted Down by Delegates', *New York Times*, 18 July 1984.

183. 'Andrew Young Booed: His Stance on Dual Primaries Irks Many Blacks' and Regina Evans, 'Dual Primary Attacked', *Sacramento Observer*, 19-25 July 1984.

184. Tony Brown, 'Is Young For Jackson's Strategy or Not?', *Carolina Peacemaker*, 28 July 1984.

185. Dudley Clendinen, 'Nation Is a Cathedral With Jackson at Pulpit', *New York Times*, 19 July 1984.

186. William G. Blair, 'Jewish Leaders Hail Jackson Unity Plea but Voice Caution', *New York Times*, 19 July 1984.

187. Clendinen, 'Nation Is a Cathedral With Jackson at Pulpit'; Kevin J. Kelley, 'Jackson is Dems' conscience despite compromises', *Guardian*, 25 July 1984; Editorial, 'If Jesse Were White?', *Carolina Peacemaker*, 28 July 1984; 'Rev. Jackson's Speech to Remember', *Sacramento Observer*, 19-25 July 1984.

188. Joe Dear, 'It's Mondale: Black Delegates Still Uneasy About Full Support', *Sacramento Observer*, 19-25 July 1984.

189. Akinshiju C. Ola, 'New dawn coming for the Rainbow Coalition?', *Guardian*, 8 August 1984.

190. Jane Perlez, 'Liberal Democrat From Queens', Bernard Weinraub, 'Geraldine Ferraro is Chosen as Running Mate' and Howell Raines, 'Mondale Decision: Praise Ignores Risks', *New York Times*, 13 July 1984; Kevin J. Kelley, 'Dems move toward middle, but miss the masses', *Guardian*, 8 August 1984; Kevin J. Kelley, 'Ferraro's platform: family, fairness and gender gap', *Guardian*, 25 July 1984.

191. Ronald Smothers, 'Jackson Applauds Mondale on "Closing the Gender Gap"', *New York Times*, 13 July 1984; Barbara Banks, Editorial, 'Mondale, Ferraro and Jackson', *Buffalo Challenger*, 18 July 1984; and Kelley, 'Jackson is Dems' conscience despite compromises'. The central irony of Ferraro's selection was that it probably would not have occurred had Jackson decided not to run for president in 1984. Black lieutenants of Jackson were quite bitter abuout this. As writer Charles G. Adams noted, 'Time and again we have seen white women step ahead of Blacks to receive that for which Blacks led the fight. Without [Jackson's] campaign Geraldine Ferraro's ascendancy would have been unthinkable and impossible.' Adams, 'The Black response to Ferraro', *Charleston Chronicle*, 28 July 1984.

192. Ola, 'New dawn coming for the Rainbow Coalition?'; Bernard Weinraub, 'Wider Role is Seen for Women and Blacks in Mondale Drive', *New York Times*, 27 July 1984.

193. See David E. Rosenbaum, 'In Four Years, Reagan Changed Basis of the Debate on Domestic Programs', *New York Times*, 25 October 1984; Joan Claybrook, 'Reagan Ballooned "Big Government"', *New York Times*, 1 November 1984; Robert Pear, 'Middle Class Shrinks as Poverty Engulfs More Families', *New York Times*, 11 December 1983; Peter T. Kilborn, 'Four Years Later: Who in us Is Better Off?', *New York Times*, 9 October 1984; Michael Kramer, 'How to Debate Ronald Reagan', *New Yorker*, 8 October 1984; Anna De Cormis, 'Why is Mondale so obsessed with the budget deficit?' *Guardian*, 17 October 1984; Jack Colhoun, 'Mondale-Ferraro: Peace candidates or cold warriors?', *Guardian*, 3 October 1984; Jack Colhoun, 'How Do You Debate When You Don't Really Disagree?', *Guardian*, 31 October 1984; and 'The Hell With Mondale: Bitter Minorities Threaten Coalition', *Village Voice*, 31 July 1984.

194. John Herbers, 'Drives to Sign Up New Voters bring surge in the rolls', *New York Times*, 29 October 1984; 'Portrait of the Electorate', *New York Times*, 8 November 1984.

195. See Pearl T. Robinson, 'Whither the Future of Blacks in the Republican Party?', *Political Science Quarterly*, vol. 97, Summer 1982, pp. 207-231.

196. Dan Siegel, 'The National Elections', *NCIPA Newsletter*, vol. 1, December 1984-January 1985, pp. 3-5.

197. 'The Rainbow Prepares To Build Permanent Force in Politics', *Southern Fight-Back*, vol. 9, November 1984, p. 5.

198. Lawrence A. Still, 'Democrats, Calls "Rainbow" Convention', *Charleston Chronicle*, 23 June 1984; 'Operation PUSH Convenes', *Sacramento Observer*, 14-20 June 1984; and Ola, 'New dawn coming for the Rainbow Coalition?'.

199. Cavanagh and Foster, *Jesse Jackson's Campaign*, pp. 12–14.

200. Genovese, *Roll, Jordan, Roll*, pp. 252-253; and Levine, *Black Culture and Black Consciousness*, pp. 50-51.

201. Hill, ed., *The Marcus Garvey and Universal Negro Improvement Association Papers, Volume I*, pp. xxxviii-xxxix. Also see Claude McKay, 'Garvey as a Negro Moses', *The Liberator*, vol. 5, April 1922, pp. 8-9; and Truman Hughes Talley, 'Marcus Garvey: The Negro Moses?', *World's Work*, vol. 41, December 1920, pp. 153-166.

202. Bill Fletcher, 'If This is Tuesday, It Must Be "Mondale": Looking at the Jackson Rainbow Coalition and the Upcoming Election', *Forward Motion*, vol. 3, October-November 1984, p. 17.

203. Cox, *Caste, Class and Race*, p. 227.

204. James, *Modern Politics*, p. 115.

Index

Bloom, Lawrence, 222
Bonaparte, Louis, 136
Bond, Julian, 22, 23, 108, 135, 165,
    249, 250, 251, 267, 271, 281, 295
Bonow, Betty, 221
Bookbinder, Hyman, 112, 291
Bosak, Alan, 120
Boseman, Benjamin A., 148, 149, 154
Boutelle, Paul, 249
Boutte, Alvin, 229
Braden, Anne, 116, 270
Bradley, Thomas, 169, 244, 281, 299
Bragg, George Freeman, 160
Brando, Marlon, 93
Brazier, Art, 206
Brazile, Donna, 108, 110, 113, 267
Brezczek, Richard J., 221, 233
Briggs, Cyril V., 69, 163
Britt, Harry, 278
Brookins, H.H., 256, 272
Brooks, Tyrone, 294
Brown, Bob, 118
Brown, Egbert Ethelred, 64
Brown, John, 41
Brown, H. 'Rap', 97
Brown, Louis, 217
Brown, Madison L., 216
Brown, Tony, 175
Bruce, Blanche K., 146–147
Bruce, John A., 64
Bruce, Roscoe Conkling, 146, 159
Bryan, William Jennings, 200
Bryant, John R., 113
Bukharin, Nicolai, 15
Bullock, Larry, 226
Bunche, Ralph, 81
Bunting, Brian, 137
Burke, Edward M., 237, 240, 243
Burke, Neil, 236
Burnham, Forbes, 66
Burnham, Loius E., 39
Bush, George, 301
Bustamante, Alexander, 13
Butler, Charles, 113
Butler, Tubal Uriah 'Buzz' 34–35, 72
Byrd, Manfred, 221
Byrne, Jane, 191, 220, 221, 222, 223–
    230, 231, 232, 240, 243

Caballera-Perez, Diana, 117
Cabral, Amilcar, ix, 21, 55

Cagan, Leslie, 116
Cain, Richard H., 148, 151, 153, 155,
    157–158
Campos, Francisco Domingos, 36–37
Carby, Hazel V., 50
Cardozo, Francis L., 147–148, 151,
    153
Carey, Archibald J., 197
Carey, Bernard, 220
Carey, James, 93
Carmichael, Stokely, 12, 23, 92, 97,
    118, 165–166, 182, 219, 285, 290
Carothers, William, 226, 230
Carson, Clayborne, 18
Carter, Jimmy, 144, 181, 183, 250, 266
Carter, Reginald, 246
Caruso, Angeline, 221
Carver, George Washington, 48
Cary, Mary Ann Shadd, 46–47
Casely-Hayford, J.E., 55, 174
Castro, Fidel, 55, 264
Cavanagh, Thomas E., 292, 304
Cayton, Horace, 193
Cermak, Anton, 203
Césaire, Aime, 174
Chamberlain, Daniel H., 154
Chapman, Frank, 116
Chase, Calvin, 161
Chavannes, Marc, 26
Chavis, Benjamin, 108, 113, 271, 274
Chilembwe, John, 34
Chisholm, Shirley, 176, 250
Chissano, Joaquim, 40
Christian, Barbara, 46
Cipriani, A.A., 41, 72
Clark, Kenneth, 101
Clark, Mark, 220
Clark, Ramsey, 108
Clark, T.A., Sr., 227
Clarke, Cheryl, 49
Clarkson, Thomas, 26
Clay, William, 166–167, 181, 187, 250
Cleaver, Elridge, 49, 249
Clewis, Richard, 233
Cloward, Richard, 15, 70–71, 80, 82,
    250
Coates, Rodney, C., 212
Cockrel, Kenneth, 171–172, 263
Coffin, William Sloan, 116
Cole, Leonard A., 177, 181
Coleman, Milton, 282, 287–288

Haughton, Jim, 271
Hayes, Charles, 206, 227, 243
Hayes, Rutherford B., 157
Haynes, George Edmund, 111
Haywood, Harry, 51
Heard, W.H., 60
Height, Dorothy, 119
Heilbroner, Robert, 133
Henson, John, 291
Hercules, F.E.M., 62
Herskovits, Melville, 6
Hertzog, J.B.M., 38
Heston, Charlton, 93
Higinio, Cynthia, Ellis, 50
Higeura, Jesus, 275
Hill, Norman, 91, 108–110, 119
Hill, Robert, 64
Hitler, Adolf, 54, 55, 137, 287
Hobsbawm, Eric, 138
Hobson, Julius, 91
Ho Chi Minh, 55, 76
Hoggard, J. Clinton, 113
Holden, Matthew, 165
Hollings, Ernest, 254, 258
Holloway, Estelle, 47
Holly, Theodore, 28
Holman, M. Carl, 254
Holt, Thomas, 149, 150, 154
Hood, James W., 147
Hood, William R., 171
Hooks, Benjamin, 108, 110, 119, 120,
    167, 179, 181, 250, 253, 265, 281
Hoover, J. Edgar, 185–186
Hope, John, 159, 160
Hopkins, Velma, 47
Houphouët-Boigny, Felix, 71–72
Hughes, Langston, 48
Humes, Marion, 221
Humphrey, Hubert, 251, 266
Hutson, D.M., 21
Hymer, Bennett, 211

Innis, Roy, 48, 97, 169

Jackson, Eugene, 271
Jackson, George 10–11
Jackson, George H., 160
Jackson, J.H., 208, 226–227
Jackson, James, 39, 51–52
Jackson, Jesse, viii, ix, 14, 35, 108,
    113, 119, 121, 123, 144, 169, 173,

187, 189, 192, 206, 222, 229, 247–
305
Jackson, Johnnie Mae, 227
Jackson, Lottie Wilson, 44
Jackson, Mahalia, 93, 207
Jacob, John E., 108, 111, 253, 256, 298
James, C.L.R., ix, x, 1, 10, 53, 55, 65,
    66, 70, 305
Jefferson, Thomas, 132, 133
Jemison, T.J., 272
Jennings, James, 178, 189
Jimenez, Jose, 243
Jimenez, Ramon, 273
Johnson, Andrew, 144
Johnson, Bernice, 93
Johnson, Charles J., 141–142
Johnson, Charles S., 111, 193
Johnson, James Weldon, 58, 65, 159,
    162
Johnson, John, 228
Johnson, John 'Mushmouth', 196, 215
Johnson, Lyndon B., 96, 113, 249, 302
Johnson, Morcedai, 60
Johnson, Wallace, 232
Jones, Clarence, 91
Jones, Dora, 47
Jones, E.J., 227, 230
Jones, Eugene K., 111
Jones, John G., 196, 246
Jones, LeRoi, 49; see Baraka, Amiri.
Jones, Thomas G., 180
Jordan, Verdon, 111, 112, 250
Julião, Francisco, 33

Kadalie, Clements, 37
Kahn, Tom, 91–92
Kamwana, Elliot, 34
Karenga, Maulana, 176, 256
Katznelson, Ira, 2
Kearns, David, T., 111
Kehler, Randy, 116
Keihl, Earl, 114
Kelly, Edmund, 233
Kelly, Edward J., 203–204, 205, 206,
    207, 226, 246
Kemp James, 227
Kennedy, John F., 89, 90, 92, 94, 251
Kennedy, Ted, 231, 235, 266, 268
Kenner, Tyrone, 240
Kenyatta, Jomo, 66, 168
Kilimanjaro, John, 286